Keys to Learning

Skills and Strategies for Newcomers

Teacher's Manual

Anna Uhl Chamot

Catharine W. Keatley

Kristina Anstrom

with

Pamela Beard El-Dinary

Longman

Keys to Learning

Skills and Strategies for Newcomers

Teacher's Manual

Consulting Reviewers

Tracy Bunker, Napa High School, Napa Valley Unified School District
Ann Hilborn, Educational Consultant, Houston, Texas
Wendy Meyers, Casey Middle School, Boulder Valley School District, Boulder, Colorado
Cher Nicolas, La Paz Middle School, Salinas Union High School District, Salinas, California
Dr. W. Dale Rees, ESL Teacher Specialist, Salt Lake City School District, Salt Lake City, Utah
Marjorie Rosenberg, Malrose Associates, LLC
Angela Seale, Educational Consultant, Houston, Texas

Thanks to Janis van Zante for contributing the tests.

Pearson Education, 10 Bank Street, White Plains, NY 10606

Vice president, primary and secondary editorial: Ed Lamprich
Publisher: Sherri Pemberton
Senior development editor: Marilyn Hochman
Development editor: Charles Green
Vice president, director of production and design: Rhea Banker
Senior production editor: Jane Townsend
Vice president, U.S. marketing: Kate McLoughlin
Senior manufacturing buyer: Edith Pullman
Photo research: Kirchoff/Wohlberg, Inc.
Cover design: Rhea Banker, Tara Mayer Raucci
Text design and composition: TSI Graphics
Text font: Minion
Illustrations: 219, 223, 226, 228 right, 229, 230 right, 231, 237, 238 right, 244 bottom, 245, 246 right, 248 left (top), 252, 258 right (bottom), 262, 265, 274, Jane McCreary; 220, 222, 228 left, 230 left, 232, 234, 236, 238 left, 240, 242, 244 top, 246 left, 248 left (bottom) and right, 250, 254, 256, 258 right (top), 260, William Waitzman.
Photos: 2 top, Getty Images; 2 middle, Charles Gupton/StockBoston; 2 bottom, Benelux Press/Index Stock Imagery; 14 top, Will & Deni McIntyre/Photo Researchers; 14 middle, Spencer Grant/PhotoEdit; 14 bottom, Jeff Greenberg/PhotoEdit; 44 top, Michael Newman/PhotoEdit; 44 middle, Jonathan Nourok/PhotoEdit; 44 bottom, Network Productions/Index Stock Imagery; 74 top, Michelle D. Bridwell/PhotoEdit; 74 middle, Getty Images; 74 bottom, CORBIS; 105 top, Gabe Palmer/CORBIS; 105 bottom, David Young-Wolff/PhotoEdit; 133 top, David Young-Wolff, PhotoEdit; 133 middle, Getty Images; 133 bottom, David Young-Wolff/PhotoEdit; 162 top, Paul A. Souders/CORBIS; 162 middle, Getty Images; 162 bottom, Rob Lewine/CORBIS; 191 top, Jorge Luján; 191 middle, Photowood/CORBIS; 191 bottom, AP/Wide World Photos; 240, Getty Images; 256, Jose Luis Pelaez/CORBIS; 264 left and right, Getty Images; 267 David Young-Wolff/PhotoEdit.

ISBN: 0-13-189222-3

Printed in the United States of America
1 2 3 4 5 6 7 8 9 10–VHG–08 07 06 05 04

Contents

Scope and Sequence

	Grammar	Phonics	Learning Strategies	Writing
Unit 1 New Friends				

Chapter 1
What's your name?
	Pronouns;
	Present tense of *be*:
	  statements; *yes/no*
	  questions
		The alphabet;
		Consonants and
		  vowels;
		Alphabetical order
			Preview	Write a
				paragraph
				about
				yourself

Chapter 2
What classes do you have?
	Present tense of *have*:
	  statements, *yes/no*
	  questions;
	Plural nouns;
	Possessive adjectives
		Short vowel
		  sounds: /a/ as
		  in *cat*, /i/ as in
		  sit, and /o/ as
		  in *hot*
			Sound out;
			Preview
				Write a
				paragraph
				about your
				favorite class

Chapter 3
This is a calculator.
	Articles: *a* and *an*;
	Demonstrative pronouns:
	  this, *that*, *these*, and
	  those;
	Possessive of singular and
	  plural nouns
		Short vowel
		  sounds: /e/ as
		  in *bed* and /u/
		  as in *cup*
			Sound out;
			Preview
				Write a
				paragraph
				about things
				in your
				backpack

Unit 2 At School				

Chapter 4
Where's the gym?
	Prepositions of location: *in*,
	  on, *under*, and *next to*;
	Where questions with *be*;
	There is and *there are*
		Consonant
		  sounds: /ch/
		  as in *lunch* and
		  /sh/ as in
		  English
			Sound out;
			Make predictions
				Write a
				paragraph
				about places
				in your
				school

Chapter 5
What's your address?
	What questions with *be*;
	Present tense of regular
	  verbs: statements;
	  yes/no questions;
	Statements with *can*;
	Yes/no questions with *can*
		Consonant blends
		  at the beginning
		  of a word, such
		  as *class*, *pretty*,
		  and *student*
			Sound out;
			Use selective
			attention
				Fill out a form
				with your
				personal
				information

Chapter 6
You were late yesterday.
	What questions with *do*;
	What + noun;
	Past tense of *be*:
	  statements; *yes/no*
	  questions
		Consonant blends
		  at the end of a
		  word, such as
		  find, *went*, and
		  best
			Sound out;
			Make predictions
				Write a
				paragraph
				about your
				day

	Grammar	Phonics	Learning Strategies	Writing
Unit 3 At Home				
Chapter 7 What are you doing?	Present continuous tense: statements; *what* questions; *yes/no* questions; Object pronouns	Long vowel sounds: /ā/ as in *came*, /ī/ as in *like*, /ō/ as in *close*, and /yoō/ as in *use*	Sound out; Make predictions	Write a dialogue about what you are doing
Chapter 8 I have to work.	Simple present tense and present continuous tense; Statements with *like, have,* and *want* + infinitive; *What* questions with *like, have,* and *want* + infinitive; *Yes/no* questions with *like, have,* and *want* + infinitive	Long vowel sound: /ā/ as in *take, wait,* and *say*	Sound out; Use what you know	Write a paragraph about a classmate
Chapter 9 You came to our party!	Past tense of regular and irregular verbs: statements; *yes/no* questions	Long vowel sound: /ē/ as in *me, read, meet, happy,* and *piece*	Sound out; Make inferences	Write a letter to a friend
Unit 4 Around Town				
Chapter 10 How much is it?	Information questions with *be*: present tense; past tense; Information questions with *do*: present tense; past tense; Questions with *how much*	Long vowel sound: /ī/ as in *hi, my, time, pie,* and *right*	Sound out; Make predictions	Write a script for a fashion show
Chapter 11 She needs some lettuce.	Count and non-count nouns; *Some* and *any*; Conjunctions: *and, but,* and *so*	Long vowel sound: /ō/ as in *go, Joe, those, coat,* and *know*	Sound out; Use selective attention	Write a paragraph about your favorite food
Chapter 12 He's the cutest guy at school.	Comparative adjectives; Superlative adjectives; Comparatives and superlatives with *more* and *most*	Long vowel sound: /yoō/ as in *use, unit,* and *few*	Sound out; Use what you know	Write words for a song

	Grammar	Phonics	Learning Strategies	Writing
Unit 5 Friends & Family				
Chapter 13 He's going to fall!	Future tense with *be going to*: statements; *yes/no* questions; information questions; Commands	Other vowel sound: / o͞o / as in *school*, *rule*, *true*, and *new*	Sound out; Make inferences	Write a dialogue about your weekend plans
Chapter 14 Hey! The lights went out!	Past continuous tense: statements; *yes/no* questions; information questions; Possessive pronouns; Questions with *whose*	Other vowel sound: / o͝o / as in *look*	Sound out; Use selective attention	Write a paragraph about something that happened to you
Chapter 15 We'll have a study group.	Future tense with *will*: statements; *yes/no* questions; information questions; Statements with *may* and *might*	Other vowel sound: / ô / as in *auditorium* and *saw*	Sound out; Personalize	Write a few paragraphs about one of your goals
Unit 6 Feelings & Hobbies				
Chapter 16 I sometimes study with my friends.	Adverbs of frequency; Adverbs of frequency with *be*; *How often* and expressions of frequency; Gerunds as objects of verbs	Other vowel sound: / oi / as in *voice* and *enjoy*	Sound out; Use what you know	Write a paragraph about a classmate's hobby or interest
Chapter 17 You should get some rest.	Statements with *should*; *Yes/no* questions with *should*; Statements with *could*; *Because* clauses	Other vowel sound: / ou / as in *out* and *now*	Sound out; Use selective attention	Write a letter giving advice to someone
Chapter 18 It was too easy.	Comparatives and superlatives: irregular adjectives; *Too* and *not enough*; Statements with *used to*; *Yes/no* questions with *used to*	Other vowel sound: / ûr / as in *hurt*, *first*, and *her*	Sound out; Make predictions	Write a story about a character

Program Overview

General Description of the Program

Student Population

Keys to Learning: Skills and Strategies for Newcomers is intended for students who need to develop language skills in order to study the content areas in an all-English curriculum. It is designed for English as a Second Language (ESL) students at the beginning level of English proficiency who also have limited literacy in their native language. Because they need to develop their skills both in and out of school, these students need literacy development that ranges from phonological awareness and the formation of letters to the tasks of writing and reading both stories and informational texts.

Literacy Focus

The main objective of *Keys to Learning* is to build the skills and experiences these adolescent English language learners need to develop literacy. *Keys to Learning* integrates both ESL and mainstream language arts literacy to bring students up to speed for academic learning. Because the focus is on reading and writing, a grammatical base is established in the first few units so that in subsequent units students can engage in more extensive and sophisticated reading and writing activities. As a result, some grammar patterns, such as the past tense, are introduced earlier in the program than in other beginning level ESL textbooks. An organized sequence of word analysis instruction helps to build the skills needed to read unfamiliar words and to spell correctly. In addition, explicit instruction in learning strategies provides students with keys to help them comprehend what they read and to remember new information and vocabulary. Listening and speaking activities complement the reading topics. Finally, a process approach to writing guides students through planning, drafting, and revising to produce written work that represents their best thinking.

Research Foundations of the Program

Keys to Learning is an outgrowth of a field-initiated study (1997–2001) called "Project Ac-

celerated Literacy" (PAL). Funded by the U.S. Department of Education's Office of Educational Research Improvement, it was the top-ranked proposal nationally of those submitted in the competing year. PAL was the first comprehensive research study to focus on the acquisition of English literacy by recent adolescent immigrants with low or no literacy in their native language. The study was conducted in fourteen high school ESL classrooms designated as literacy level classes for students with low native language literacy and/or interrupted prior education. Each classroom was studied for an entire academic year. Both standardized tests and research-developed tests were used as pre- and post-test measures.

The results showed wide variability in students' actual native language literacy levels at the onset of the study. Some of these secondary school students were reading at a second grade level in their native language, while others were reading at grade level. Most students could successfully decode words in their native language but could not comprehend what they were decoding. At post-test, all students had made significant progress in developing English literacy, with greater progress made by students who had started with higher literacy levels in their native language.

Two major tasks of the PAL study were (1) to develop an English literacy curriculum that would provide secondary students with the skills and strategies needed to be successful in reading and writing, and (2) to create lessons that would be appropriate to the interests and maturity level of these students. Participating teachers began with differing philosophical and methodological views about teaching reading and writing to secondary school students. A common curriculum was eventually developed through collaboration, a study of research on literacy development at different ages, and a sharing of teaching experiences including learning strategies that really work in the classroom. The result was a balanced approach that included both authentic and quasi-authentic reading, practice with word-attack skills, vocabulary development, explicit learning strategy instruction, and a process approach to writing. Teachers decided on the scope and sequence of content topics, which included typical beginning ESL topics and some content-based topics. This literacy curriculum was then field-tested for two years. The researchers collected weekly teacher comments on the curriculum as it was taught and observed participating classrooms on a regular basis. The PAL curriculum was then revised based on teacher evaluations and classroom implementation notes, and it has formed the basis for *Keys to Learning*.

Components of the Program

The program *Keys to Learning: Skills and Strategies for Newcomers* contains these components.

Student Book

The Student Book includes six thematic units. The units are tied together through a story line that follows a diverse group of fictional ESL students through their school year. Supported by dialogues and readings throughout each chapter, the story line is both entertaining and closely related to students' experiences. Supporting materials include the following: Getting Started, Content Readings, Vocabulary Handbook, Grammar Handbook, Word Analysis, Writing Process, How to Use a Dictionary, Learning Strategy Chart, Glossary, and Topical Index.

Teacher's Manual

The Teacher's Manual offers complete teaching suggestions for each chapter of the Student Book. References to corresponding Workbook practice exercises and to the supporting materials provided in the back of the Student Book are also included. Answers to all Student Book exercises are highlighted in boxes on the corresponding Teacher's Manual pages, and an icon indicates when audio segments are to be used. Also included are a Scope and Sequence chart, information on basic teaching techniques, and a Workbook Answer Key.

Graphic Organizers provide visual support for vocabulary, grammar, word study, reading, and writing lessons.

Before students begin the course, a Diagnostic Test assesses what areas students know (and how well) and what areas they need improvement in. Chapter Tests focus on assessing learning of the dialogue vocabulary, grammar, word study, and reading vocabulary. Unit Tests assess the overall learning of these areas for each unit, with a focus on grammar, reading, and writing. Answer keys are provided for all tests. The Introduction to Tests (pages 217–218) discusses the purpose of the tests and offers guidelines for administering and grading the tests.

Audio Program

The audio program is available in two formats—audio CDs and audiocassettes. The program includes the chapter dialogues, vocabulary, conversations, and readings, plus the Focus on Content readings. There is also a segment for the Diagnostic Test.

Workbook

The Workbook provides further practice and reinforcement of language skills. Workbook activities correspond to the various sections in each chapter of the Student Book. Supportive Reader's Companion pages give students further guidance for comprehending the Focus on Content readings that are included in the Student Book. Additional grammar exercises are also provided.

Handwriting Practice Sheets give students practice writing numerals and letters (uppercase, lowercase, print, and cursive).

Overview of the Student Book

About the Authors

Anna Uhl Chamot is professor of secondary education and faculty advisor for ESL in the Department of Teacher Preparation and Special Education at the George Washington University. She is a researcher and teacher educator in content-based second-language learning and language-learning strategies. She co-designed and has written extensively about the Cognitive Academic Language Learning Approach (CALLA) and implemented the CALLA model in the Arlington public schools in Virginia. She was principal investigator of a recent study on literacy development in adolescent English language learners with low literacy in their native language, a study that ultimately led to the development of this book. She is co-author of the *Shining Star* program.

Catharine W. Keatley is associate director of the National Capital Language Resource Center for the George Washington University, Georgetown University, and The Center for Applied Linguistics. She taught English as a Foreign Language with the Peace Corps in Senegal, received her M.A. from New York University in remedial reading and learning disabilities, and, after traveling and living in a number of different countries, received her Ph.D. from the University of Hong Kong where she studied cognitive psychology with a focus on bilingual memory. She served as co-project director for Dr. Chamot's research study on literacy development.

Kristina Anstrom is the assistant director of the Center for Equity and Excellence in Education at The George Washington University. She has been involved in the education of English language learners as a teacher, researcher, and teacher educator. She has worked with mainstream teachers and teacher educators at the K–12 and university levels to help them design more inclusive curricula and learning environments for English language learners. She served as co-project director for Dr. Chamot's research study on literacy development.

Organization of the Student Book

The Student Book opens with the Getting Started unit. This unit exposes students to basic vocabulary and language used in day-to-day communication, also known as Basic Interpersonal Communicative Skills, or BICS (Cummins, 1981).

There are six main units with three chapters in each unit (eighteen chapters total). The chapters are divided into the following sections: Getting Ready; Listening and Reading; Vocabulary; Grammar 1; Grammar 2; Word Study; Grammar 3; Reading; Writing; Learning Log.

After students complete each of the main units, teachers have the option of presenting one of the Focus on Content readings (these are grouped together in the back of the Student Book). These readings focus on academic content areas so students can put their emerging literacy skills into practice.

Overview of a Teacher's Manual Chapter

The organization for each Teacher's Manual chapter parallels that of the corresponding Student Book chapter. Each chapter in the Teacher's Manual starts with a list of objectives for language, literacy, and learning strategies. These objectives are followed by a complete lesson for each section of the Student Book chapter and guidelines for tailoring instruction to students' individual needs (see the Reaching All Students section on the next page).

The instructional suggestions in the Teacher's Manual are based on the CALLA model of instruction (see Chamot, in press, 1996; Chamot & O'Malley, 1994, 1996, 1999; Chamot, Barnhardt, El-Dinary & Robbins, 1999), de-

scribed in the next section. Headings in the Teacher's Manual show how the teaching information is organized according to CALLA's instructional sequence: Preparation, Presentation, Practice, Self-Evaluation, and Expansion.

CALLA Instruction

The Cognitive Academic Language Learning Approach (CALLA) is an instructional model that integrates current research-supported educational innovations. The CALLA model integrates content, academic language, and learning strategies. Content subject matter includes language arts as well as history, math, science, and social studies. Academic language development in CALLA focuses on literacy across the curriculum. CALLA provides explicit instruction in learning strategies that will help students meet national curriculum standards, learn both language and content, and become independent learners who can evaluate their own learning. CALLA is designed to accelerate academic achievement for English language learning (ELL) students, and has been applied in ESL, EFL, and foreign language instruction. The theoretical framework of CALLA is a cognitive-social learning model that emphasizes the role of students' prior knowledge, the importance of collaborative learning, and the development of metacognitive awareness and self-reflection.

The instructional framework of CALLA assists teachers in integrating its three components: high-priority curriculum content, academic language and literacy development, and explicit learning strategies instruction. This instructional framework is task-based and has five phases in which teachers combine the three components of content, language, and learning strategies.

In the **Preparation** stage, teachers first assess students' prior knowledge of the topic, their language proficiency in the skills to be taught, and their current learning strategies for this type of task. Teachers also share the lesson objectives and develop vocabulary needed for the task.

In the **Presentation** stage, teachers then use a variety of techniques to make new information and skills clear and accessible to students. Explanations, demonstrations, modeling, and visual support are among the methods teachers may use to present a lesson.

In the **Practice** stage, students use the new information, skills, and strategies in activities that involve collaboration, problem solving, inquiry, and hands-on experiences.

In the **Self-Evaluation** stage, students assess their own proficiency with the content, language, and learning strategies introduced in the lesson.

Finally, in the **Expansion** stage, students engage in activities that make connections between different school subjects and apply what they have learned to their own lives.

The CALLA instructional model also incorporates scaffolding. Through detailed explanations and modeling, the teacher provides a great deal of initial instructional support. As students become increasingly proficient, they are encouraged to apply the skills and strategies independently. Because students may need occasional support with skills and strategies that have already been introduced, however, the five instructional phases are recursive, allowing for flexibility in lesson planning and implementation.

Lesson Flexibility and Individualized Instruction

The Teacher's Manual includes specific, sometimes scripted lesson plans to provide a scaffold for teachers who are new to strategies instruction. Research in professional development with teachers implementing strategies instruction shows that these supports can provide a springboard for teachers learning the approach (El-Dinary, 2002). Just as students learn best when they "own" vocabulary words and expand their learning in ways that are personally meaningful, so teachers use strategies instruction most effectively when they make it their own.

Therefore, the Teacher's Manual has built-in instructional flexibility to meet teachers' and students' needs. Each section of the Teacher's Manual includes suggestions for optional activities and ways of reaching students with different learning strengths and styles. All of these activities are optional supplements to the lesson and are designed to be used at the teacher's discretion. These optional activities add flexibility to the course length, depending on how few or how many are used. These suggested activities are indicated by the following bold headings:

Optional Activities These notes give ideas for ways to extend the practice by way of activities, drills, and games.

Reaching All Students These notes give specific instruction on how to reach students who may need additional help, who are ready for more of a challenge, or who prefer a specific learning modality. The Reaching All Students sections are targeted to the following student groups:

- **Emergent learners** (students with limited proficiency and/or confidence with English language learning) The term Emergent learners parallels the use of the term emergent literacy to describe the processes of learning to read and write. The activities here provide extra support through the scaffolding activities of modeling, coaching, and guided practice.

- **Advanced learners** (students who are relatively proficient in English) These activities offer additional challenges as well as opportunities for students to provide peer modeling.

- **Auditory learners** (students who learn most easily through listening and speaking activities) These activities include reading written instructions aloud, having students complete activities orally before putting them in writing, and encouraging students to say new words while they write them.

- **Visual learners** (students who learn most easily through visual information) Activities include writing information on the board and using posters as well as other visual displays of information. For conversational exercises, students may also refer to written information for support and prompting.

- **Kinesthetic learners** (students who learn most easily through movement and dramatization) Activities include acting out dialogues and readings as well as presenting information orally in front of the class. Students may also physically manipulate objects or written words to support the learning of grammar structures or to reinforce the meanings of new vocabulary.

Teaching Suggestions

This section outlines suggested teaching procedures for each type of lesson activity contained in the Student Book. Strategy names in parentheses indicate points at which you can introduce and reinforce appropriate learning strategies.

How to Use the Getting Started Unit

The lessons in the Getting Started unit are designed as vocabulary review, with the understanding that some material may be new for some students. The vocabulary in this unit forms the building blocks for future units. For each Getting Started lesson, adapt the length and intensity of instruction to students' needs for that topic. If students already know the material, pick only one or two short activities for review.

How to Use the Unit Openers

Begin the preview by reading the unit title. (In later units, have students read the title.) Use the theme-related photos to elicit vocabulary and expressions already familiar to students and to introduce new words and expressions. Start by having students call out words they know for objects and situations in the photos *(Use Selective Attention);* write these on the board. Introduce new vocabulary by asking and answering questions about the pictures. As students work through the unit, have them take on the task of asking and answering questions about the photos while you provide support as needed. The unit preview can also include opportunities to connect the topic to students' own experiences *(Use What You Know)* and/or to make predictions about what they will learn in the unit *(Make Predictions).* Complete the preview by reading the unit goals and answering any questions students may have.

How to Teach the Opening Dialogues

Prepare students for the opening dialogue by having them identify words they know from the accompanying illustration *(Use Selective Attention).* Write the words on the board as students say them. Follow this by pointing to other items in the picture and asking what they are. Elicit the responses. Have students repeat them. **Present** the dialogue first by having students listen to you or the audio segment while they look at the illustrations. Then have students answer the prelistening question. Finally, have students read the dialogue to themselves. For emergent learners, read the story aloud as they follow along and stop after each section to ask comprehension questions *(Self-Evaluation).*

How to Teach the Pair and Group Practice

Practice the dialogue by having students read it aloud in pairs *(Cooperation);* scaffold students' reading as needed through teacher or peer modeling and through coaching while students read. Then form heterogeneous small groups so that students of varying abilities can work together to read one of the roles in the dialogue. As an option, have each group act out the dialogue for the class, and then have them **Self-Evaluate** their performance. Refer students to the Workbook pages for additional comprehension exercises related to the dialogue.

How to Teach Vocabulary

The vocabulary lessons present key words that may be new to students and provide a variety of exercises to help students learn their meanings. Students need to use new words in various contexts before the words become part of their own vocabularies. Encountering new words in a meaningful context and utilizing all four language modalities—listening, reading, speaking, and writing—can help students achieve fluency with new vocabulary.

First, **Prepare** students by having them identify the vocabulary items they already know and select the words they will need to study *(Use Selective Attention).* Encourage students to look for cognates, or words that are similar to words in their native language *(Use What You Know),* and to make guesses about probable word meanings, based on the chapter topic and the dialogue story line *(Make Inferences).*

Then, students can progress through the steps outlined on the Word Analysis pages at the back of the Student Book (pages 250–251). At this stage, students should be encouraged to recognize the patterns that occur in words, a strategy that will help them with their decoding and spelling skills.

Students can then be encouraged to work together *(Cooperate)* to **Practice** the new vocabulary. Have them find words and expressions in the dialogue that will help them understand their meanings. Then give them the opportunity to **Self-Evaluate** by identifying the words that are new to them. Encourage students to say the words and expressions as they write them *(Rehearsal).* Refer students to the Workbook pages for additional vocabulary practice.

Have students **Expand** their learning of new vocabulary by choosing a set of words "to own." They should strive to incorporate them into their own speaking and writing as well as recognize them in reading and listening. Students should be encouraged to use additional strategies with their "owned words," which can include looking up definitions in a dictionary or thesaurus *(Use Resources)* or working with a partner to quiz each other in order to keep track of their individual progress in learning vocabulary *(Self-Evaluation).* Students may also be asked to use the new words in sentences that they generate based on their own experiences *(Use What You Know).*

How to Teach Grammar 1, 2, 3

Prepare students to learn the new grammar structure through an introductory dialogue, as described in the teacher's notes for each grammar lesson. The dialogue connects the grammar structure to the familiar characters of the book and, in many cases, to the content of the chapter *(Use What You Know)*.

Present the content of the grammar chart by re-creating the grammar chart on the board or on a poster; for some charts it may be useful to leave the verb blank and then write in verbs one at a time as you discuss them. Explain the layout of the chart, and then have students read aloud the examples from the chart *(Rehearsal)*.

Practice the grammar structure using the written and oral exercises provided. Review the answers to give students an opportunity to **Self-Evaluate** what they have learned *(Self-Evaluation)*. Refer students to the Workbook pages (both the main chapters and the material in the back of the Workbook) for additional practice.

After giving students initial practice in re-producing the grammar structure, have students **Expand** their learning by creating original con-versations, writing original sentences, or otherwise connecting the grammar structure to their own interests and experiences *(Use What You Know)*.

How to Teach Word Study

Prepare students for learning new sound-letter relationships by reviewing letter names and pre-viously learned patterns as needed. Write words on the board that illustrate the grapheme/phoneme correspondence in the cur-rent lesson, and have students identify the consonants and vowels.

Present the target grapheme-phoneme cor-respondence, referring to the presentation box in the Student Book. Guide students through the steps of the strategy *Sound Out* to identify the target sound-letter relationships. As students try sounding out words, give them a chance to self-correct any mistakes before giving feedback on their pronunciation. If students are struggling with forming a given sound, Blevins (1998) pro-vides intensive instruction in phonics, including physical descriptions of how each sound is formed.

Have students **Practice** pronouncing the target phonemes by using the strategy *Sound Out,* along with a series of illustrations, to de-code a list of words. This can be done as a class or individually *(Cooperation)*. Then have them read sentences that include words with the let-ter-sound relationship, again, as a large class or individually. Use the dictation exercise provided in the teacher's notes as an opportunity to prac-tice writing words with the letter-sound relationship. Have students **Self-Evaluate** their

performance on the dictation *(Self-Evaluation)*. Students can then **Expand** their learning either by looking for the letter-sound relationships in the Opening Dialogue, or by creating their own list of words with the target sound *(Use What You Know)*.

Refer students to the Workbook pages for additional practice with letters, sounds, and word families. If your students require additional resources, Blevins (1998) provides intensive in-struction in phonics.

How to Teach Reading

Before You Read **Prepare** students for the reading selection by having them look at the title and illustrations. Have them discuss what's hap-pening in the pictures.

Learning Strategy If a learning strategy is introduced, **Present** it explicitly before the reading. (See How to Teach Learning Strategies, page xiv.)

Read This! As an option, unless the focus strategy is to *Make Inferences* about the meanings of new words, or unless the teacher prefers to have students face new vocabulary only in the context of the reading itself, introduce new vo-cabulary students will encounter in the reading to further **Prepare** them to read. Emphasize that the focus is on overall meaning rather than on decoding and defining every word. Remind stu-dents to apply the learning strategies as they read. If desired, **Present** a scaffold for reading by first reading the story aloud or playing the audio as students follow along in their textbooks. As they become more proficient, you can have stu-dents model by reading aloud for the class. If your students are ready for independent reading, skip this step and have them read silently. While students **Practice** silent reading, circulate to pro-vide coaching on strategy use and to help with difficult sections. Encourage students to first try to apply learning strategies, and then ask for clar-ification when they do not understand and cannot figure out the meaning of any part of a reading selection *(Use Resources)*.

After You Read After students read the selection, guide them through the exercises to **Self-Evaluate** their comprehension and use of the strategy. After completing the comprehen-sion exercises, students should check their own work by looking back over the reading selection to find out which questions were answered cor-rectly. Have students revise any incorrect answers *(Self-Evaluation)*. **Expand** students' learning by discussing how they could apply the strategy to other types of reading and other con-tent areas. Refer students to the Workbook pages for additional comprehension exercises related to the reading.

How to Teach Writing

The Writing sections of the Student Book and Teacher's Manual walk students through the steps of planning, drafting, revising, and making a final copy of their work. The Writing Process pages in the back of the Student Book (pages 252–255) offer additional instruction on these steps.

Before You Write **Prepare** students for the writing assignment by reading the assignment instructions. Point out the checklists that will provide students with strategies to guide them through the process of writing. **Present** the assignment by having students study the writing model. Have students **Practice** planning strategies by following the Before I Write checklist (*Plan/Organize/Take Notes*). When scaffolding is needed, model following the writing checklists or call on a volunteer for peer modeling.

Write This! Have students **Practice** strategies for writing a draft by following the While I Write checklist to create a draft in their notebooks. Provide modeling and coaching as needed.

After You Write Have students **Self-Evaluate** their writing by following the While I Write checklist (*Self-Evaluate*). Encourage students to evaluate their successive drafts critically so that the final draft is representative of their best and most thoughtful effort. Provide modeling and coaching as needed. Have students seek input from peers to identify any additional changes that might be needed (*Cooperate*). Then have them write a final copy of the assignment.

Students can **Expand** their learning through a related assignment that connects new skills to their own interests (*Use What You Know*). Encourage students to think of ways they could use this type of writing in their own lives. The Workbook provides an expansion writing activity for each chapter.

A note on evaluating students' writing: The main objective is to have students communicate their ideas and practice various writing formats. In some cases this understanding will be expressed in inaccurate or incomplete English. Respond to the intended meaning your students are trying to communicate. At the same time, make note of frequent errors so that you can plan corrective lessons.

How to Use the Learning Log

Prepare students for the Learning Log by explaining its structure and purpose. Each section of the log helps students **Self-Evaluate** how well they have learned the material in the chapter (*Self-Evaluation*). Students are also encouraged to choose strategies for learning that may be difficult for them. **Present** and **Practice** the Learning Log activities in each section, as follows:

Vocabulary Read the vocabulary aloud with students, and note the word categories in the chart. Ask students to copy the words and expressions, including the category headings, into their notebooks. Then have them underline the words and expressions they don't know. Discuss with students different strategies they could use to unlock the meanings of unfamiliar words. (Examples: Look up the meanings in a dictionary; find the words and expressions in textbook dialogues and reread the sentences in which they appear; ask a classmate to explain the meaning.) Have students work with a classmate to compare their word lists; encourage them to help each other learn the new words and expressions. See How to Teach Vocabulary on page xi if students require additional instruction. As students learn the meanings of the new words and expressions, have them write checkmarks next to them to track their progress. Remind them to use their "owned" words in their speaking or writing every day. (See How to Teach Vocabulary, page xi.)

Language and Learning Strategies Have students copy the sentences into their notebooks. Call on a volunteer to read the sentences aloud, and make sure students understand their meaning. Then have them put a checkmark next to the items they know how to do. If a significant number of students indicate that they have not learned a particular concept or strategy, review that material with the whole class. Otherwise, have students form study groups with others who need review. Circulate among the groups and offer assistance as needed.

Self-Evaluation Questions Have students answer the Self-Evaluation Questions in their notebooks. Then call on students to read their answers to the class. Note their responses on the board. Write students' responses to question 4 on a poster and return it to them later to see how well the suggested strategies worked.

You can **Expand** the Learning Log checklists by having advanced students keep a learning diary in which they write open-ended reflections on their learning. Other students may wish to keep learning diaries in their native language, introducing English as they gain proficiency. Students can share these learning diary entries with the class, or just with the teacher (with the teacher adding comments). They can also keep them private for their own use.

How to Teach the Focus on Content Lessons

Reading to learn is a skill students need across the curriculum, and students often need to be explicitly taught to transfer the strategies they learn in the language classroom to other academic subjects. The Focus on Content lessons offer practice in reading for information, reading for the main idea, skimming, scanning, making inferences, and drawing conclusions. Each lesson includes (1) prereading strategy use instructions; (2) a Before You Go On mid-reading comprehension question, and; (3) postreading comprehension checks.

Tell students that these reading selections are similar to the readings they will find in regular textbooks, but that some vocabulary may be unfamiliar. Their goal should be to get as much meaning as possible from what they read, rather than to know every word. Explain that their learning strategies can help them understand what they read. The Teacher's Manual offers suggestions for integrating learning strategies into the Focus on Content lessons. You may wish to include additional strategy instruction as suggested below.

- To activate students' prior knowledge, have them recall what they already know about the topic (*Use What You Know*). As students purposefully relate their experiences and knowledge to the new information they acquire through reading, they build a deeper understanding of the content.
- Students can also use strategies to help them remember information they read. They can take notes of important facts while they read (*Take Notes*) and also develop summaries of the reading, either orally or in writing (*Summarize*). Students who need help practicing summarizing can develop their summaries in pairs or groups (*Cooperate*).

How to Teach Learning Strategies

Learning strategy boxes and icons indicate to both students and teacher that one or more strategies should be used to assist in the accompanying activity.

When a new strategy is introduced, you can **Prepare** students by pointing out ways in which they're already using the strategy as a classroom activity or in other contexts. For example, point out to students that they probably get ideas about a story when they read the title and look at any pictures or illustrations. Explain that they can now learn to do this intentionally as part of the strategy *Make Predictions*.

When students encounter a strategy in a subsequent lesson, ask them what they remember about the strategy and its use. Refer students to the list of steps in their texts. Offer additional explanations and modeling when needed (**Present**). Encourage students to use the strategy with the activity that follows the Learning Strategy box. Provide coaching as necessary (**Practice**). After they have completed the activity, discuss how well students believe they used the strategy, whether it helped them complete the task, and with what other tasks they could use the strategy. Encourage them to include activities and assignments in other classes (**Self-Evaluate** and **Expand**).

Although initial strategy explanations and modeling are explicit, teacher reminders to use strategies should become gradually less direct and prescriptive. Fading explicit strategy reminders will support students in the transition toward independent strategy use.

How to Use the Student Book Supporting Materials

The back of the Student Book includes several supporting materials: Content Readings, Vocabulary Handbook, Grammar Handbook, Word Analysis, Writing Process, How to Use a Dictionary, Learning Strategy Chart, Glossary, and Topical Index.

Let students know that the **Vocabulary Handbook** lists common words they may find useful in the following categories: Free-Time Activities, Adjectives, Colors and Shapes, Clothes, Food, Daily Activities, Family, Money and Units of Measurement, Your School, Your Home, School Subjects, and Weather. The Student Book and Teacher's Manual provide point-of-use page references for the Vocabulary Handbook, particularly for writing assignments and conversational exercises. Refer students to and/or present the appropriate pages whenever students may need support with vocabulary for these topics.

The **Grammar Handbook** covers the major grammar topics in *Keys to Learning*. The handbook consists of simple definitions of the grammar points, followed by sample sentences. These pages are a good reference for instruction when you are reviewing the grammar topics. The Teacher's Manual includes point-of-use page references for the Grammar Handbook.

The **Learning Strategy Chart** provides a list of the learning strategies and their definitions. When asking students to consider strategies they can use for a learning task, refer them to this chart as needed for reminders of the choices that are available to them.

The **Word Analysis** section teaches students how to look at new words and try to recognize patterns that will help them decode the words and remember their spellings. At first students will need careful guidance as they carry out these steps, but gradually they will become more adept at making their own analyses, thus bringing them further down the path of being independent readers.

The **Writing Process** section provides elaboration on the steps of the writing process. Examples are provided about what good writers are thinking during each stage of writing: prewriting, writing, revising, editing, and publishing. Refer students to this checklist whenever they are ready for more detailed instruction and/or need additional support in planning, drafting, revising, or editing beyond what is provided in the writing assignment in the Student Book.

The section **How to Use a Dictionary** provides students with instructions on how to use reference materials, walking them through sample pages of these two resources. When students need to use a dictionary, use "teachable moments" to introduce this section and to provide reminders that these resources are available.

Tell students that the **Topical Index** can help them quickly locate information on a given content topic, grammar structure, strategy, or skill. When students face assignments that integrate previously learned content or skills, encourage them to locate the information they need. During the Learning Log exercises, encourage students to locate topics they need to review. The Topical Index is also a good reference for teachers in locating grammar topics (e.g., present progressive tense) and subject categories (e.g., dates).

References

Blevins, Wiley. (1999). *Phonemic Awareness Activities for Early Reading Success.* New York: Scholastic.

Chamot, A. U. (in press). "The Cognitive Academic Language Learning Approach (CALLA): An Update." In P. A. Richard-Amato & M. A. Snow (eds.), *The Multicultural Classroom: Readings for Content-Area Teachers, Second Edition.* White Plains, N.Y.: Longman.

Chamot, A. U. (1996). "The Cognitive Academic Language Learning Approach (CALLA): Theoretical Framework and Instructional Applications." In J. E. Alatis (ed.), *Georgetown University Round Table on Languages and Linguistics 1996,* pp. 108–115. Washington, D.C.: Georgetown University Press.

Chamot, A. U. (1995). "Implementing the Cognitive Academic Language Learning Approach: CALLA." *Bilingual Research Journal, 19* (3 & 4): pp. 379–394.

Chamot, A. U. & O'Malley, J. M. (1999). "The Cognitive Academic Language Learning Approach: A Model for Linguistically Diverse Classrooms." In K. Biacindo (ed.), *Perspectives: Educational Psychology,* pp. 39–51. Boulder, Colo.: Coursewise Publishing.

Chamot, A. U., & O'Malley, J. M. (1996). "The Cognitive Academic Language Learning Approach (CALLA): A Model for Linguistically Diverse Classrooms." *The Elementary School Journal, 96* (3): pp. 259–273.

Chamot, A. U., & O'Malley, J. M. (1996). "Implementing the Cognitive Academic Language Learning Approach: Issues and Options." In R. Oxford (ed.), *Language Learning Strategies Around the World,* pp. 167–173. Manoa: University of Hawaii Press.

Chamot, A. U., & O'Malley, J. M. (1994). *The CALLA Handbook: Implementing the Cognitive Academic Language Learning Approach.* White Plains, N.Y.: Addison Wesley Longman.

Chamot, A. U. & Steeves, K. A. (2004). *Land, People, Nation: A History of the United States, Books 1 and 2.* White Plains, N.Y.: Pearson Education.

Chamot, A. U. & Steeves, K. A. (2001). "Designing History Lessons for English Language Learners Using the CALLA model." *The Social Studies Review, Journal of the California Council for the Social Studies, 40* (1): pp. 22–27.

Chamot, A. U., Barnhardt, S., El-Dinary, P. B. & Robbins, J. (1999). *The Learning Strategies Handbook.* White Plains, N.Y.: Addison Wesley Longman.

Cummins, J. (1981). "The Role of Primary Language Development in Promoting Success for Limited English Proficient Students." In *Schooling and Language Minority Students: A Theoretical Framework.* Los Angeles: Evaluation, Dissemination, and Assessment Center, California State University, Los Angeles.

El-Dinary, P. B. (2002). "Challenges of Implementing Transactional Strategies Instruction for Reading Comprehension." In C. C. Block & M. Pressley, (eds.), *Comprehension Instruction: Research-Based Best Practices.* New York: Guilford Press.

GETTING STARTED

Unit Opener, pages 2–3

Preview

- Read aloud the unit title, "Getting Started." Tell students that this unit is about the basics of English.

- Have students look at the photos and identify the people and the settings. Provide help as needed. (A student entering a school, a teacher and students reading the school newspaper, students working together on a computer.) Write the descriptions of the people and the settings on the board as students say them.

- Help students identify the different items in the photos. (Examples: school, classroom, computer, desk.) Write the names of the items on the board as students say them.

- Point to key objects in the photos, one at a time, and ask, "What's this?" or "What are these?" Then model the response. "It's (a computer)." or "They're (newspapers)." Write the responses on the board.

- Continue the procedure above, calling on volunteers to answer the questions. Then call on volunteer pairs to ask and answer the questions.

- Read the unit goals aloud as students follow along in their texts. Answer any questions they may have.

Introductions, page 4

Preparation

Tell students that in this lesson they will practice introducing themselves to each other in English. Through the practice, they will get to meet their classmates and learn their names.

Presentation

Exercise A

- Refer students to the sample name in their texts. Point to the words as you say, "Isabel Estrada." Point to *Isabel* and say, "*Isabel* is the student's first name." Point to *Estrada* and say, "*Estrada* is the student's last name, or family name."

- Have students write their first and last name in their notebooks.

    Reaching All Students—Emergent Learners: Call on an advanced student to say and then write his or her first and last name on the board as a model. Then work individually with students who need help understanding the directions.

- Call on several students to say and write their first and last name on the board.

Practice

Exercise B

- 🎧 Have students listen to the dialogue, or read the dialogue aloud to them. Have them look at the illustration as they listen.

- Read the dialogue aloud with an advanced student as the other students follow along in their texts.

- Have students read the dialogue aloud with you.

    Optional Activity: Have one side of the classroom read part A; have the other side read part B. Then have the sides switch parts and read the dialogue again.

Exercise C

- Have students who can read on their own form pairs. Have them take turns reading both parts of the dialogue aloud. Provide help as needed.

    Reaching All Students—Emergent Learners: Work with emergent readers in small groups. Model each sentence and have individual students "echo" your reading; that is, have them repeat each sentence after you. Make sure that students look at the sentences as you read them.

- Have students work in pairs, substituting their own names to practice introducing themselves to each other.

    Reaching All Students—Emergent Learners: Write the dialogue on the board, leaving blanks for the students' information.
    A: Hello.
    B: Hi. What's your name?
    A: My name is ___ .
    B: I'm ___ . Nice to meet you.
    A: Nice to meet you, too.
    Have the students in one pair state their names. Fill in the blanks with their names. Have the pair read the dialogue aloud. Repeat the procedure with a second pair of students if needed.

    Reaching All Students—Kinesthetic Learners: Call on volunteer pairs to act out the dialogue, using their own names for the rest of the class.

Exercise D

- Have students look at the illustration in their texts. Read the names aloud as you point to each person.

- 🎧 Have students listen and say the names.

- Have students form new pairs. Have them practice the dialogue from Exercise B, substituting the names from the illustration. Have them repeat until each student has used all of the names.

    Reaching All Students—Emergent Learners: Work with two advanced students through a model dialogue. Leave the dialogue on the board with blanks for the substitutions if needed.

    Reaching All Students—Kinesthetic Learners: Call on volunteer pairs to act out the dialogue, using names from the illustration, for the rest of the class.

Expansion

Exercise E

- Have students close their texts and stand up.

- Have students practice the dialogue with their own names to meet as many classmates as they can.

Classroom Objects, page 5

Preparation

- Tell students that in this lesson they will practice the English names of objects in the classroom.

Presentation

Exercise A

- Have students listen to the names of the classroom objects, or read the names aloud to them. Have students look at the illustration as they listen. Point to each item as it is said.
- Have students read the names of the objects aloud with you.

  Optional Activity: Point to objects in the illustration, one at a time, and call on the class or individual students to say the name of the object.

Exercise B

- Have students look at the illustration in their texts. Call on volunteers to say the names of a few of the objects. Write the names on the board.
- Have students take out their notebooks and write the names of the classroom objects in the illustration. Encourage them to double-check their spelling against the names in their texts.

  Reaching All Students—Emergent Learners: Have students work in pairs or small groups. Provide help as needed.

- Review the answers as a class. Call on an advanced student to share his or her list with the class.

Answers
Order may vary:

a chalkboard	a pencil
a table	a pen
a chair	an eraser
a book	a bookcase
a notebook	

Practice

Exercise C

- Have students listen to the dialogue, or read the dialogue aloud to them. Have them look at the illustration as they listen.
- Read the dialogue aloud with an advanced student as the other students follow along in their texts.
- Have students read the dialogue aloud with you.

  Optional Activity: Have one side of the classroom read part A; have the other side read part B. Then have the sides switch parts and read the dialogue again.

Exercise D

- Have students who can read on their own form pairs. Have them take turns reading both parts of the dialogue aloud. Provide help as needed.

  Reaching All Students—Emergent Learners: Work with emergent readers in small groups. Model each sentence and have individual students "echo" your reading; that is, have them repeat each sentence after you. Make sure that students look at the sentences as you read them.

- Have students work in pairs to take turns practicing the dialogue using other classroom objects in the illustration in Exercise A. Have one student point to an item in the picture and ask, "What's this?" Have the second student answer and then point to and ask about another item.

  Reaching All Students—Emergent Learners: Write the dialogue on the board, leaving blanks for the information students will supply.
  A: What's this?
  B: It's ____ .
  Work with two advanced students through a model dialogue. Have the pair demonstrate pointing to objects and taking turns asking and answering.
  Reaching All Students—Kinesthetic Learners: Call on volunteer pairs to act out their original dialogues for the rest of the class.

Expansion

  Optional Activity: Explain the following game and demonstrate it with a group before having students play it. Divide students into groups of four or five, and have each group of students stand in a circle. Have each group choose someone to start. Have the first student say, "This is (a book)." while pointing to and saying the name of the object in the classroom. Have the second student clap two times and add a second object: "This is (a book), and this is (a pen)." while pointing to and saying the name of both objects in the classroom. Continue around the circle, with each student adding an object. If a student makes a mistake or pauses for more than three seconds, he or she must sit down. Encourage students to move as quickly as they can and to start around the circle again, adding as many objects as possible. Have students start the list again if they have already named all the objects they can think of. The last student standing wins.

Classroom Commands, page 6

Preparation

Tell students that in this lesson they will practice following and giving different English commands they will use every day in the classroom.

Presentation

Exercise A

- 🎧 Have students listen to the classroom commands, or read the commands aloud to them. Have them look at the illustrations as they listen.
- Have students read the commands aloud with you.

  Optional Activity: Point to the illustrations, one at a time, and call on the class or individual students to say the command.

Practice

Exercise B

Say the commands, in order, with both the class and you performing them at the same time. Then say the commands at random, and have the class perform them on their own.

  Optional Activity: After students have mastered the commands illustrated, make slight variations in the commands using the names of classroom objects students learned in the previous lesson. (Examples: Get your [pen/eraser/book/notebook]. Close your [notebook]. Open your [book].)

Exercise C

- 🎧 Have students listen to the dialogue, or read the dialogue aloud to them. Have them look at the illustration as they listen.
- Read the dialogue aloud with an advanced student as the other students follow along in their texts.
- Have students read the dialogue aloud with you.

  Optional Activity: Have one side of the classroom read part A; have the other side read part B. Then have the sides switch parts and read the dialogue again.

Exercise D

- Have students who can read on their own form pairs. Have them take turns reading both parts of the dialogue aloud. Provide help as needed.

  Reaching All Students—Emergent Learners: Work with emergent readers in small groups. Model each sentence and have individual students "echo" your reading; that is, have them repeat each sentence after you. Make sure that students look at the sentences as you read them.

- Have students practice the dialogue again, substituting other commands and using their partner's last name with "Mr." or "Ms."

  Reaching All Students—Emergent Learners: Write the dialogue on the board, leaving blanks for the information students will supply.
  A: ___ .
  B: Okay, Mr./Ms. ___ .
  Work with two advanced students through a model dialogue. Have the pair demonstrate pointing to objects and taking turns asking and answering.

  Reaching All Students—Kinesthetic Learners: Call on volunteer pairs to act out their original dialogues for the rest of the class.

Expansion

  Optional Activity: Explain the following game and demonstrate it with a group before having the whole class play it. Divide students into groups of four to six, and have each group choose a leader. Have the leader give an introduction using his or her last name, for example, "I'm Mr./Ms. (Estrada)." Then have the leader give commands to the other group members. The group members should follow the commands and say, "Okay, Mr./Ms. (Estrada)." Encourage the leader to move quickly. After six commands, have the leader pick the student who was the best at following the directions. That student is the next leader.

Days of the Week, page 7

Preparation

Tell students that in this lesson they will practice the English names for the days of the week.

Presentation

Exercise A *(See Transparency 81.)*

- 🎧 Have students listen and say the names of the days of the week, or read the names aloud to them. Point to each word (on a poster, the board, or in the text) as it is said.

- 🎧 Have students listen to the names of the days of the week a second time, following along in their texts.

- Have students read the names of the days of the week aloud with you.

  🎧 **Optional Activity:** Sing the song "Days of the Week" to the tune of the theme song from the TV series *The Addams Family.* (If you don't know the tune, just chant the lyrics.) Write the words on the board and point to the words as you sing them. Then point to the words again as students sing along with you.

    There's Monday and there's Tuesday
    There's Wednesday and there's Thursday
    There's Friday and there's Saturday
    And then there's Sunday
    Days of the week (snap, snap)
    Days of the week (snap, snap)
    Days of the week, days of the week, days
      of the week (snap, snap)

Practice

Exercise B

- 🎧 Have students listen to the dialogue, or read the dialogue aloud to them. Have them look at the illustration as they listen.

- Read the dialogue aloud with an advanced student as the other students follow along in their texts.

- Have students read the dialogue aloud with you.

Optional Activity: Have one side of the classroom read part A; have the other side read part B. Then have the sides switch parts and read the dialogue again.

Exercise C

- Have students who can read on their own form pairs. Have them take turns reading the parts of the dialogue aloud. Provide help as needed.

  Reaching All Students—Emergent Learners: Work with emergent readers in small groups. Model each sentence and have individual students "echo" your reading; that is, have them repeat each sentence after you. Make sure that students look at the sentences as you read them.

- Have students practice the dialogue again, substituting other days of the week.

  Reaching All Students—Emergent Learners: Write the dialogue on the board, leaving blanks for the information students will supply.
  A: What day is it?
  B: It's ___ .
  Work with two advanced students through a model dialogue.

  Reaching All Students—Kinesthetic Learners: Call on volunteer pairs to act out their original dialogues for the rest of the class.

Exercise D

- Have students write the names of the days of the week in order in their notebooks. Refer them to their texts for help with spelling.

- To review the answers, call on students, one at a time, to write the name of a day of the week on the board in order, beginning with Monday.

Expansion

Exercise E

- Read the directions aloud as students follow along in their texts.

- Have students work in pairs to play the game. Have them take turns, keeping score in their notebooks. Encourage them to work quickly.

Reaching All Students—Emergent Learners: Write the exchange on the board, leaving blanks for the information students will supply.

A: Today is ___ . Tomorrow is . . .
B: ___ .

Work with two advanced students through a model dialogue. Have the pair demonstrate taking the different parts. Encourage them to move quickly, until one student makes a mistake. Demonstrate writing points on the board.

<u>**Optional Activity:**</u> Explain the following game and demonstrate it with a group before having students play it. Have students form groups of four to six and stand in a circle. Have students go around the circle, saying the names of the days of the week in order. Have students continue going around the circle, starting again with the name of the first day of the week. Have students sit down if they make a mistake or can't answer in three seconds. The last person standing is the winner.

The Alphabet, page 8

Preparation

Tell students that in this lesson they will practice the letters of the alphabet in English. Refer students to the title "The Alphabet" and to the letters of the alphabet in their texts. Have them repeat the title "The Alphabet." Point out that the letters are capital letters and small letters.

Presentation

Exercise A

- Have students listen to and say the names of the letters of the alphabet, or read the names of the letters aloud to them and have them repeat them after you. Point to each letter (on a poster, the board, or in the text) as it is said.

- Have students read the names of the letters of the alphabet aloud with you. Work on specific pronunciation problems at this point. Do this section at a brisk pace to hold students' interest.

<u>**Optional Activity:**</u> Have students work in pairs to take turns reading the names of the letters of the alphabet.

Practice

Exercise B

- Have students listen to "The ABC Song," or sing the song aloud to them.

> **Teacher:** ABCDEFG
> **Students [echoing teacher]:** ABCDEFG
> **Teacher:** HIJKLMNOP
> **Students [echoing teacher]:** HIJKLMNOP
> **Teacher:** LMNOPQRST
> **Students [echoing teacher]:** LMNOPQRST
> **Teacher:** UVWXYZ
> **Students [echoing teacher]:** UVWXYZ

Point to each letter (on a poster, on the board, or in the text) as it appears in the song. Tell students that the song can help them to remember the names of the letters and their order in the alphabet.

- Have students sing "The ABC Song" along with you or the CD (or tape).

<u>**Optional Activity:**</u> Make a set of index cards, each card with a letter of the alphabet. Do two sets if needed, to make sure there are enough cards so that each student gets at least one. Distribute the cards to students. First, play or sing "The ABC Song." Have students stand and sing the name of their letter as it appears in the song. Then begin again without your voice or the CD, asking each student to stand and sing the name of his or her letter to complete the song.

Exercise C

- Have students listen to the dialogue, or read the dialogue aloud to them. Have them look at the illustration as they listen.

- Read the dialogue aloud with an advanced student as the other students follow along in their texts.

- Have students read the dialogue aloud with you.

<u>**Optional Activity:**</u> Have one side of the classroom read part A; have the other side read part B. Then have the sides switch parts and read the dialogue again.

Exercise D

- Have students who can read on their own form pairs. Have them take turns reading both parts of the dialogue aloud. Provide help as needed.

> **Reaching All Students—Emergent Learners:** Work with emergent readers in small groups. Model each sentence and have individual students "echo"

your reading; that is, have them repeat each sentence after you. Make sure that students look at the sentences as you read them. Have students also spell their names aloud for practice if needed.

- Have students work in pairs to practice the dialogue again, spelling their own names.

    Reaching All Students—Emergent Learners: Write the dialogue on the board, leaving blanks for the information students will supply.
    A: How do you spell your name?
    B: ___ .
    Work with two advanced students through a model dialogue.

    Reaching All Students—Kinesthetic Learners: Call on volunteer pairs to act out their original dialogues for the rest of the class.

Expansion
Exercise E

Have students take out their notebooks and a pencil. Divide them into pairs. Have students take turns asking each other how to spell their name. Have them write down the name in their notebooks. Then have them check each other's written work, making any necessary corrections.

    Reaching All Students—Emergent Learners: Work with two advanced students through a model conversation. Have them demonstrate writing down each other's name, checking each other's work, and making any necessary corrections.

    Optional Activity: Do the preceding exercise as a game. Have students work quickly to pair with as many classmates as possible to write down the most names. At the end of the exercise, the student with the most names wins.

    Optional Activity: Explain the following game and demonstrate it with a group before having the other students play it. Have students form pairs. Have one student in each pair look at page 7 in the text (Days of the Week). Have the other student in each pair look at page 5 in the text (Classroom Objects). Then have the pairs take turns asking each other to spell the names of the days of the week or the names of seven classroom objects. Have students give themselves one point for each correct answer, keeping score

in their notebooks. The student with the most points wins.

Numbers 1–20, page 9

Preparation

Tell students that in this lesson they will practice the English names for the numbers 1 through 20.

Presentation
Exercise A

- Have students listen to the names of the numbers, or read the names aloud to them. Point to each numeral (on a poster, the board, or in the text) as it is said.
- Have students read the names of the numbers aloud with you.

    Optional Activity: Write the numerals 1 to 20 on the board, one at a time, and call on the class or individual students to say them.

Practice

Exercise B *(See Transparencies 6–7.)*

- Have students write the numerals 1 to 20, one numeral per line, on a sheet of paper in their notebooks. Demonstrate by writing a few numerals on the board.
- Next, have students write the number word next to each numeral. Demonstrate with a few numerals on the board. Encourage students to use their texts for help with spelling.
- Review the answers as a class by having students say the numbers from 1 to 20. If there are more than 20 students, have students start with the number 1 again after they have reached 20. If there are fewer than 20 students, have the students each take turns again and continue until they reach 20.

Exercise C

- Have students listen to the dialogue, or read the dialogue aloud to them. Have them look at the illustration as they listen.
- Read the dialogue aloud with an advanced student as the other students follow along in their texts.
- Have students read the dialogue aloud with you.

Optional Activity: Have one side of the classroom read part A; have the other side read part B. Then have the sides switch parts and read the dialogue again.

Exercise D

- Have students who can read on their own form pairs. Have them take turns reading both parts of the dialogue aloud. Provide help as needed.

   Reaching All Students—Emergent Learners: Work with emergent readers in small groups. Model each sentence and have individual students "echo" your reading; that is, have them repeat each sentence after you. Make sure that students look at the sentences as you read them.

- Have students practice the dialogue again, substituting their own ages.

   Reaching All Students—Emergent Learners: Write the dialogue on the board, leaving blanks for the information students will supply.
   A: How old are you?
   B: I'm ___ .
   Work with two advanced students through a model dialogue.

   Reaching All Students—Kinesthetic Learners: Call on volunteer pairs to act out their original dialogues for the rest of the class.

Expansion
Exercise E

- Have students close their texts and stand up.
- Have them use the dialogue to find out the age of as many classmates as they can.

   Optional Activity: Do the exercise below as a game with students writing in the name and age of as many classmates as possible. Write the following dialogue on the board:
   A: How do you spell your name?
   B: ___ .
   A: How old are you?
   B: I'm ___ .
   Have students compete to write down the most names and ages. At the end of the exercise, the student with the most names and ages is the winner.

Numbers 20–100, page 10

Preparation
Tell students that in this lesson they will practice the English names for the numbers 20 through 100.

Presentation
Exercise A

- Have students listen to the names of the numbers, or read the names aloud to them. Point to each numeral (on a poster, the board, or in the text) as it is said.
- Have students read the names of the numbers aloud with you.
- Write numerals on the board from Student Book page 10, one at a time, and call on the class or individual students to say them. After covering these numerals, write the numerals 31 through 40, one at a time, on the board and call on the class or individual students to name them.

   Optional Activity: Divide students into groups of four to six. Have them go around their group saying the numbers from 20 to 100. Have students coach each other as needed.

Practice
Exercise B *(See Transparency 7.)*

- Have students number a sheet of paper in their notebooks from 1 to 12. Then have them copy the numerals. Demonstrate by writing the first few items on the board.
- Next, have students write the number word for each numeral they wrote. Demonstrate on the board for the first few items. Encourage students to use their texts for help with spelling.

   Reaching All Students—Emergent Learners: Have students work in pairs or small groups to identify the names of the numerals and to write the corresponding number words.

- Review the answers as a class. Call on students to say and write their answers on the board.

Exercise C

- 🎧 Have students listen to the dialogue, or read the dialogue aloud to them. Have them look at the illustration as they listen.

- Read the dialogue aloud with an advanced student as the other students follow along in their texts.

- Have students read the dialogue aloud with you.

  Optional Activity: Have one side of the classroom read part A; have the other side read part B. Then have the sides switch parts and read the dialogue again.

Exercise D

- Have students who can read on their own form pairs. Have them take turns reading both parts of the dialogue aloud. Provide help as needed.

  Reaching All Students—Emergent Learners: Work with emergent readers in small groups. Model each sentence and have individual students "echo" your reading; that is, have them read each sentence after you. Make sure that students look at the sentences as you read them.

- Have students practice the dialogue again, substituting other numbers and the correct answer to the math problem.

  Reaching All Students—Emergent Learners: Write the dialogue on the board, leaving blanks for the information students will supply.
  A: What's ___ plus ___ ?
  B: It's ___ .
  Work with two advanced students through a model dialogue. Encourage students to solve the math problem their classmate gives them in their notebooks if needed.

  Reaching All Students—Kinesthetic Learners: Call on volunteer pairs to act out their original dialogues for the rest of the class.

Expansion

Optional Activity: Explain the following game and demonstrate it with a group before having students play it. Tell students that they are going to play a math game. Divide the class into two teams. Have students on Team A and B line up to take turns asking and answering math problems. Have a student from Team A give a math problem using two numbers between 1 and 49. Have the first player from Team B try to answer the math problem. If the answer is correct, Team B gets a point. Then Team B gives a math problem to the first player from Team A. Keep score on the board. Continue in the same manner as time allows or until a team reaches a specified number of turns.

Time, page 11

Preparation

Tell students that in this lesson they will practice telling the time in English.

Presentation

Exercise A (See Transparency 84.)

- 🎧 Have students listen to the times, or read the times aloud to them. Point to each clock face as the time is said.

- Have students read the times aloud with you.

  Optional Activity: Bring in a time-teaching clock that can be set for any time, or use a digital or analog clock that is easy to set. Set the clock to different times and call on the class or individual students to tell the time.

Practice

Exercise B

- Have students number a sheet of paper in their notebooks from 1 to 12. Have them copy the times. Demonstrate by writing the first few items on the board.

- Next, have students write the time word for each item. Demonstrate on the board for the first few items. Encourage students to use page 10 in their texts for help with spelling.

  Reaching All Students—Emergent Learners: Have students work in pairs or small groups to identify the names of the times and to write them.

- Review the answers as a class. Call on students to say and write their answers on the board.

Answers
1. 7:15 seven fifteen
2. 9:35 nine thirty-five
3. 3:20 three twenty
4. 5:45 five forty-five
5. 8:00 eight o'clock
6. 6:05 six oh five
7. 11:25 eleven twenty-five
8. 2:10 two ten
9. 1:55 one fifty-five
10. 12:33 twelve thirty-three
11. 4:48 four forty-eight
12. 10:02 ten oh two

Exercise C

- 🎧 Have students listen to the dialogue, or read the dialogue aloud to them. Have them look at the illustration as they listen.

- Read the dialogue aloud with an advanced student as the other students follow along in their texts.

- Have students read the dialogue aloud with you.

  Optional Activity: Have one side of the classroom read part A; have the other side read part B. Then have the sides switch parts and read the dialogue again.

Exercise D

- Have students who can read on their own form pairs. Have them take turns reading both parts of the dialogue aloud. Provide help as needed.

  Reaching All Students—Emergent Learners: Work with emergent readers in small groups. Model each sentence and have individual students "echo" your reading; that is, have them repeat each sentence after you. Make sure that students look at the sentences as you read them.

- Have students practice the dialogue again, substituting different times.

  Reaching All Students—Emergent Learners: Write the dialogue on the board, leaving blanks for the information students will supply.
  A: What time is it?
  B: It's ___ .
  Work with two advanced students through a model dialogue.

Reaching All Students—Kinesthetic Learners: Call on volunteer pairs to act out their original dialogues for the rest of the class.

Expansion

Optional Activity: Explain the following game and demonstrate it with a group before having students play it. Have students form groups of four to six and stand or sit in a circle. Have each group choose a leader. The group leader thinks of a time. The next student tries to guess the time. The leader says "earlier" or "later." The students go around the circle. The first student to guess the correct time is the new group leader.

Months of the Year, page 12

Preparation

Tell students that in this lesson they will practice the English names for the months of the year.

Presentation

Exercise A

- 🎧 Have students listen to the names of the months, or read the names aloud to them. Point to each word as it is said.

- Have students read the names of the months aloud with you.

  Optional Activity: Have students number a sheet of paper in their notebooks from 1 to 12. Then, for each numeral, have them write the name of the corresponding month, for example, 1. January, 2. February. Demonstrate by writing the first few months on the board.

  Reaching All Students—Kinesthetic Learners: Play a Total Physical Response game using "Birthdays," either as a song or as a chant. Write the words to the song on the board. Point to the words while you sing or chant them. Have students stand up and sit down when their birthday month is mentioned. Then have the class sing or chant the song with you.

  Birthdays! Birthdays! They're such fun!
  Stand up when I say the month your birthday's in.

(continued)

January stand up. January sit down.
February stand up. February sit
   down.
March stand up. March sit down.
April stand up. April sit down.

May stand up. May sit down.
June stand up. June sit down.
July stand up. July sit down.
August stand up. August sit down.

September stand up. September sit
   down.
October stand up. October sit down.
November stand up. November
   sit down.
December stand up. December
   sit down.

Practice
Exercise B

- 🎧 Have students listen to the dialogue, or read the dialogue aloud to them. Have them look at the illustration as they listen.
- Read the dialogue aloud with an advanced student as the other students follow along in their texts.
- Have students read the dialogue aloud with you.

   Optional Activity: Have one side of the classroom read part A; have the other side read part B. Then have the sides switch parts and read the dialogue again.

Exercise C (See Transparency 81.)

- Have students who can read on their own form pairs. Have them take turns reading both parts of the dialogue aloud. Provide help as needed.

   Reaching All Students—Emergent Learners: Work with emergent readers in small groups. Model each sentence and have individual students "echo" your reading; that is, have them repeat each sentence after you. Make sure that students look at the sentences as you read them.

- Have students practice the dialogue again, substituting different months.

   Reaching All Students—Emergent Learners: Write the dialogue on the board, leaving blanks for the information students will supply.

A: What month is it?
B: It's ___ .
Work with two advanced students through a model dialogue.

Reaching All Students—Kinesthetic Learners: Call on volunteer pairs to act out their original dialogues for the rest of the class.

Expansion

Optional Activity: Explain the following game and demonstrate it with a group before having students play it. Have students form groups of four to six. Have each group choose a leader. Have the group leader say a number from 1 to 12. The first student to say the name of the corresponding month gets one point. Have students keep a tally of their points in their notebooks. After 12 items, the student with the most points is the new group leader.

Dates, page 13

Preparation

Tell students that in this lesson they will practice the English names of dates, using ordinal numbers. Refer students to the ordinal numbers in their texts.

Presentation
Exercise A

- 🎧 Have students listen to the names of the ordinal numbers, or read the names aloud to them. Point to each numeral (on a poster, the board, or in the text) as it is said.
- Have students read the names of the ordinal numbers aloud with you.

Optional Activity: Write the ordinal numerals on the board or a poster. Point randomly to numbers and call on the class or individual students to say the names of the numbers.

Optional Activity: Have students say the ordinal numbers from 1st to 31st. If there are fewer than 31 students, have the students begin again and continue until they reach 31st. If there are more than 31 students, have students continue with higher ordinal numbers.

Practice

Exercise B

- 🎧 Have students listen to the dialogue, or read the dialogue aloud to them. Have them look at the illustration as they listen.
- Read the dialogue aloud with an advanced student as the other students follow along in their texts.
- Have students read the dialogue aloud with you.
  Optional Activity: Have one side of the classroom read part A; have the other side read part B. Then have the sides switch parts and read the dialogue again.

Exercise C (See Transparency 81.)

- Have students who can read on their own form pairs. Have them take turns reading both parts of the dialogue aloud. Provide help as needed.
  Reaching All Students—Emergent Learners: Work with emergent readers in small groups. Model each sentence and have individual students "echo" your reading; that is, have them repeat each sentence after you. Make sure that students look at the sentences as you read them.
- Have students practice the dialogue again, substituting different dates.
  Reaching All Students—Emergent Learners: Write the dialogue on the board, leaving blanks for the information students will supply.
  A: What's the date?
  B: It's ___ .
  Work with two advanced students through a model dialogue. Encourage students to use page 12 in their texts to review the names of the months if needed.
  Reaching All Students—Kinesthetic Learners: Call on volunteer pairs to act out their original dialogues for the rest of the class.

Exercise D

- Have students number a sheet of paper in their notebooks from 1 to 4. Have them copy the birth date for each person next to the appropriate number. Demonstrate by writing the first item on the board.

- Have students spell out the months and days for each birth date they wrote in their notebooks. Demonstrate on the board for the first item. Encourage students to use page 12 in their texts for help with spelling.
- Call on volunteers to say and write their answers on the board.

> **Answers**
> 1. 4/10 April tenth
> 2. 12/30 December thirtieth
> 3. 4/7 April seventh
> 4. 6/13 June thirteenth

Exercise E

Explain to students that dates can also be written as follows: November 18, June 4, etc.

Expansion

Optional Activity: Write the following dialogue on the board:
A: When's your birthday?
B: It's ___ .
A: How do you spell your name?
B: ___ .
Read the dialogue aloud. Then have students read the dialogue aloud with you. Tell students that they will use the dialogue to ask and answer questions about their classmates' birth dates. They will write their classmates' birth dates and names in their notebooks. Work with two advanced students through a model dialogue. Have each student write the other's numerical birth date and name on the board. Then have them check for correctness. Have students stand and pair with as many different classmates as possible. Have them write their classmates' birth dates and names in their notebooks. Encourage students to show their classmates what they wrote and make corrections if needed. Do this activity as a game if desired. The winner is the student with the most birth dates.

UNIT 1 NEW FRIENDS

Unit Opener, pages 16–17

Preview

- Read aloud the unit title, "New Friends." Tell students that this unit is about meeting people and making new friends. Tell students that they will be making new friends in this class, too.

- Have students look at the photos and identify the people and the settings. Point to the students in the photo and ask, "Are they students?" Elicit the response. (Yes, they are.) Point to the students in the hall and ask, "Where are they?" Elicit the response. (They're at school.) Write the questions and responses on the board as students say them.

- Point to key objects in the photos, one at a time, and ask, "What is this?" or "What are these?" Elicit the response. (It's [milk]. *or* They're [books].) Write the questions and responses on the board as students say them.

- Read the unit goals aloud as students follow along in their texts. Answer any questions they may have.

- Refer students to pages 14 and 15, where the characters in the readings throughout the book are introduced.

Chapter 1
What's your name?

Objectives

Language:
- Listen to a dialogue for comprehension.
- Understand familiar vocabulary and grammar structures by listening to a dialogue.
- Develop new vocabulary and grammar structures by listening to a dialogue.
- Act out a dialogue.
- Use pronouns correctly.
- Use the present tense of *be* in affirmative statements, negative statements, and *yes/no* questions.
- Use contractions of pronouns and the simple present tense of *be*.
- Say the names of the letters of the alphabet.
- Make original conversations using new vocabulary and grammar structures.
- Discuss character's feelings.
- Discuss personal experiences.
- Evaluate one's own learning of new vocabulary, grammar, and oral language.

Literacy:
- Read a dialogue for comprehension.
- Understand familiar vocabulary and grammar structures by reading a dialogue.
- Develop new vocabulary and grammar structures by reading a dialogue.
- Complete and write sentences using pronouns correctly.
- Complete and write affirmative and negative statements using contractions of pronouns and the present tense of *be*.
- Write affirmative and negative answers to *yes/no* questions with the present tense of *be*.
- Write the letters of the alphabet, using uppercase and lowercase letters.
- Write one's name.
- Alphabetize words.
- Read a short story for comprehension.
- Understand familiar vocabulary and grammar structures by reading a short story.

- Develop new vocabulary and grammar structures by reading a short story.
- Act out a short story.
- Plan, write, revise, edit, proofread, and make a final copy of a descriptive paragraph about oneself.
- Capitalize and punctuate sentences correctly.
- Evaluate one's own learning of reading skills, reading comprehension, and writing skills.

Learning Strategies:
- Use cooperation with a classmate to read a dialogue.
- Use cooperation with a small group to act out a dialogue.
- Use cooperation with a classmate to alphabetize names.
- Use one's own experience to comprehend a short story.
- Use cooperation with a small group to act out a short story.
- Use cooperation with a classmate to check a paragraph one has written.
- Identify easy and difficult material in a chapter and the different ways to learn the difficult material.

Opening Dialogue, pages 18–19

Getting Ready

Preparation *(See Transparency 17.)*

- Have students look at the illustrations and identify the words they know for the people and objects they see. (Examples: teacher, students, desk, book, globe.) Write the words on the board as students say them.

  Reaching All Students—Visual/ Kinesthetic Learners: Have students point to these objects in the classroom as they say the words.

- Point to the objects in the pictures, one at a time, and ask, "What is this?" Elicit the response. (It is a [globe].) Have students repeat.

- Point to the teacher in the picture on page 18 and ask, "Who is this?" Elicit the response. (He is the teacher.) Have students repeat. Point to the students in the picture and ask, "Who are they?" Elicit the response. (They are students.)

Listening and Reading

Good Morning

Presentation

Exercise A

- Read the directions and the prelistening question aloud as students follow along in their texts.
- Have students listen to the dialogue, or read the dialogue aloud to them. Have them look at the appropriate illustrations as they listen.
- Ask the prelistening question, "What is the teacher's name?" Call on a volunteer to answer. (The teacher's name is Mr. Gomez.)

Exercise B

Have students read the dialogue. Point out to students that the asterisks in the dialogue signal a change in scene. Provide help with content, vocabulary, etc. as needed.

> **Reaching All Students—Emergent Learners:** Work with emergent learners in small groups while the other students work independently. Read aloud as students follow along in their texts. Monitor their comprehension by interrupting the reading with questions such as, "Where is Mr. Gomez from?" (He is from the United States.) "Who are Carlos and Carmen?" (They are brother and sister.) "Where are they from?" (They are from Mexico.) "Who is very nervous?" (Maria is very nervous.)

Pair and Group Work

Exercise A

- Read the dialogue with an advanced student while the other students follow along in their texts.
- Have students who can read on their own form pairs. Have them take turns reading the dialogue. Provide help as needed.

> **Reaching All Students—Emergent Learners:** Work with emergent readers in small groups. Model each sentence and have individual students "echo" your reading; that is, have them repeat each sentence after you. Make sure that

students look at the sentences as you read them.

Exercise B

Divide the class into groups of five. Group students heterogeneously so that each group is made up of average readers, weak readers, and strong readers. For each group, have each student choose a role for him- or herself from the dialogue. Encourage each group to practice acting out the dialogue several times. Circulate among the groups. Offer assistance as needed.

> **Reaching All Students—Kinesthetic Learners:** Have each group act out the dialogue dramatically for the rest of the class. Then have them evaluate their performance.

Vocabulary

Practice

Exercise A *(See Transparency 82.)*

Have students read and say the words and expressions. Provide assistance with pronunciation as needed. Then have them write the words and expressions in their notebooks.

> **Reaching All Students—Auditory Learners:** Encourage students to say the words and expressions as they write them in their notebooks.

Exercise B *(See Transparency 85.)*

- Have students turn to page 250 in their texts.
- Call on a volunteer to read Step 1 aloud as the other students follow along.
- Model with an advanced student asking for and giving the spelling of the first two words in the word box on page 19.
- Have students work in pairs asking for and giving the spelling of words and expressions in the word box on page 19.

Exercise C

Have students find the words and expressions in the dialogue. Have them read the sentences.

Exercise D

- Have students choose two words from the word box. Then have them write a sentence using each word.

> **Reaching All Students—Emergent Learners:** Work with students in small groups. Guide them in creating two

sentences, each one using a new vocabulary word. Write the sentences on the board. Have students copy the sentences into their notebooks.

- Call on volunteers to read their sentences aloud.

Answers
Answers will vary.

Grammar 1, page 20

Pronouns

Preparation

- Have students look at the illustrations and the pronouns printed below them.
- Pointing to the illustrations in the text, read aloud each of the pronouns and have students repeat them after you: *I, you, she, he, it, we, you, they.*

Presentation

- Prepare display cards with each of the pronouns: *I, you, she, he, it, we, you, they.*
- Call on two volunteers—a boy and a girl.
- Hold up the "*I*" card and point to yourself, as in the illustration in the text. Say, "*I* am (your name)."
- Hold up the "*you*" card and stand facing one of the volunteers so that the class sees the profile of you and the volunteer. Say, while looking at the student and using an open palm gesture, "*You* are (student's name)." Have students repeat.
- Hold up the "*she*" card. From the side, use an open palm gesture toward the female student, and say, "*She* is (female student's name)." Have students repeat.
- Hold up the "*he*" card. From the side, use an open palm gesture toward the male student, and say, "*He* is (male student's name)." Have students repeat.
- Hold up the "*it*" card. Use an open palm gesture toward the chalkboard or another classroom object and say, "*It* is a (chalkboard)." Have students repeat.
- Hold up the "*we*" card and stand facing one of the volunteers, so that the class sees the profile of you and the volunteer. Say, while looking at the student and using an open

palm circle gesture toward yourself and the student, "*We* are (student's name and your name)." Then use an open palm circle gesture toward yourself and the whole class, saying, "*We* are (your name's) class." Have students repeat.

- Hold up the "*you*" card and make an open palm circle gesture toward the two volunteers while facing them. Say, "*You* are (first student's name and second student's name)." Have students repeat. Then use an open palm circle gesture toward all the students, saying, "*You* are students."
- Hold up the "*they*" card and make an open palm circle gesture toward the two volunteers, while facing the class as if introducing the volunteers. Say, "*They* are (first student's name and second student's name)." Have students repeat. Then use an open palm circle gesture toward the rest of the class, while looking at the volunteers as if introducing the class. Say, "*They* are students."
- Have students look again at the illustrations and pronouns in their texts. Explain that pronouns are words that refer to people, places, and objects without stating their names. Say, "Instead of saying, '(female student's name) is in our class,' I can say, '*She* is in our class.'"

Practice
Exercise A

- Have students number a sheet of paper in their notebooks from 1 to 5. Demonstrate on the board if needed.
- Explain that students will match the items in the left-hand column with the correct pronouns in the right-hand column.
- Call on a volunteer to read the first item with the sample answer. Ask the student to explain why the answer is correct.
- Have students write the letters for the remaining answers in their notebooks.
- Review the answers with the class.

Answers

1. (c) we	**3.** (a) you	**5.** (e) he
2. (d) they	**4.** (b) she	

Exercise B

- Have students copy the five sets of sentences into their notebooks.

- Call on a volunteer to read the first set of sentences. Ask the student to explain why the sample answer is correct.
- Have students complete the remaining sentences by writing the correct pronoun in each sentence.

  Reaching All Students—Emergent Learners: First, have students do the exercise orally, using the illustrations and pronouns for reference. Then have them copy the sentences into their notebooks. Have them complete the sentences. Provide help as needed.

- Review the answers with the class.

Answers		
1. She	3. It	5. He
2. They	4. We	

Optional Activity: Have students work in small groups to write three pairs of sentences about the characters and objects introduced in the "Good Morning" dialogue on pages 18–19. The first sentence in each pair should include the name of the character or object; the second sentence should use the corresponding pronoun. Provide help as needed.

Examples:
1. <u>Carmen</u> is a student. <u>She</u> is from Mexico.
2. <u>Carlos</u> is from Mexico. <u>He</u> is Carmen's brother.

Call on volunteers to read their pairs of sentences.

Reaching All Students—Emergent Learners: Provide pairs of sentences. Have students complete the second sentence in each pair by writing the correct pronoun in the blank.

Examples:
1. <u>Carmen</u> is a student. *<u>She</u>* is from Mexico.
2. <u>Carlos</u> is from Mexico. *<u>He</u>* is Carmen's brother.

Grammar 2, page 21

Present Tense of *be*: Statements

Preparation

- Write the following dialogue on the board as a way of presenting the grammar focus in context.

Carlos: This is Carmen. She's my sister.
Carmen: And he's my brother, Carlos. We're from Mexico. We're not from El Salvador.

- Read the dialogue aloud as students follow along.

  Reaching All Students—Advanced Learners: Call on an advanced pair of students to read the dialogue aloud.

Presentation

- Copy the first part of the grammar chart onto the board.
- Read aloud across the first row, "I am from Mexico." Have students repeat. Follow the same procedure with the other rows in this part: "You are from Mexico. He is from Mexico. She is from Mexico. It is from Mexico," and so on.
- Copy the second part of the grammar chart onto the board.
- Read across the first row, "I am not from Mexico." Have students repeat.
- Follow the same procedure with the other rows in this part.
- Say, "In English, some verbs have a short form, called a *contraction*." Write the word *contraction* on the board. Then copy the contractions chart onto the board. Read aloud the sentences in the first part of the grammar chart. Then read the same sentences aloud, substituting the contractions for the long forms. Point to the contractions on the board as you say them in the sentences. Have students repeat after you.
- Follow the same procedure for the second part of the grammar chart.
- Explain to students that most people use contractions when speaking. They also use the contractions in informal (friendly) writing, such as letters or notes to friends.
- Have students work in pairs or small groups. First, have them read one of the sentences from the first part of the grammar chart. Then have them substitute the contraction for the long form. Have them follow the same procedure for the second part of the grammar chart.

  Reaching All Students—Emergent Learners: Work with students in small groups, pointing out where they should look in the charts.

Exercise A

- Have students copy the five sentences into their notebooks.
- Call on a volunteer to read aloud the first sentence with the sample answer. Have the student explain why the answer is correct.
- Have students complete the remaining sentences in their notebooks with the given pronoun and the correct form of *be*. Remind them to use contractions.

   Reaching All Students—Emergent Learners: First, have students do the exercise orally, using both parts of the grammar chart for reference. Then have them copy the sentences into their notebooks. Have them complete the sentences. Provide help as needed.

- Review the answers with the class.

Answers

1. They're	3. It's	5. We're
2. I'm	4. He's	

Exercise B

- Call on a volunteer to read aloud the first sentence without the sample answer. Ask the class, "Is the sentence in the affirmative or the negative?" (Affirmative.) Then ask the same volunteer to read aloud the sample answer. Ask the class, "Is the sample answer in the affirmative or the negative?" (Negative.)
- Follow the same procedure for the second sentence.
- Remind students that they have to change each sentence from the negative to the affirmative or from the affirmative to the negative.
- Have students complete items 3–5 in their notebooks.

   Reaching All Students—Emergent Learners: First, have students do the exercise orally, using both parts of the grammar chart for reference. Remind them to change each sentence from the negative to the affirmative or from the affirmative to the negative. Then have them copy the sentences into their notebooks. Have them complete the exercise. Provide help as needed.

- Review the answers with the class.

Answers

1. He's not a teacher.
2. I'm from Peru.
3. You're not a student.
4. She's not my sister.
5. It's pretty.

Word Study, page 22

The Alphabet

Presentation

Display the alphabet on the board or a poster and have students say the names of the letters as you point to them. Work on specific pronunciation problems of letters as needed. Do this section at a brisk pace so that it holds students' interest. (Keep the alphabet accessible.)

Practice

Exercise A

Have students work in pairs or small groups. Have them say the letters of the alphabet as they point to the letters in the chart in their texts.

   Optional Activity: Have students listen to the "ABC Song" as you point to the corresponding letters on the board or the poster (see lyrics on page 7.) Then have them sing along.

Exercise B *(See Transparencies 1–5 and 8–15.)*

- Have students look at the chart of capital letters and lowercase letters in their texts. Explain that there are special situations in which capital letters are used, such as at the beginning of a name or a country. Write on the board: *Mr. Gomez is from the United States.* Underline the capital letters.
- Have students write the alphabet, using capital letters, in their notebooks.
- Have students write the alphabet, using lowercase letters, in their notebooks.

Consonants and Vowels

Preparation

Tell students that in English, sounds can be divided into two main groups: consonants and vowels. Consonants are "closed sounds," with the lips, teeth, or tongue blocking part of the air from the breath to form the sound. (Give a spoken example, such as /t/. Explain that when we make this sound, the tongue is behind the teeth, blocking part of the air. Have students repeat /t/.) Vowel sounds are "open sounds" that don't block the air from the breath. (Give an example, such as /a/. Explain that when we make this sound, the air flow isn't stopped. Have students repeat /a/.)

Practice
Exercise A

- Review the consonant letters with students, pointing to the letters in the alphabet on the board. Have students repeat.

- Review the sounds of the consonants, using the chart below for reference. Write the letter, corresponding sound (or sounds), and example word (or words) on the board. After you say each letter, sound, and example word, have students repeat. Underline the consonants that stand for more than one sound as you reach them in your presentation.

- *b* stands for the sound /b/ as in *boy*.
- *c* does not have its own sound. It can stand for many sounds. A common one is the sound /k/ as in *cat*; *c* with an *a* or *o* after it always represents the sound /k/. Another common sound for *c* is /s/ as in *city*; this is the sound *c* has when it is followed by *e* or *i*.
- *d* stands for /d/ as in *dog*.
- *f* usually stands for the sound /f/ as in *fit*. An important exception is the word *of*, in which *f* stands for the sound /v/.
- *g* can stand for the sound /g/ as in *game* or the sound /j/ as in *gym*.
- *h* stands for /h/ as in *hat*.
- *j* stands for /j/ as in *job*.
- *k* stands for /k/ as in *kiss*.
- *l* stands for /l/ as in *late*.
- *m* stands for /m/ as in *map*.
- *n* stands for /n/ as in *name*.
- *p* stands for /p/ as in *pen*.
- *q* does not have its own sound. It represents the sound /k/. It usually appears in the combination *qu* to represent the blended sound /kw/ as in *quiet*.
- *r* stands for /r/ as in *room*.
- *s* can stand for the sound /s/ as in *sad* or /z/ as in *is*.
- *t* stands for /t/ as in *top*.
- *v* stands for /v/ as in *van*.

- *w* stands for /w/ as in *wait*.
- *x* usually stands for the sound /ks/ as in *fox*. At the beginning of a word, *x* stands for the sound /z/, as in the beginning of the word *Xerox*. In some words, you pronounce the letter name *x*, as in *x-ray*.
- *y* can act as a vowel or consonant. When *y* acts as a consonant, it stands for the sound /y/ as in *yes*.
- *z* stands for /z/ as in *zero*.

Reaching All Students—Kinesthetic Learners: Have students work in small groups to experiment with different consonants, making notes of where the breath is blocked (for example, lips, teeth, or tongue). Call on groups to share some of their observations with the class.

Optional Activity: Dictate words beginning with each consonant (most common sound) in random order. Have students write the letter for the consonant sound they hear at the beginning of each word. Tell students that they will learn about the sounds of consonants in different combinations throughout the course.

Exercise B

- Review the vowel letters with students, pointing to the letters in the alphabet on the board. Have students repeat.

- Tell students that throughout the course they will learn rules for pronouncing vowels in words.

Expansion

Discuss and demonstrate the importance of vowels and consonants in singing. (Have demonstrations by you, by some musically inclined students, or by the whole class. Consider listening to popular music samples.)
1. Have students experiment with singing tones on various vowels and consonants.
2. Ask, "Which are easier to sing—vowels or consonants?" (Vowels.)
3. Ask, "What happens when you sing consonants?" (They stop the sound.)

Exercise C

Have students write their names in their notebooks. Tell them to begin with a capital letter, using small letters for the rest of their names. Refer them to the names in their texts as examples for how to write a name.

Optional Activity: Ask students to write ten other words that begin with the same letter as their names. Tell them that they can look through the chapter for words or they can think of other words they know that start with that letter. Write an example on the board, using your own name as a model. Have students share their answers with the class.

Answers
Answers will vary.

Alphabetical Order

Presentation

- Tell students that often information is organized in alphabetical order.

- Have students brainstorm places they might need to look up information in alphabetical order (dictionary, encyclopedia, phone book, filing system, etc.).

- Ask students if they can think of any situations in which they might need to put information in alphabetical order (address book, filing system, class lists, etc.).

- Point out that often lists have words that start with the same letter. In that case, they will need to look at the second letter in each word to see which comes first. If the first two letters are the same, then they will need to look at the third letter, and so on. Refer students to the example under Exercise A—<u>Carl</u>os, <u>Carm</u>en.

Practice
Exercise A

- Have students number a sheet of paper in their notebooks from 1 to 8.

- Refer them to the list of names in the exercise. Ask them to write the names in alphabetical order. Remind students that if the first letter is the same for two words, they should look at the second letter to see which word comes first. If the second letter is the same for two words, they should look at the third letter, and so on.

  Reaching All Students—Emergent Learners: Have students work in pairs or small groups, coaching them as needed.

- Call on students to read their alphabetized lists and explain their answers by referring to the alphabet on the board or poster.

Answers

Bic	Liliana	Pablo
Carlos	Maria	Samir
Carmen	Mei	

Exercise B

- Have students call out their first names in the order in which they're seated while you write their names on the board or a poster.

- Have students form pairs. Have them write the names on the board or poster in alphabetical order in their notebooks.

  Reaching All Students—Emergent Learners: Work with students in small groups, referring them to the alphabet chart in their texts.

- Call on a student to read the first few names on his or her list, then call on another student to add the next few names, and so on. Write the answers on the board or poster as students say them.

- Have students compare their lists to the list generated by the class and make any necessary corrections.

Expansion

- Have students bring in an existing or created list in alphabetical order (for example, their address book, a class list from another class, an invitation list, a list of vocabulary words, etc.).

- Have students share their lists with the class and explain why the alphabetical order of the lists is useful.

Grammar 3, page 23

Present Tense of *be*: *Yes/No* Questions

Presentation

- Copy the grammar chart onto the board or a poster.

- Explain that this chart shows students how they can ask and answer *yes/no* questions using *be*. Point to the first part of the chart and say, "This part of the chart shows how to ask the questions." Read the first line, "Am I from Mexico?" Point to the middle part and say, "This part shows how to answer the questions if the answer is *yes*." Read the first line, "Yes, you are." Point to the last part of the chart and say, "This part shows how to answer the questions if the answer is *no*." Read the first line, "No, you're not."

- Have students study the grammar chart. Ask them to read silently across the rows in each part of the chart, using words in each column to make a question or short answer.

- Call on individual students to read aloud one or two of the questions and answers they made from the words in the columns.

    Optional Activity: Call on three advanced students to come to the front of the room. Have the first student read the question from the first row of the first part of the chart while you point to the words on the board, "Am I from Mexico?" Have the second volunteer read the *yes* answer from the first row of the second part of the chart while you point to the words, "Yes, you are." Then have the third volunteer read the *no* answer from the first row of the third part of the chart, while you point to the words, "No, you're not."

    Have students work in groups of three to continue the activity for the remaining rows.

Practice

Exercise A

- Have students copy items 1–5 on a sheet of paper in their notebooks.

- Call on an advanced student to read item 1 and the sample answer.

- Have students write the short answers to the remaining items in their notebooks.

- Review the answers as a class.

Answers

1. No, he's not.
2. Yes, he is.
3. Yes, they are.
4. No, she's not.
5. *Answers will vary. Possible answers:* No, I'm not. Yes, I am.

Exercise B

First, have students read the conversation on their own. Then have them listen to the conversation.

Exercise C

- Have students work in pairs.

- Have each student in a pair select a role—A or B. Then have the pair practice the conversation in Exercise B.

- Have the students in each pair switch roles. Then have them practice the conversation again.

- Have students substitute their own information in the conversations. Have them practice the new conversations.

    Reaching All Students—Emergent Learners: Work with students in pairs or small groups. Guide them in substituting their own information in the conversations. Then write the conversations on the board. Have the students practice the new conversations.

Reading, pages 24–25

Before You Read

Preparation

Tell students that the Before You Read activities can help them get ready to read for better understanding.

Practice *(See Transparency 19.)*

- Have students look at the illustrations and read the title of the story. Then ask, "How does Maria feel?" Write their answers on the board under the heading "Maria feels . . ." (Possible answers: scared, worried, nervous, shy.) Keep these posted during the reading.

- Divide the class into pairs. Ask students, "How do you feel in a new school? Talk about it with your classmate."

- After pair discussion time, call on a few volunteers to share their ideas. Write their answers on the board under the heading, "We feel . . ." Keep these posted during the reading.

Read This!

A New School

Preparation

Note: Students will encounter the following new words in the reading: *El Salvador, school, say, new.*

Practice

- 🎧 Have students listen to the story, or read it aloud to them. As you read, point out how Maria is feeling. (Nervous.) Then compare this to students' responses on the board under the heading "Maria feels . . ." Also, compare this to students' responses under the heading "We feel . . ."

- Have students read the story with a classmate. Pair students so that a proficient reader is partnered with a less proficient reader. Provide help with content, vocabulary, etc. as needed.

- Have students retell the story to a classmate. The listener can retell what the classmate says. Teach this technique by modeling it with a proficient student.

  Reaching All Students—Emergent Learners: Work with emergent readers in small groups while the other students work independently in pairs. Read aloud as students follow along in their texts. Monitor their comprehension by interrupting the reading with questions such as, "Where is Maria from?" (She is from El Salvador.) "What language does she speak?" (She speaks Spanish.) "Who is her teacher?" (Mr. Gomez is her teacher.) "Where are Carlos and Carmen from?" (They are from Mexico.) "Who is nervous?" (Maria is nervous.) "Why is she nervous?" (She is in a new school.) Encourage students to answer using complete sentences.

After You Read

Preparation

Tell students that the After You Read activities can help them make sure they understood what they read.

Practice

Exercise A

Divide the class into groups of three. Have students assign themselves roles—the first student plays the part of Maria, the second plays Carmen, and the third, Carlos. Group students heterogeneously so that each group is made up of average readers, weak readers, and strong readers. Tell students to read the words in quotation marks to act out the story. (Write quotation marks on the board to illustrate.)

Reaching All Students—Emergent Learners: Write just the quoted dialogue on the board or on a poster.
Example:
> **Maria:** My . . . my . . . my name is . . . is . . . umm . . .
> **Carmen:** Wow! She's *very* nervous. What's her name?
> **Carlos:** She's very *pretty!* What *is* her name?

Reaching All Students—Kinesthetic Learners: Have one or two groups act out the story for the whole class.

Self-Evaluation

Exercise B

- On the board, write the sentence *Maria is a student at Washington School.* Ask students whether the sentence is true or false. (True.) Ask students to identify the statement in the story that supports their response. (She is a new student at Washington School.) Write the word *True* after the sentence on the board.

- Next, write the sentence *Carmen is a teacher.* on the board. Ask students whether the sentence is true or false. (False.) Ask students to look for information in the story that shows that Carmen is not a teacher. After students give their answers, read the supporting statement in the story. (Her [Maria's] teacher is Mr. Gomez.) Write the word *False* after the sentence on the board.

- Have students number a sheet of paper in their notebooks from 1 to 5.

- Have students work in pairs to find the answers to the *true/false* statements. Each student should write the correct answer, either *True* or *False*, next to the correct number. Tell them to look for supporting evidence in the story.

- Have pairs share their answers with the rest of the class. Encourage each pair to explain why they chose *True* or *False* as their answers, using sentences from the story for support.

- Have students check their answers and count the number correct. Have them write their scores in their notebooks to keep track of their progress.

Answers

1. True	3. False	5. True
2. False	4. True	

Writing, page 26

Before You Write

Preparation *(See Transparencies 26–27.)*

- Explain to students that they will write a paragraph introducing themselves. Tell them that there is a series of steps to follow to help them write their paragraph.

- Discuss with students the meaning of the checklist headings: Before I Write, While I Write, and After I Write. As you go through each explanation, have students follow along by looking at the appropriate checklist box.

- Explain to students that Before I Write is a checklist that helps them to plan what they will write. It makes sure that they understand the writing assignment, their topic (what they want to write about), and the information that they want to include about their topic.

- Explain to students that While I Write is a checklist that asks them to apply the rules of writing, such as beginning a sentence with a capital letter and ending it with a period.

- Explain to students that After I Write is a checklist that asks them to review their written work. It also asks them to check their use of capital letters and periods.

Practice

Exercise A

- Refer students to the handwritten paragraph in their texts. Tell students that Pablo has written a paragraph introducing himself.

- Ask students if they have ever had to introduce themselves. Ask them if they have ever had to introduce themselves in writing, for example, in a letter to a pen pal or in an e-mail to a key pal.

- Read the paragraph aloud as students follow along in their texts. Then read each sentence and have students repeat while following along in their texts.

Exercise B

- Have students study the Before I Write checklist.

- Model the process of following the Before I Write checklist. First, read the sample aloud. Next, think aloud about what you would write if you were introducing yourself. Then

answer the questions with your own information, writing your notes on the board.

- Ask a proficient student to write notes on the board in response to the last step in the Before I Write box.

- Ask students to follow the Before I Write checklist. Tell them to take notes in their notebooks as suggested in the checklist.

    Reaching All Students—Emergent Learners: Group students who might have difficulty with the assignment and work with them. Guide them in answering the questions and in writing their notes in their notebooks.

Write This!

Presentation

- Draw students' attention to the While I Write checklist.

- Model following the While I Write checklist. Write your paragraph about yourself on the board, referring back to the notes you wrote earlier on the board. As you write, do a "think aloud" about how you are following the While I Write checklist. For example, point out, "I'm starting the sentence with a capital letter. I'm ending my sentence with a period." As you model, deliberately make the mistakes of not capitalizing one proper name and leaving out one period. (You will later model making a correction in After I Write.) If students correct you as you go, correct the mistake and tell students that you can make these kinds of corrections either during or after writing.

Practice

- Have students write their paragraphs in their notebooks, following the While I Write checklist and using the notes they took in the previous exercise.

- Circulate while students are writing to answer questions about new words or to offer other assistance.

    Reaching All Students—Emergent/ Cooperative Learners: Have students work cooperatively in small groups. Circulate among the groups. Offer assistance as needed.

After You Write

Practice

Exercise A

- Model following the steps in the After I Write checklist, correcting the errors you made in your paragraph on the board.
- Have students use the After I Write checklist to evaluate their writing. Have them correct their errors.

Exercise B

- Divide the class into pairs. Have students read their paragraphs to their partners.
- Have students make suggestions for improvement.
- Have students make any necessary corrections to their paragraphs.

Exercise C

Have students make a final copy of their paragraphs in their notebooks.

> **Optional Activity:** Divide the class into small groups, preferably of students who do not yet know each other well. Have students read their paragraphs aloud to their groups.

Expansion

Have students write a pen-pal letter (or key-pal e-mail) to introduce themselves. They could send letters within the class, across classes, or to students in other cities or countries.

Learning Log, page 27

See How to Use the Learning Log on page xiii. *(See Transparencies 20 and 62.)*

Chapter 2
What classes do you have?

Objectives

Language:

- Listen to a dialogue for comprehension.
- Understand familiar vocabulary and grammar structures by listening to a dialogue.
- Develop new vocabulary and grammar structures by listening to a dialogue.
- Act out a dialogue.
- Use the present tense of *have* in affirmative statements, negative statements, and *yes/no* questions.
- Use the contractions *don't* and *doesn't* with *have*.
- Form plural nouns by adding *-s* or *-es*.
- Use possessive adjectives correctly.
- Evaluate one's own learning of new vocabulary, grammar, and oral language.

Literacy:

- Read a dialogue for comprehension.
- Understand familiar vocabulary and grammar structures by reading a dialogue.
- Develop new vocabulary and grammar structures by reading a dialogue.
- Write sentences using new vocabulary.
- Complete and write sentences with the present tense of *have* in affirmative statements and negative statements.
- Write sentences using the contractions *don't* and *doesn't* with *have*.
- Write *yes/no* questions with the present tense of *have*.
- Decode words with short vowel sounds /a/, /i/, and /o/.
- Form the plural of nouns by adding *-s* or *-es*.
- Complete sentences using the correct possessive adjectives.
- Read a short story for comprehension and to solve a math problem.
- Understand familiar vocabulary and grammar structures by reading a short story.
- Develop new vocabulary and grammar structures by reading a short story.

- Plan, write, revise, edit, proofread, and make a final copy of a descriptive paragraph about one's favorite class.
- Indent the first line of a paragraph and capitalize the name of a language.
- Evaluate one's own learning of reading skills, reading comprehension, and writing skills.

Learning Strategies:

- Use cooperation with a classmate to read a dialogue and study new vocabulary.
- Use cooperation with a small group to act out a dialogue.
- Use the strategy *Sound Out* to decode words.
- Use pictures to help understand a short story.
- Use cooperation with a classmate to check a paragraph one has written.
- Evaluate one's own learning of the strategy *Sound Out*.
- Identify easy and difficult material in a chapter and the different ways to learn the difficult material.

Opening Dialogue, pages 28–29

Getting Ready

Preparation *(See Transparency 17.)*

- Have students look at the illustrations and identify the words they know for the people and objects they see. (Examples: teachers, students, doors, classrooms.) Write the words on the board or a poster as students say them.

    Reaching All Students—Visual/ Kinesthetic Learners: Have students locate the objects in the classroom. Have them come up and point to the objects as they say the words.

- Ask students if they can recall the names of the characters in the illustrations. (Carmen, Liliana, and Maria.) Write the names of the characters on the board or a poster.
- Have students look again at the illustration on page 28. Ask, "What word do you see written in the picture?" (English.) Write the response on the board.

- Point to the illustrations and ask, "What are the girls reading?" Elicit the response. (They're reading their class schedules.)

Listening and Reading

Our Schedules

Presentation

Exercise A

- Read the directions and the prelistening question aloud as students follow along in their texts.
- Have students listen to the dialogue, or read the dialogue aloud to them. Have students look at the appropriate illustrations as they listen.
- Ask the prelistening question, "What is Carmen's favorite class?" Call on a volunteer to answer. (Math is Carmen's favorite class.)

Exercise B

Have students read the dialogue. Provide help with content, vocabulary, etc. as needed.

Reaching All Students—Emergent Learners: Work with emergent learners in small groups while the other students work independently. Read aloud as students follow along in their texts. Monitor their comprehension by interrupting the reading with questions such as, "What class does Liliana have now?" (Liliana has P.E. now.) "Do Liliana and Carmen eat lunch together?" (No. Liliana and Carmen don't eat lunch together.) "What classes do they have together?" (They have math, science, and music together.) "Do Liliana, Carmen, and Maria have almost the same classes?" (Yes, they do. *or* Yes, they have almost the same classes.)

Pair and Group Work

Exercise A

Have students who can read on their own form pairs. Have one student take the roles of Carmen and Maria; have the other student take the role of Liliana. Have them practice reading the dialogue. Provide help as needed.

Reaching All Students—Emergent Learners: Work with emergent readers in small groups. Model each sentence and have individual students "echo" your reading. Make sure that students look at the sentences as you read them.

Exercise B

Divide the class into groups of three. Group students heterogeneously so that each group is made up of average readers, weak readers, and strong readers. For each group, have each student choose a role for him- or herself from the dialogue. Encourage each group to practice the dialogue several times. Circulate among the groups. Offer assistance as needed.

Reaching All Students—Kinesthetic Learners: Choose one or more groups to act out the dialogue in front of the class.

Vocabulary

Practice

Exercise A

Have students read and say the words and expressions. Provide assistance with pronunciation as needed. Then have them write the words and expressions in their notebooks.

Reaching All Students—Auditory Learners: Encourage students to say the words and expressions as they write them in their notebooks.

Exercise B *(See Transparency 85.)*

- Have students turn to page 250 in their texts.
- Call on a volunteer to read Step 1 aloud as the other students follow along.
- Model with an advanced student asking for and giving the spelling of the first two words in the word box on page 29.
- Have students work in pairs asking for and giving the spelling of words and expressions in the word box on page 29.

Exercise C

Have students find the words and expressions in the dialogue. Have them read the sentences.

Exercise D

- Have each student choose three words from the words in the word box. Have them write three sentences in their notebooks, using these new words.
- Call on students to read their sentences to the class.

> **Answers**
> *Answers will vary.*

Grammar 1, page 30

Present Tense of *have*: Affirmative Statements

Preparation

- Write the following line of dialogue on the board as a way of presenting the grammar focus in context.
  Carmen: I *have* seven classes. Carlos *has* seven classes, too. Our schedules are almost the same.
- Read the dialogue aloud as students follow along. Then have students read it aloud with you.

Presentation

- Have students study the grammar chart. Ask them to read silently across the rows, using a word or words in each column to make a sentence.
- Call on individual students to read aloud one or two of the sentences they made from the words in the columns.

Practice

Exercise A

- Have students look at the realia for Exercise A. Ask, "What are these?" Call on a volunteer to answer. (They are Carmen's and Carlos's schedules.)
- Have students copy the sentences into their notebooks.
- Read the first sentence aloud. Ask, "Is that statement true or false?" Call on a volunteer to answer. (True.) Ask the student to explain why the answer is true. (They both have English period 3.) Have students write *True* next to the first sentence in their notebooks.
- Call on advanced students, one at a time, to read each of the remaining sentences. Have students write their answers in their notebooks.
- Call on students to give their answers, asking them to explain how they figured them out.

Answers		
1. True	**3.** False	**5.** False
2. True	**4.** True	

Exercise B

- Have students copy the five sentences into their notebooks.
- Call on a volunteer to read the first sentence with the sample answer.
- Have students complete the remaining sentences by writing the correct form of *have* in each sentence.

  Reaching All Students—Emergent Learners: First, have students do the exercise orally, using the grammar chart for reference. Then have them copy the sentences into their notebooks. Have them complete the sentences. Provide help as needed.

- Review the answers with the class.

Answers		
1. have	**3.** have	**5.** has
2. have	**4.** have	

Grammar 2, page 31

Present Tense of *have*: Negative Statements

Preparation

Write the following dialogue on the board as a way of presenting the grammar focus in context.

Liliana: *Do* you *have* P.E. now?
  Mei: No, I *don't have* P.E. now. I *have* lunch.
Liliana: Oh, our schedules are different.

  Reaching All Students—Kinesthetic Learners: Call on volunteers to act out the dialogue.

Presentation

- Have students study the grammar chart. Ask them to read silently across the rows, using a word or words in each column to make a sentence.
- Have students look at the contractions box next to the chart. Explain that the contraction, or short form, of *do not* is *don't*; the contraction of *does not* is *doesn't*. Have students repeat "don't have" and "doesn't have" after you.

- Call on individual students to read aloud one or two of the sentences they made from the words in the columns.
- Copy onto the board the chart from Present Tense of *have*: Affirmative Statements, page 30 in the Student Book, and the chart from Present Tense of *have*: Negative Statements, page 31 in the Student Book.
- As a class, have students generate a rule for using *have* in affirmative and negative statements. Write the rule on the board. (Example: In affirmative statements, the verb *have* changes to match the subject. In negative statements, the verb *do* changes to match the subject while *have* stays in the base form.)

Practice

- Call on a volunteer to read item 1 aloud (without the sample answer) as the other students follow along in their texts. Then say, "We can change the sentence to a negative statement by saying, 'Liliana doesn't have P.E. now.'"
- Have students copy items 1 to 5 into their notebooks, skipping two lines for two new sentences after each one. (Note: In this exercise they will be adding one sentence, and in the next exercise they will be adding another sentence.) After the first sentence, have them write "Liliana doesn't have P.E. now." Write both sentences for item 1 on the board as a model.
- Have students write the remaining negative statements in their notebooks.

  Reaching All Students—Emergent Learners: First, have students do the exercise orally, using the grammar chart for reference. Then have them write the sentences in their notebooks. Provide help as needed.

  Reaching All Students—Cooperative Learners: Have students work in pairs or small groups to complete the exercise.

- Review the answers with the class.

Answers
1. Liliana doesn't have P.E. now.
2. Carmen doesn't have math with Liliana.
3. Maria and Liliana don't have English class together.
4. I don't have math after lunch.
5. You don't have seven classes.

Present Tense of *have*: *Yes/No* Questions

Presentation

- Have students look at the grammar chart at the bottom of page 31. Explain that the chart shows how they can ask and answer *yes/no* questions with *have*.
- Point to the first part of the chart and say, "This part shows how to ask the questions." Point to the middle part and say, "This part shows how to answer the questions if the answer is *yes*." Point to the last part of the chart and say, "This part shows how to answer the questions if the answer is *no*."
- Have students study the grammar chart. Ask them to read silently across the rows using a word or words in each column to make a question or short answer.
- Call on individual students to read aloud one of the questions and corresponding short answers they made from the words in the columns.

  Reaching All Students—Advanced Learners: Call on two advanced students. Pointing to the words on the chart in your text, read the question from the first row of the chart with the pronoun *I:* "Do I have math after lunch?" Have the first student read the *yes* answer from the first row: "Yes, you do." Then have the second student read the *no* answer from the first row: "No, you don't."

- Have students work in groups of three. The first student in each group will read the question from the first row with the pronoun *I:* "Do I have math after lunch?" The second student will read the *yes* answer from the first row: "Yes, you do." Then the third student will read the *no* answer from the first row: "No, you don't." Have students repeat for the remaining pronouns.
- Have students work in pairs or small groups to develop rules that tell how to make *yes/no* questions, affirmative statements, and negative statements with the present tense of *have*. Call on students to give their rules. Then write the rules on the board. Examples:
  - Questions—*Do* + subject + *have* + object. The verb *do* matches the subject. The verb *have* stays in the base form.

- Affirmative statements—Subject + *have* + object. The verb *have* matches the subject.
- Negative statements—Subject + *don't/doesn't* + *have* + object. *Don't/doesn't* matches the subject. The verb *have* stays in the base form.

Practice

- Have students look at the sentences in the first exercise on page 31 in their texts. Have them read item 1 (without the sample answer) aloud with you. Then say, "We can change the sentence to a question: Does Liliana have P.E. now?" Have students repeat the question.
- Have students turn to the page in their notebooks where they wrote the sentences and the negative statements for the first exercise on page 31. In the remaining space for item 1, have them write "Does Liliana have P.E. now?" Write the question on the board as a model.
- Have students write the remaining questions in their notebooks.

  Reaching All Students—Emergent Learners: First, have students do the exercise orally, using the grammar chart for reference. Then have them write the questions in their notebooks. Provide help as needed.

- Review the answers with the class.

Answers
1. Does Liliana have P.E. now?
2. Does Carmen have math with Liliana?
3. Do Maria and Liliana have English class together?
4. Do I have math after lunch?
5. Do you have seven classes?

Reaching All Students—Advanced Learners: Have students work in small groups. Have them look again at Exercise A on page 30. Then have them change the statements into questions and write the questions with short answers in their notebooks. Refer them to the grammar charts on pages 30 and 31 for help. Call on volunteers to read their questions and answers aloud. (Note: Students may need additional help with item 4.)

Answers
1. Do Carlos and Carmen have the same English class?
   Yes, they do.
2. Does Carlos have music after lunch?
   Yes, he does.
3. Do Carmen and Carlos have math together?
   No, they don't.
4. Does Carlos have art, then history?
   (or Does Carlos have history after art? *or* Does Carlos have art before history?)
   Yes, he does.
5. Do Carmen and Carlos have the same P.E. class?
   No, they don't.

Expansion

- Have a pair of advanced students come to the front of the room and compare their class schedules aloud for the class. Encourage them to use as many of the new vocabulary words as possible. Write the new vocabulary words on the board as students use them.
- Have students work in pairs or small groups to compare their schedules.

  Reaching All Students—Emergent Learners: Group together students who need additional help and guide them in comparing their schedules.

Word Study, page 32

Presentation

- Write the following words on the board: *cat, sit, hot.*
- Read the words one at a time. Have students repeat each word after you. Then have students look at the explanation box in the text. Read the explanations aloud as students follow along in their texts.
- Have students look at the Learning Strategy box. Point out that the learning strategy is called *Sound Out* and that it can help them sound out new words.
- Read the *Sound Out* explanation and example as students follow along in their texts.
- As a class, have students practice the strategy *Sound Out* with the word *bat*. Be sure they first say the sounds of the letters separately (/b/ /a/ /t/) and then blend the sounds to read the word *(bat).*

- Write the words below on the board. Have students use the learning strategy *Sound Out* to read them.

1. *dad*		3. *lip*		5. *hop*	
2. *man*		4. *six*		6. *pot*	

Practice
Exercise A

- Have students use the learning strategy *Sound Out,* as well as the pictures, to read the words with the short vowel sounds /a/, /i/, and /o/.

   Reaching All Students—Emergent Learners: Do this exercise as a class if students need help sounding out the words. After students have an approximation of the pronunciation, say the words correctly to provide a model.

   Optional Activity: Have students close their texts. Ask them to number a page in their notebooks from 1 to 8. Ask them to listen carefully to the words you read and to write the words. Then dictate the following words:

1. big		5. mat
2. hat		6. hot
3. cap		7. map
4. pig		8. hit

- After the dictation, write the words on the board. Then have students check their words.
- Have students record the number of correct words in their notebooks; for example, *I wrote (7) out of 8 dictated words with short vowel sounds /a/, /i/, and /o/ correctly.* Write this example on the board as a model.

Exercise B

- First, have students read the sentences aloud. Then have them copy the sentences into their notebooks. Last, have them circle the letters that stand for the short vowel sounds /a/, /i/, and /o/.
- Review the answers as a class.

Answers
1. Maria h(a)s a pretty h(a)t.
2. Samir h(a)s my c(a)p.
3. (I)t (i)s a very b(i)g p(i)g.
4. (I)s the m(a)p (i)n your book?
5. My lunch (i)s h(o)t.
6. H(i)t the ball w(i)th your b(a)t.

Expansion
Exercise C

- Have students skim the dialogue on pages 28–29 for two words with the short vowel sound /a/ and two words with the short vowel sound /i/. Have them write the words in their notebooks.
- Review the answers as a class.

Answers
Answers will vary. Possible answers:

math	class	is	it's

Grammar 3, page 33

Plural Nouns

Preparation

- Write the word *student* on the left side of the board. Write the word *students* on the right side.
- Call on four volunteers. Have one student stand in front of the word *student.* Have the other three students stand in front of the word *students.*
- Read the word *student* aloud while using an open palm gesture to point to the student in front of the word. Have students repeat the word after you. Then read the word *students* (emphasizing the /s/ sound at the end of the word) while using an open palm gesture to point to the students in front of the word. Have students repeat the word after you.

Presentation

- Have students look at the first grammar chart.
- Review with students that a noun names a person, place, thing, or idea.
- Tell students that when a noun names just one, for example, *book,* it is called a singular noun. When it names more than one, for example, *books,* it is called a plural noun.
- Read the grammar rule at the top of the chart as students follow along in their texts.
- Read the singular form of each noun and then its plural form. Have students repeat each pair after you.
- Have students look at the second grammar chart.

- Read the grammar rule at the top of the chart as students follow along in their texts.
- Read the singular form of each noun and then its plural form. Have students repeat each pair after you.

Practice

- Have students write the six nouns in their notebooks. Tell them these are *singular* nouns that they can make *plural* by adding *-s* or *-es*. Have students write the plural of each noun in their notebooks, next to the singular. Write the first item and the sample answer on the board as an example.
- Review the answers with the class.

Answers

1. brothers **3.** classes **5.** desks
2. pencils **4.** boxes **6.** schedules

Expansion

Reaching All Students—Kinesthetic/ Visual Learners: Hand out a sticky note or index card with tape to each student. Have each student write a *singular* noun on the sticky note, representing something he or she would like to have more than one of. (Or, if you prefer, just have students write a singular noun representing something in the classroom.)

- Call on a volunteer to tape his or her noun to the board.
- Call on another volunteer to come up to the board with his or her pen or pencil. First, have the student make the previous student's noun plural by adding *-s* or *-es*. Then ask the class if the plural form is correct. Next, have that student place his or her noun on the board.
- Continue with each student forming the plural of the previous student's noun, then adding his or her own noun.
- At the end, the student who posted the first noun forms the plural of the last noun.

Possessive Adjectives

Preparation

- Write the following line of dialogue on the board as a way of presenting the grammar focus in context.

Mei: This is our class pet. It's a turtle. *Its* name is Mr. Bigsley.

- Read the text aloud as students follow along. **Optional Activity:** Call on a volunteer to act out the text.

Presentation

- Have students look at the grammar chart.
- Point out the headings: Subject Pronoun and Possessive Adjective.
- Read aloud across the rows as students follow along in their texts.
- Call on volunteers to read aloud across the rows.

Practice

- Have students look at the illustration and discuss what they see. (A family; a father and mother; two sons and a daughter.)
- Have students copy the sentences into their notebooks. Have them write the correct possessive adjective to complete each sentence.

Reaching All Students—Emergent Learners: First, do the exercise orally with them. Then have them copy the incomplete sentences in their notebooks. Have them complete the sentences with the correct possessive adjectives. Provide help as needed.

Answers

1. My **3.** Her **5.** His
2. my **4.** our **6.** Their

Expansion

Have students bring in pictures of their pets or special objects. Have them work in small groups to write sentences describing their pets and objects and their classmates' pets and objects. Encourage them to use possessive adjectives in their descriptions.

Answers

Answers will vary. Sample answers:
These are <u>our</u> fish.
He is <u>my</u> cat.
<u>Her</u> hamster is brown.
This is <u>their</u> car.

Reading, pages 34–35

Before You Read

Preparation

Remind students that the Before You Read activities can help them get ready to read for better understanding.

Presentation

Call on an advanced student to read the directions under the heading Before You Read.

Practice

Divide students into pairs. Then have them follow the directions by looking at the illustration and answering the questions: "What class is this?" "How do you know?" (It's a math class. The teacher is writing a math problem on the board. Mei has a protractor. Students are looking at their math books.)

Read This!

The Math Class

Preparation

Note: Students will encounter the following new words in the reading: *also, Arabic, China, Chinese, day, every, language, Puerto Rico, Lebanon, not very good at.*

Practice

- Have students listen to the story, or read it aloud to them.
- Have students read the story silently on their own. Provide help with content, vocabulary, etc. as needed.

  Reaching All Students—Emergent Learners: Work with emergent learners in small groups while the other students work independently. Read aloud as students follow along in their texts. Monitor their comprehension by interrupting the reading with questions such as, "How many students are boys?" (Four students are boys.) "How many students are girls?" (Five students are girls.) "Who loves math?" (Carmen loves math.) "What languages does Mrs. Garcia speak?" (She speaks Spanish and English.) "Where is Mei from?" (She is from China.) "What language does she speak?" (She speaks Chinese.) "Where is Samir from?" (He is from Lebanon.) "What language does he speak?" (He speaks Arabic.) Encourage students to answer the questions using complete sentences.

After You Read

Preparation

Remind students that the After You Read activities can help them make sure they understood what they read.

Self-Evaluation
Exercise A

- Have students take out their notebooks. Have them solve the math problem and write the answer in their notebooks.

  Reaching All Students—Emergent/ Cooperative Learners: Have students work in pairs or small groups.

- Call on a volunteer to give the answer to the math problem. Ask how many students agree with the answer and how many disagree. Have the volunteer come to the board and explain how he or she figured out the answer.

Answer
Nine (four boys + five girls = nine students)

Exercise B

- Have students number a sheet of paper in their notebooks from 1 to 5.
- On the board, write the first sentence from the exercise: *Carmen and Liliana are good at math.* Ask students to tell whether the sentence is true or false. (True.) Ask students to identify the statement in the story that supports their response. *(Carmen and Liliana are very good at math.)* Have students write *True* next to item 1 in their notebooks.
- Have students answer the remaining statements as *True* or *False*. Have them write the answers in their notebooks.
- Ask pairs to check each other's answers. Encourage each pair to explain why they chose *True* or *False* as their answer, using sentences from the story for support.

- Call on students to share their answers with the rest of the class.
- Have students write their scores in their notebooks to keep track of their progress.

Answers
1. True	**3.** False	**5.** True
2. False	**4.** True	

Writing, page 36

Before You Write

Preparation *(See Transparencies 28–29.)*

- Tell students that they are going write a paragraph about their favorite class. Explain that the Before I Write, While I Write, and After I Write checklists will guide them through the process of writing their paragraphs.
- Review with students the meaning of the checklist headings: Before I Write, While I Write, and After I Write.

Practice
Exercise A

- Focus students' attention on the handwritten paragraph. Call on an advanced student to read the paragraph aloud while the other students follow along in their texts.
- Call on a volunteer to tell what the paragraph is about. (The writer's favorite class.)
- Ask students to explain what kinds of information the student included in the paragraph. (The student's favorite class, the teacher's name, the number of boys and girls in the class, a sentence explaining how much the student likes the class.) Write their answers on the board.
- Have students brainstorm other information the student could have included in the paragraph. Write responses on the board (for example, why the student likes the teacher [he is smart and funny], why the student likes the class [it is interesting], why the student likes the other students [they are fun]).
- Draw students' attention to the Before I Write checklist.
- Model following the Before I Write checklist. Recall your favorite class when you were

your students' age. Write your notes on the board.

- Have students follow the Before I Write checklist and take notes in their notebooks. If they wish, they can also include other kinds of information they brainstormed earlier.

    Reaching All Students—Emergent Learners: Group students who might have difficulty with the assignment and work with them. Guide them in taking notes about the information to include in their paragraphs.

Write This!

Presentation

- Draw students' attention to the While I Write checklist.
- Model following the While I Write checklist. Refer to the notes you took earlier about your favorite class at their age. As you write, do a "think aloud" about how you are following the While I Write checklist. In writing your paragraph, make a mistake with the plural form of a noun. If students catch the mistake, circle it and say, "I can correct that later."

Practice

- Have students write their paragraphs in their notebooks. They should use their notes as a guide. They should also use the While I Write checklist for help.

    Reaching All Students— Emergent/Advanced Learners: Encourage emergent learners to keep the paragraph simple. Encourage advanced learners to include more details in their paragraphs.

- Circulate while students are writing, and encourage them to ask you for help with new words if they need it.

After You Write

Presentation

- Draw students' attention to the After I Write checklist.
- Model following the After I Write checklist, checking your own paragraph on the board. Correct the mistake you made with the plural form of the noun if you didn't correct it earlier.

Practice

Exercise A

Have students use the After I Write checklist to evaluate their writing. Have them circle and then correct their errors.

Exercise B

Have students read their paragraphs to a classmate. Encourage them to make suggestions for improvement.

Exercise C

Have students make a final copy of their paragraphs in their notebooks.

Learning Log, page 37

See How to Use the Learning Log on page xiii. *(See Transparencies 20 and 63.)*

Chapter 3
This is a calculator.

Objectives

Language:
- Listen to a dialogue for comprehension.
- Understand familiar vocabulary and grammar structures by listening to a dialogue.
- Develop new vocabulary and grammar structures by listening to a dialogue.
- Use the articles *a* and *an* correctly.
- Use demonstrative pronouns *this, that, these,* and *those* correctly.
- Use the contraction *that's*.
- Form the possessive of singular and plural nouns.
- Make original conversations using new vocabulary and grammar structures.
- Discuss a character's feelings.
- Evaluate one's own learning of new vocabulary, grammar, and oral language.

Literacy:
- Read a dialogue for comprehension.
- Understand familiar vocabulary and grammar structures by reading a dialogue.
- Develop new vocabulary and grammar structures by reading a dialogue.
- Write sentences using new vocabulary.
- Complete sentences with the articles *a* and *an*.
- Complete sentences with demonstrative pronouns *this, that, these,* and *those*.
- Decode words with short vowel sounds /e/ and /u/.
- Complete sentences with the possessive of singular and plural nouns.
- Read a short story for comprehension.
- Understand familiar vocabulary and grammar structures by reading a short story.
- Develop new vocabulary and grammar structures by reading a short story.
- Act out a short story.
- Plan, write, revise, edit, proofread, and make a final copy of a descriptive paragraph about the contents of one's backpack.
- Indent the first line of a paragraph.
- Use *a* before words that begin with a consonant sound. Use *an* before words that begin with a vowel sound.
- Use number words to tell how many items there are.
- Evaluate one's own learning of reading skills, reading comprehension, and writing skills.

Learning Strategies:
- Use cooperation with a classmate to read a dialogue and study new vocabulary.
- Use cooperation with a classmate to practice conversations.
- Use the strategy *Sound Out* to decode words.
- Use pictures to understand a short story.
- Use cooperation with a classmate to act out a short story.
- Use cooperation with a classmate to check a paragraph one has written.
- Evaluate one's own learning of the strategy *Sound Out*.
- Identify easy and difficult material in a chapter and the different ways to learn the difficult material.

Opening Dialogue, pages 38–39

Getting Ready

Preparation *(See Transparency 17.)*

- Have students look at the illustrations and identify the words they know for the people and objects they see. Write the words on the board or on a poster. Read the words and have students repeat them after you.

  Reaching All Students—Visual/ Kinesthetic Learners: Display the objects in the illustrations on a desk or table in the front of the classroom. Call on volunteers to come up to the objects. Have them point to the objects as they say the words.

- Point to the objects in the illustrations that students didn't mention and ask, "What's this?" Write the responses on the board or on a poster. Read the responses and have students repeat them after you.

Listening and Reading

Maria's Teacher

Presentation

Exercise A

- Read the directions and the prelistening question aloud as students follow along in their texts.
- Have students listen to the dialogue, or read the dialogue aloud to them. Have students look at the appropriate illustrations as they listen.
- Ask the prelistening question, "Who has Carmen's backpack?" Call on a volunteer to answer. (Carlos has Carmen's backpack.)

Exercise B

Have students read the dialogue. Provide help with content, vocabulary, etc. as needed.

> **Reaching All Students—Emergent Learners:** Work with emergent learners in small groups while the other students work independently. Read aloud as students follow along in their texts. Monitor their comprehension by interrupting the reading with questions such as, "What does Maria have?" (She has a calculator.) "Are the English words for math class easy or hard for Maria?" (The words are hard.) "What words does Carmen teach Maria?" (She teaches Maria the words *calculator* and *protractor.*) "Is the backpack Maria's?" (No, it isn't.)

Pair Work

Practice

Have students who can read on their own form pairs. Have each student in a pair take a role in the dialogue and read it aloud. Provide help as needed.

> **Reaching All Students—Emergent Learners:** Work in small groups with students who cannot read on their own. Model each sentence and have individual students "echo" your reading. Make sure that students look at the sentences as you read them.

> **Reaching All Students—Kinesthetic Learners:** Choose one or more pairs to act out the dialogue in front of the class. If available, give the actors props for the dialogue: calculator, protractor, eraser, backpack, folders, binders, notebooks.

Vocabulary

Practice

Exercise A

Have students read and say the words and expressions. Provide assistance with pronunciation as needed. Then have them write the words and expressions in their notebooks.

> **Reaching All Students—Auditory Learners:** Encourage students to say the words and expressions as they write them in their notebooks.

Exercise B *(See Transparency 85.)*

- Have students turn to page 250 in their texts.
- Call on a volunteer to read Step 1 aloud as the other students follow along.
- Model with an advanced student asking for and giving the spelling of the first two words in the word box on page 39.
- Have students work in pairs asking for and giving the spelling of words and expressions in the word box on page 39.

Exercise C

Have students find the words and expressions in the dialogue. Have them read the sentences.

Exercise D

- Have each student choose four words from the words in the word box. Have them write four sentences in their notebooks, using these new words.
- Call on volunteers to read their sentences to the class.

> **Answers**
> *Answers will vary.*

Grammar 1, page 40

Articles: *a* and *an*

Preparation

- Write the following line of dialogue on the board as a way of presenting the grammar focus in context.
  Bic: I have *a* pencil. I also have *an* eraser.
- Read the dialogue aloud as students follow along.

- Call on an advanced student to read the dialogue aloud for the rest of the class.

Presentation

- Have students look at the first grammar chart.
- Read aloud the rules and the examples as students follow along in their texts.
- Reread aloud the article *a* and the nouns in the first part of the chart one at a time. Have students repeat the article and noun after you.
- Follow the same procedure for the article *an* and the nouns in the second part of the chart.

    Reaching All Students—Advanced Learners: Call on volunteers to give examples of nouns that take the article *a* and examples of nouns that take the article *an.*

- Have students look at the second grammar chart.
- Read aloud the names of the vowels and the names of the consonants. Read the Remember note as students follow along in their texts.

    Reaching All Students—Cooperative Learners: Pair students and have them discuss the rule for using *a* or *an* before nouns. Have them quiz each other with a few examples. Be sure they review that sometimes *y* can make a vowel sound.

Practice

Exercise

- Read the first sentence with the sample answer aloud. Then call on a volunteer to explain why *an* is correct. (The noun *umbrella* begins with a vowel sound. We use *an* before a noun that begins with a vowel sound.)

    Reaching All Students—Auditory and Visual Learners: Write *umbrella* on the board. Then underline the *u.* Say, "umbrella." Have students repeat. Write the article *an* before the word. Say, "an umbrella." Have students repeat.

- Have students copy the incomplete sentences into their notebooks. Have them complete the sentences by writing the correct article in the blank.

Reaching All Students—Auditory Learners: Call on advanced students to read each of the remaining sentences (without the answers) before students write their answers.

Reaching All Students—Emergent/ Cooperative Learners: Have students work in pairs to complete the exercise.

- Call on volunteers to give and explain their answers.

Answers		
1. an	**3.** an	**5.** an
2. a	**4.** a	

Demonstrative Pronouns: *this* and *that*

Preparation

Have students look at the illustrations in their texts. Point out that in the first illustration, the orange is close to the girl. In the second picture, the apple is far away.

Presentation

- Read the text under the illustrations aloud while students follow along in their texts. "*This* is an orange." "*That* is an apple." Then have students read aloud with you.
- Point out that we use *this* to refer to something or someone close to us. We use *that* to refer to something or someone far away.
- Refer students to the contraction box. Explain that the contraction, or short form, of *that is* is *that's.* Tell them that *That is an apple* means the same thing as *That's an apple.*
- Point out that *this is* does not have a contraction.

Practice

Exercise A

First, have students read the conversation on their own. Then have them listen to the conversation.

Optional Activity: Assign role A to yourself. Assign role B to an advanced student. As you say your line, point to a backpack you are holding in your hands. As the advanced student says his or her line, have him or her point to his or her backpack on a chair a short distance away.

Exercise B

- Have students work in pairs to practice the conversation.
- Encourage students to make new conversations, using their own information about items in the classroom. Be sure they know the pronoun they should use for an item close to them (*this*) and the pronoun they should use for an item far away (*that*).

> **Reaching All Students—Emergent Learners:** Help students brainstorm a list of items in the room to use in their conversations. Then work with them in small groups to help them practice their original conversations.

> **Reaching All Students—Kinesthetic Learners:** Encourage students to pick up or point to the items as they use *this* and *that*.

Grammar 2, page 41

Demonstrative Pronouns: *these* and *those*

Preparation

- Have students look at the illustrations in their texts. Point to the picture on the left and ask, "What is the boy holding?" Call on a volunteer to respond. (He is holding pens.) Point to the picture on the right and ask, "What is the boy pointing to?" Call on a volunteer to respond. (He is pointing to erasers.)
- Point out that in the first illustration the pens are close to the boy. In the second illustration, the erasers are far away.

Presentation

- Read the text under the illustrations aloud as students follow along in their texts. Then have students read aloud with you.
- Ask students to tell which plural demonstrative pronoun they should use for items that are close to them (these) and which plural demonstrative pronoun they should use for items that are far away from them (those).

Practice

Exercise A

- Call on a volunteer to read item 1 with the sample answer aloud as the other students follow along in their texts.

- Ask, "Why do we say *these* instead of *those*?" (The girl is holding the pencils; they are close to her.) Ask, "Why do we say *these* instead of *this*?" (She has more than one; *these* is the correct demonstrative pronoun to use with a plural noun.)
- Have students copy the incomplete sentences into their notebooks. Then have them complete them by writing *these* or *those* in the blanks.

> **Reaching All Students—Emergent Learners:** First, have students do the exercise orally, using the example illustrations and text for reference. Then have them copy the incomplete sentences into their notebooks. Last, have them complete the sentences. Provide help as needed.

> **Reaching All Students—Cooperative Learners:** Have students work in pairs or small groups to complete the exercise.

- Review the answers with the class.

Answers
1. These	3. Those	5. Those
2. These	4. These	6. Those

Exercise B

- Have students copy the sentences into their notebooks.
- Call on a volunteer to read the first sentence with the sample answer aloud and to explain why the answer is correct.
- Have students complete the remaining sentences by writing the correct demonstrative pronoun in each sentence.

> **Reaching All Students—Cooperative Learners:** Have students work in small groups to complete the activity. Each group should be able to explain why the answers are correct. Provide help as needed.

- Review the answers with the class.

Answers
1. Those	3. This	5. Those
2. This	4. That	6. These

Word Study, page 42

Short Vowel Sounds: /e/ and /u/

Presentation

- Have students look at the explanation box in their texts. Read the explanations aloud as students follow along in their texts.
- Write the learning strategy *Sound Out* with the steps below on the board.
  Use the strategy Sound Out to learn new words.
  Example:
  1. Sound out the letters.   b-e-d
  2. Read the word.   bed
- Read the learning strategy and example as students follow along.
- As a class, have students practice the learning strategy *Sound Out* with the word *bed*. Be sure they first say the sounds of the letters separately (/b/ /e/ /d/) and then blend the sounds to read the word *bed*.
- Write the words below on the board. Have students use the learning strategy *Sound Out* to read them.
  1. yes   *3. cut*
  2. get   *4. hug*

Practice
Exercise A

Have students use the learning strategy *Sound Out* (page 32 in the text), as well as the pictures, to read the words with short vowel sounds /e/ and /u/.

> **Reaching All Students—Emergent Learners:** Complete the activity as a class. After students have an approximation of the pronunciation, say the words correctly to provide a model.

Exercise B

- First, have students read the sentences aloud. Then have them copy the sentences into their notebooks. Last, have them circle the letters that stand for the short vowel sounds /e/ and /u/.
- Review the answers as a class.

Answers
1. Mei has a new p(u)p.
2. Carm(e)n and Carlos are on the b(u)s.
3. Is that your p(e)t?
4. This is Pablo's p(e)n.
5. Liliana has t(e)n dollars.
6. It's hot in the s(u)n.

Optional Activity: Ask students to number a page in their notebooks from 1 to 8. Then ask them to listen carefully to the words you read and to write the words next to the correct numbers. Then dictate the following words:

1. run		5. pet	
2. pen		6. bus	
3. ten		7. sun	
4. pup		8. net	

- After the dictation, write the words on the board. Then have students check their words.
- Have students record the number of correct words in their notebooks; for example, *I wrote (7) out of 8 dictated words with the short vowel sounds /e/ and /u/ correctly*. Write this example on the board as a model.

Expansion
Exercise C

- Have students skim the dialogue on pages 38–39 for two words with the short vowel sound /e/ and one word with the short vowel sound /u/. Have them write the words in their notebooks.
- Review the answers as a class.

Answers
Answers will vary. Possible answers:
excuse   ten   fun

Grammar 3, page 43

Possessive of Singular and Plural Nouns

Presentation

- Have students look at the first set of illustrations and the text below them.
- Read the text aloud as students follow along in their texts. Then write *Keiko's pens* and *Martin's backpack* on the board.

- Explain that a possessive noun shows ownership, or who owns something. In *Keiko's pens*, *Keiko's* shows that Keiko owns the pens. In *Martin's backpack*, *Martin's* shows that Martin owns the backpack.
- Point out that the words *Keiko's* and *Martin's* are singular possessive nouns.
- Explain that we form the possessive of a singular noun by adding an apostrophe and *s* (*'s*) to the end of the noun.

    Reaching All Students—Visual Learners: Write examples of other singular possessive nouns on the board. Use examples from your own class; for example, (teacher's) class, (student's) workbook, and (principal's) office.
- Have students look at the second set of illustrations and the text below them.
- Read the text aloud as students follow along in their texts. Then write *the girls' umbrellas* and *the boys' caps* on the board. Explain that in *the girls' umbrellas*, *girls'* shows that the girls own the umbrellas. In *the boys' caps*, *boys'* shows that the boys own the caps.
- Point out that the words *girls'* and *boys'* are plural possessive nouns.
- Explain that we form the possessive of a plural noun by adding an apostrophe (') to the end of the noun.

    Reaching All Students—Visual Learners: Write examples of other plural possessive nouns on the board; for example, *the students' cafeteria, the parents' meeting*, and *the teachers' desks.*

Practice
Exercise A
- Call on a volunteer to read item 1 aloud as the other students follow along in their texts. Call on another volunteer to explain how the possessive was formed. (An apostrophe and *s* (*'s*) were added to *Carlos*.)
- Have students copy the incomplete sentences into their notebooks. Then have them fill in the blanks with the possessive form of the noun in parentheses.

    Reaching All Students—Emergent/ Cooperative Learners: Have students work in pairs or small groups to complete the activity. Provide help as needed.
- Review the answers with the class.

Expansion
- Have students bring in a special object or set of objects from home, or have them use an object or set of objects from their desks. Have students use sticky notes or index cards with tape on the back to label their objects with their names.
- Set up one table or desk at the front of the room and another one some distance away. Have students place their objects on one of the two tables.
- Call on an advanced student to come up to a table with the objects. Have him or her pick up or point to an object or set of objects. Then have him or her make a statement about the object or set of objects and its owner. Examples of statements include: "This is Alice's pen." "These are David's books." "That is Nicole's notebook." "Those are Tyler's pencils."
- Continue by calling on other volunteers.

Exercise B
- Have students copy items 1–5 into their notebooks.
- Call on an advanced student to read aloud item 1 as the other students follow along in their texts. Have the student explain why the possessive noun *Pablo's* is correct. (The wallet belongs to Pablo. To form the possessive of a singular noun, we add an apostrophe plus *s* to the end of the word.)
- Have students complete the remaining sentences by writing *'s* or *'* in the blanks to form the possessive of a singular noun or a plural noun.

    Reaching All Students—Emergent/ Cooperative Learners: Have students work in pairs or small groups to complete the activity. Provide help as needed.
- Review the answers with the class.

Reading, pages 44–45

Before You Read

Practice (See Transparency 17.)

- Have students look at the picture of Carlos.
- Call on an advanced student to read the questions aloud as the other students follow along in their texts.
- Have students work in pairs to discuss their answers to the questions. (He's looking for something. He seems worried.).

Read This!

Carlos's Backpack

Preparation

Note: Students will encounter the following new words in their reading: *answer, ask, big, book, comb, pen, pencil, problem, some, worried, again*.

Practice

- Have students listen to the story, or read it aloud to them.
- Have students read the story silently on their own. Provide help with content, vocabulary, etc. as needed.

    Reaching All Students—Emergent Learners: Work with emergent learners in small groups while the other students work independently. Read aloud as students follow along in their texts. Monitor their comprehension by interrupting their reading with questions such as, "What does Mr. Gomez have?" (He has a student's backpack.) "How does Carlos feel?" (He is worried. *or* He has a problem.) "The wallet in the backpack has ten dollars. Is it Carlos's wallet?" (No, it isn't. Carlos's wallet has eight dollars.) "Is it Carlos's backpack?" (No, it isn't. It's Carmen's backpack.) Encourage students to answer the questions using complete sentences.

After You Read

Practice

Exercise A

Divide the class into pairs. Have students in each pair decide who will play the part of Mr.

Gomez and who will play the part of Carlos. Remind students to read the words in quotation marks to act out the story.

Reaching All Students—Emergent/ Visual Learners: Write just the quoted dialogue on the board or on a poster to guide students.
Example:
Mr. Gomez: Hi, Carlos. Are you okay?
    Carlos: Oh, hello, Mr. Gomez. No, I'm not okay. I have a problem.
Reaching All Students—Kinesthetic Learners: Have one or two groups act out the story for the whole class.

Self-Evaluation

Exercise B

- Call on a student to read the first sentence with the sample answer aloud to the class. Ask students where in the story they found the answer. (The second sentence in the story.) Have students work in pairs to complete the activity.
- Have them complete the remaining sentences by writing the answers in their notebooks. Encourage them to find the support for their answers in the story.
- Call on students to share their answers with the rest of the class.
- Have students write their scores in their notebooks to keep track of their progress.

Answers	
1. b. a student's	**3.** b. a problem
2. c. worried	**4.** b. Carmen's

Writing, page 46

Before You Write

Preparation (See Transparencies 30–31.)

- Tell students that they are going write two paragraphs: one about the things in their backpack, the other about the things in their friend's backpack. Remind them that the Before I Write, While I Write, and After I Write checklists will guide them through the process of writing their paragraphs.
- Ask students when they will use each of the checklists and how each one will help them.

Presentation/Practice
Exercise A

- Focus students' attention on the handwritten paragraphs. Call on an advanced student to read the paragraphs aloud while the other students follow along in their texts.
- Ask students what the paragraphs are about. (The first paragraph is about the things in the writer's backpack; the second paragraph is about the things in the friend's backpack.) Ask them what kinds of information the student included in the paragraphs. (The things in the backpacks and the number of things in the backpacks.)
- Brainstorm with students the vocabulary they will need to include in a paragraph about the things in their backpacks and the things in their friends' backpacks. Write their responses on the board.

Exercise B

- Draw students' attention to the Before I Write checklist.
- If possible, take out your own backpack, book bag, or briefcase. Model each of the planning points in the checklist, using the contents of your own bag as an example. For the section about a friend's backpack, call on a volunteer to share with the class some of the contents of his or her backpack.
- Have students follow the Before I Write checklist and take notes in their notebooks.

   Reaching All Students—Emergent Learners: Group students who might have difficulty with the assignment and work with them. Guide them in taking notes about the contents of their backpacks and their friends' backpacks.

Write This!
Presentation

- Draw students' attention to the While I Write checklist.
- Model each of the writing points in this checklist, referring to the notes you took about the contents of your backpack and the contents of a student's backpack for Exercise B. As you write, do a "think aloud" about how you are following the While I Write

checklist. In writing your paragraphs, make a mistake with the use of *a* or *an* to correct later. If students catch the mistake, circle it and say, "I can correct that later."

Practice

- Have students write their paragraphs in their notebooks. They should use their notes as a guide. They should also use the While I Write checklist for help. They can refer back to page 40 (lesson on *a* and *an*) for the lists of vowels and consonants, if necessary.

   Reaching All Students—Emergent/ Advanced Learners: Encourage emergent learners to keep the paragraphs simple. Encourage advanced learners to include more details in their paragraphs.
- Circulate while students are writing, and encourage them to ask for help with new words if they need it.

After You Write
Presentation

Draw students' attention to the After I Write checklist. Model each of the points in the checklist, checking your own paragraphs on the board. Correct the mistake you made with the use of *a* or *an* if you didn't correct it earlier.

Practice
Exercise A

Have students use the After I Write checklist to evaluate their writing. Have them circle and then correct their errors.

Exercise B

Have students read their paragraphs to a classmate. Encourage them to make suggestions for improvement.

Exercise C

Have students make a final copy of their paragraphs in their notebooks.

Learning Log, page 47

See How to Use the Learning Log on page xiii. *(See Transparencies 20 and 64.)*

UNIT 2 AT SCHOOL

Unit Opener, pages 48–49

Preview

- Read aloud the unit title, "At School." Tell students that this unit is about places in school, students at school, and friends at school.

- Have students look at the photos and identify the people and the settings. Write their responses on the board. (Example: *She's a student. She's in her art class. She's making something out of clay.*) Read the responses, one at a time, as students follow along.

- Pointing to each of the photos, one at a time, ask a question beginning with *Where is* or *Where are.* For example, ask, "*Where are* the students?" Then give the response, "They're in (art class)."

  Reaching All Students—Advanced Learners: Call on pairs of advanced students, one pair at a time, to ask and answer questions about the people and the settings. (Examples: He's a teacher. Where is he? He's in his classroom.)

- Read the unit goals aloud as students follow along in their texts. Answer any questions they may have.

Chapter 4
Where's the gym?

Objectives

Language:
- Listen to a dialogue for comprehension.
- Understand familiar vocabulary and grammar structures by listening to a dialogue.
- Develop new vocabulary and grammar structures by listening to a dialogue.
- Act out a dialogue.
- Use prepositions of location: *in, on, under,* and *next to.*
- Use *Where* questions with *be.*
- Use *There is (There's)* and *There are.*
- Use the contractions *Where's* and *There's.*
- Make original conversations using new vocabulary and grammar structures.
- Evaluate one's own learning of new vocabulary, grammar, and oral language.

Literacy:
- Read a dialogue for comprehension.
- Understand familiar vocabulary and grammar structures by reading a dialogue.
- Develop new vocabulary and grammar structures by reading a dialogue.
- Write sentences using new vocabulary.
- Complete sentences with prepositions of location: *in, on, under,* and *next to.*
- Complete *Where* questions with *be.*
- Write sentences answering *Where* questions with *be.*
- Decode words with the consonant sounds /ch/ and /sh/.
- Complete and write sentences with *There is (There's)* and *There are.*
- Read a short story for comprehension.
- Understand familiar vocabulary and grammar structures by reading a short story.
- Develop new vocabulary and grammar structures by reading a short story.
- Plan, write, revise, edit, proofread, and make a final copy of a descriptive paragraph about places in one's school.
- Use location words, *has/have,* and *There is/There are* to describe places in one's school.

- Evaluate one's own learning of reading skills, reading comprehension, and writing skills.

Learning Strategies:
- Use cooperation with a classmate to read a dialogue and study new vocabulary.
- Use cooperation with a small group to act out a dialogue.
- Use cooperation with a classmate to practice conversations.
- Use the strategy *Sound Out* to decode words.
- Use the strategy *Make Predictions* to understand a short story.
- Use cooperation with a classmate to check a paragraph one has written.
- Evaluate one's own learning of the strategies *Make Predictions* and *Sound Out.*
- Identify easy and difficult material in a chapter and the different ways to learn the difficult material.

Opening Dialogue, pages 50–51

Getting Ready

Preparation *(See Transparency 17.)*

- Have students look at the illustrations and identify any words they know for the objects in the illustrations. Write the words on the board or a poster. Read the words, one at a time, as students follow along.

- Point to objects in the illustrations that student didn't mention and ask, "What's this?" Write the responses on the board or a poster. Read the responses as students follow along.

- Ask students if they can recall the names of the characters in the illustrations. (Pablo, Mei, and Liliana.) Write the names of the characters on the board or a poster. Read the responses as the students follow along.

Listening and Reading

Lost at School

Presentation

Exercise A

- Read the directions and the prelistening question aloud as students follow along in their texts.

- Have students listen to the dialogue, or read the dialogue aloud to them. Have students look at the appropriate illustrations as they listen.
- Ask the prelistening question, "Does Pablo have gym with Liliana?" Call on a volunteer to respond. (No, he doesn't.)

Exercise B

Have students read the dialogue. Provide help with content, vocabulary, etc. as needed.

> **Reaching All Students—Emergent Learners:** Work with emergent learners in small groups while the other students work independently. Read aloud as students follow along in their texts. Monitor their comprehension by interrupting the reading with questions such as, "Where is the gym?" (It's across from the cafeteria.) "Who is lost?" (Pablo is lost.) "Who has P.E. now?" (Pablo and Liliana have P.E. now.) "Where is Pablo's P.E. class?" (It's in the other gym.) "Are there three gyms in Pablo's school?" (Yes, there are.)

Pair and Group Work

Practice
Exercise A

Have students who can read on their own form pairs. Have one student in the pair take the roles of Pablo and Mei; have the other student take the roles of Liliana and Samir. Then have them read the dialogue aloud. Provide help as needed.

> **Reaching All Students—Emergent Learners:** Work in small groups with emergent readers. Model each sentence and have individual students "echo" your reading. Make sure that students look at the sentences as you read them.

Exercise B

Have students form groups of four. Group students heterogeneously so that each group is made up of average readers, weak readers, and strong readers. Have each student choose a role in the dialogue. Have students practice acting out the dialogue in their groups.

> **Reaching All Students—Kinesthetic Learners:** Choose one or more groups to act out the dialogue in front of the class.

Vocabulary

Practice
Exercise A

Have students read and say the words and expressions. Provide assistance with pronunciation as needed. Then have them write the words and expressions in their notebooks.

> **Reaching All Students—Auditory Learners:** Encourage students to say the words and expressions as they write them in their notebooks.

Exercise B (See Transparencies 85–86.)

- Have students turn to page 250 in their texts.
- Have students work through Step 1 (recognizing letters) with the words in the box on page 51 if further practice is needed.
- Call on a volunteer to read Step 2 aloud as the other students follow along.
- Model the exercise by saying how many syllables are in the first two words in the box on page 51 (*gym* has 1 syllable, *downstairs* has 2 syllables).
- Write *downstairs* on the board, and show how the two syllables are divided by drawing a slash between "down" and "stairs."
- Have students work in pairs, saying how many syllables are in each word in the box on page 51. Answer students' questions as needed.

Exercise C

Have students find the words and expressions in the dialogue. Have them read the sentences.

Exercise D

- Have each student choose five words from the words in the word box. Have them write five sentences in their notebooks, using these new words.
- Call on volunteers to read their sentences to the class.

> **Answers**
> *Answers will vary.*

Grammar 1, page 52

Prepositions of Location: *in, on, under, next to*

Preparation

Demonstrate the four location words *(in, on, under, next to)* using objects in the classroom. For example, place a pen on a book and say, "The pen is *on* the book." Have the class repeat after you.

Presentation

- Have students study the illustrations and the text below them.
- Call on a volunteer to read the sentence below the first illustration. Continue by calling on other volunteers to read the other sentences.

Practice

Exercise

- Have students look at the first illustration. Call on a volunteer to read the first sentence with the sample answer aloud.
- Have students copy the sentences into their notebooks. Have them fill in the blanks with the correct preposition: *in, on, under,* or *next to.*

   Reaching All Students—Auditory Learners: Call on advanced students to read the sentences (without the answers) before students write their answers.

   Reaching All Students—Emergent/ Cooperative Learners: Have students work in pairs to complete the activity.

- Review the answers with the class.

Answers		
1. under	3. on	5. under
2. next to	4. in	6. on

Grammar 2, page 53

Where Questions with *be*

Preparation

- Write the following dialogue on the board as a way of presenting the grammar focus in context.

Pablo: *Where are* Carmen and Liliana?
  Mei: They*'re* in the gym.
Pablo: *Where's* the gym?
  Mei: It*'s* on the second floor.

- Read the dialogue aloud as students follow along.
- Call on two advanced students to dramatize the dialogue for the rest of the class.

Presentation

- Have students look at the grammar chart in their texts.
- Explain that the first part of the grammar chart shows them how to ask *Where* questions with *be.* The second part shows them how to answer the questions. Model forming two questions and two answers. (Examples: Where is she? She is in the gym. / Where are they? They are in the gym.)
- Have students study the first part of the chart. Ask them to read silently across this part, using a word in each column to make a question.
- Have students follow the same procedure for the second part of the chart to make answers.

   Reaching All Students—Cooperative Learners: Have students work in pairs. Have the first student make a question, reading across the first row. Then have the second student make a question, reading across the second row. Have them repeat for the remaining rows. Then have them follow the same procedure for the answers.

- Call on individual students to read aloud one or two of the questions and answers they made from the words in the columns.
- Refer students to the contraction box, and explain that *Where's* is the contraction, or shortened form, of *Where is.* Ask, "Where is the gym?" Then ask, "Where's the gym?" Explain that both questions are right: *Where is* is formal (for many school writing assignments); *Where's* is casual (for everyday speaking situations).

Practice

Exercise A

- Call on a volunteer to read the first question with the sample answer aloud. Call on another volunteer to explain why the sample answer is correct. (The noun *stairs* replaces the pronoun *they* in the grammar chart. Therefore, the sentence takes the plural form of the verb *be* [*are*]).

- Have students copy the items into their notebooks. Have them fill in the blanks with the correct form of *be (is or are)*.

   Reaching All Students—Auditory Learners: Call on advanced students to read the sentences (without the answers) before students write their answers.

   Reaching All Students—Emergent Learners: Work with students in small groups, guiding them to see which pronoun from the chart correctly replaces the noun or nouns. Then have them use the chart to find the correct form of *be*.

- Review the answers with the class.

Answers

1. are   **3.** are   **5.** is
2. is   **4.** is

Exercise B *(See Transparency 83.)*

- Explain that in this exercise, students will write the answers to the questions listed, using information about their own school. They can use vocabulary from the box or their own words.

- Read the question in the example aloud. Call on a student to read the response.

- Have students write their responses to questions 1–5 in their notebooks.

   Reaching All Students—Emergent Learners: First, have students do the exercise orally, either using the vocabulary from the box or their own words. Then have them copy the questions into their notebooks. Have them write responses to the questions. Provide help as needed.

- Review the answers with the class.

Answers

Answers will vary. Possible answers:
1. It's on the second floor.
2. It's next to the cafeteria.
3. It's in room 275.
4. It's next to the library.
5. It's in the next building.

Word Study, page 54

Consonant Sounds: /ch/ and /sh/

Preparation

- Write the words *lunch* and *English* on the board.
- Call on volunteers to identify the names of the consonants and vowels in the words.
- Pronounce the words and have students repeat them after you.

Presentation

- Point to the word *lunch* on the board. Call on a volunteer to identify the first sound (/l/), the second sound (/u/), the third sound (/n/), and the fourth sound (/ch/).
- Ask students, "How many sounds does the word have?" (Four.) "How many letters does the word have?" (Five.)
- To help students understand why the word has five letters but only four sounds, underline the consonants *ch* in the word. Call on a volunteer to pronounce the sound (/ch/).
- Explain that the consonants *ch* together stand for one sound. Explain that consonant combinations like *ch* are called consonant digraphs. Consonant digraphs are two consonants that come together in a word and stand for one sound.
- Point out that the consonant digraph *ch* can appear at the beginning, in the middle, or at the end of words.
- Follow the same procedure for the word *English*.

Practice
Exercise A

Have students use the learning strategy *Sound Out* (page 32 in the text), as well as the pictures, to read the words with the consonant sounds /ch/ and /sh/.

   Reaching All Students—Emergent Learners: Complete this activity as a class if students need help. After students have an approximation of the pronunciation, say the words correctly to provide a model.

Exercise B

- First, have students read the sentences aloud. Then have them copy the sentences into their notebooks. Last, have them circle the letters that stand for the consonant sounds /ch/ and /sh/.
- Review the answers as a class.

Answers
1. Where is your lun(ch)?
2. Please (sh)ut the door.
3. That is a very pretty di(sh).
4. Carmen's hat is on the ben(ch).
5. Are they on that (sh)ip?
6. Does Bic have two fi(sh)?

Optional Activity: Ask students to number a page in their notebooks from 1 to 8. Then ask them to listen carefully to the words you read and to write the words next to the correct numbers. Then dictate the following words:

1. bench   5. chin
2. lunch   6. shut
3. dish   7. inch
4. ship   8. fish

- After the dictation, write the words on the board. Then have students check their words.
- Have students record the number of correct words in their notebooks; for example, *I wrote (7) out of 8 dictated words with the consonant sounds /ch/ and /sh/ correctly.* Write this example on the board as a model.

Expansion
Exercise C

- Have students look at Exercise A. Have them choose two words with the consonant sound /ch/ and two words with the consonant sound /sh/. Have them write a sentence for each word in their notebooks.

  Reaching All Students—Emergent Learners: Review the meanings of the words in Exercise A. Model a sample sentence on the board. Then have students write the sentences in their notebooks. Provide help as needed.
- Have students share their sentences with the class.

Answers
Answers will vary.

Optional Activity: Have students draw two columns in their notebooks. Have them write /ch/ at the top of one column and /sh/ at the top of another column (model this on the board). Have students write as many words as they can that begin or end with each consonant sound. (Set a time limit of 5–10 minutes.) Encourage students to use a dictionary, their texts, or their vocabulary lists for help.

  Reaching All Students—Auditory Learners: Encourage students to say the words aloud as they write them.
- Have students share their lists with the class.

Answers
Answers will vary.

Grammar 3, page 55

There is and *there are*

Preparation

- Write the following dialogue on the board as a way of presenting the grammar focus in context.
  Liliana: *There are* three gyms in this school.
  Pablo: Are there three cafeterias, too?
  Liliana: No, *there's* only one cafeteria, silly.
- Read the dialogue aloud as students follow along.
- Call on two advanced students to dramatize the dialogue for the rest of the class.

Presentation

- Have students look at the grammar chart. Read across each row in the first part as students follow along in their texts. Point out that we use *There is* before a singular noun. Read across each row in the second part as students follow along in their texts. Point out that we use *There are* before a plural noun.
- Read the Remember note at the bottom of the chart as students follow along in their texts.
- Point out that *There's* is the contraction, or shortened form, of *There is*. Explain that the following two statements mean the same thing: *There's a locker. There is a locker.*

- Have students read silently across each row in the first part of the chart. Then have them read silently across each row in the second part of the chart.

    Reaching All Students—Auditory/Cooperative Learners: Have pairs of students take turns reading sentences from the chart. Have the first student read a *There is* sentence from the first part. Then have the second student read a *There are* sentence from the second part. Have them continue for the remaining sentences.

- Call on volunteers to read the sentences they made to the rest of the class.
- Call on students to read the *There is* sentences from the chart, substituting *There's* for *There is*.

Practice

Exercise A

- Call on a volunteer to read item 1 with the sample answer aloud as the other students follow along in their texts. Ask the student to explain why the answer is correct. (The noun *girls* is plural; therefore, we use the plural form *There are*.)
- Have students copy the sentences into their notebooks. Then have them fill in the blanks with *There is* or *There are*. For this activity, tell the students *not* to use the contraction for *There is* (*There's*).

    Reaching All Students—Emergent Learners: First, have students do the exercise orally, using the grammar chart for reference. Then have them copy the sentences into their notebooks. Have them complete the activity. Provide help as needed.

    Reaching All Students—Cooperative Learners: Have students work in pairs or small groups to complete the activity.

- Review the answers with the class.

Answers

1. There are
2. There is
3. There is
4. There are
5. There are

Exercise B

- Tell students that they will write their own sentences about their class and their school, using *There's* and *There are*.

- Model writing three sentences each about your class and your school, using *There's* and *There are*.
    Examples:
    There's a map on the wall.
    There are books on the teacher's desk.
    There's a backpack under the student's desk.
    There's a computer lab next to the library.
    There are long tables in the cafeteria.
    There's a gym on the first floor.

    <u>Optional Activity:</u> Have the class develop the examples. Write them on the board.

- Have students write their own sentences in their notebooks.

    Reaching All Students—Emergent Learners: Have students start by copying one of the examples generated as a class. Then have them create two more sentences on their own, in pairs, or in small groups.

- Call on volunteers to read their sentences aloud.

Answers
Answers will vary.

Exercise C

- Read the directions and the example as students follow along in their texts.
- Have students study the illustration. Then, in their notebooks, have them write five sentences about the illustration. Remind them to use *in*, *on*, and *next to* in their sentences. Also remind them to use *There's* with a singular noun and *There are* with a plural noun.

    Reaching All Students—Emergent Learners: Have students look at the illustration and identify the words they know for the objects in the picture. Write the words on the board. Include the article or adjective with the word, for example, *a computer*, *three books*, and *a long desk*. Next, read the example sentence as students follow along in their texts. Then call on volunteers to create sentences about the picture, using phrases on the board. Provide help as needed. Last, have students copy the sentences into their notebooks.

- Review the answers as a class.

Reading, pages 56–57

Before You Read

Presentation (See Transparency 22.)

- Explain to students that when we make predictions, we say what we think is going to happen next in a certain situation. To do that, we use information or clues that are available to us.

- Point out to students that they can make predictions about a story's events or characters. The predictions can help them understand the story better.

- Have students look at the Learning Strategy box *Make Predictions*. Read the information aloud as students follow along in their texts.

- Have students look at the Before You Read section in their texts. Read aloud the general direction line and the steps as students follow along.

Practice

Have students work in pairs to complete the activity. Remind them that they can change their prediction if they learn new information or find new clues.

Read This!

I Love School!

Preparation

Note: Students will encounter the following new words in the reading: *a lot of, auditorium, chair, classroom, library, like, live, nice, small, table, use, go, I come from [Peru].*

Practice

- 🎧 Have students listen to the story, or read it aloud to them.

- Have students read the story silently on their own. Provide help with content, vocabulary, etc. as needed.

Reaching All Students—Emergent Learners: Work with emergent learners in small groups while the other students work independently. Read aloud as students follow along in their texts. Monitor their comprehension by interrupting the reading with questions such as, "Where is Liliana from?" (She's from Peru.) "What school does she go to?" (She goes to Washington School.) "Are there many classrooms in the school?" (Yes, there are.) "Does Liliana like computers?" (Yes, she does.) "Does Liliana have eight classes?" (No, she doesn't. She has seven classes.) "Does Liliana like all her classes?" (Yes, she does.) Encourage students to answer the questions using complete sentences.

After You Read

Preparation

Remind students that the After You Read activities can help them be sure they understood what they read.

Self-Evaluation

Exercise A

- Read the questions aloud as students follow along in their texts.

  Reaching All Students—Visual Learners: Write the four questions from Exercise A on the board.

- Divide students into pairs. Have them discuss their responses. Provide help as needed.

- Call on volunteers to give their responses. Write them on the board.

Exercise B

- Have students take out their notebooks and number a sheet of paper from 1 to 5.

- Read the example aloud, "Liliana is a teacher." Ask, "Is that statement true or false?" Call on a volunteer to answer. (False.) Ask the student to find the supportive statement in the story. (Liliana says, "I am a student.") Tell students that they will need to write correct statements for any false ones. Read the correct statement in the example. (Liliana is a student.)

- Have students complete the activity.

  Reaching All Students—Auditory Learners: Call on advanced students to read the sentences. Have students write their answers in their notebooks.

- Call on students to give their answers and write them on the board. Be sure they also give the supporting statements from the story.
- Have students count the number of correct answers and write that number in their notebooks.

Answers
1. True
2. True
3. False. Liliana is sixteen years old.
4. False. Liliana likes all her classes.
5. True

Expansion

Encourage students to use the strategy *Make Predictions* with their science and social studies readings. Later, have them explain how the strategy helped them understand the readings better.

Writing, page 58

Before You Write

Preparation *(See Transparencies 17 and 32–33.)*

Tell students that they are going write a paragraph about the different places in their school. Tell them that the Before I Write, While I Write, and After I Write checklists provide *strategies* to guide them through the process of writing their paragraphs.

Presentation/Practice
Exercise A

- Focus students' attention on the handwritten paragraph.

   Reaching All Students—Auditory Learners: Call on an advanced student to read the paragraph aloud to the class while the other students follow along in their texts.

- Call on a volunteer to tell what the paragraph is about. (It's a description of Liliana's school.) Ask them what kinds of information Liliana included in her paragraph. (Places in her school, her favorite place,

what her favorite place has, what she does there.)

- Brainstorm with students the vocabulary they will need to include in a paragraph about places in their school. Write their responses on the board.
- Refer students to page 230 in their Vocabulary Handbooks for the names of the different places in a school.
- Draw students' attention to the Before I Write checklist.
- Model following the steps in the Before I Write checklist to plan your own sample paragraph.
- Have students follow the Before I Write checklist and take notes in their notebooks.

   Reaching All Students—Emergent Learners: Group students who might have difficulty with the assignment and work with them. Guide them in following the steps in the checklist.

Write This!

Presentation

- Draw students' attention to the While I Write checklist.
- Model following the While I Write checklist. Refer to the notes you took in your earlier modeling. As you write, do a "think aloud" about how you are following the While I Write checklist. Model making errors with *has/have* or *there is/there are*. If students catch the mistakes, circle them and say, "I can correct these errors later."

Practice

- Have students write their paragraphs in their notebooks, using their notes as a guide. They should also use the While I Write checklist for help. If needed, they can also refer back to the grammar charts earlier in the chapter.

   Reaching All Students—Emergent/ Advanced Learners: Encourage emergent learners to keep the paragraph simple. Encourage advanced learners to include more details in their paragraphs.

- Circulate while students are writing, and encourage them to ask for help with new words if they need it.

After You Write

Presentation

- Draw students' attention to the After I Write checklist.
- Model following the steps in the After I Write checklist, checking your own paragraph. Correct any mistakes you made with *has/have* or *there is/there are*.

Practice

Exercise A

Have students use the After I Write checklist to evaluate their writing. Have them circle and then correct their errors.

Exercise B

Have students read their paragraphs to a classmate. Encourage them to make suggestions for improvement.

Exercise C

Have students make a final copy of their paragraphs in their notebooks.

Learning Log, page 59

See How to Use the Learning Log on page xiii. *(See Transparencies 20 and 65.)*

Chapter 5
What's your address?

Objectives

Language:
- Listen to a dialogue for comprehension.
- Understand familiar vocabulary and grammar structures by listening to a dialogue.
- Develop new vocabulary and grammar structures by listening to a dialogue.
- Act out a dialogue.
- Use the present tense of *What* questions with *be*.
- Use the present tense of regular verbs in *yes/no* questions and in affirmative and negative statements.
- Use *can* in *yes/no* questions and in affirmative and negative statements.
- Use the contractions *what's, don't, doesn't,* and *can't.*
- Make original conversations using new vocabulary and grammar structures.
- Ask for and give information.
- Evaluate one's own learning of new vocabulary, grammar, and oral language.

Literacy:
- Read a dialogue for comprehension.
- Understand familiar vocabulary and grammar structures by reading a dialogue.
- Develop new vocabulary and grammar structures by reading a dialogue.
- Read *What* questions with *be* and match them with answers.
- Complete and write *yes/no* questions and affirmative and negative statements using the present tense of regular verbs.
- Decode words with consonant blends.
- Complete and write *yes/no* questions and affirmative and negative statements with *can.*
- Read a short story for comprehension.
- Understand familiar vocabulary and grammar structures by reading a short story.
- Develop new vocabulary and grammar structures by reading a short story.

- Plan, write, revise, edit, proofread, and make a final copy of a personal information form.
- Capitalize the names of people, streets, and cities; use the abbreviation *St.* for *Street* and *Apt.* for *Apartment;* and abbreviate the names of states.
- Evaluate one's own learning of reading skills, reading comprehension, and writing skills.

Learning Strategies:
- Use cooperation with a classmate to read a dialogue and study new vocabulary.
- Use cooperation with a small group to act out a dialogue.
- Use cooperation with a classmate to practice conversations.
- Use the strategy *Sound Out* to decode words.
- Use the strategy *Use Selective Attention* to understand a short story.
- Use cooperation with a classmate to check a form one has filled out.
- Evaluate one's own learning of the strategies *Use Selective Attention* and *Sound Out.*
- Identify easy and difficult material in a chapter and the different ways to learn the difficult material.

Opening Dialogue, pages 60–61

Getting Ready

Preparation *(See Transparency 17.)*
- Have students look at the illustrations and identify the words they know for objects in the illustrations. Have students identify the characters. (Samir, Pablo, Liliana, Carmen, and Carlos.) Write the words on the board or a poster. Read the words, one at a time, and have students repeat each one after you.
- Point to objects in the illustrations that students didn't mention and ask, "What's this?" Write the responses on the board or a poster. Read the responses and have students repeat them after you.

Listening and Reading

The Party

Presentation

Exercise A

- Read the directions and the prelistening question aloud as students follow along in their texts.

  Reaching All Students—Visual Learners: Have a map available, along with photos, to illustrate new vocabulary (for example, *map, fire station, building, party*).

- Have students listen to the dialogue, or read the dialogue aloud to them. Have students look at the appropriate illustrations as they listen.

- Ask the prelistening question, "Who is having a party?" Call on a volunteer to respond. (Carmen and Carlos are having a party.)

Exercise B

Have students read the dialogue. Provide help with content, vocabulary, etc. as needed.

Reaching All Students—Emergent Learners: Work with emergent learners in small groups while the other students work independently. Read aloud as students follow along in their texts. Monitor their comprehension by interrupting the reading with questions such as, "Where is Carmen and Carlos's party?" (It's at their house.) "What's their address?" (It's 316 Fifth Street.) "Where is Carmen and Carlos's house?" (It's next to a building.) "Who can go to the party together?" (Pablo and Liliana can go to the party together.) "Who cannot go to the party?" (Maria cannot go to the party.)

Pair and Group Work

Practice

Exercise A

Have students who can read on their own form pairs. Have one student read one section of the dialogue while the other one follows along in the text. Then have them switch. Provide help as needed.

Reaching All Students—Emergent Learners: Work in small groups with students who cannot read on their own. Model each sentence and have individual students "echo" your reading. Make sure that students look at the sentences as you read them.

Exercise B

Have students form groups of six. Group students heterogeneously so that each group is made up of average readers, weak readers, and strong readers. Have each student choose a role in the dialogue. Have students practice acting out the dialogue in their groups.

Reaching All Students—Kinesthetic Learners: Choose one or more groups to act out the dialogue in front of the class.

Vocabulary

Practice

Exercise A

Have students read and say the words and expressions. Provide assistance with pronunciation as needed. Then have them write the words and expressions in their notebooks.

Exercise B *(See Transparencies 85–86.)*

- Have students turn to page 250 in their texts.
- Have students work through Step 1 (recognizing letters) with the words in the box on page 61 if further practice is needed.
- Have students work in pairs, saying how many syllables are in each word. Answer students' questions as needed.

Exercise C

Have students find the words and expressions in the dialogue. Have them read the sentences aloud.

Exercise D

Have students work in pairs. Have each student in a pair choose a word from the word box to illustrate. Then have each student guess the other student's word.

Grammar 1, page 62

What Questions with *be*

Preparation

- Write the following dialogue on the board as a way of presenting the grammar focus in context.

  Sophie: *What's that?*

      Mei: It's a map to Carlos and Carmen's house.

- Read the dialogue aloud as students follow along.

- Call on two advanced students to dramatize the dialogue for the rest of the class.

Presentation

- Have students look at the grammar chart in their texts.

- Point out that the left part of the chart shows *What* questions with *be*. The right part of the chart shows the answers to the questions.

- Have students read across each row in the left section of the chart.

- Next, have students read each question and corresponding answer. (Example: What is that? / It is a map.)

  Reaching All Students—Visual/Auditory Learners: Copy the chart onto the board. Call on volunteers to read aloud across each row in the left part of the chart. Then call on volunteers to read aloud each question and corresponding answer. As students read aloud, point to the corresponding rows.

- Direct students' attention to the contractions box. Explain that the contraction of *What is* is *What's*.

- Call on students to read the *What is* questions from the chart, substituting *What's* for *What is*.

Practice

Exercise A

- Call on a volunteer to read item 1 aloud as the other students follow along in their texts. Have another student read the answer.

- Have students number a sheet of paper from 1 to 5. Have them write the letter of the correct answer next to the number.

Reaching All Students—Emergent/Auditory Learners: Call on volunteers to read the list of questions and the list of answer choices aloud.

Reaching All Students—Cooperative Learners: Have students work in pairs or small groups to complete the activity.

Reaching All Students—Advanced/Emergent Learners: Follow this procedure as part of the review for advanced students or as additional support for emergent students. Call on a volunteer to read item 2. Then call on another volunteer to provide the answer. (a. They're my sister's books.) Ask the student to explain why the answer isn't "c. It's my schedule." (*Those* in the question indicates a plural; *it's* is singular.)

- Review the answers with the class.

Answers		
1. e	**3.** b	**5.** d
2. a	**4.** c	

Exercise B

Have students listen to the conversation, or read the dialogue aloud to them. Have students look at the illustration as they listen. Provide help with content, vocabulary, etc. as needed.

Exercise C

- Have students work in pairs. Have one student read part A in the dialogue and the other, part B.

  Reaching All Students—Emergent Learners: Work with students in small groups. Provide help with unfamiliar words.

- Next, have pairs make new conversations using their own information.

- Have students consult the Vocabulary Handbook (page 232) for other school subjects.

- Call on two advanced students to model new conversations, using other school subjects and other teachers' names.

  Reaching All Students—Emergent Learners: Work with students in small groups. Provide help with unfamiliar words.

Grammar 2, page 63

Present Tense of Regular Verbs: Statements

Preparation

- Write the following dialogue on the board as a way of presenting the grammar focus in context.

  Liliana: I *want* some new shoes for the party. My shoes are old and boring.

  Carmen: You *don't need* new shoes, Liliana. Carlos *needs* new shoes.

- Read the dialogue aloud as students follow along.
- Call on two advanced students to dramatize the dialogue for the rest of the class.

Presentation

- Have students look at the grammar chart in their texts. Explain that the left part of the chart shows affirmative statements—"*yes* statements." The right part shows negative statements—"*no* statements."

  Reaching All Students—Visual Learners: Copy the chart onto the board. Point to each part of the chart as you name it.

- Have students read silently across each row of the Affirmative Statements part of the chart.
- Have students read silently across each row of the Negative Statements part of the chart.

  Reaching All Students—Auditory/ Cooperative Learners: Have pairs of students take turns reading sentences from the chart. Have the first student read an affirmative sentence from the left part of the chart. Then have the second student read the corresponding negative sentence from the right part of the chart. Have them continue for the remaining sentences.

- Have students note that the verb after *he, she,* and *it* has a final *-s*.
- Have students work in pairs or small groups to develop a rule that tells how to make negative statements with regular verbs. Call on students to give their rule. Then write the rule on the board. (Example: Subject + *do not (does not)* + verb + object. The verb *do*

should match its subject. The second verb should be in the base form.)

- Call on volunteers and have each one read a sentence from the chart.
- Direct students' attention to the contractions box in their texts. Explain that the contraction of *do not* is *don't* and the contraction of *does not* is *doesn't*.
- Call on students to read the Negative Statements part of the chart again, substituting the long forms for the contractions.

Practice

Exercise

- Read the first sentence with the sample answer aloud. Have students repeat. Call on a volunteer to explain why the answer is correct. (*Maria* replaces *she* in the chart. The verb takes a final *-s* [*speaks*].)
- Have students copy the sentences into their notebooks. Have them fill in the blanks with the correct form of the verb.

  Reaching All Students—Auditory Learners: Call on advanced students to read each of the remaining sentences (without the answers) before students write their answers.

  Reaching All Students—Emergent Learners: First, have students do the exercise orally. Then have them copy the incomplete sentences into their notebooks. Have them complete the sentences with the correct form of the verb. Provide help as needed, showing them how to use the chart to find the answers.

- Review the answers with the class.

Answers	
1. speaks	**4.** doesn't speak
2. live	**5.** don't like
3. wants	

Present Tense of Regular Verbs: *Yes/No* Questions

Presentation

- Have students look at the grammar chart in their texts. Explain that the left part of the chart shows *yes/no* questions for the regular verb *need,* the middle part shows affirmative answers, and the right part shows negative answers. Have students read silently across each row of each part.

> **Reaching All Students—Visual Learners:** Copy the chart on the board. Point to each part of the chart as you name it.

> **Reaching All Students—Auditory/Cooperative Learners:** Have groups of three students take turns reading the questions and answers across the chart. Have the first student read the question, the second student read the affirmative answer, and the third student read the negative answer.

- Call on volunteers to read the questions and answers from the chart. This time, have students respond appropriately to the questions; for example, "Do I need new shoes?" "Yes, you do." / "No, you don't."

Practice

- Tell students that they will write three *yes/no* questions using the regular verbs *speak, like,* and *need.* They will then ask a classmate their questions. Their classmate will answer the questions.
- Call on a student to read the example aloud. Have students write the example in their notebooks.
- Have students brainstorm topics they could ask about for each verb—*speak, like,* and *need.* Write the topics on the board.

> **Reaching All Students—Emergent Learners:** After students select a topic, ask them to generate the question. For example, "Italian—Do you speak Italian?" Then write the questions on the board.

> **Reaching All Students—Advanced Learners:** Write the topics only. Have students generate their own questions.

- Have students write their three questions in their notebooks.
- Pair students to ask each other their questions. Have them answer their classmate's questions orally.
- Have pairs share their questions and answers with the class.

Answers
Answers will vary. Possible answers include:
Do you speak Spanish?
Do you like computers?
Do you need more time?

Word Study, page 64

Consonant Blends

Preparation

- Write the word *block* on the board.
- Call on volunteers to identify the names of the consonants and vowel in the word.
- Pronounce the word and have students repeat it after you.
- Ask students to identify the first sound (/b/), the second sound (/l/), the third sound (/o/), and the last sound (/k/). Then have them blend all the sounds together to pronounce the word. (Block.)
- Underline the consonants *bl* in *block* and ask students to pronounce the sounds. Ask them if they hear the sound /b/. (Yes.) Ask them if they hear the sound /l/. (Yes.) Ask them if both sounds blend together. (Yes.)
- Review with students that the consonants *ck* at the end of the word *block* are called a consonant digraph. A consonant digraph consists of two consonants that come together in a word and stand for one sound. (See Chapter 4, Word Study, page 54 in the Student Book.)

Presentation

- Have students look at the instruction box in the text. Read aloud the information as students follow along.
- Reread the examples aloud, one at a time. Have students repeat each one after you.

Practice

Exercise A

Have students use the learning strategy *Sound Out,* as well as the pictures, to read the words with consonant blends.

> **Reaching All Students—Emergent Learners:** Complete this activity as a class if students need help. After students have an approximation of the pronunciation, say the words correctly to provide a model.

Exercise B

- First, have students read the sentences aloud. Then have them copy the sentences into their notebooks. Last, have them circle the consonant blends.

- Review the answers as a class.

Optional Activity: Have students close their texts. Ask them to number a page in their notebooks from 1 to 8. Then ask them to listen carefully to the words you read and to write the words. Then dictate the following words:

1. flag
2. clock
3. dress
4. glass
5. black
6. drums
7. class
8. swim

- After the dictation, write the words on the board. Then have students check their words.
- Have students record the number of correct words in their notebooks; for example, *I wrote (7) out of 8 dictated words with consonant blends correctly.* Write this example on the board as a model.

Exercise C

- Have students look at Exercise A. Have them choose two words with consonant blends. Then have them write a sentence for each word in their notebooks.

    Reaching All Students—Emergent Learners: Review the meanings of the words in Exercise A. Model a sample sentence on the board. Then have students write the sentences in their notebooks. Provide help as needed.

- Have students share their sentences with the class.

Answers
Answers will vary.

Optional Activity: Have students copy the consonant blends from Exercise A into their notebooks (*dr, bl, cl, sw, fl,* and *gl*). Then have them write as many words as they can that begin with each consonant blend. (Set a time limit of 5–10 minutes.) Encourage students to use a dictionary, the text, or their vocabulary lists for help.

Reaching All Students—Auditory Learners: Encourage students to say the words aloud as they write them.

Have students share their lists with the class.

Answers
Answers will vary.

Grammar 3, page 65

Statements with *can*

Preparation

- Write the following dialogue on the board as a way of presenting the grammar focus in context.

    Carmen: *Can* you come to our party?
    Mei: Yes, I *can* come.
    Maria: I'm sorry, but I *can't* come.

- Read the dialogue aloud as students follow along.
- Call on three advanced students to dramatize the dialogue for the rest of the class.

Presentation

Reaching All Students—Visual Learners: Copy the chart onto the board. Point to each section of the chart as you name it.

- Have students look at the grammar chart. Explain that the left part of the chart shows affirmative statements with *can*—when the answer is *yes.* The right part shows negative statements with *can*—when the answer is *no.*
- Have students read silently across each row of each part, first reading the affirmative statements on the left, then reading the negative statements on the right.

    Reaching All Students—Auditory/ Cooperative Learners: Have pairs of students take turns reading sentences from the chart. Have the first student read an affirmative sentence from the left part of the chart. Then have the second student read a negative sentence from the right part of the chart. Have them continue for the remaining sentences.

- Call on volunteers to read sentences from the chart.

- Have students look at the contractions box. Explain that *can't* is the contraction of *cannot*.

Practice

Exercise

- Read the first sentence with the sample answer aloud. Have students repeat. Point out that the answer *can't* is negative.
- Have students copy the sentences into their notebooks. Have them fill in the blanks with the correct answer—*can* or *can't*. Have them use the grammar chart for reference.

   Reaching All Students—Auditory Learners: Call on advanced students to read each of the remaining sentences (without the answers) aloud before students write their answers.

   Reaching All Students—Emergent Learners: First, have students do the exercise orally. Then have them copy the incomplete sentences into their notebooks. Have them complete the sentences with the correct answer—*can* or *can't*. Provide help as needed.

   Reaching All Students—Emergent/ Cooperative Learners: Have students work in pairs to complete the activity.

- Review the answers with the class.

```
Answers
1. can't        3. can't        5. can't
2. can          4. can
```

Yes/No Questions with *can*

Presentation

   Reaching All Students—Visual Learners: Copy the chart onto the board. Point to each section of the chart as you name it.

- Have students look at the grammar chart. Explain that the left part of the chart shows *yes/no* questions with *can* (read the first line as an example). The middle section shows affirmative answers (read the first line). The right part shows negative answers (read the first line).
- Have students read silently across each row of one section at a time.
- As a class, have students develop rules that tell how to make *yes/no* questions and affirmative and negative statements with *can*.

Have them refer to both grammar charts on page 65 in the text. Call on students to give their rules. Then write the rules on the board. (Example: For questions, the form is *Can* + subject + verb in the base form + object? For affirmative statements, the form is Subject + *can* + verb in the base form + object. For negative statements, the form is Subject + *can't* + verb in the base form + object.)

   Reaching All Students—Auditory/ Cooperative Learners: Have groups of three students take turns reading sentences from the chart. Have the first student read the question, the second student read the affirmative answer, and the third student read the negative answer. Point out that this is just for practice of form—the answer to "Can *you* come to the party?" is either "Yes, *I* can." *or* "No, *I* can't."

- Call on volunteers to read the questions and answers from the chart. This time, have students respond appropriately to the questions rather than just reading across the chart. (Example: "Can I come to the party?" "Yes, you can.")

Practice

Exercise A

- Read the directions aloud as students follow along in their texts.
- Have students number a sheet of paper in their notebooks from 1 to 5.
- Point out that this exercise is for practice of form (word order) in *yes/no* questions with *can*.
- Read item 1 with the sample answer aloud as students follow along in their texts.
- Have students change the statements for items 2–5 into questions, using the grammar chart for reference.
- Review the answers as a class. As you review the answers, point out that *Bic* replaces *he* in the grammar chart (item 2) and *Samir and Liliana* replace *they* (item 3).

   Reaching All Students—Emergent Learners: First, have students do the exercise orally, using the grammar chart for reference. Point out the word order in the question (*Can* + subject + base form of verb + object). Also, point out that *Bic* replaces *he* (item 2) in the chart and *Samir and Liliana* replace *they* (item 3). Next, have students copy the sentences into their notebooks. Then have them complete the activity. Provide help as needed.

Answers
1. Can you answer this question?
2. Can Bic speak English and Chinese?
3. Can Samir and Liliana come to the party?
4. Can we play the drums?
5. Can it swim?

Exercise B

- Tell students that they will write five *yes/no* questions with *can,* using a new topic—not "the party." Call on a student to read the example aloud. Have students write the example in their notebooks.
- Have students brainstorm other topics they could ask questions about. Write the topics on the board. (Possible topics include sports, musical instruments, languages, games, and academic subjects.)

    Reaching All Students—Emergent Learners: After students select a topic, ask them to generate the question. For example, "soccer—Can you play soccer?" Then write the questions on the board.

    Reaching All Students—Advanced Learners: Write the topics only, having students generate their own questions.
- Have students write their five questions in their notebooks.
- Pair students to ask each other their questions. Have them answer their classmate's questions orally.
- Have pairs share their questions and answers with the class.

Answers
Answers will vary. Possible answers include:
1. Can you play football?
2. Can you play the guitar?
3. Can you speak Italian?
4. Can you add fractions?
5. Can you go to the movies?

Reading, pages 66–67

Before You Read

Presentation

- Have students look at the Learning Strategy box. Read the information in the box aloud as students follow along.
- Explain that *Use Selective Attention* can help them find information they need. To use the strategy, they need to look for key ideas and words as they read.
- Have students look at the Before You Read section. Read the text aloud as students follow along.

Practice

Ask students to brainstorm a list of ideas or words that could answer the question, "Why can't Maria go to the party on Saturday?" Write students' responses on the board. Read them aloud, and have students repeat them after you. (Examples: She's busy. She has homework. She has other plans.)

Read This!

Maria's Job

Preparation

Note: Students will encounter the following new words in the reading: *chef, children, job, money, practice, time, baby-sit, dance, eat, happy, little, sad, about, really, seriously, still, sadly.*

Practice

Have students listen to the story, or read it aloud to them. Provide help with content, vocabulary, etc. as needed. Remind students to *Use Selective Attention* to answer the question, "Why can't Maria go to the party?"

Reaching All Students—Emergent Learners: Work with emergent learners in small groups while the other students work independently. Read aloud as students follow along in their texts. Monitor their comprehension by interrupting the reading with questions such as, "Why is Maria sad?" (She cannot go to the party on Saturday.) "Why can't Maria go to the party?" (She has a job on Saturday.) "What does Maria do on Saturdays?" (She baby-sits three children.) Encourage students to answer the questions using complete sentences.

After You Read

Self-Evaluation

Exercise A

- Read the directions aloud as students follow along in their texts.
- Write the Before You Read question on the board. *(Why can't Maria go to the party on Saturday?)* Read it aloud as students follow along.
- Call on a volunteer to tell if he or she was able to *Use Selective Attention* to find the answer to the question. Then ask the student to read the key idea from the story that helps to answer the question. ("I have a job on Saturday.") Have the student write the answer on the board. (She has a job on Saturday.)
- Have students discuss their answers with a classmate.

Exercise B

- Read the directions aloud as students follow along in their texts.
- Call on a volunteer to explain the three possible answer choices for this true/false activity. (True, false, I don't know.)
- Explain to students that they should write *I don't know* if the information in the statement is *not* in the story. Say, "If one statement were 'Samir likes enchiladas,' you would write *I don't know* because the information is not in the reading."
- Have students number a sheet of paper in their notebooks from 1 to 5. Then have them complete the activity.

    Reaching All Students—Emergent Learners: Read the first item aloud. Have students repeat. Ask, "Is the answer *true, false,* or *I don't know?*" Call on a student to answer. (False.) Ask students to find the supporting information in the story. Call on a volunteer to read it. ("Maria cannot go to the party on Saturday.")

    Reaching All Students—Auditory Learners: Call on advanced students to read the remaining sentences. Have students write their answers in their notebooks.

- Call on students to give their answers. Ask them to explain how they figured them out. Ask students if they were able to

Use Selective Attention to help them find the answers to the questions.

- Have students count the number of correct answers and write that number in their notebooks.

Answers
(Supporting statements are in parentheses.)
1. False ("Maria cannot go to the party on Saturday.")
2. False (Carlos says, "A party is fun!")
3. True (Maria says, "I love my job.")
4. True (Samir says, "I baby-sit my little brothers and sisters.")
5. I don't know.

Expansion

Have students brainstorm ways they could *Use Selective Attention* in their other classes. Write their responses on a poster or chart. Have students refer to the chart from time to time to see how they can apply the learning strategy in their other classes.

Writing, page 68

Before You Write

Preparation *(See Transparencies 34–35.)*

Tell students that they are going to fill out a form with their personal information. Remind them that the checklists Before I Write, While I Write, and After I Write will guide them through the process of filling out and checking the form.

Exercise A

- Focus students' attention on the Personal Information Form.

    Reaching All Students—Auditory Learners: Call on an advanced student to read the form aloud while the other students follow along in their texts.

- Call on a volunteer to describe the kind of writing in the form. (Personal information: names, address, phone numbers.)
- Call on another volunteer to tell how this writing is different from writing they've done before. (The other writing consisted of paragraphs written on a particular topic.)
- Brainstorm with students the vocabulary they will need for the form. Write their responses on the board.

Exercise B

- Draw students' attention to the Before I Write checklist.
- Model following the Before I Write checklist. Use fictional information or the information printed on the form in the text. Write the information on the board.
- Have students follow the Before I Write checklist and take notes in their notebooks. Circulate to answer questions about capitalization, spelling, and abbreviations.

> **Reaching All Students—Emergent Learners:** Work with students in small groups. Guide them in following the steps in the checklist.

Write This!

Presentation

- Have students copy the printed part of the form into their notebooks.
- Draw students' attention to the While I Write checklist. Call on volunteers to read aloud the points in the checklist.

> **Reaching All Students—Visual Learners:** Copy the Personal Information Form, with the model responses omitted, on the board.

- Model following the While I Write checklist. Use information from your earlier notes on the board. As you write, do a "think aloud" about how you are following the While I Write checklist. Model making errors in capitalization, spelling, and abbreviations to correct later.

Practice

- Have students fill in the forms in their notebooks, using their notes and the While I Write checklist for help.
- Circulate while students are writing and encourage them to ask for help.

After You Write

Presentation

- Draw students' attention to the After I Write checklist. Call on volunteers to read aloud the points in the checklist.
- Model following the checklist. Correct the errors in capitalization, spelling, and abbreviations you made earlier.

Practice

Exercise A

Have students use the After I Write checklist to evaluate their writing. Have them circle and then correct their errors.

Exercise B

Have students read their forms to a classmate. Have them evaluate their classmate's suggestions for improvement. Have them make any necessary changes.

Exercise C

Have students write a final copy of the form in their notebooks.

Expansion

- Bring in samples of real forms; for example, job applications, sign-up sheets for school activities, and surveys.
- Have students fill out the forms with their own information.

> **Reaching All Students—Emergent/Advanced Learners:** Have emergent learners work in groups. Have advanced learners work independently.

- Encourage students to bring to class any forms that they need help filling out.

Learning Log, page 69

See How to Use the Learning Log on page xiii. *(See Transparencies 20 and 66.)*

Chapter 6
You were late yesterday.

Objectives

Language:

- Listen to a dialogue for comprehension.
- Understand familiar vocabulary and grammar structures by listening to a dialogue.
- Develop new vocabulary and grammar structures by listening to a dialogue.
- Act out a dialogue.
- Use *What* questions with *do*.
- Use *What* questions with object + *do*.
- Use the past tense of *be* in *yes/no* questions and affirmative and negative statements.
- Use the contractions *wasn't* and *weren't*.
- Make original conversations using new vocabulary and grammar structures.
- Ask for and give information.
- Evaluate one's own learning of new vocabulary, grammar, and oral language.

Literacy:

- Read a dialogue for comprehension.
- Understand familiar vocabulary and grammar structures by reading a dialogue.
- Develop new vocabulary and grammar structures by reading a dialogue.
- Write a mini-dialogue using new vocabulary.
- Write *What* questions with *do*.
- Write *What* questions with object + *do*.
- Decode words with final consonant blends.
- Write *yes/no* questions and affirmative and negative statements using the past tense of *be*.
- Read a fictional student's journal for comprehension.
- Understand familiar vocabulary and grammar structures by reading a fictional student's journal.
- Develop new vocabulary and grammar structures by reading a fictional student's journal.
- Plan, write, revise, edit, proofread, and make a final copy of a personal journal entry.

- Use details, describing words, and the past tense of *be* to write a journal entry.
- Evaluate one's own learning of reading skills, reading comprehension, and writing skills.

Learning Strategies:

- Use cooperation with a classmate to read a dialogue and study new vocabulary.
- Use cooperation with a small group to act out a dialogue.
- Use cooperation with a classmate to practice conversations.
- Use the strategy *Sound Out* to decode words.
- Use the strategy *Make Predictions* to understand a fictional student's journal.
- Use cooperation with a classmate to check a paragraph in one's personal journal.
- Evaluate one's own learning of the strategies *Make Predictions* and *Sound Out*.
- Identify easy and difficult material in a chapter and the different ways to learn the difficult material.

Opening Dialogue, pages 70–71

Getting Ready

Preparation *(See Transparency 17.)*

- Have students look at the illustrations and identify the objects and characters they know. Write the words on the board or a poster. Read the words, one at a time, and have students repeat each one after you.
- Ask students, "How does Mr. Gomez look?" (Angry.) "How does Carmen look?" (Sorry, upset, worried.) Write students' responses on the board or poster. Have students repeat each one after you.
- Point out to students that there is a character in the illustrations they have not seen before. Explain that they can *Use Selective Attention* as they read to find out who the new character is.

Listening and Reading

Late Again

Presentation

Exercise A

- Read the directions and the prelistening question aloud as students follow along in their texts.
- Have students listen to the dialogue, or read the dialogue aloud to them. Have students look at the appropriate illustrations as they listen.
- Explain any vocabulary words that students do not understand.
- Ask the prelistening question, "What time does class start?" Call on a volunteer to respond. (It starts at ten o'clock.)

Exercise B

Have students read the dialogue. Provide help with content, vocabulary, etc. as needed.

Reaching All Students—Emergent Learners: Work with emergent learners in small groups while the other students work independently. Read aloud as students follow along in their texts. Monitor their comprehension by interrupting the reading with questions such as, "Who is late for class?" (Carmen is late for class.) "What time does class start?" (Class starts at ten o'clock.) "What time is it now?" (It's ten minutes after ten o'clock.) "Why is Carmen late?" (She was with a new student.) "What is the new student's name?" (Her name is Sophie.) "What languages does Sophie speak?" (She speaks English, Haitian Creole, and French.)

Pair and Group Work

Practice

Exercise A

Have students who can read on their own form pairs. Have one student in the pair take the roles of Mr. Gomez and Sophie; have the other student take the roles of Carmen and Carlos. Then have them read the dialogue aloud. Provide help as needed.

Reaching All Students—Emergent Learners: Work in small groups with emergent readers. Model each sentence and have individual students "echo" your

reading. Make sure that students look at the sentences as you read them.

Exercise B

Have students form groups of four. Group students heterogeneously so that each group is made up of average readers, weak readers, and strong readers. Have each student choose a role in the dialogue. Have students practice acting out the dialogue in their groups.

Reaching All Students—Kinesthetic Learners: Choose one or more groups to act out the dialogue in front of the class.

Vocabulary

Presentation

- Read the vocabulary words and expressions aloud and have students repeat them.
- Check students' understanding of the words and expressions.

Practice

Exercise A

Have students read and say the words and expressions. Provide assistance with pronunciation as needed.

Exercise B *(See Transparencies 85–86.)*

- Have students turn to page 250 in their texts.
- Have students work through Step 1 (recognizing letters) with the words in the box on page 71, if further practice is needed.
- Have students work in pairs, saying how many syllables are in each word. Answer students' questions as needed.

Exercise C

Have students find the words and expressions in the dialogue. Then have them read the sentences.

Reaching All Students—Auditory Learners: Encourage students to say the words and expressions as they write them in their notebooks.

Exercise D

- Have each student choose five words from the words in the word box. Then have them write a mini-dialogue in their notebooks, using those words.

- Have students practice their dialogue with a classmate.

Grammar 1, page 72

What Questions with *do*

Preparation

- Write the following dialogue on the board as a way of presenting the grammar focus in context.
  Maria: *What do you need?*
    Bic: I *need* a piece of paper.
- Read the dialogue aloud as students follow along.
- Call on two advanced students to dramatize the dialogue for the rest of the class.

Presentation

- Have students look at the grammar chart in their texts.
- Explain that the left section of the chart shows *What* questions with *do*.
- Read aloud each *What* question with *do*. Have students repeat each question after you.
- Have students work in pairs or small groups to develop a rule that explains how to make *What* questions with *do*. Call on volunteers to give their rules. Then write the rule on the board. (Example: *What* + *do* + subject + verb in the base form. The verb *do* should match its subject. The second verb should be in the base form.)
- Have students look at the right part of the chart.
- Explain that the right part gives the long answers to the *What* questions with *do* in the left part of the chart.
- Read aloud each answer. Have students repeat each answer after you.
- Have students note that the verb form for *he* and *she* ends in a final -*s (needs)*.
- Have students work in pairs. Have the first student read a question from the left section of the chart. Then have the second student read the corresponding answer from the right section. Have them continue until they have asked and answered all the questions.

Practice
Exercise A

- Have students number a sheet of paper in their notebooks from 1 to 5.

- Read aloud the sample question and response with the sample answers. Have students repeat after you.
- Call on a volunteer to explain why the sample answers are correct. (The verb *do* matches the subject *Carlos and Pablo*; the verb *like* matches the subject *they*.) Refer students to the grammar chart for reference.
- Have students complete the activity by filling in the blanks with the correct form of *do* and the correct form of the main verbs.

  Reaching All Students—Emergent Learners: First, have students do the exercise orally. Then have them write the answers in their notebooks. Provide help as needed.

  Reaching All Students—Auditory Learners: Call on advanced students to read each of the remaining questions and responses (without the answers) before students write their answers.

  Reaching All Students—Cooperative Learners: Have students work in pairs to complete the activity.

- Review the answers with the class.

Answers		
1. do, like	**3.** does, likes	**5.** do, have
2. do, need	**4.** do, want	

Exercise B

- Tell students that they will need to write the question that goes with each sentence listed in the activity.
- Have students number a sheet of paper in their notebooks from 1 to 5.
- Read the first sentence aloud. Have students repeat after you.
- Call on a volunteer to read the question and explain why it is correct. (The main verb is the same one as in the answer *(have)*. The verb *does* matches the subject *he*.) Refer students to the grammar chart for reference.
- Have students complete the activity by writing the question for each sentence listed.

  Reaching All Students—Auditory Learners: Call on advanced students to read each of the remaining sentences before students write their questions.

  Reaching All Students—Emergent Learners: First, have students do the exercise orally. Then have them write the questions in their notebooks. Provide help as needed.

Reaching All Students—Cooperative Learners: Have students work in pairs to complete the activity.

- Review the questions with the class.

Answers
1. What does he have?
2. What do the students need?
3. What does Mr. Gomez need?
4. What do you have?
5. What do you need?

Grammar 2, page 73

What + Noun

Preparation

- Write the following dialogue on the board as a way of presenting the grammar focus in context.
  Carmen: *What class do* you have next?
  Sophie: I *have* P.E.
- Read the dialogue aloud as students follow along.
- Call on two advanced students to dramatize the dialogue for the rest of the class.

Presentation

- Have students look at the grammar chart. Point out that the left part shows how to make *What* + noun questions. The right part shows the answers to the questions in the left part.
- Have students read silently across each row of the left part of the chart, forming the questions with the correct words in the columns.

  Reaching All Students—Cooperative Learners: Have pairs of students take turns reading the questions from the chart.

- Call on volunteers and have them read the questions from the chart.
- Have students work in pairs or small groups to develop a rule that tells how to make *What* + noun questions. Call on students to give their rule. Then write the rule on the board. (Use *What* + noun + *do* + subject + the base form of the verb. The form of *do* must match its subject.)

- Call on a volunteer to read across the first row of both parts of the chart, forming both the question and the answer. (Example: *What language do I speak? / I speak French.*)
- Continue the process by calling on other volunteers to read across the rows of both parts of the chart.

  Reaching All Students—Cooperative Learners: Have pairs of students take turns reading across the rows of both parts of the chart.

Practice

Exercise A

- Have students number a sheet of paper in their notebooks from 1 to 5.
- Explain to students that they are going to match a phrase in the left-hand column with a phrase in the right-hand column to make a *What* question with *do*.
- Call on a volunteer to read the example. *(What color do you like?)* Ask the student to identify the phrase from the left-hand column *(What color)* and the phrase from the right-hand column *(do you like?)*.
- Have students complete the activity by matching the phrases and writing the questions in their notebooks.

  Reaching All Students—Emergent Learners: First, have students do the exercise orally. Then have them write the answers in their notebooks. Provide help as needed.

- Call on volunteers to read their questions aloud. Encourage the other students to check their sentences and make any needed corrections in their notebooks.

  Reaching All Students—Visual Learners: Have the volunteers write their sentences on the board in addition to reading them aloud.

Answers
1. What color do you like?
2. What time do you eat lunch?
3. What languages do they speak?
4. What class does she have after math?
5. What books do I have in my backpack?

Preparation

Exercise B

Call on a volunteer to tell what is happening in the photo. (Students are eating lunch in the cafeteria.)

Presentation

 Have students listen to the conversation, or read it aloud with an advanced student.

Practice

Exercise C

- Have students work in pairs to practice the conversation in Exercise B.

- Have students make new conversations, using their own information about what time they participate in other activities. First, guide the class in brainstorming other activities they could include in their conversations; for example, having soccer practice, working after school, doing homework, and going to bed. Write students' responses on the board. Next, ask them to tell what time they participate in these activities. Write the times on the board. Then say the activities and the times. Have students repeat them after you. Last, have students work in pairs to make new conversations using the new information. Encourage them to try several different conversations.

- Refer students to page 227 of the Vocabulary Handbook for other daily activities.

    Reaching All Students—Emergent Learners: Work with students in small groups to complete this activity.

    <u>Optional Activity:</u> Call on volunteer pairs to dramatize their conversations for the rest of the class.

Expansion

- Have students work in pairs.

- Have one student in each pair write a note asking his or her classmate a *What* question with object + *do*. Have the classmate write a reply. Then have them reverse roles.

- Write a model of a question and reply on the board. (See the models provided in the sample answers that follow.)

    Reaching All Students—Emergent Learners: Work with students in small groups to complete this activity.

- Call on pairs to share their questions and replies with the class. Have them write them on the board.

> **Answers**
> *Answers will vary. Sample answers:*
> What instrument do you play in the band?
> I play the trumpet.
> What activity do you have after school today?
> I have dance class.

Word Study, page 74

Consonant Blends

Preparation

- Write the word *bulb* on the board. Say, "bulb."
- Call on volunteers to identify the names of the consonants and vowel in the word.
- Pronounce the word and have students repeat it after you.

Presentation

- Point to the word *bulb* on the board again. Call on a volunteer to identify the first sound (/b/), the second sound (/u/), the third sound (/l/), and the fourth sound (/b/). Have students say all the sounds and blend them together to form the word.

- Underline the consonants *lb* in *bulb* and have students pronounce the sounds. Ask, "Do you hear the (/l/) sound?" (Yes.) Ask, "Do you hear the (/b/) sound?" (Yes.) Ask, "Do both sounds blend together?" (Yes.)

- Refer students to the instruction box in their texts. Read the sentences aloud as students follow along. Have the class repeat the three example words.

Practice

Exercise A

Have students use the learning strategy *Sound Out*, as well as the pictures, to read the words with final consonant blends.

Reaching All Students—Emergent Learners: Complete this activity as a class. After students have an approximation of the pronunciation, say the words correctly to provide a model.

Exercise B

- First, have students read the sentences aloud. Then have them copy the sentences into their notebooks. Last, have them circle the consonant blends that come at the end of a word.

- Review the answers as a class. Note that the contraction *don't* in item 2 has a consonant blend also.

Answers

1. Where is my red be(lt)?
2. I don't have a gi(ft) for Carlos.
3. Do you like this la(mp)?
4. That is a pretty pla(nt)!
5. Do you have my ma(sk)?
6. My mother can't find a sta(mp).

Optional Activity: Have students close their texts. Ask them to number a page in their notebooks from 1 to 8. Then ask them to listen carefully to the words you read and to write the words. Then dictate the following words:

1. tent   5. mask
2. lamp   6. plant
3. hand   7. stamp
4. gift   8. belt

- After the dictation, write the words on the board. Then have students check their words.

- Have students record the number of correct words in their notebooks; for example, *I wrote (7) out of 8 dictated words ending with consonant blends correctly.* Write this example on the board as a model.

Expansion

Exercise C

- Have students look at Exercise A. Have them choose three words with consonant blends that come at the end of a word. Have them write a sentence for each word in their notebooks.

    Reaching All Students—Emergent Learners: Review the meanings of the words in Exercise A. Model a sample sentence on the board. Then have students write the sentences in their notebooks. Provide help as needed.

- Have students share their sentences with the class.

Answers
Answers will vary.

Optional Activity: Have students copy the letters that stand for the consonant blends from Exercise A into their notebooks (*ft, sk, lt, nd, mp, nt*). Have students write as many words as they can that end with the blends. (Set a time limit of 5–10 minutes.) Encourage students to use a dictionary, the text, or their vocabulary lists for help.

Reaching All Students—Auditory Learners: Encourage students to say the words aloud as they write them.

Have students share their lists with the class.

Answers
Answers will vary.

Grammar 3, page 75

Past Tense of *be*: Statements

Preparation

- Write the following dialogue on the board as a way of presenting the grammar focus in context.

    Carlos: Mr. Gomez *was* pretty angry with you.

    Carmen: I know, but I *was* with a new student. She *was* lost.

    Carlos: I know, Carmen, but you *were* late yesterday, too.

- Read the dialogue aloud as students follow along.

- Call on two advanced students to dramatize the dialogue for the rest of the class.

Presentation

- Have students look at the grammar chart in their texts.

- Explain that the left part of the chart shows affirmative statements with the past tense of *be*. The right part shows negative statements with the past tense of *be*.

- Have students first study the Affirmative Statements part of the chart. Have them read silently across each row of the part, using the word or words in each column to make a statement.

- Have students follow the same procedure for the right part of the chart to make negative statements.

    Reaching All Students—Cooperative Learners: Have pairs of students take turns reading sentences from the chart.

Have the first student make an affirmative statement from the left part of the chart, then have the second student make a negative statement from the right part of the chart. Have them repeat this procedure for the remaining rows.

- Call on volunteers to read an affirmative or negative statement from the chart.
- Refer students to the contractions box. Explain that *wasn't* is the contraction of *was not* and *weren't* is the contraction of *were not*. Say, "I wasn't late yesterday." Have students repeat. Say, "We weren't late yesterday." Have students repeat.

Practice

Exercise A

- Tell students that in this exercise they will change statements from the affirmative to the negative. Also point out that they will use contractions *(wasn't and weren't)* in the exercise.
- Read the first affirmative statement aloud. Have students repeat.
- Ask, "How do you change that to a negative statement?" (Change *was* to *wasn't*.) Call on a student to read the sample answer. Read the sample answer again and have students repeat.
- Have students change the statements from the affirmative to the negative and write the negative statements in their notebooks. Remind them to use *wasn't* or *weren't* in their answers.

    Reaching All Students—Cooperative Learners: Have students work in pairs to complete the exercise.
- Call on students to write their answers on the board.

Answers
1. Carmen wasn't late to class.
2. We weren't with a new student.
3. Liliana and Mei weren't in school yesterday.

Exercise B

- Tell students that in this exercise they will change statements from the negative to the affirmative.
- Read the first sentence aloud. Have students repeat.

- Ask, "How do you change that to an affirmative statement?" (Change *wasn't* to *was*.) Call on a student to read the sample answer.
- Have students change the statements from the negative to the affirmative and write the affirmative statements in their notebooks.

    Reaching All Students—Cooperative Learners: Have students work in pairs to complete the exercise.
- Call on students to write their answers on the board.

Answers
1. Pablo was sick yesterday.
2. Maria was in English class.
3. Carlos and Bic were at lunch.

Past Tense of *be*: Yes/No Questions

Presentation

- Have students look at the grammar chart. Explain that the left part of the chart shows *yes/no* questions with the past tense of *be*. Read the first row aloud as students follow along in their texts. Explain that the middle part shows affirmative answers. Read the first row aloud. Explain that the right part shows negative answers. Read the first row aloud.
- Have students read silently across each row of the chart, using the word or words in each column to make a question, then an affirmative short answer, then a negative short answer.

    Reaching All Students—Auditory/ Cooperative Learners: Have students work in groups of three. Have the first student make a question, the second make an affirmative answer, and the third make a negative answer. Have them repeat this procedure for the remaining rows.
- Call on volunteers to read questions and affirmative and negative answers from the chart.

Practice

Exercise

- Tell students that they will write five *yes/no* questions with the past tense of *be*. Explain that they will then ask the questions to a classmate. Call on a student to read the example question and answer aloud. Have students write the example in their notebooks.

- As a class, have students brainstorm other topics they can ask questions about. Write the topics on the board. (Examples: in the cafeteria, in science class, in the library, with [Joan], excited, nervous, angry.) Provide additional words as needed.

  Reaching All Students—Advanced Learners: Call on several advanced students to give examples of questions.

  Reaching All Students—Emergent Learners: After students select a topic, ask them to generate the question. For example, "in the library—Were you in the library yesterday?" Then write the questions on the board.

- Have students write their five *yes/no* questions in their notebooks.

- Pair students. Have them take turns asking and answering their questions.

- Call on pairs to share their questions and answers with the class.

Answers
Answers will vary.

Reading, pages 76–77

Before You Read

Preparation *(See Transparency 22.)*

- Tell students they will use the learning strategy *Make Predictions* to understand the story.
- Have students look at the Before You Read section. Call on volunteers, one at a time, to read the strategy steps.

Practice

Have students work in pairs to follow the strategy steps. Call on students to share their predictions with the class. Write the students' predictions on the board.

Read This!

My Journal

Preparation

Note: Students will encounter the following new words in the reading: *tomorrow, birthday, test, watch, angry, bad, early, easy, hard, on time, minutes.*

Practice

- 🎧 Have students listen to the story, or read it aloud to them. Remind students to check their predictions as they read the journal.

- Have students read the journal silently on their own. Provide help with content, vocabulary, etc. as needed. Ask students individually if the reading fits their predictions.

  Reaching All Students—Emergent Learners: Work with emergent learners in small groups while the other students work independently. Read aloud as students follow along in their texts. Monitor their comprehension by interrupting the reading with questions such as, "Was Mr. Gomez angry on Monday?" (No, he wasn't.) "When is the math test?" (It's Tuesday / tomorrow.) "Is Carmen nervous about the math test?" (No, she's not.) "Was Carmen late for math class on Tuesday?" (No, she wasn't.) "Was the math test hard?" (No, it wasn't.) "Was Mr. Gomez angry on Tuesday?" (Yes, he was.) "When is the English test?" (It's tomorrow / Wednesday.) "Is Carmen nervous?" (Yes, she is.) "Was Carmen on time for math and English on Wednesday?" (No, she wasn't.) "What does Carmen want for her birthday?" (She wants a watch.) Encourage students to answer the questions using complete sentences.

After You Read

Self-Evaluation
Exercise A

  Reaching All Students—Visual Learners: Write the four questions from Exercise A on the board.

- Read the questions aloud. Have students repeat. Call on volunteers to give their responses.

- Have students discuss their answers with a classmate.

Exercise B

- Tell students that for this exercise they will choose the answer that correctly completes each sentence.

- Have students number a sheet of paper in their notebooks from 1 to 4.

- Read item 1 aloud. Have students repeat. Ask, "Is the answer a. *hard,* b. *easy,* or c. *silly?*" Call on a student to answer. (b. *easy.*) Ask the student to find the supportive statement from the journal.

  > **Reaching All Students—Auditory Learners:** Call on advanced students to read each of the remaining sentences before students write their answers.

- Have students write the letter and word of the correct answer for items 1–4 in their notebooks.

- Call on students to give their answers. Write them on the board. Be sure they also give the supporting statements from the journal.

- Have students count the number of correct answers and write that number in their notebooks.

Answers

1. b. easy	**3.** b. late
2. c. English	**4.** a. angry

Expansion

Ask students how the strategy *Make Predictions* helped them understand the paragraphs in Carmen's journal.

Writing, page 78

Before You Write

Preparation

Exercise A *(See Transparencies 36–37.)*

- Tell students that they are going to write a paragraph in their journal about their day. Remind them that the Before I Write, While I Write, and After I Write checklists provide *strategies* to guide them through the process of writing their paragraphs.

- Focus students' attention on the handwritten journal entry.

  > **Reaching All Students—Auditory Learners:** Call on an advanced student to read the journal entry aloud as the other students follow along in their texts.

- Ask students what kind of writing this is. (A paragraph in a journal about one's day.) Ask them what kinds of information the student included in the sample journal (What kind of day it was, what happened, what happened to other people, how the student and other people felt.) Write students' responses on the board.

- Brainstorm with students the vocabulary they could include in their own journal entries. Write students' responses on the board. Provide additional words as needed.

Presentation

Exercise B

- Tell students that they are going to write their own journal entry. If needed, remind them that the Before I Write, While I Write, and After I Write checklists provide strategies that will guide them through the writing process.

- Draw students' attention to the Before I Write checklist.

- Model following the steps in the Before I Write checklist to plan your own sample paragraph.

- Have students follow the Before I Write checklist and take notes in their notebooks.

  > **Reaching All Students—Emergent Learners:** Work with students in small groups. Guide them in following the steps in the checklist.

Write This!

Presentation

- Draw students' attention to the While I Write checklist.

- Model following the While I Write checklist. Refer to the notes you took in your earlier modeling. As you write, do a "think aloud" about how you are following the While I Write checklist.

Practice

- Have students write their journal entries in their notebooks, using their notes and the While I Write checklist for help. If needed, they can also refer back to the grammar charts in the chapter.

- Circulate while students are writing and encourage them to ask you for help with new words.

After You Write

Presentation

- Draw students' attention to the After I Write checklist.
- Model following the steps in the After I Write checklist, checking your own paragraph.

Practice

Exercise A

Have students use the After I Write checklist to evaluate their writing. Have them circle and then correct their errors.

Exercise B

Have students read their paragraph to a classmate. Encourage them to make suggestions for improvement.

Exercise C

Have students write a final copy of their paragraph in their notebooks.

Expansion

Encourage students to keep a journal for the next two weeks, using the format introduced here.

Learning Log, page 79

See How to Use the Learning Log on page xiii. *(See Transparencies 20 and 67.)*

UNIT 3 AT HOME

Unit Opener, pages 80–81

Preview

- Call on a student to read the unit title, "At Home." Tell students that this unit is about kids who are having a party in their home. Ask students if they like to have parties and/or go to parties.

- Have students look at the photos and identify the people and the settings. (A family eating dinner together at home, a girl talking on the phone, a boy reading in his bedroom.) Write the descriptions of the people and the settings on the board as the students say them.

- Help students identify the different items in the photos. Write the names of the items on the board as students say them.

- Point to the people in the photos, one at a time, and ask, "What is (<u>he</u>) doing?" Elicit responses and write them on the board.
  Optional Activity: Call on pairs of advanced students, one pair at a time, to ask and answer questions about what the people in the photos are doing.

- Read the unit goals aloud as students follow along in their texts. Answer any questions they may have.

Chapter 7
What are you doing?

Objectives

Language:

- Listen to a dialogue for comprehension.
- Understand familiar vocabulary and grammar structures by listening to a dialogue.
- Develop new vocabulary and grammar structures by listening to a dialogue.
- Act out a dialogue.
- Use the present continuous tense in affirmative and negative statements, *What* questions, and *yes/no* questions.
- Use contractions with the present continuous tense.
- Use object pronouns in statements and *yes/no* questions.
- Make original conversations using new vocabulary and grammar structures.
- Ask for and give information.
- Evaluate one's own learning of new vocabulary, grammar, and oral language.

Literacy:

- Read a dialogue for comprehension.
- Understand familiar vocabulary and grammar structures by reading a dialogue.
- Develop new vocabulary and grammar structures by reading a dialogue.
- Write a dialogue using new vocabulary.
- Complete and write affirmative and negative statements, *What* questions, and *yes/no* questions in the present continuous tense.
- Write sentences using contractions with the present continuous tense.
- Decode words with the long vowel sounds /ā/, /ī/, /ō/, and /yōō/.
- Complete and write statements and *yes/no* questions using object pronouns.
- Read a short story for comprehension.
- Understand familiar vocabulary and grammar structures by reading a short story.
- Develop new vocabulary and grammar structures by reading a short story.

- Plan, write, revise, edit, proofread, and make a final copy of a dialogue.
- Use names, pronouns, and the present continuous tense to write a dialogue.
- Evaluate one's own learning of reading skills, reading comprehension, and writing skills.

Learning Strategies:

- Use cooperation with a classmate to read a dialogue and study new vocabulary.
- Use cooperation with a small group to act out a dialogue.
- Use cooperation with a classmate to practice conversations.
- Use the strategy *Grouping* to learn new vocabulary.
- Use the strategy *Sound Out* to decode words.
- Use the strategy *Make Predictions* to understand a short story.
- Use cooperation with a classmate to check a dialogue one has written.
- Evaluate one's own learning of the strategies *Grouping, Make Predictions,* and *Sound Out.*
- Identify easy and difficult material in a chapter and the different ways to learn the difficult material.

Opening Dialogue, pages 82–83

Getting Ready

Preparation *(See Transparency 17.)*

- Have students look at the illustrations and identify any words they know for the objects or actions in the illustrations. Write the words on the board or a poster. Read the words, one at a time, and have students repeat each one after you.
- Point to objects and actions in the illustrations that student didn't mention and ask, "What's this?" or "What's he doing?" Write the responses on the board or a poster. Read the responses and have students repeat them after you.

Listening and Reading

Help for Carlos

Presentation

Exercise A

- Read the directions and the prelistening question aloud as students follow along in their texts.
- Have students listen to the dialogue, or read the dialogue aloud to them. Have students look at the appropriate illustrations as they listen.
- Explain any vocabulary words that students do not understand.
- Ask the prelistening question, "Who is Carolina?" Call on a volunteer to respond. (She's Carlos and Carmen's sister.)

Exercise B

Have students read the dialogue. Provide help with content, vocabulary, etc. as needed.

Reaching All Students—Emergent Learners: Work with emergent learners in small groups while the other students work independently. Read aloud as students follow along in their texts. Monitor their comprehension by interrupting the reading with questions such as, "What is Carlos asking for?" (He's asking for help.) "Who is he asking for help?" (He's asking his sisters and brother—Carmen, David, Carolina.). "What is Carolina doing?" (She's washing her hair.) "Who comes to help Carlos?" (Grandma does.)

Pair and Group Work

Practice

Exercise A

Have students who can read on their own form pairs. Have one student in the pair take the role of Carlos; have the other student take all the other roles (Carmen, David, Mother, and Grandma). Then have them read the dialogue aloud. Provide help as needed.

Reaching All Students—Emergent Learners: Work in small groups with emergent readers. Model each sentence and have individual students "echo" your reading. Make sure that students look at the sentences as you read them.

Exercise B

Have students form groups of five. Group students heterogeneously so that each group is made up of average readers, weak readers, and strong readers. Have each student choose a role in the dialogue. Have students practice acting out the dialogue in their groups.

Reaching All Students—Kinesthetic Learners: Choose one or more groups to act out the dialogue in front of the class.

Vocabulary

Presentation

- Read the vocabulary words aloud and have students repeat them.
- Check students' understanding of the words.

Practice

Exercise A

Have students read and say the words and expressions. Provide assistance with pronunciation as needed.

Exercise B *(See Transparencies 85–86.)*

- Have students turn to page 250 in their texts.
- Have students work through Steps 1–2 (recognizing letters and finding syllables) with the words in the box on page 83 if further practice is needed.
- Call on a volunteer to read Step 3 aloud as the other students follow along in their texts.
- Model the exercise by pointing out words in the word box on page 83 whose letters or letter combinations follow the patterns described in Step 3 (silent letters or double letters), or make unexpected sounds. For example, point out how the letters "igh" in "light" make the long vowel sound /i/, as in "I" and "nice". Also point out how the letters "oo" sound different in the words "bedroom" and "cook". (Note: Some letters or letter combinations that students encounter in the word box will be taught in later Word Study lessons. It isn't necessary to explain these new sounds in too much detail at this point in the lesson. Just give students the opportunity to observe the different patterns, and to make notes about them. The more reading opportunities they have, the more they will be able to recognize and un-

derstand the various patterns they encounter.)

- Have students work in pairs, identifying other letters or letter combinations that follow patterns or make unexpected sounds. Encourage students to ask questions and to discover as much as they can on their own.

Exercise C

Have students find the words and expressions in the dialogue. Then have them read the sentences.

Presentation
Exercise D

- Have students write the following categories in their notebooks as you write them on the board: *Verbs, Family Names, Rooms in a House, Things in a House, Other Words.*
- Have students look at the dialogue and find one word for the *Verb* category. Call on a volunteer to read the verb he or she found. Have students write that verb under the category *Verb* in their notebooks.

Practice

- Have students work in pairs to complete each category in their notebooks.
- Call on five volunteers and assign each one a category. Have the students write the words for their category on the board.
- As you check each category on the board, have students write any words they missed in their notebooks.
- For each category, ask students if they found other words not written on the board. Write correct responses on the board.

Answers
Possible answers include:

Verbs		Family Names
help	changing	sister
making	calm down	mother
cleaning	cooking	mama
come/coming	burning	grandmother
washing	turn off	grandma

Rooms in a House	Other Words
bedroom	busy
kitchen	hair
	I mean
Things in a House	right now
bed	Oh dear!
windows	enchiladas
lightbulb	
stove	

Grammar 1, page 84

Present Continuous Tense: Statements

Preparation

- Write the following dialogue on the board as a way of presenting the grammar focus in context.

    Liliana: Hi, Carmen! What *are* you *doing* right now?

    Carmen: I'*m cleaning* the house. We'*re getting ready* for the party!

- Read the dialogue aloud as students follow along.
- Call on two advanced students to dramatize the dialogue for the rest of the class.

Presentation

- Have students look at the grammar chart in their texts.
- Tell them that this chart shows how to talk about what people are doing right now. Explain any new words.
- Call on individual students to read aloud across each row in the chart, omitting the *not*.
- As a class, have students develop a rule for how to form a sentence in the present continuous. Write their response on the board. (Example: Subject + *(be)* + verb + *ing* + object. The verb *be* matches the subject. The second verb has -*ing* at the end.)
- Call on individual students to read aloud across each row in the chart, including the *not*.
- Refer students to the verb box. Tell students that the verb box includes verbs in the base form and then in the present continuous form. Read the verbs and have students follow along in their texts.
- Refer students to the contractions box. Remind students that *isn't* is the contraction of *is not*, and *aren't* is the contraction of *are not*. Say, "She isn't making the bed." Have students repeat. Say, "They aren't making the bed." Have students repeat. Remind students that *is not* and *are not* are formal (for many school writing assignments); *isn't* and *aren't* are casual (for everyday speaking situations).

Practice

Exercise A

- Have students copy the sentences into their notebooks.
- Call on a volunteer to read the first sentence with the sample answer. Ask the student to explain why the answer is correct. (The verb form *is eating* matches the subject *She*.)
- Have students complete the remaining sentences by writing the correct form of the verb in each sentence. Encourage students to use the sentences in the chart as models. Provide help as needed.

  Reaching All Students—Emergent Learners: First, have students do the exercise orally. Then have them copy the sentences into their notebooks. Have them complete the sentences. Provide help as needed.

- Review the answers with the class.

Answers

1. is eating	4. are cleaning
2. are writing	5. am making
3. is washing	6. are getting

Exercise B

- Have students look at item 1 in Exercise A. Ask how they would rewrite it, using *isn't* or *aren't*. Call on a student to write the answer on the board. (*She isn't eating lunch.*) Ask the student to explain why *isn't* is correct. (The verb form *isn't* matches the subject *She*.)
- In their notebooks, have students rewrite the remaining five sentences from Exercise A, using *isn't* or *aren't*.
- Review the answers with the class.

Answers

1. She isn't eating lunch.
2. We aren't writing in our notebooks.
3. He isn't washing his hair.
4. They aren't cleaning the classroom.
5. She isn't making the bed.
6. They aren't getting ready for school.

Grammar 2, page 85

Present Continuous Tense: *What* Questions

Preparation

- Write the following dialogue on the board as a way of presenting the grammar focus in context.

  Carlos: *What are* you *doing?*
  Carmen: I'm *washing* dishes. And guess what? You're *drying* them.

- Read the dialogue aloud as students follow along.
- Call on two advanced students to dramatize the dialogue for the rest of the class.

Presentation

- Have students look at the grammar chart.
- Explain that the left part of the chart shows how to ask questions about what people are doing right now.
- Explain that the right part of the chart shows how to tell what people are doing right now.
- Call on individual volunteers to read aloud across each row—first in the left part of the chart, then in the right part.
- As a class, have students develop a rule for how to form a *What* question in the present continuous. Write their response on the board. (Example: *What* + *(be)* + subject + verb + *ing*. The verb *be* matches the subject. The second verb has *-ing* at the end.)
- Have students look at the contractions box.
- Point out that *What's* is the contraction of *What is*. Explain that the contraction and the long form mean the same thing.
- Write the following example sentences on the board: *What's he cleaning? What is he cleaning?* Read them aloud as students follow along. Then have students read them aloud.

Practice

Exercise

- Tell students that this exercise has the answers, but not the questions. Explain that they will write the question that goes with each answer.
- Have students number a sheet of paper in their notebooks from 1 to 5.

- Read the first statement aloud. Have students repeat.
- Call on a volunteer to read the question (response) and to explain how it was formed. (*What* + (*be*) + subject [*Liliana*] + verb + *ing*.)
- Have students write the questions in their notebooks to correspond with the answers in the exercise.

> **Reaching All Students—Auditory Learners:** Call on advanced students to read each of the remaining sentences before students write their questions.

> **Reaching All Students—Emergent Learners:** First, have students do the exercise orally. Then have them write the answers in their notebooks. Provide help as needed.

> **Reaching All Students—Cooperative Learners:** Have students work in pairs to complete the activity.

- Review the answers with the class.

Answers
1. What's Liliana reading?
2. What's David cleaning?
3. What are Mom and Dad making?
4. What are you eating?
5. What are you studying?

Present Continuous Tense: *Yes/No* Questions

Preparation

Exercise A

Have students look at the illustration. Point to the girl and ask students, "What is she doing?" (She's making cookies.) Write the question and answer on the board. Have students repeat. Point to the boy and ask, "Is he studying?" (No, he's not. He's talking on the phone.) Write the question and answer on the board. Have students repeat.

Presentation

- Have students look at the grammar chart.
- Tell students that the left part of the chart shows how to ask *yes/no* questions about what people are doing right now. Point out that the middle and right part of the chart show how to give affirmative and negative short answers. Model forming two questions with affirmative and negative answers.

(Are you studying? Yes, I am./No, I'm not. Is she studying? Yes, she is./No, she's not.)

- Have students first study the left part of the chart. Ask them to read silently across the left part, using a word in each column to make a question.
- Have students follow the same procedure for the middle and right parts of the chart to make affirmative and negative answers.

> **Reaching All Students—Cooperative Learners:** Have students work in pairs. Have the first student make a question, reading across the left part of the chart. Then have the second student make an affirmative and a negative answer, reading across the middle and right parts. Have them repeat for the remaining rows.

- Call on an individual student to read aloud one of the questions in the left part of the chart. Call on a second student to provide an affirmative answer and a third student to provide a negative answer from the middle and right parts. Repeat this for two or three questions.
- As a class, have students develop a rule for how to form a *yes/no* question in the present continuous. Write their response on the board. (Example: *yes/no* question = (*be*) + subject + verb + *ing*? The verb *be* matches the subject. The second verb has *-ing* at the end. Response = *Yes*, + subject + (*be*); or *No*, + subject + (*be*) + *not*. The verb *be* matches the subject.)
- 🎧 Have students listen to the conversation, or read it aloud with an advanced student.

Practice

Exercise B

- Have students work in pairs to practice the conversation in Exercise A.
- Tell students they can make new conversations, using their own information. Guide the class in brainstorming other activities they could include in their conversations. (Examples: practicing the piano, working, eating lunch, going to sleep). Write students' responses on the board. Have students repeat. Then have students work in pairs to practice creating original conversations. Encourage them to try several different

conversations, using ideas the class generated or their own ideas.

- Refer students to page 222 of the Vocabulary Handbook for other activities. Remind them to put the activities in the present continuous tense. Work through a couple of examples with verbs from the Vocabulary Handbook.

  Reaching All Students—Emergent Learners: Work with students in small groups to complete the activity.

  Reaching All Students—Auditory/ Advanced Learners: Have advanced students dramatize their conversations for the rest of the class.

Word Study, page 86

Long Vowel Sounds: /ā/, /ī/, /ō/, /yōō/

Preparation

- Write the words *came, like, close,* and *use* on the board.
- Call on volunteers to identify the names of the consonants and vowels in the words.
- Pronounce the words and have students repeat them after you.

Presentation

- Underline the vowel *a* in *came* and ask students to pronounce the sound (/ā/). Repeat for the vowel sounds in the words *like, close,* and *use*.
- Point to the word *came* on the board again. Call on a volunteer to identify the first sound (/c/), the second sound (/ā/), and the third sound (/m/).
- Ask students, "How many sounds does the word have?" (Three.) "How many letters does the word have?" (Four.)
- To help students understand why the word has four letters but only three sounds, underline the vowel *e* in the word. Point out that the *e* does not represent a sound in the word *came*. Instead, it acts as a marker or signal that the vowel before it probably stands for a long vowel sound—in this case, the sound /ā/. Write on the board *a_e*. Repeat the example with the words *like, close,* and *use*.
- Refer students to the instruction box in their texts. Tell them that the sounds /ā/, /ī/, /ō/, and /yōō/ are called long vowel sounds. Ex-

plain that vowels can represent either a long sound or a short sound. The long sound sounds the same as the name of the letter: /ā/, /ī/, /ō/, /yōō/. The short sound is different: /a/ as in *cat,* /e/ as in *bet,* /i/ as in *sit,* /o/ as in *hot,* /u/ as in *cut.*

- Call on students to read the sentences in the instruction box. Have the class repeat the example word in each sentence.

Practice
Exercise A

Have students work in pairs to use the learning strategy *Sound Out,* as well as the pictures, to read the words with long vowel sounds /ā/, /ī/, /ō/, and /yōō/.

  Reaching All Students—Emergent Learners: Complete this activity as a class if students need help. After students have an approximation of the pronunciation, say the words correctly to provide a model.

Exercise B

- First, have students read the sentences aloud. Then have them copy the sentences into their notebooks. Last, have them circle the spellings for the long vowel sounds /ā/, /ī/, /ō/, and /yōō/.
- Review the answers as a class.

Answers
1. That dress is very c(u)t(e)!
2. Does Anna have f(i)v(e) dollars?
3. Jan is eating c(a)k(e).
4. Pl(ea)se turn to p(a)g(e) ten in your books.
5. Where is Samir's b(i)k(e)?
6. Kevin has a r(o)s(e) for Kelly.

Optional Activity: Have students close their texts. Ask them to number a page in their notebooks from 1 to 8. Then ask them to listen carefully to the words you read and to write the words. Then dictate the following words:

1. nose   5. bike
2. cake   6. cute
3. cube   7. rose
4. five   8. page

- After the dictation, write the words on the board. Then have students check their words.
- Have students record the number of correct words in their notebooks; for example,

I wrote (7) out of 8 dictated words with the long vowel sounds /ā/, /ī/, /ō/, and /yōō/ correctly. Write this example on the board as a model.

Expansion
Exercise C

- Have students look at Exercise A. Have them choose one word for each of the long vowel sounds /ā/, /ī/, /ō/, and /yōō/. Have them write a sentence for each word in their notebooks.

> **Reaching All Students—Emergent Learners:** Review the meanings of the words in Exercise A. Model a sample sentence on the board. Then have students write the sentences in their notebooks. Provide help as needed.

- Have students share their sentences with the class.

Answers
Answers will vary.

Optional Activity: Have students play the game "Transformations with silent *e*." Write words on the board that have one meaning as they are, but another meaning with silent *e* at the end. Have a volunteer choose one of the words and read it as it is. Have another volunteer write an *e* at the end of the word and read the new word. Examples include: *cap, cape; cut, cute; dim, dime; man, mane; rob, robe.*

> **Reaching All Students—Visual Learners:** Illustrate some of the transformations on index cards. (Examples: a can on one side, a cane on the other; a cub on one side; a cube on the other.)

Grammar 3, page 87

Object Pronouns

Preparation

- Write the following dialogue on the board as a way of presenting the grammar focus in context.
  Carmen: Where's Grandma? Is she with Carlos?
  Mama: Yes, she's helping *him.*
- Read the dialogue aloud as students follow along.

- Call on two advanced students to dramatize the dialogue for the rest of the class.

Presentation

- Please note that the pointing in the following activity is done with an open palm gesture.
- Prepare display cards with each of the object pronouns: *me, you, her, him, it, us, you, them.*
- Call on two volunteers—a boy and a girl.
- Hold up the "*me*" card, and point to yourself. Say, "I am pointing to *me*."
- Hold up the "*you*" card and stand facing one of the volunteers so that the class sees the profile of you and the volunteer. Say, while looking and pointing at the student, "I am pointing to *you*." Have students repeat.
- Hold up the "*her*" card. From the side, point toward the female student and say, "I am pointing to *her*." Have students repeat.
- Hold up the "*him*" card. From the side, point toward the male student and say, "I am pointing to *him*." Have students repeat.
- Hold up the "*it*" card. Point toward the chalkboard or another classroom object and say, "I am pointing to *it*." Have students repeat.
- Hold up the "*us*" card and stand facing one of the volunteers, so that the class sees the profile of you and the volunteer. Say, while pointing toward yourself and the student, "I am pointing to *us*." Have students repeat.
- Hold up the "*you*" card and point toward all the students, saying, "I am pointing to *you*." Have students repeat.
- Hold up the "*them*" card and point toward the two volunteers, while facing the class as if introducing the volunteers. Say, "I am pointing to *them*." Have students repeat.
- Have students look at the first grammar chart in their texts. Explain that an object pronoun takes the place of a noun and serves as the object in the sentence. Say, "Instead of saying, 'I'm helping (male student's name),' I can say, 'I'm helping *him*.'"
- Have students read silently across each row to make sentences.
- Call on individual students to read aloud one or two of the sentences they made from the word or words in the columns.

- Have students look at the second grammar chart. Read aloud the Remember note at the bottom of the chart as students follow along.
- Have students silently study the object and subject pronouns in the chart.
  Optional Activity: Say a subject pronoun at random. Then call on the class to say the object pronoun.

Practice

Exercise A

- Have students copy the five sentences into their notebooks.
- Call on a volunteer to read the first sentence with the sample answer. Ask the student to explain why the answer is correct. (*Them* replaces the noun phrase *the dishes*.)
- Have students complete the remaining sentences by writing the correct object pronoun in each sentence.

  Reaching All Students—Emergent Learners: First, have students do the exercise orally. Then have them copy the sentences into their notebooks. Have them complete the sentences. Provide help as needed.

- Review the answers with the class.

Answers

1. them	**3.** it	**5.** me
2. her	**4.** it	

Exercise B

- Have students read the first sentence from Exercise A. Ask students how they could turn the statement into a *yes/no* question. Call on a volunteer to write the question on the board and explain how he or she formed it. (Example: *(Be)* + subject pronoun + verb + *ing* + object pronoun?) Then have the student write a short affirmative answer to the question and explain how he or she formed the answer. Last, have the student write a short negative answer and explain how he or she formed it.

  Reaching All Students—Emergent Learners: Have the class develop a rule for forming affirmative and negative short answers. (Example: *Yes,* + subject + *(be)*. The form of the verb *be* should match the subject. *No,* + subject + *(be + not)*. The form of the verb *be* should

match the subject. The *(be + not)* can be written as a contraction.)

- Have students copy the question for the first item into their notebooks. Have them write questions for the remaining sentences. Tell them that they can write either an affirmative or a negative short answer to each question.

  Reaching All Students—Emergent Learners: First, have students do the exercise orally. Then have them write the questions and short answers into their notebooks. Provide help as needed.

- Review the answers with the class.

Answers

Students may offer affirmative or negative responses.

1. Is she drying them?
   Yes, she is./No, she isn't.
2. Are we helping her?
   Yes, we are./No, we aren't.
3. Is he burning them?
   Yes, he is./No, he isn't.
4. Is he eating it?
   Yes, he is./No, he isn't.
5. Is she helping me?
   Yes, she is./No, she isn't.

Reading, pages 88–89

Before You Read

Preparation (See Transparency 22.)

- Tell students that they will be using the learning strategy *Make Predictions* to understand the story.
- Have students look at the Before You Read section. Call on students to read the strategy steps.

Practice

Have students work in pairs to follow the strategy steps. Call on students to share their predictions with the class. Write the students' predictions on the board.

Read This!

Getting Ready

Preparation

Note: Students will encounter the following new words in the reading: *entranceway, living room, bathroom, door, rug, floor, get ready, knock, sweep, vacuum, blue, turn* [= *to change*], *later, cool.*

Practice

Have students listen to the story or read it aloud to them. Provide help with content, vocabulary, etc. as needed. Ask students individually if the reading fits their predictions.

Reaching All Students—Emergent Learners: Work with emergent learners in small groups while the other students work independently. Read aloud as students follow along in their texts. Monitor their comprehension by interrupting the reading with questions such as, "What is the family doing?" (They're getting ready for the party.) "What is their father doing?" (He's vacuuming the rug in the hallway.)"What is their mother doing?" (She's sweeping the floor in the entrance-way.) "What is Carolina doing?" (She's washing her hair in the bathroom.) "What do Carmen and Carlos need time to do?" (They need time to get ready.) "What time is it now?" (It's three o'clock.) "When does the party start?" (The party starts at seven o'clock.) "Why is Carolina crying?" (Her hair is turning blue.) Encourage students to answer the questions using complete sentences.

After You Read

Self-Evaluation
Exercise A

Reaching All Students—Visual Learners: Write the four questions from Exercise A on the board.

Read the questions aloud. Have students repeat. Call on volunteers to give their responses. Have students discuss their answers with a classmate.

Exercise B

- Have students number a sheet of paper in their notebooks from 1 to 5.
- Read the first item aloud, "The grandmother is getting ready for the party." Have students repeat. Ask, "Is that statement true or false?" Call on a student to answer. (True.) Ask the student to find the supportive answer in the story. ("Their grandmother is cooking enchiladas in the kitchen.") Point out that in

this exercise, they will write a correct sentence for any items that are false.

Reaching All Students—Emergent Learners: Answer the second item as a class or with a small group of students, as an example of how to make a false statement correct. (Carlos and Carmen are angry.)

Reaching All Students—Auditory Learners: Call on advanced students to read the remaining sentences.

- Have students write their answers in their notebooks.
- Call on students to give their answers and write them on the board. Be sure they also give the supporting statements from the story.
- Have students count the number of correct answers and write that number in their notebooks.

Answers
1. True
2. False. Carlos and Carmen are angry.
3. True
4. False. Carmen is angry at Carolina.
5. False. Carlos and Carmen are not ready for their party.

Expansion

Have students develop a plan for how they will use *Make Predictions* in another class. Have them write their plan in their notebooks. (Example: Look at the pictures and the title of a reading. Look for words I know in the reading. Make a prediction about the reading.) Have them write a checkmark in their notebooks when they have completed their plan.

Writing, page 90

Before You Write

Preparation (See Transparencies 38–39.)

Tell students that they are going write a dialogue about two people talking on the phone. Remind them that the Before I Write, While I Write, and After I Write checklists provide *strategies* to guide them through the process of writing their dialogues.

Practice

Exercise A

- Focus students' attention on the handwritten dialogue.

   Reaching All Students—Auditory Learners: Call on two advanced students to read the dialogue aloud while the other students follow along in their texts.

- Ask students what kind of writing this is and how it is different from what they've written before. (A dialogue, all conversation.) Ask them what kinds of information are included in the sample dialogue. (Questions and answers, what people are doing, an invitation, hellos and good-byes.) Write students' responses on the board.

- Brainstorm a structure with students that they will use for their dialogues, based on the example. (Examples: a greeting, questions and answers about what the people are doing, an invitation, saying "good-bye.")

- Brainstorm with students the vocabulary they could include in their own dialogues. Write students' responses on the board.

- Refer students to page 222 of the Vocabulary Handbook for activities they could include in the dialogue.

Exercise B

- Draw students' attention to the Before I Write checklist.

- Model following the steps in the Before I Write checklist to plan your own sample paragraph.

- Have students follow the Before I Write checklist and take notes in their notebooks.

   Reaching All Students—Emergent Learners: Work with students in small groups. Guide them in following the steps in the checklist.

Write This!

Presentation

- Draw students' attention to the While I Write checklist.

- Model following the While I Write checklist. Refer to the notes you took in your earlier modeling. As you write, do a "think aloud" about how you are following the While I Write checklist.

Practice

- Have students write their dialogues in their notebooks, using their notes and the While I Write checklist for help. If needed, they can also refer back to the grammar charts in the chapter.

- Circulate while students are writing and encourage them to ask for help with new words.

After You Write

Presentation

- Draw students' attention to the After I Write checklist.

- Model following the steps in the After I Write checklist, checking your own dialogue.

Practice

Exercise A

Have students use the After I Write checklist to evaluate their writing. Have them circle and then correct their errors.

Exercise B

Have students read their dialogues to a classmate. Encourage them to make suggestions for improvement.

Exercise C

Have students write a final copy of their dialogues in their notebooks.

Expansion

Have students work in pairs to practice the dialogues they wrote.

   Reaching All Students—Kinesthetic Learners: Have a few pairs of students act out their dialogues for the class.

Learning Log, page 91

See How to Use the Learning Log on page xiii.
(See Transparencies 20 and 68.)

Chapter 8
I have to work.

Objectives

Language:

- Listen to a dialogue for comprehension.
- Understand familiar vocabulary and grammar structures by listening to a dialogue.
- Develop new vocabulary and grammar structures by listening to a dialogue.
- Act out a dialogue.
- Use both the simple present and the present continuous.
- Use *like*, *have*, and *want* plus the infinitive in affirmative and negative statements, *What* questions, and *yes/no* questions.
- Make original conversations using new vocabulary and grammar structures.
- Ask for and give information.
- Evaluate one's own learning of new vocabulary, grammar, and oral language.

Literacy:

- Read a dialogue for comprehension.
- Understand familiar vocabulary and grammar structures by reading a dialogue.
- Develop new vocabulary and grammar structures by reading a dialogue.
- Write questions using new vocabulary.
- Complete sentences with the simple present and present continuous.
- Complete and write affirmative and negative statements with *like*, *have*, and *want* plus the infinitive.
- Decode words with the long vowel sound /ā/.
- Complete and write *What* questions and *yes/no* questions with *like*, *have*, and *want* plus the infinitive.
- Read a short story for comprehension.
- Understand familiar vocabulary and grammar structures by reading a short story.
- Develop new vocabulary and grammar structures by reading a short story.
- Discuss information gained from reading a short story.
- Write interview questions.
- Take notes during an interview.

- Plan, write, revise, edit, proofread, and make a final copy of a descriptive paragraph about a classmate.
- Capitalize the name of a country in a descriptive paragraph.
- Use *he* or *she* in place of the name of a person in a descriptive paragraph.
- Use *likes*, *wants*, and *has* plus the infinitive in a descriptive paragraph.
- Evaluate one's own learning of reading skills, reading comprehension, and writing skills.

Learning Strategies:

- Use cooperation with a classmate to read a dialogue and study new vocabulary.
- Use cooperation with a small group to act out a dialogue.
- Use cooperation with a classmate to practice conversations.
- Use the strategy *Sound Out* to decode words.
- Use the strategy *Use What You Know* to read and understand a story.
- Use cooperation with a classmate to check a paragraph one has written.
- Evaluate one's own learning of the strategies *Use What You Know* and *Sound Out*.
- Identify easy and difficult material in a chapter and the different ways to learn the difficult material.

Opening Dialogue, pages 92–93

Getting Ready

Preparation (See Transparency 17.)

- Have students look at the illustrations and identify the characters.
- Point to each character, one at a time, and ask, "What is (Maria) doing?" Have students repeat. Then model the response, "She's talking on the telephone." Have students repeat.
- Ask the questions again and call on volunteers to answer.

   Reaching All Students—Advanced Learners: Call on pairs of advanced students, one pair at a time, to ask and answer the questions.

- Have students identify any other words they know for the objects or actions in the illustrations, using complete sentences. If needed, model complete sentences. Write the sentences on the board or a poster. Read the sentences and have students repeat them after you.

Listening and Reading

The Telephone Calls

Presentation

Exercise A

- Read the directions and the prelistening question aloud as students follow along in their texts.
- Have students listen to the dialogue, or read the dialogue aloud to them. Have students look at the appropriate illustrations as they listen.
- Ask the prelistening question, "How many boys call Maria?" Call on a volunteer to respond. (Three boys call Maria.)

Exercise B

Have students read the dialogue. Provide help with content, vocabulary, etc. as needed.

> **Reaching All Students—Emergent Learners:** Work with emergent learners in small groups while the other students work independently. Read aloud as students follow along in their texts. Monitor their comprehension by interrupting the reading with questions such as, "When is Carlos's party?" (It's tonight.) "What does Maria have to do tonight?" (She has to work.) "What does Pablo ask Maria?" ("Would you like to go to the party with me tonight?") "Who calls Maria next?" (Samir does.) "Who can baby-sit for Maria?" (Her mother can.)

Pair and Group Work

Exercise A

Have students who can read on their own form pairs. Have one student in the pair take the role of Maria; have the other student take all the other roles (Carlos, Mother, Pablo, and Samir). Then have them read the dialogue aloud. Provide help as needed.

> **Reaching All Students—Emergent Learners:** Work in small groups with

emergent readers. Model each sentence and have individual students "echo" your reading. Make sure that students look at the sentences as you read them.

Exercise B

Have students form groups of five. Group students heterogeneously so that each group is made up of average readers, weak readers, and strong readers. Have each student choose a role in the dialogue. Have students practice acting out the dialogue in their groups.

> **Reaching All Students—Kinesthetic Learners:** Choose one or more groups to act out the dialogue in front of the class.

Vocabulary

Presentation

- Read the vocabulary words and expressions aloud and have students repeat them.
- Check students' understanding of the words and expressions.

Practice

Exercise A

Have students read and say the words and expressions. Provide assistance with pronunciation as needed.

Exercise B *(See Transparencies 85–87.)*

- Have students turn to page 250 in their texts.
- Have students work through Steps 1–2 (recognizing letters and finding syllables) with the words in the box on page 93, if further practice is needed.
- Have students work in pairs on Step 3, identifying letters or letter combinations that follow patterns or make unexpected sounds. Encourage students to ask questions and to discover as much as they can on their own.

Exercise C

Have students find the words or expressions in the dialogue. Then have them read the sentences.

Exercise D

- Have each student choose three words from the word box. Have the students write three questions to ask a classmate, using these words.

- Have students work in pairs. Have them take turns asking and answering the questions they wrote.
- Call on pairs to share their questions and answers with the class.

Answers
Answers will vary.

Grammar 1, page 94

Simple Present Tense and Present Continuous Tense

Preparation

- Write the following dialogue on the board as a way of presenting the grammar focus in context.

  Liliana: What *are* you *doing?*
  Sophie: *I'm studying.*
  Liliana: Really? Do you *study* every Saturday morning?
  Sophie: Yes, I do. I *study* in the morning. I *have* dance class in the afternoon.

- Read the dialogue aloud as students follow along.
- Call on two advanced students to dramatize the dialogue for the rest of the class.

Presentation

- Have students look at the grammar chart. Direct students to look at the Remember note at the bottom of the chart. Read it aloud while students read along silently. Explain any new words.
- Call on individual students to read aloud down the simple present column.
- Follow the same procedure for the present continuous column.
- Call on individual students to read aloud across each row in the chart to compare the sentences.
- As a class, have students tell you the rules for using both the simple present and the present continuous. Write their responses on the board. (Use the simple present to tell what you usually do. Use the present continuous to tell what you are doing right now.)

Practice
Exercise A

- Have students copy the six sentences (two sentences per item) into their notebooks.
- Call on a volunteer to read the first sentence with the sample answer. Have the student explain why the present continuous is used in the sentence. (It tells us what Carlos and Carmen are doing now.)
- Have students complete the remaining sentences by writing the correct form of the verb in each sentence.

  Reaching All Students—Emergent Learners: First, have students do the exercise orally. Then have them copy the sentences into their notebooks. Have them complete the sentences. Provide help as needed.

  Reaching All Students—Cooperative Learners: Have students work in pairs to complete the activity.

- Review the answers with the class.

Answers
1. are cleaning, are getting ready
2. is talking, calls
3. plays, is playing

Practice
Exercise B

 Have students listen to the conversation, or read it aloud with an advanced student.

Optional Activity: Assign role A to an advanced student. Assign role B to yourself. Mime talking on the phone (hand "holding phone" to ear). Have pairs do the same in Exercise C below.

Exercise C

- Have students work in pairs to practice the conversation in Exercise B.
- Tell students they can now make new conversations, using their own information. Guide the class in brainstorming other activities they could include in their conversations. (For example, eating lunch, studying, and cleaning my room.) Write students' responses on the board.
- Refer students to page 222 of the Vocabulary Handbook for other activities. Work through a couple of examples with verbs from the Vocabulary Handbook.

- Have students work in pairs to practice creating original conversations. Encourage them to try several different conversations, using ideas the class generated or their own ideas.

    Reaching All Students—Emergent Learners: Work with students in small groups to complete the activity.

    Reaching All Students—Auditory/Advanced Learners: Have advanced students dramatize their conversations for the rest of the class.

Grammar 2, page 95

Sentences with *like, have,* and *want* + Infinitive

Preparation

- Write the following dialogue on the board as a way of presenting the grammar focus in context.
    Carmen: Can Maria come to the party?
    Carlos: No, she can't. She *has to* work.
- Read the dialogue aloud as students follow along.
- Call on two advanced students to dramatize the dialogue for the rest of the class.

Presentation

- Have students look at the Affirmative Statements part of the grammar chart. Ask them to read silently across that section, using a word or words in each column to make a sentence.
- Call on individual students to read aloud one or two of the sentences they made from the words in the columns.
- As a class, have students develop a rule for how to make affirmative statements with *like, have,* and *want* plus the infinitive. Write their responses on the board. (Example: Subject + *like/want/have* + *to* + verb. The first verb should match the subject. The second verb should be in the base form. *To* + the base form of a verb is called the "infinitive.")
- Have students look at the Negative Statements part of the grammar chart. Ask them to read silently across that section, using a word or words in each column to make a sentence.

- Call on individual students to read aloud one or two of the sentences they made from the words in the columns.
- As a class, have students develop a rule for how to make negative statements with *like, have,* and *want* plus the infinitive. Write their responses on the board. (Example: Subject + *don't/doesn't* + *like/want/have* + *to* + verb. *Don't* or *doesn't* matches the subject.)

Exercise A

- Call on a volunteer to read the first sentence with the sample answer aloud as the other students follow along in their texts. Have the student explain why the answer is correct. (The sentence is negative, and *doesn't want* matches the subject.)
- Have students copy the sentences into their notebooks. Have them write the correct form of the verb in parentheses to complete each negative or affirmative sentence.

    Reaching All Students—Emergent Learners: First, have students do the exercise orally. Then have them copy the sentences into their notebooks. Have them complete the sentences. Provide help as needed.

- Review the answers with the class.

Answers

1. doesn't want	4. doesn't have
2. have	5. likes
3. want	

Exercise B

- Read the directions and the example for item 1 as students follow along in their texts. Call on volunteers to give examples of other things they have to do. Read the directions and the examples for the second and third items and call on volunteers to give their own examples. Provide assistance as needed.
- Have students complete the exercise by creating new sentences and writing them in their notebooks.

    Reaching All Students—Emergent Learners: Have students copy the following sentences into their notebooks. Call on volunteers to give examples of verbs they can use in each of the blanks. Provide assistance as needed. Write student responses on the board. Then have students complete their sentences.

1. I have to _____.
2. My friend (_____) wants to _____.
3. My friend (_____) and I like to _____.

- Call on volunteers to write their completed sentences on the board and read them aloud.

Answers
Answers will vary.

Word Study, page 96

Long Vowel Sound: /ā/

Preparation

- Write the words *take, wait,* and *say* on the board.
- Call on volunteers to identify the names of the consonants and vowels in the words.
- Pronounce the words and have students repeat them after you.

Presentation

- Explain to students that they are going to study the three most common spellings for the long vowel sound /ā/: *a_e, ai,* and *ay.*
- Begin by reviewing the spelling *a_e.*
- Point to the word *take* on the board. Say the word. Then call on a volunteer to identify the first sound (/t/), the second sound (/ā/), and the third sound (/k/).
- Ask students, "How many sounds does the word have?" (Three.) "How many letters does the word have?" (Four.)
- To help students understand why the word has four letters but three sounds, underline the vowel *e* in the word. Point out that the *e* does not represent a sound in the word *take.* Instead, it acts as a marker or signal that the vowel before it probably stands for a long vowel sound—in this case, the long vowel sound /ā/. Underline *a_e* in the word *take* on the board.
- Next, point to the word *wait* on the board. Say the word. Then call on a volunteer to identify the first sound (/w/), the second sound (/ā/), and the third sound (/t/).
- Ask students, "How many sounds does the word have?" (Three.) How many letters does the word have?" (Four.)
- To help students understand why the word has four letters but only three sounds, un-

derline the vowels *ai* in the word. Point out that the two vowels stand for the long vowel sound /ā/.

- Explain that the vowel combination *ai* is a vowel digraph. Vowel digraphs are vowels that appear together in a word and stand for one vowel sound.
- Last, point to the word *say* on the board. Say the word. Then call on a volunteer to identify the first sound (/s/) and then the second sound (/ā/).
- Ask students, "How many sounds does the word have?" (Two.) "How many letters does the word have?" (Three.)
- To help students understand why the word has three letters but only two sounds, underline the vowels *ay* in the word.
- Point out that the two vowels *ay* stand for the long vowel sound /ā/. Explain that the vowel combination *ay* is also a vowel digraph.
- Have students look at the instruction box in their texts. Read the sentence aloud as students follow along. Have students repeat the three example words: *take, wait,* and *say.*

Practice
Exercise A

Have students work in pairs to use the learning strategy *Sound Out,* as well as the pictures, to read the words with long vowel sound /ā/.

Reaching All Students—Emergent Learners: Complete this activity as a class. After students have an approximation of the pronunciation, say the words correctly to provide a model.

Exercise B

- First, have students read the sentences aloud. Then have them copy the sentences into their notebooks. Last, have them circle the letters that stand for the long vowel sound /ā/.
- Review the answers as a class.

Answers
1. Paco wants to buy a gr**ay** hat.
2. You can have lunch by the l**a**k**e**.
3. Do you want to pl**ay** this g**a**m**e** with me?
4. Can you m**ai**l these letters, please?
5. We have to t**a**k**e** the six o'clock tr**ai**n.
6. Mr. Gomez is not from Sp**ai**n.

Optional Activity: Have students close their texts. Ask them to number a page in their notebooks from 1 to 8. Then ask them to listen carefully to the words you read and to write the words. Then dictate the following words:

1. day
2. train
3. mail
4. game
5. gray
6. Spain
7. play
8. lake

- After the dictation, write the words on the board. Then have students check their words.
- Have students record the number of correct words in their notebooks; for example, *I wrote (7) out of 8 dictated words with the long vowel sound /ā/ correctly.* Write this example on the board as a model.

Expansion
Exercise C

- Have students look at Exercise A. Have them choose two words with the long vowel sound /ā/. Have them write a sentence for each word in their notebooks.

   Reaching All Students—Emergent Learners: Review the meanings of the words in Exercise A. Write a sample sentence for one of the words on the board. Then have students write the three sentences in their notebooks. Provide help as needed.

- Have students share their sentences with the class.

> **Answers**
> *Answers will vary.*

Optional Activity: On a sheet of paper in their notebooks, have students head columns with the spellings for the long vowel sound /ā/: *a_e, ai, ay.* Then have them write as many words as they can that have these spellings for the long vowel sound /ā/. (Set a time limit of 5–10 minutes.) Encourage students to use a dictionary, the text, or their vocabulary lists for help.

   Reaching All Students—Auditory Learners: Encourage students to say the words aloud as they write them.

Have students share their lists with the class.

> **Answers**
> *Answers will vary.*

Grammar 3, page 97

What Questions with *like*, *have*, and *want* + Infinitive

Preparation

- Write the following dialogue on the board as a way of presenting the grammar focus in context.

   Pablo: Maria, *what do* you *like to do* after school?

   Maria: I *like to paint* and *draw.* But I can't today.

   Pablo: Why not? *What do* you *have to do?*

   Maria: I *have to baby-sit.*

- Read the dialogue aloud as students follow along.
- Call on two advanced students to dramatize the dialogue for the rest of the class.

Presentation

- Ask, "What do you like to do after school?" Write the question on the board. Then call on a volunteer to respond. (Example: I like to watch TV after school.) Write the response on the board. Then ask, "What does (Nela) like to do after school?" Write the question on the board. Then call on another volunteer to respond. (Example: [Nela] likes to watch TV after school.) Write the response on the board. Continue by asking *What* questions with *have* and *want* plus the infinitive. (Examples: What do you have to do after school? What do you want to do after school?) Write the questions on the board. Then call on volunteers to respond. Write their responses on the board.
- Have students look at the grammar chart. Point out that the chart shows them how to make *What* questions with *like, have,* and *want* plus the infinitive. Ask students to read silently across the chart, using a word or words in each column to make a *What* question.
- Call on individual students to read aloud one or two of the *What* questions and answers they made from the words in the chart.

- Have students work in pairs or small groups to develop a rule that explains how to make *What* questions with *like*, *have*, or *want* plus the infinitive. Call on students to give their rule. Then write the rule on the board. (Example: *What + do/does + subject + like (have/want) + the infinitive form of the verb.* The form of *do* must match its subject.)

Practice

Exercise

- Have a volunteer read question 1 with the sample answer aloud as the other students follow along in their texts. Ask the student to explain why the answer is correct. (*Does* matches the subject, *Maria*.)

- Have students copy the *What* questions into their notebooks. Then have them write *do* or *does* to complete each sentence.

   Reaching All Students—Emergent Learners: First, have students do the exercise orally. Then have them copy the sentences into their notebooks. Have them complete the exercise. Provide help as needed.

- Review the answers with the class.

Answers		
1. does	**3.** does	**5.** do
2. do	**4.** does	

Yes/No Questions with *like*, *have*, and *want* + Infinitive

Presentation

- Have students look at the grammar chart. Ask them to read silently across the chart, using a word or words in each column to make a *yes/no* question.

- Call on individual students to read aloud one or two of the *yes/no* questions they made.

- Have students work in pairs or small groups to develop a rule that explains how to make *yes/no* questions with *like*, *have*, or *want* plus the infinitive. Call on students to give their rule. Then write the rule on the board. (Example: *Do/Does + subject + like/have/want + infinitive.*)

- Ask students, "Do you like to watch TV?" Write the question on the board. Then call on a volunteer to respond. (Example: Yes, I

do. / No, I don't.) Write the response on the board. Then ask, "Does (Sandra) like to watch TV? Write the question on the board. Call on a volunteer to respond. (Example: Yes, she does. / No, she doesn't.) Write the response on the board. Continue the procedure by asking *yes/no* questions with *have* and *want*. (Examples: Do you have to study after school? Do you want to go to a party?)

Practice

Exercise

- Tell students that they will write five *yes/no* questions with *like*, *want*, and *have* plus the infinitive to ask a classmate.

- Call on a student to read the example aloud. Have students write the example in their notebooks.

- Write *like to*, *want to*, and *have to* on the board. For each item, have students brainstorm topics they could ask questions about. Write the topics on the board. Provide additional words as needed.

   Reaching All Students—Advanced Learners: Call on several advanced students to give examples of questions for the topics.

- Have students write their five questions in their notebooks.

- Pair students. Have them take turns asking and answering their questions.

- Call on pairs to share their questions and answers with the class.

Answers
Answers will vary.

Reading, pages 98–99

Before You Read

Presentation *(See Transparency 20.)*

- Explain to students that when we read we can use what we already know about people and places to help us understand the story better.

- Have students look at the Learning Strategy box *Use What You Know*. Read the information aloud as students follow along in their texts.

Practice

- Have students look at the Before You Read section in their texts. Read aloud the first instruction as students follow along. Have students look at the illustrations and read the title of the story. Ask, "Who is this story about?" Call on a volunteer to respond. (Maria.)

- Read the second instruction from Before You Read aloud as students follow along. Have students close their books so that they do not look at the story. Ask the class questions about Maria to give students ideas about what to discuss. Write the questions on the board as you ask them, but don't elicit responses. (Examples: Where is Maria from? What language does she speak? Where does she live now? Is Maria a new student? Do the other students like her? Who are Maria's friends? What work does Maria sometimes do?)

- Have students work in pairs to discuss what they remember about Maria from earlier chapters.

- Call on volunteers to share what they discussed. Write their responses on the board.

- Have students open their books. Read the last line of the instruction section aloud. Point out that they can use what they know about Maria to help them understand the story better.

Read This!

Maria

Preparation

Note: Students will encounter the following new words in the reading: *family, home, homesick, homework, nights, picture, draw, feel, learn, miss, paint, show, most, shy, sometimes.*

Practice

Have students listen to the story or read it aloud to them. Provide help with content, vocabulary, etc. as needed. Ask students individually if the strategy *Use What You Know* is helping them understand the story.

Reaching All Students—Emergent Learners: Work with emergent learners in small groups while the other students work independently. Read aloud as students follow along in their texts. Monitor their comprehension by interrupting the reading with questions such as, "How does Maria feel most of the time?" (She feels happy most of the time.) "How does Maria feel sometimes?" (She feels sad and homesick sometimes.) "Who does she miss?" (She misses her friends and her big sister). "Is English hard for her?" (Yes, it is.) "What does Maria do after her homework?" (She paints and draws.) "What is she drawing tonight?" (She's drawing a picture of her friends in El Salvador.) "Why doesn't Maria want to show her art to other people?" (Because she's shy.) "Does Maria like to baby-sit?" (Yes, she does.) Encourage students to answer the questions using complete sentences.

After You Read

Self-Evaluation

Exercise A *(See Transparency 20.)*

- Read the directions aloud as students follow along in their texts.

- Write the first question on the board. Have students discuss three things they already knew about Maria with a classmate. When students have finished, call on volunteers to share their information with the class.

- Write the second question on the board. Have students respond with *yes* or *no*.

- Write the third question on the board. Have students discuss three new things they learned about Maria with a classmate. When students have finished, call on volunteers to share their responses.

Answers
Answers will vary.

Exercise B

- Read the directions aloud as students follow along in their texts. Call on a volunteer to read the example sentence.

- Ask students whether the sentence is true or false. (False.) Ask students to identify the statement in the story that supports their response. ("She really likes children.")

- Tell students that they are going to write their own *true/false* statements. Write the first one together as a class. First, locate information in the story and ask volunteers for a *true* statement about that information. (Example: Maria is fifteen years old.) Then locate other information in the story and ask volunteers for a *false* statement about that information. (Example: She lives with her family in a house.) Write the statements on the board and write *True/False* next to each one. Circle *True* next to the first sentence and *False* next to the second one. For example:

1. *Maria is fifteen years old.*   ⟨True⟩ False
2. *She lives with her family in a house.*   True ⟨False⟩

- Have students work in pairs to write five more *true/false* statements. Remind students that three statements should be true and two statements should be false.

- Ask each pair of students to exchange their papers with a nearby pair of students. Tell pairs to circle *True* or *False* for each sentence.

- Have pairs exchange and check each other's papers. Have students write a checkmark next to correct answers and an X next to incorrect answers. Then have pairs return the papers.

- Have pairs share several *true/false* statements with the rest of the class.

- Have students count the number of correct answers and write that number in their notebooks.

Writing, page 100

Before You Write

Preparation *(See Transparencies 40–41.)*

- Tell students that they are going to interview a classmate and write a paragraph about him or her. Explain *interview*. (In an interview, one person asks another person questions.)

- Remind them that the checklists Before I Write, While I Write, and After I Write will guide them through the writing.

Exercise A

Focus students' attention on the handwritten paragraph. Explain to students that a classmate of Alberto interviewed him and then wrote the paragraph about him.

> **Reaching All Students—Auditory Learners:** Call on an advanced student to read the paragraph aloud while the other students follow along in their texts.

Exercise B

- Draw students' attention to the Before I Write checklist.

- Have students study the paragraph in Exercise A. Then ask them what questions they would have to ask to get the information that is in the paragraph. Write their questions on the board. (Examples: Where are you from? How old are you? Where do you live? What do you like to do? What do you want to be? Do you have to study hard?)

- Brainstorm with students several other questions they could ask a classmate in an interview. (Examples: What languages do you speak? What's your address? Do you like to play soccer? Do you like to dance?) Write these questions on the board.

- Have students write five to ten interview questions in their notebooks. Provide help as needed.

Exercise C

- Model asking a proficient student some of the questions on the board. As the student answers, model taking notes on the board. Point out that in note taking only the most important words are written down.

- In pairs, have students interview each other and take notes in their notebooks.

> **Reaching All Students—Emergent Learners:** Work with students in small groups. Have them write only three to five questions. Guide them in asking their questions and taking notes.

Write This!

Presentation

- Draw students' attention to the While I Write checklist.

- Model following the While I Write checklist. Refer to the notes you took in your earlier modeling. As you write, do a "think aloud" about how you are following the While I Write checklist. Model using the student's name more often than necessary so that you can later model substituting *he* or *she*.

Practice

- Have students write their paragraphs in their notebooks, using their notes and the While I Write checklist for help.

- Circulate while students are writing and encourage them to ask for help with new words.

After You Write

Presentation

- Draw students' attention to the After I Write checklist.
- Model following the steps in the After I Write checklist, checking your own paragraph. Point out a place where you can substitute *he* or *she* for the student's name.

Practice

Exercise A

Have students use the After I Write checklist to evaluate their writing. Have them circle and then correct their errors.

Exercise B

Have students read their paragraphs to the classmate they interviewed. Encourage them to make suggestions for improvement.

Exercise C

Have students write a final copy of their paragraphs in their notebooks.

Expansion

Reaching All Students—Auditory Learners: Have advanced students read their paragraphs aloud for the class.

Learning Log, page 101

See How to Use the Learning Log on page xiii. *(See Transparencies 20 and 69.)*

Chapter 9
You came to our party!

Objectives

Language:

- Listen to a dialogue for comprehension.
- Understand familiar vocabulary and grammar structures by listening to a dialogue.
- Develop new vocabulary and grammar structures by listening to a dialogue.
- Act out a dialogue.
- Use the past tense of regular and irregular verbs in affirmative and negative statements.
- Use the past tense of regular and irregular verbs in *yes/no* questions.
- Make original conversations using new vocabulary and grammar structures.
- Evaluate one's own learning of new vocabulary, grammar, and oral language.

Literacy:

- Read a dialogue for comprehension.
- Understand familiar vocabulary and grammar structures by reading a dialogue.
- Develop new vocabulary and grammar structures by reading a dialogue.
- Write sentences using new vocabulary.
- Complete and write sentences with the past tense of regular and irregular verbs in affirmative and negative statements.
- Write *yes/no* questions with the past tense of regular and irregular verbs.
- Decode words with the long vowel sound /ē/.
- Read a short story for comprehension.
- Understand familiar vocabulary and grammar structures by reading a short story.
- Develop new vocabulary and grammar structures by reading a short story.
- Plan, write, revise, edit, proofread, and make a final copy of a letter.
- Use correct formatting for a letter, including the date, greeting, closing, and signature.
- Evaluate one's own learning of reading skills, reading comprehension, and writing skills.

Learning Strategies:

- Use cooperation with a classmate to read a dialogue and study new vocabulary.
- Use cooperation with a small group to act out a dialogue.
- Use cooperation with a classmate to practice conversations.
- Use the strategy *Sound Out* to decode words.
- Use the strategy *Make Inferences* to read and understand a story.
- Use cooperation with a classmate to check a letter one has written.
- Evaluate one's own learning of the strategies *Make Inferences* and *Sound Out*.
- Identify easy and difficult material in a chapter and the different ways to learn the difficult material.

Opening Dialogue, pages 102–103

Getting Ready

Preparation *(See Transparency 17.)*

- Have students look at the illustrations and identify the characters. Then ask them to name the objects in the illustrations. Write the names and the words on the board or a poster. Say the names and words. Have students repeat.

- Ask students to make sentences about what they see and what the people are doing. Write students' responses on the board. If needed, model complete sentences. Read the sentences and have students repeat them after you.

  Reaching All Students—Emergent Learners: Point to each character, one at a time, and ask, "What is (Carmen) doing?" Have students repeat. Call on students to respond. If needed, model the response. (She's welcoming Maria and Paco to the party.) Have students repeat.

  Reaching All Students—Advanced Learners: Call on pairs of advanced students, one pair at a time, to ask and answer the questions.

Listening and Reading

Maria and Paco

Presentation

Exercise A

- Read the directions and the prelistening question aloud as students follow along in their texts.
- Have students listen to the dialogue, or read the dialogue aloud to them. Have students look at the appropriate illustrations as they listen.
- Explain any vocabulary that students do not understand.
- Ask the prelistening question, "How old are Carmen and Carlos?" Call on a volunteer to respond. (They are both sixteen.)

Exercise B

Have students read the dialogue. Provide help with content, vocabulary, etc. as needed.

Reaching All Students—Emergent Learners: Work with emergent learners in small groups while the other students work independently. Read aloud as students follow along in their texts. Monitor their comprehension by interrupting the reading with questions such as, "Who is baby-sitting for Maria?" (Maria's mother is baby-sitting for Maria.) "Whose birthday is it?" (It's Carmen's and Carlos's birthday.) "Are Carmen and Carlos twins?" (Yes, they are.) "Who does Maria introduce?" (She introduces Paco.) "Did Pablo talk to Paco?" (No, he didn't. Carmen did.) "Does Carmen like to dance?" (Yes, she does.) "Who wants to dance with Carmen?" (Paco does.) "Who wants to dance with Maria?" (Carlos, Pablo, and Samir do.)

Pair and Group Work

Practice

Exercise A

Have students who can read on their own form pairs. Have one student in the pair take the role of Carmen and Carlos; have the other student take all other roles (Maria, Paco, Samir, and Pablo). Then have them read the dialogue aloud. Provide help as needed.

Reaching All Students—Emergent Learners: Work in small groups with emergent readers. Model each sentence and have individual students "echo" your reading. Make sure that students look at the sentences as you read them.

Exercise B

Have students form groups of six. Group students heterogeneously so that each group is made up of weak readers, average readers, and strong readers. Have each student choose a role in the dialogue. Have students practice acting out the dialogue in their groups.

Reaching All Students—Kinesthetic Learners: Choose one or more groups to act out the dialogue in front of the class.

Vocabulary

Presentation

- Read the vocabulary words and expressions aloud and have students repeat them.
- Check students' understanding of the words and expressions.

Practice

Exercise A

Have students read and say the words and expressions. Provide assistance with pronunciation as needed. Then have students copy the words and expressions into their notebooks.

Exercise B *(See Transparencies 85–87.)*

- Have students turn to page 250 in their texts.
- Have students work through Steps 1–2 (recognizing letters and finding syllables) with the words in the box on page 103 if further practice is needed.
- Have students work in pairs on Step 3, identifying letters or letter combinations that follow patterns or make unexpected sounds. Encourage students to ask questions and to discover as much as they can on their own.

Exercise C

Have students find the words or expressions in the dialogue. Have them read the sentences.

Exercise D

- Tell students that they will write a dialogue with five words from the word box in their notebooks.

- Have students choose the names of two characters for their dialogues. Have them write the dialogues in their notebooks using five words or expressions from the word box.

    Reaching All Students—Emergent Learners: Work with students in small groups.

    Reaching All Students—Advanced Learners: Challenge advanced students to use as many words from the list as they can.

- Have students work in pairs to read their dialogues.

    Reaching All Students—Kinesthetic Learners: Call on pairs to act out one of their dialogues for the rest of the class.

Answers
Answers will vary.

Grammar 1, page 104

Past Tense of Regular Verbs: Affirmative Statements

Preparation

- Write the following dialogue on the board as a way of presenting the grammar focus in context.
    Carmen: Are you having fun, Liliana?
    Liliana: Oh, yes! I *danced* with Pablo for a long time. Then I *talked* to Maria, and she *introduced* me to Paco.
    Carmen: Isn't Paco cute? I *danced* with him!
    Liliana: Lucky you!
- Read the dialogue aloud as students follow along.
- Call on two advanced students to dramatize the dialogue for the rest of the class.

Presentation

- Have students look at the first grammar chart. Tell students that this grammar chart shows how to talk about actions that happened in the past; for example, what they did yesterday, last night, or last Saturday or Sunday.
- Read the explanation and examples in the chart aloud while students read along silently. Then have students read silently across each row in the chart to make sentences.

- Call on individual students to read aloud one or two of the sentences they made.
- Ask students if they notice anything different about past-tense sentences as compared with present-tense sentences. (The same verb form is used for all subjects in past-tense sentences.) Have students compare to previous grammar charts if necessary.
- Have students look at the second grammar chart. Point out that the chart contains the rules for forming the past tense of regular verbs. Read the rules and examples aloud as students follow along in their texts.

Practice
Exercise A

- Have students write the regular verbs for items 1 to 10 in their notebooks.
- Call on a volunteer to read the sample answer for item 1. Have the student explain how to form the past tense of *play*. Have him or her refer to the rules in the second grammar chart, if necessary. (Add *-ed*. Since there isn't a consonant before the *y*, we don't change the *y* to an *i* before adding *-ed*.)
- Have students write the past tense for items 1 to 10 in their notebooks.

    Reaching All Students—Emergent Learners: First, have students do the exercise orally. Then have them write the answers in their notebooks. Provide help as needed.

    Reaching All Students—Cooperative Learners: Have students complete the exercise in pairs or small groups.

- Review the answers with the class.

Answers

1.	played	6.	studied
2.	asked	7.	laughed
3.	introduced	8.	liked
4.	looked	9.	arrived
5.	danced	10.	loved

Exercise B

- Read the first sentence with the sample answer aloud. Have students repeat. Call on a volunteer to explain how to form the answer. (Add *-ed* to *play*.)
- Have students copy the sentences into their notebooks. Have them complete the

sentences by writing the correct form of the verb in parentheses in each sentence. Encourage students to refer to the rules in the second grammar chart.

> **Reaching All Students—Emergent Learners:** First, have students do the exercise orally. Then have them write the answers in their notebooks. Provide help as needed.

- Review the answers with the class.

Answers
1. played   4. cleaned
2. liked   5. studied
3. talked

<u>Optional Activity:</u> Have students write three true sentences about what they did *yesterday, last night, on Saturday,* or *on Sunday*. Write these expressions of time on the board. Tell them to use three past-tense verbs from Exercise A. Model the activity by writing on the board a true sentence about something you did.

- Have students write their sentences in their notebooks.

> **Reaching All Students—Emergent Learners:** Work with emergent learners in a small group, guiding them through the exercise.

- Call on volunteers to write their completed sentences on the board and read them aloud.

Grammar 2, page 105

Past Tense of Irregular Verbs: Affirmative Statements

Preparation

- Write the following dialogue on the board as a way of presenting the grammar focus in context.

  Carlos: Do you like the enchiladas? I *made* them.

  Bic: They're pretty good. But I love the pizza. I *ate* three slices!

- Read the dialogue aloud as students follow along.
- Call on two advanced students to dramatize the dialogue for the rest of the class.

Presentation

- Tell students that the rule for forming the past tense by adding *-ed* applies only to regular verbs. Irregular verbs have a different form for the past tense. In the dialogue on the board, point out the past-tense form of *make (made)* and the past-tense form of *eat (ate)*.
- Tell students they will need to memorize the past-tense forms for irregular verbs.
- Have students look at the first grammar chart. Ask them to read silently across the chart to make sentences.
- Call on individual students to read aloud one or two of the sentences they made.
- Have students look at the second grammar chart. Read aloud across the chart, saying the present-tense and past-tense forms of each verb as students follow along. Have students repeat the verbs after you.
- Have students silently study the chart.
- Prepare two large display cards. Write the words *every day* on one; write the word *yesterday* on the other.
- Hold up the card with the words *every day* and say one of the verbs in the present tense from the chart, chosen at random. Have students repeat after you. Then hold up the card with the word *yesterday,* and have students say the past-tense form of the verb. Repeat students' responses, correcting pronunciation if necessary. Continue the procedure with the other verbs from the chart.

Exercise A

- Call on a volunteer to read item 1 aloud as the other students follow along in their texts. Have the student explain why the answer is correct. (The past tense of *teach* is *taught.*)
- Have students copy the sentences into their notebooks and write the correct form of the verb in parentheses to complete each sentence.

  > **Reaching All Students—Emergent Learners:** First, have students do the exercise orally. Then have them copy the sentences into their notebooks and complete them. Provide help as needed.

• Review the answers with the class.

Exercise B

• Call on a student to read the instructions for the exercise. Call on another student to read the example.

> **Reaching All Students—Advanced Learners:** Have an advanced student model the exercise by writing a past-tense sentence on the board and reading it aloud.

• Have students complete the exercise by creating three new sentences, each one using a different past-tense irregular verb from the chart in their texts. Have them write the sentences in their notebooks.

> **Reaching All Students—Emergent Learners:** Work with emergent learners in a small group, guiding them through the exercise.

• Call on volunteers to write their completed sentences on the board and read them aloud.

Answers

Answers will vary.

Word Study, page 106

Long Vowel Sound: /ē/

Preparation

• Write the words *me, read, meet, happy,* and *piece* on the board.
• Call on volunteers to identify the names of the consonants and vowels in the words.
• Pronounce the words and have students repeat them after you.

Presentation

• Explain to students that they are going to study the five most common spellings for the long vowel sound /ē/. Write these spellings on the board: *e, ea, ee, y,* and *ie.*
• Begin by reviewing the spelling *e.*
• Point to the word *me* on the board. Say the word. Then call on a volunteer to identify

the first sound (/m/) and the second sound (/ē/).

• Ask students, "How many sounds does the word have?" (Two.) "How many letters does the word have?" (Two.)
• Point to the word *read* on the board. Then call on a volunteer to identify the first sound (/r/), the second sound (/ē/), and the third sound (/d/).
• Ask students, "How many sounds does the word have?" (Three.) "How many letters does the word have?" (Four.)
• To help students understand why the word has four letters but only three sounds, underline the vowels *ea* in the word. Point out that the two vowels stand for the long vowel sound /ē/.
• Explain that the vowel combination *ea* is a vowel digraph. Vowel digraphs are vowels that appear together in a word and stand for one vowel sound.
• Follow the same procedure for the words *meet, happy,* and *piece.*

Practice

Exercise A

Have students use the learning strategy *Sound Out,* as well as the pictures, to read the words with long vowel sound /ē/.

> **Reaching All Students—Emergent Learners:** Complete this activity as a class if students need help. After students have an approximation of the pronunciation, say the words correctly to provide a model.

Exercise B

• First, have students read the sentences aloud. Then have them copy the sentences into their notebooks. Last, have them circle the letters that stand for the long vowel sound /ē/.
• Review the answers as a class. Point out that items 1, 5, and 6 each have two words with the long vowel sound (/ē/).

Optional Activity: Have students close their texts. Ask them to number a page in their notebooks from 1 to 8. Then ask them to listen carefully to the words you read and to write the words. Then dictate the following words:

1. me   5. field
2. clean   6. tree
3. city   7. baby
4. meat   8. feet

- After the dictation, write the words on the board. Then have students check their words.
- Have students record the number of correct words in their notebooks; for example, *I wrote (7) out of 8 dictated words with long vowel sound /ē/ correctly.*

Exercise C

- Have students skim the dialogue on pages 102–103, looking for five words with the long vowel sound /ē/. Be sure students look for the spellings they learned: *e, ea, ee, y,* and *ie.* Last, have them write the five words in their notebooks.
- Have students share their lists with the class.

Answers

Answers will vary. Possible answers include:

part(y)   Sh(e)'s
happ(y)   W(e)'re
s(ee)   sixt(ee)n
bab(y)-sitting   m(ee)t
m(e)

Optional Activity: In their notebooks, have students head five columns with these spellings for the long vowel sound /ē/: *e, ea, ee, y,* and *ie.* Then have them write as many words as they can under the correct headings. (Set a time limit of 5–10 minutes.) Encourage students to use a dictionary, the text, or their vocabulary lists for help.

Reaching All Students—Auditory Learners: Encourage students to say the words as they write them.

Have students share their lists with the class.

Grammar 3, page 107

Past Tense: Negative Statements

Preparation

- Write the following dialogue on the board as a way of presenting the grammar focus in context.

  Carmen: Maria *didn't go* to work. She came to the party.
  Mother: That's great.
  Carmen: But she *didn't come* alone.
  Mother: Poor Carlos!

- Read the dialogue aloud as students follow along.
- Call on two advanced students to dramatize the dialogue for the rest of the class.

Presentation

- Have students look at the grammar chart. Explain that the left section of the chart shows affirmative statements with the past tense of regular and irregular verbs. Explain that the right section shows negative statements with the past tense. Model forming two positive and two negative statements, using words in the columns in the chart. Refer students to the Remember note at the bottom of the chart; read this aloud as students follow along in their texts.
- Have students read silently across each row of the chart—first the affirmative statement on the left, then the negative statement on the right.

  Reaching All Students—Auditory/ Cooperative Learners: Have pairs of students take turns reading sentences from the chart. Have the first student read an affirmative sentence from the left part of the chart. Have the second student read a negative sentence from the right part of the chart. Continue for the remaining rows.

- Call on individual students to read aloud one or two of the sentences they made from the chart.
- Refer students to the contraction box. Point out that *didn't* is the contraction of *did not.* Call on individual students to read negative statements from the chart, substituting *didn't* for *did not.*

Practice

Exercise

- Tell students that in this exercise, they will change statements from the affirmative to the negative.
- Read the first sentence aloud. Have students repeat.
- Ask, "How do you change that to a negative statement?" Call on a student to read the answer and explain how it was formed. (The contraction *didn't* was added before the base form of the verb.)
- Have students change the remaining statements from the affirmative to the negative. Have them write the answers in their notebooks.

> **Reaching All Students—Auditory Learners:** Call on advanced students to read the sentences (without the answers) before students write their answers.

> **Reaching All Students—Cooperative Learners:** Have students work in pairs to complete the activity.

- Call on students to write their answers on the board and read them aloud.

Answers
1. Carlos didn't call Pablo last night.
2. Carmen didn't help her mother with the housework.
3. Liliana and Bic didn't go to the movies yesterday.
4. Samir didn't do his homework at the library.
5. Sophie didn't like her mother's new shoes.

Past Tense: *Yes/No* Questions

Presentation

- Have students look at the grammar chart. Explain that the left part of the chart shows *yes/no* questions in the past tense. (Read the first row example.) The middle part shows affirmative answers. (Read the first row example.) The right part shows negative answers. (Read the first row example.)
- Have students read silently across each row of each part of the chart.

> **Reaching All Students—Auditory/ Cooperative Learners:** Have groups of three students take turns reading sentences from the chart. Have the first

student read the question, the second student read the affirmative answer, and the third student read the negative answer.

- Call on volunteers to read the questions and answers they made for the rest of the class.
- Have students work in pairs or small groups to develop rules that tell how to make *yes/no* questions and affirmative or negative short answers with the past tense.
- Call on individual students to give their rules. Write the rules on the board. (Examples: Questions = *Did* + subject + verb; *Did* stays the same for all subjects; the second verb is in the base form. Affirmative short answers = *Yes,* + subject + *did*; *did* stays the same for all subjects. Negative short answers = *No,* + subject + *did not (didn't)*; *did* stays the same for all subjects.)

Practice

Exercise

- Tell students that they will use the statements in the previous exercise to write five *yes/no* questions in the past tense.
- Call on a student to read the example aloud. Have students write the example in their notebooks.
- Have students change the remaining statements from the previous exercise to questions. Have them write the questions in their notebooks.
- Review the answers with the class.

Answers
1. Did Carlos call Pablo last night?
2. Did Carmen help her mother with the housework?
3. Did Liliana and Bic go to the movies yesterday?
4. Did Samir do his homework at the library?
5. Did Sophie like her mother's new shoes?

Expansion

- Tell students that they will write three *yes/no* questions about yesterday to ask a classmate.
- As a class, brainstorm topics students could ask questions about. Write the topics on the board. Provide additional words as needed.

> **Reaching All Students—Advanced Learners:** Call on several advanced students to give examples of questions.

Reaching All Students—Emergent Learners: After students select a topic, ask them to generate the question. For example, "clean your room—Did you clean your room yesterday?" Then write the questions on the board.

- Have students write their questions in their notebooks.
- Pair students. Have them take turns asking and answering their questions.
- Call on pairs to share their questions and answers with the class.

Reading, pages 108–110

Before You Read

Presentation

- Explain to students that when we read, we can often guess what new words or ideas mean by looking at the other words or sentences around them.
- Have students look at the Learning Strategy box *Make Inferences*. Read the information aloud as students follow along.
- Have students look at the Before You Read section in their texts. Call on volunteers to read the steps for the strategy.

Read This!

A Fun Party

Preparation

- For this chapter, do not preteach vocabulary; allow students to use the strategy *Make Inferences* to understand new words.
- Call on a student to read the title of the story.
- Have students look at the illustrations and study them silently. Tell students that they can also use the illustrations to help them guess, or make inferences, about new words and ideas.

Presentation

Read the first paragraph of the story "A Fun Party" aloud as students follow along in their texts. As you read, stop to do a "think aloud," demonstrating how to use the strategy *Make Inferences* to help you understand the words *everybody*, *delicious*, and *grandson*. For example, say, "The word *everybody* is new." Write

this word on the board and have students write it in their notebooks. Say, "The sentence says 'Everybody at Carlos and Carmen's birthday party had fun.' The sentences after say 'People laughed and talked.' 'The music was good.' 'People danced.' I know *every* means *each* or *all*, so I think *everybody* means *all the people*." Follow the same procedure with the words *delicious* and *grandson*. (Other new words in the story are: *guitar, beautiful, song, wonderful, embarrassed, cute, agreed, boyfriend, promised,* and *midnight*.)

Practice

Have students listen to the story, or read it aloud to them. Provide help with content, vocabulary, etc. as needed. Remind them to write new words in their notebooks and use the strategy *Make Inferences* to guess the meaning of the words. Circulate to answer questions.

Reaching All Students—Emergent Learners: Work with emergent learners in small groups while the other students work independently. Guide them in using the strategy *Make Inferences* for each of the new words.

After You Read

Self-Evaluation

Exercise A

- Refer students to After You Read. Read the question in item 1 aloud. On the board, write the headings *New Word* and *Inference*. Call on volunteers to say what new words they found in the story. Write each word on the board and ask what inference the student made about the meaning. Write this on the board and ask what information in the reading let them make that inference.
- Have students write the words and inferences in their notebooks.
- Refer students to item 2. Read it aloud as students follow along. Call on a volunteer to answer the questions.

Answers
1. *Answers will vary.*
2. Paco is Maria's brother. Paco says to Maria, "We have to go home." and "We promised Mama, Maria."

Exercise B

- Read the instructions aloud as students follow along. Point out that in this exercise, they will write a past-tense sentence that answers each question.
- Have students number a sheet of paper in their notebooks from 1 to 5.
- Read item 1 aloud. Have students repeat. Call on a student to read the answer. Ask the student to find the supportive statements in the story. ("People laughed and talked." "People danced." "People ate a lot.")

  Reaching All Students—Auditory Learners: Call on advanced students to read the remaining questions aloud before students write their answers in their notebooks.
- Have students write their answers in their notebooks.
- Call on students to give their answers and write them on the board. Be sure they also give the supporting statements from the story.
- Have students count the number of correct answers and write that number in their notebooks.

Answers
1. They talked, danced, and ate.
2. She danced with her grandson.
3. He played his guitar and sang songs.
4. She said, "He's very cute!"
5. They promised their mother.

Expansion

Have students brainstorm the ways they can use the strategy *Make Inferences* in their other classes. Write their responses on a poster. Have students refer to the poster from time to time.

Writing, page 110

Before You Write

Preparation *(See Transparencies 24 and 42–43.)*

- Explain to students that they are going to write a letter to a friend.
- Ask students, "Whom do you write letters to?" and "What do you write about in your letters?"

Practice
Exercise A

- Focus students' attention on the handwritten letter.

  Reaching All Students—Auditory Learners: Call on an advanced student to read the letter aloud to the class while the other students follow along in their texts.
- Call on volunteers to identify the date (November 6, 2004), the greeting (Dear Sara,), the closing (Your friend,), and the signature (Liliana).
- Ask what the letter is about. (A description of Carlos and Carmen's birthday party.) Ask them what kinds of information Liliana included in her letter. (When and where the party was, what she and others did at the party, what she ate, and a question for her friend.)

Exercise B

- Call on an advanced student to read the Before I Write checklist.
- Have students brainstorm events that they could write about. Write their responses on the board. Then have them brainstorm information about the events that they could include in their letters. Write their responses on the board.
- Refer students to pages 222 and 227 of the Vocabulary Handbook for free-time activities and daily routines as needed.
- Have students follow the Before I Write checklist to take notes in their notebooks.

  Reaching All Students—Emergent Learners: Work with students in small groups. Guide them in following the steps in the checklist.

Write This!

Presentation

- Draw students' attention to the While I Write checklist. Call on volunteers to read aloud the points in the checklist.
- Explain and model on the board each of the writing points in this section while you write a brief sample letter. As you write, do a "think aloud" about how you are following the While I Write checklist.

Practice

- Have students write their letters in their notebooks. They should use their notes and the While I Write checklist as guides. If needed, they can also refer to the grammar charts earlier in the chapter.
- Circulate while students are writing and encourage them to ask for help with new words.

After You Write

Presentation

Exercise A

- Draw students' attention to the After I Write checklist.
- Model following the steps in the After I Write checklist, checking your own letter on the board.

Practice

Have students use the After I Write checklist to evaluate their writing. Have them circle and then correct their errors.

Exercise B

Have students read their letters to a classmate. Encourage them to make suggestions for improvement.

Exercise C

Have students make a final copy of their letters in their notebooks.

Expansion

- Encourage students to use the letter format whenever they write letters to family and friends.
- For e-mail correspondence, point out that the letter format can be easily adapted:
  1. Do not include the date.
  2. Align the greeting, closing, and signature with the left margin.
  3. Do not indent the paragraphs; align them with the left margin.
  4. Skip a line after each paragraph.

Learning Log, page 111

See How to Use the Learning Log on page xiii.
(See Transparencies 20 and 70.)

UNIT **4** AROUND TOWN

Unit Opener,
pages 112–113

Preview

- Call on a student to read the unit title, "Around Town." Tell students that this unit is about activities around town.

- Have students look at the photos and identify the people and the settings. (Teens walking through town together, two teens shopping for hats.) Write the descriptions of the people and the settings on the board as the students say them.

- Help students identify the different items in the photos. Write the names of the items on the board as students say them.

- Point to the people in the photos, one at a time, and ask, "What is (<u>he</u>) doing?" Have students repeat. Then model the response. "(<u>He's</u> <u>shopping</u>)." Have students repeat. Write responses on the board.

  <u>Optional Activity:</u> Call on pairs of advanced students, one pair at a time, to ask and answer questions about what the people in the photos are doing.

- Read the unit goals aloud as students follow along in their texts. Answer any questions they may have.

Chapter 10
How much is it?

Objectives

Language:

- Listen to a dialogue for comprehension.
- Understand familiar vocabulary and grammar structures by listening to a dialogue.
- Develop new vocabulary and grammar structures by listening to a dialogue
- Act out a dialogue.
- Ask information questions with *be* and *do* in the present and past tenses.
- Ask *How much* questions with *be* and *do*.
- Make original conversations using new vocabulary and grammar structures.
- Evaluate one's own learning of new vocabulary, grammar, and oral language.

Literacy:

- Read a dialogue for comprehension.
- Understand familiar vocabulary and grammar structures by reading a dialogue.
- Develop new vocabulary and grammar structures by reading a dialogue.
- Draw pictures of new vocabulary.
- Complete and write information questions with *be* and *do* in the present and past tenses.
- Decode words with the long vowel sound /ī/.
- Complete and write *How much* questions with *be* and *do*.
- Read a short story for comprehension.
- Understand familiar vocabulary and grammar structures by reading a short story.
- Develop new vocabulary and grammar structures by reading a short story.
- Plan, write, revise, edit, proofread, and make a final copy of a script.
- Use contractions, adjectives, and information questions to write a script for a fashion show.
- Evaluate one's own learning of reading skills, reading comprehension, and writing skills.

Learning Strategies:

- Use cooperation with a classmate to read a dialogue and study new vocabulary.
- Use cooperation with a small group to act out a dialogue.
- Use cooperation with a classmate to practice conversations.
- Use the strategy *Sound Out* to decode words.
- Use the strategy *Make Predictions* to understand a short story.
- Use cooperation with a classmate to check a script one has written.
- Evaluate one's own learning of the strategies *Make Predictions* and *Sound Out*.
- Identify easy and difficult material in a chapter and the different ways to learn the difficult material.

Opening Dialogue, pages 114–115

Getting Ready

Preparation *(See Transparency 17.)*

- Have students look at the illustrations and identify the characters. Then ask them to name the items in the illustrations. Write the names and the words on the board or a poster. Have students repeat.

- Ask students to make sentences about what they see and what the people are doing. Write students' responses on the board. If needed, model complete sentences. Read the sentences, and have students repeat them after you.

  Reaching All Students—Emergent Learners: Point to each character, one at a time, and ask, "What is (<u>Carlos</u>) doing?" Have students repeat. Call on students to respond. If needed, model the response. (<u>He's</u> <u>shopping</u>.) Have students repeat. Then ask students to make other sentences about what they see and what the people are doing.

Listening and Reading

Pablo's New Clothes

Presentation

Exercise A

- Read the directions and the prelistening question aloud as students follow along in their texts.

- Have students listen to the dialogue, or read the dialogue aloud to them. Have students look at the appropriate illustrations as they listen.

- Explain any vocabulary words that students do not understand.

- Ask the prelistening question, "Does Pablo have a new job?" Call on a volunteer to respond. (No, not exactly.)

Exercise B

Have students read the dialogue. Provide help with content, vocabulary, etc. as needed.

Reaching All Students—Emergent Learners: Work with emergent learners in small groups while the other students work independently. Read aloud as students follow along in their texts. Monitor their comprehension by interrupting the reading with questions such as, "What does Pablo need?" (He needs a shirt and a pair of pants.) "Why does Pablo need new clothes?" (It's a secret.) "Who helps Pablo find the shirts?" (The salesclerk does.) "What color shirt does Pablo want?" (He wants a dark color.) "How much is the shirt?" (It's $15.95) "Does Pablo need casual pants?" (No, he doesn't.) "What pair of pants does Pablo like?" (He likes the dark blue pair.) "What does Pablo need to do?" (He needs to try on the pants.) "Where can Carlos meet Pablo?" (He can meet him at the fountain.)

Pair and Group Work

Practice

Exercise A

Have students who can read on their own form pairs. Have one student in the pair take the role of Pablo; have the other student take the roles of Carlos and the salesclerk. Then have them read the dialogue aloud. Provide help as needed.

Reaching All Students—Emergent Learners: Work in small groups with emergent readers. Model each sentence and have individual students "echo" your reading. Make sure that students look at the sentences as you read them.

Exercise B

Have students form groups of three. Group students heterogeneously so that each group is made up of a weak reader, an average reader, and a strong reader. Have each student choose a role in the dialogue. Have students practice acting out the dialogue in their groups.

Reaching All Students—Kinesthetic Learners: Choose one or more groups to act out the dialogue in front of the class.

Vocabulary

Presentation

- Read the vocabulary words and expressions aloud and have students repeat them.

- Check students' understanding of the words and expressions.

Practice

Exercise A

Have students read and say the words and expressions. Provide assistance with pronunciation as needed. Then have students copy the words and expressions into their notebooks.

Exercise B *(See Transparencies 85–87.)*

- Have students turn to page 250 in their texts.

- Have students work through Steps 1–2 (recognizing letters and finding syllables) with the words in the box on page 115 if further practice is needed.

- Have students work in pairs on Step 3, identifying letters or letter combinations that follow patterns or make unexpected sounds. Encourage students to ask questions and to discover as much as they can on their own.

Exercise C

Have students find the words and expressions in the dialogue. Have them read the sentences aloud.

Exercise D

- Read the instructions aloud and model the game with an advanced student. Draw a picture on the board and have the student guess which word you are drawing the picture for.
- Pair students. Have students take turns drawing and guessing the words. Circulate to encourage students and provide help.
- Have several students draw their pictures on the board. Call on volunteers to guess which words the students have illustrated.

Grammar 1, page 116

Information Questions with *be*: Present Tense

Preparation

- Write the following dialogue on the board as a way of presenting the grammar focus in context:
  Carlos: *Who's that girl?*
  Pablo: She's in my music class.
  Carlos: *What's her name?*
  Pablo: Her name is Jasmine.
  Carlos: *How old is she?*
  Pablo: I don't know, Carlos! Stop asking so many questions!
- Read the dialogue aloud as students follow along. Then have the class read aloud with you.
- Call on two advanced students to dramatize the dialogue for the rest of the class.

Presentation

- Have students look at the grammar chart. Tell them that this chart shows how to make information questions with *be* in the present tense. Tell them that information questions ask *Who? What? When? Where? Why?* and *How?* Explain any new words.
- Call on pairs of students to read aloud across each row in the chart. Have one student read the question in the left part of the chart and the other read the answer in the right part of the chart.
- Have students look at the contractions box. Read the contractions aloud as students follow along. Have them repeat. Remind students that these contractions are casual (for everyday speaking situations).

- Call on volunteers to read the questions in the chart again, substituting the contractions where appropriate.

Practice

- Have students look at the photograph of the birthday party. Have students identify the event, people, and items in the photograph. (A girl is having a birthday party with her friends. There's a birthday cake and candles. Everyone looks happy.)
- Tell students that they will write questions about the party in the photograph. Explain that the exercise has the answers but not the questions. They will need to write the question that goes with each answer, using the information question word in parentheses at the end of each line.
- Have students number a sheet of paper in their notebooks from 1 to 5.
- Read the first statement aloud and the information question word in parentheses. Have students repeat.
- Have students write the questions in their notebooks to correspond with each answer in the exercise.

    Reaching All Students—Auditory Learners: Call on advanced students to read each of the sentences aloud before students write their questions.

    Reaching All Students—Emergent Learners: First, have students do the exercise orally. Then have them write the answers in their notebooks. Provide help as needed.

    Reaching All Students—Cooperative Learners: Have students work in pairs to complete the activity.

- Review the answers with the class.

Answers
1. What is her name?
2. Why is she happy?
3. Where is the party?
4. Who made the cake?
5. How is Akiko feeling?

Information Questions with *be*: Past Tense

Presentation

Have students look at the grammar chart. Read the information aloud as students follow along.

Reaching All Students—Emergent Learners: Review the past tense of *be* by writing the pronouns *I, you, he/she, it, we, you,* and *they* on the board. Have students write these in their notebooks. Ask students to tell you the past-tense form of *be* for each pronoun. Write students' responses on the board and have students write them next to the pronouns in their notebooks.

Practice

- Tell students that the questions in this exercise are missing the information question word and the past tense of *be*. Explain that they will need to complete each question based on the given answer.
- Call on a volunteer to read the sample question and answer for item 1. Ask the student why *How* is the information question word used. (The answer to the question is "It was great!")
- Have students write the questions in their notebooks, completing each question with the correct information question word and the correct past-tense form of *be*. Point out that students do not need to write the answers to the questions in their notebooks.

    Reaching All Students—Emergent Learners: First, have students do the exercise orally. Then have them write the answers in their notebooks. Provide help as needed.

    Reaching All Students—Cooperative Learners: Have students work in pairs to complete the activity.

- Review the responses with the class.

Answers
1. How was
2. Why were
3. Where was
4. When was
5. What was

Grammar 2, page 117

Information Questions with *do*: Present Tense

Preparation

- Write the following dialogue on the board as a way of presenting the grammar focus in context:

    Maria: *Where do* you *want* to go first?
    Mother: Let's go to Bowman's department store.
    Maria: *What do* we *need* there?
    Mother: You need new gym shoes. Your old ones are too small.

- Read the dialogue aloud as students follow along. Then have the class read aloud with you.
- Call on two students to dramatize the dialogue for the rest of the class.

Presentation

- Have students look at the grammar chart. Tell them that this chart shows how to ask information questions with *do*. Explain any new words.
- Call on pairs of students to read aloud across each row in the chart. Have one student read the question on the left part of the chart and the other read the answer on the right part of the chart.
- Have a volunteer describe the rule for forming an information question with *do*. Write the rule on the board. (Example: Information question word + *(do/does)* + subject + verb. *Do* matches the subject. The main verb is in the base form.)

Practice
Exercise

- Tell students that this exercise has the answers, but not the questions. They will need to write the question that goes with each answer, using the information question word in parentheses at the end of the line.
- Have students number a sheet of paper in their notebooks from 1 to 5.
- Read the first statement and the information question word in parentheses aloud. Have students repeat.
- Call on a student to read the question (sample answer). Have the student explain why the question is correct.

- Have students write the questions in their notebooks.

  Reaching All Students—Auditory Learners: Call on advanced students to read each of the sentences before students write their questions.

  Reaching All Students—Emergent Learners: First, have students do the exercise orally. Then have them write the answers in their notebooks. Provide help as needed.

  Reaching All Students—Cooperative Learners: Have students work in pairs to complete this activity.

- Review the responses with the class.

Answers
1. Where does he come from?
2. What do Mr. Gomez's students study?
3. When do you get to school?
4. Who do you see?
5. How do his shoes look?

Information Questions with *do*: Past Tense

Presentation

- Have students look at the grammar chart. Read the information aloud as students follow along.
- Have a volunteer describe the rule for forming an information question with *do* in the past tense. Write the rule on the board. (Example: Information question word + *did* + subject + verb. *Did* does not change. The main verb is in the base form.)
- Have students look again at the grammar chart at the top of the page. Call on pairs to change the questions and answers in the chart from the present tense to the past tense. Have one student transform the question in the left part of the chart and the other student transform the answer in the right part of the chart.

Practice

Exercise

- Tell students that in this exercise they will write a dialogue about their dinner last night. Explain that they will use their own information and information questions with *do* in the past tense.
- Call on a student to read the example aloud. Ask several students what time they ate din-

ner last night. Have students write the example in their notebooks, using the real time that they ate dinner.

- As a class, brainstorm possible questions students could use in their dialogues for each of the information question words. (Examples: Where did you eat dinner? Who did you eat dinner with? What did you eat? How was it?/How were they?)
- Have students write their dialogues in their notebooks.

  Reaching All Students—Emergent Learners: Work with students in small groups to complete the activity.

- Have students work in pairs. Have students take a role in each other's dialogue. Have them practice reading their dialogues.
- Call on pairs to read aloud one or both of their dialogues for the rest of the class.

Answers
Answers will vary.

Word Study, page 118

Long Vowel Sound: /ī/

Preparation

- Write the words *hi, my, time, pie,* and *right* on the board.
- Call on volunteers to identify the names of the consonants and the vowels in the words.
- Pronounce the words and have students repeat them after you.

Presentation

- Explain to students that they are going to study the five most common spellings for the long vowel sound /ī/: *i, y, i_e, ie,* and *igh.*
- Begin by reviewing the spelling *i.*
- Point to the word *hi* on the board. Say the word. Then call on a volunteer to say the first sound (/h/) and the second sound (/ī/).
- Ask students, "How many sounds does the word have?" (Two.) "How many letters does the word have?" (Two.)
- Follow the same procedure for the words *my, time, pie,* and *right.*

Practice

Exercise A

Have students use the learning strategy *Sound Out*, as well as the pictures, to read the words with long vowel sound /ī/.

> **Reaching All Students—Emergent Learners:** Complete this activity as a class. After students have an approximation of the pronunciation, say the words correctly to provide a model.

Exercise B

- First, have students work in pairs to read the sentences aloud. Then have them copy the sentences into their notebooks. Last, have them circle the letters that stand for the long vowel sound /ī/.

- Review the answers as a class. Point out that items 3, 4, and 6 have two words each with the long vowel sound /ī/.

> **Answers**
> 1. Are you baking a p(ie)?
> 2. Turn r(igh)t at the gym.
> 3. Wh(y) does he need a new t(ie)?
> 4. (I) need a d(i)m(e).
> 5. What s(i)z(e) dress does she wear?
> 6. We can go to the movies on Fr(i)day n(igh)t.

Optional Activity: Have students close their texts. Ask them to number a page in their notebooks from 1 to 8. Then ask them to listen carefully to the words you read and to write the words. Then dictate the following words:

1. tie	5. child
2. cry	6. night
3. pie	7. size
4. right	8. dime

- After the dictation, write the words on the board. Then have students check their words.

- Have students record the number of correct words in their notebooks; for example, *I wrote (7) out of 8 dictated words with the long vowel sound /ī/ correctly.*

Exercise C

- Have students skim the dialogue on pages 114–115, looking for four words with the long vowel sound /ī/. Be sure they look for the spellings they learned: *i, y, i_e, ie,* and *igh*. Last, have them write the four words in their notebooks.

- Have students share their lists with the class.

> **Answers**
> *Answers will vary. Possible answers include:*
>
> | | | |
> |---|---|---|
> | find | Right | like |
> | Why | ninety | try |
> | I | five | |

Optional Activity: In their notebooks, have students head five columns with these spellings for the long vowel sound /ī/: *i_e, y, i, ie,* and *igh*. Then have them write as many words as they can under the correct headings. (Set a time limit of 5–10 minutes.) Encourage students to use a dictionary, the text, or their vocabulary lists for help.

> **Reaching All Students—Auditory Learners:** Encourage students to say the words aloud as they write them.

Have students share their lists with the class.

Grammar 3, page 119

Questions with *how much*

Preparation

- Write the following dialogue on the board as a way of presenting the grammar focus in context:

> **Maria:** *How much are* these?
> **Clerk:** They're $59.95.
> **Mother:** That's too expensive! *How much do* these *cost?*
> **Clerk:** Those are $34.95.
> **Mother:** That's better. Try these on, Maria.

- Point out that the demonstrative pronouns *these* and *those* in the dialogue refer to a pair of shoes.

- Read the dialogue aloud as students follow along. Then have the class read aloud with you.

- Call on two students to dramatize the dialogue for the rest of the class.

Presentation

- Have students look at the first grammar chart. Tell them that this chart shows how to ask *How much* questions with the verb *be*.

- Read aloud across each row in the chart. Have students repeat after you.

- As a class, have students develop a rule for how to form a *How much* question with *be*.

Write the rule on the board. (Example: *How much* + *(be)* + subject. *Be* matches the subject. Use *this* and *that* for singular items. Use *these* and *those* for plural items.)

- Have students look at the second grammar chart. Tell them that this chart shows students how to ask *How much* questions with the verb *do*.
- Read aloud across each row in the chart. Have students repeat after you.
- As a class, have students develop a rule for how to form a *How much* question with the verb *do*. Write the rule on the board. (Example: *How much* + *(do/does)* + subject + *cost?* *Do* matches the subject. The main verb is in the base form.)

Practice

Exercise A

- Have students copy the five sentences into their notebooks.
- Call on a volunteer to read the first sentence with the sample answer.
- Have the student explain why the sample answer is correct. (The verb *be* agrees with the subject.)
- Have students complete the remaining sentences by writing the correct form of the verb in each sentence.

    Reaching All Students—Emergent Learners: First, have students do the exercise orally. Then have them copy the sentences into their notebooks. Have them complete the sentences. Provide help as needed.

- Review the answers with the class.

Answers		
1. is	**3.** are	**5.** do
2. does	**4.** is	

Exercise B

Have students listen to the conversation. Provide help with content, vocabulary, etc. as needed.

   Reaching All Students—Emergent Learners: Work with emergent learners in small groups while other students work independently. Read aloud as students follow along in their texts.

Exercise C

Divide the class into pairs. Have each pair practice the dialogue in Exercise B. Have students turn to page 225 in the Vocabulary Handbook. Explain that some clothing items are singular and some are plural. Name several singular clothing items, for example, a shirt, a dress, and a skirt. Ask students whether they use *this/that* or *these/those* for these items. (*This/that.*) Call on volunteers to tell you the names of the other singular clothing items on the page. Then ask students to tell you the names of the plural clothing items on the page. (Pants, socks, shoes, shorts.) Ask students whether they use *this/that* or *these/those* for these items. (*These/those.*)

Reading, pages 120–121

Before You Read

Presentation (See Transparency 22.)

- Tell students that they will use the learning strategy *Make Predictions* to understand the story.
- Have students look at the Before You Read section. Call on volunteers to read the strategy steps.

Practice

- Have students work independently through Steps 1–4. Have them write their predictions in their notebooks.

    Reaching All Students—Emergent Learners: Have students do the activity in pairs. Circulate to guide students and answer questions.

- Call on individual students to share their predictions with the class (Step 5). Write students' predictions on the board.

Read This!

A Forty-Dollar Dress

Preparation

Note: Students will encounter the following new words in the reading: *skirt, sweater, department store, price tag, supermarket, buy, cost, shop, only, suddenly, dress, fountain, color, find.*

Practice

- 🎧 Have students listen to the story, or read it aloud to them. Provide help with content, vocabulary, etc. as needed. Remind students to check their predictions as they read the story.

- Have students read the story silently on their own. Circulate to answer questions. Ask students individually if the reading fits their predictions, or if they changed their predictions.

  Reaching All Students—Emergent Learners: Work with emergent learners in small groups while the other students work independently. Read aloud as students follow along in their texts. Monitor their comprehension by interrupting the reading with questions such as, "Where did Carmen, Mei, and Maria go?" (They went to a department store.) "How much was the first dress?" (It was a hundred and fifty dollars.) "How much money does Maria have?" (She only has forty dollars.) "How much are the sweater and skirt together?" (They're fifty dollars.) "Do Mei and Carmen like the forty-dollar dress?" (No, they don't.) "Where does Mei have to be at three o'clock?" (She has to be at the supermarket.) "Who has to meet Pablo at six o'clock?" (Maria, Carmen, and Mei do.) Encourage students to answer the questions using complete sentences.

After You Read

Self-Evaluation

Exercise A

Read the first question aloud. Have students write their answers in their notebooks. Then call on individual students to give their answers. Follow the same procedure for the remaining questions.

Answers

Answers will vary.

Exercise B

- Have students number a sheet of paper in their notebooks from 1 to 5.

- Read the first question aloud. Call on a volunteer to answer. Write the answer on the board. *(Carmen and Mei did.)* Ask the student to identify the supportive statement in the story. ("Carmen and Mei went shopping with her.")

  Reaching All Students—Auditory Learners: Call on advanced students to read the remaining questions before students write their answers.

- Have students write their answers in their notebooks.

  Reaching All Students—Emergent Learners: Have students work in pairs, or work with them in a small group, to complete the exercise.

- Call on students to give their answers and write them on the board. Be sure they also give the supporting statements from the story.

- Have students count the number of correct answers and write that number in their notebooks.

Answers

1. Carmen and Mei went shopping with her.
2. It was a hundred and fifty dollars. / Maria only had forty dollars.
3. It wasn't a good color for Maria.
4. She's meeting her sister, Amy, there. / They have to buy some things for her grandmother.
5. They have to be at the fountain.

Expansion

In their notebooks, have students turn to the plan they developed in Chapter 7 for using *Make Predictions* in another class. Call on volunteers to name the class and to describe how they used the strategy. Encourage all students to use the strategy in another class.

Writing, page 122

Before You Write

Preparation *(See Transparencies 44–45.)*

Tell students that they are going to write a script for a school fashion show. Explain that a script for a fashion show is the dialogue that the performers use.

Practice

Exercise A

- Focus students' attention on the handwritten script.

  Reaching All Students—Auditory Learners: Call on three advanced students to read the script aloud while the other students follow along in their texts.

- Ask students what kind of information is included in the sample script. (Descriptions of people, clothing, colors, and prices.) Write students' responses on the board.

Exercise B

- Call on an advanced student to read the Before I Write checklist.

- As a class, have students generate a structure they will use for their scripts, based on the example. (A welcome/introduction. Naming the first model. Describing the outfit. Repeat for the second model. A conclusion/invitation to buy the outfit.)

- Refer students to pages 224 and 225 in the Vocabulary Handbook for a list of colors and clothes they could include in their script.

- Have students follow the Before I Write checklist and take notes in their notebooks.

  Reaching All Students—Emergent Learners: Work with students in small groups. Guide them in following the steps in the checklist.

Write This!

Presentation

- Draw students' attention to the While I Write checklist. Call on volunteers to read aloud the points in the checklist.

- Explain and model on the board each of the writing points in this section while you write a sample script on the board. As you write, do a "think aloud" about how you are following the While I Write checklist.

Practice

- Have students write their scripts in their notebooks, using their notes and the While I Write checklist for help.

- Circulate while students are writing and encourage them to ask you for help with new words.

After You Write

Exercise A

- Draw students' attention to the After I Write checklist. Call on students to read aloud the points in the checklist.

- Have students use the After I Write checklist to evaluate their writing. Have them circle and then correct any errors.

Exercise B

Have students read their scripts to a classmate. Encourage them to make suggestions for improvement.

Exercise C

Have students write a final copy of their scripts in their notebooks.

Expansion

Have students work in small groups to practice reading the scripts they wrote.

Reaching All Students—Kinesthetic Learners: Have a few groups of students act out one or more of their scripts for the class.

Learning Log, page 123

See How to Use the Learning Log on page xiii.
(See Transparencies 20 and 71.)

Chapter 11
She needs some lettuce.

Objectives

Language:
- Listen to a dialogue for comprehension.
- Understand familiar vocabulary and grammar structures by listening to a dialogue.
- Develop new vocabulary and grammar structures by listening to a dialogue.
- Act out a dialogue.
- Use count and non-count nouns.
- Use *some* and *any* as adjectives.
- Use the coordinating conjunctions *and, but,* and *so.*
- Make original conversations using new vocabulary and grammar structures.
- Evaluate one's own learning of new vocabulary, grammar, and oral language.

Literacy:
- Read a dialogue for comprehension.
- Understand familiar vocabulary and grammar structures by reading a dialogue.
- Develop new vocabulary and grammar structures by reading a dialogue.
- Write sentences using new vocabulary.
- Complete sentences using count and non-count nouns.
- Complete and write sentences using *some* and *any* as adjectives.
- Decode words with the long vowel sound /ō/.
- Complete sentences with coordinating conjunctions *and, but,* and *so.*
- Read a short story for comprehension.
- Understand familiar vocabulary and grammar structures by reading a short story.
- Develop new vocabulary and grammar structures by reading a short story.
- Act out a short story.
- Plan, write, revise, edit, proofread, and make a final copy of a descriptive paragraph.
- Connect ideas with *and,* tell how many, and tell how often when writing about a favorite food.

- Evaluate one's own learning of reading skills, reading comprehension, and writing skills.

Learning Strategies:
- Use cooperation with a classmate to read a dialogue and study new vocabulary.
- Use cooperation with a small group to act out a dialogue.
- Use cooperation with a classmate to practice conversations.
- Use the strategy *Sound Out* to decode words.
- Use the strategy *Use Selective Attention* to understand a short story.
- Use cooperation with a classmate to check a paragraph one has written.
- Evaluate one's own learning of the strategies *Use Selective Attention* and *Sound Out.*
- Identify easy and difficult material in a chapter and the different ways to learn the difficult material.

Opening Dialogue, pages 124–125

Getting Ready

Preparation
- Remind students that keeping a picture dictionary is a good way to learn new words.
- Have students look at the Getting Ready section. Read the directions aloud as students follow along in their texts.
- Have students look at the illustrations in their texts. In their notebooks, have them draw simple pictures of the foods in the illustrations.
- Pointing to the foods in the illustrations one at a time, ask, "What's this?" or "What are these?" Provide help as needed. Write the responses on the board. Read them aloud, and have students repeat after you.

Listening and Reading

I'm So Hungry!

Presentation

Exercise A

- Read the directions and the prelistening question aloud as students follow along in their texts.

- Have students listen to the dialogue, or read the dialogue aloud to them. Have students look at the appropriate illustrations as they listen.

- Explain any vocabulary that students do not understand.

- Ask the prelistening question, "Does Mei's grandmother need any broccoli?" Call on a volunteer to respond. (No, she doesn't.)

Exercise B

Have students read the dialogue. Provide help with content, vocabulary, etc. as needed.

Reaching All Students—Emergent Learners: Work with emergent learners in small groups while the other students work independently. Read aloud as students follow along in their texts. Monitor their comprehension by interrupting the reading with questions such as, "Does Mei's grandmother need any broccoli?" (No, she doesn't.) "Does she need lettuce?" (Yes, she does.) "What else does she need?" (She needs a gallon of milk and a dozen eggs.). "Who is so hungry?" (Carmen is so hungry.) "What does Carmen eat?" (She eats crackers.) "How much does the food cost?" ($57.04.) "What do they have time to do?" (They have time to eat something.) "Why isn't Carmen hungry anymore?" (She ate crackers!)

Pair and Group Work

Practice

Exercise A

Have students who can read on their own form pairs. Have one student in the pair take the roles of Carmen and Maria; have the other student take the roles of Mei, Amy, and the cashier. Then have them read the dialogue aloud. Provide help, as needed.

Reaching All Students—Emergent Learners: Work in small groups with students who cannot read on their own.

Model each sentence and have individual students "echo" your reading. Make sure that students look at the sentences as you read them.

Exercise B

Have students form groups of five. Group students heterogeneously so that each group is made up of weak readers, average readers, and strong readers. Have each student choose a role in the dialogue. Have students practice acting out the dialogue in their groups.

Reaching All Students—Kinesthetic Learners: Choose one or more groups to act out the dialogue in front of the class.

Vocabulary

Practice

Exercise A

Have students read and say the words and expressions. Provide assistance with pronunciation as needed. Then have students write the words and expressions in their notebooks.

Exercise B (See Transparencies 85–87.)

- Have students turn to page 250 in their texts.

- Have students work through Steps 1–2 (recognizing letters and finding syllables) with the words in the box on page 125, if further practice is needed.

- Have students work in pairs on Step 3, identifying letters or letter combinations that follow patterns or make unexpected sounds. Encourage students to ask questions and to discover as much as they can on their own.

Exercise C

Have students find the words and expressions in the dialogue. Have them read the sentences aloud.

Exercise D

- Have each student choose five words from the words in the word box. Have them write five sentences in their notebooks, using these new words.

- Call on students to read their sentences to the class.

Answers
Answers will vary.

Expansion

Prepare index cards, each one listing one of the food items from the word box *(potato, carrot, lettuce, broccoli, milk, egg,* and *cracker)*. Hand out the cards to individual students. Have each student draw an illustration of his or her item on the board. Call on volunteers to guess the words illustrated.

Grammar 1, page 126

Count and Non-Count Nouns

Preparation

- Write the following dialogue on the board as a way of presenting the grammar focus in context.

  Mei: I'm thirsty! I need *a glass of lemonade.*
  Sophie: Let's go to Ricky's.
  Mei: Okay. Do you want some lemonade, too?
  Sophie: No, I want *a glass of milk.*
  Mei: Let's have some cookies, too.

- Read the dialogue aloud as students follow along. Then have the class read aloud with you.
- Call on two students to dramatize the dialogue for the rest of the class.

Presentation

- Have students look at the grammar charts.
- Call on a student to read aloud the information at the top of the first chart. Then call on a pair of students to read across each example in the chart. Have students note the use of *a, an,* and numerals before count nouns.
- Call on a student to read aloud the information at the top of the second chart. Then call on a pair of students to read across each example in the chart. Have students note the use of expressions of measure before non-count nouns. Last, have a student read the Remember note.

Practice
Exercise A

- Have students create two columns in their notebooks—*Count Nouns* and *Non-Count Nouns.*
- Call on a student to read aloud the first example and explain why it is correct. Have the student refer to the grammar chart if necessary.

- Have students write the nouns from the box in the correct columns in their notebooks.

  Reaching All Students—Auditory Learners: Call on a student to read each of the nouns in the box aloud before students write their responses.
  Reaching All Students—Emergent/ Cooperative Learners: Have students work in pairs. Provide help as needed.
  Reaching All Students—Advanced Learners: In addition to completing the chart, have students write a sentence for each noun. Write a sample sentence on the board.

- Review the answers with the class.

Answers

Count Nouns	Non-Count Nouns
potato	milk
onion	bread
carrot	lettuce
cookie	cheese
apple	rice

Optional Activity: For non-count nouns, review possible expressions of measure to go with them. Have students write the non-count nouns with these expressions.

Answers
Answers will vary. Possible answers:

Non-Count Nouns
a piece of lettuce
a slice of cheese, a pound of cheese
a cup of milk, a gallon of milk
a slice of bread, a piece of bread
a cup of rice, a pound of rice

Optional Activity: Give each student an index card. Ask half the class to write a count noun (in the singular or plural form) on their card; ask the other half to write a non-count noun. Collect the cards. Then shuffle and redistribute them. Have students, in turn, state whether their noun is a count or non-count noun. If it is a count noun, have them say it again with a numeral. If it is a non-count noun, have them say it again with an expression of measure.

  Reaching All Students—Advanced Learners: Have students use the noun on their card in a sentence.

Exercise B

- Have students look at the illustration. Ask them what the boy is doing. (He is making lunch.) Have students repeat.
- Tell students that they need to complete the paragraph about the boy's lunch with the names of the food items and drinks from the grammar charts. Tell them to use the illustration for help in choosing the words.
- Have students copy the paragraph into their notebooks. Then have them complete the paragraph by filling in the blanks with the names of the food items or drinks.

  Reaching All Students—Emergent Learners: First, have students name the food items and drinks in the illustration. Then have them complete the exercise orally. Last, have them copy the paragraph into their notebooks and fill in the blanks with words from the grammar charts. Provide help as needed.

- Review the answers with the class.

Answers		
bread	carrot	milk
cheese	crackers	

Expansion

- Tell students they will write their own paragraphs about making lunch, using their own information about what they like to eat.
- Refer students to page 222 of the Vocabulary Handbook for the names of additional food items and drinks.
- As a class, brainstorm the names of food items and drinks students could use in their paragraphs. Have students specify the number for count nouns (*an apple*) and the expression of measure for non-count nouns (*a piece of cheese*). Write students' responses on the board. Read the phrases, and have students repeat after you.
- Model writing a sample paragraph on the board. Use the paragraph in Exercise B as a model. (I am making my lunch. I need two slices of bread and a piece of beef for a sandwich. I also want to eat an apple and four cookies. I also need a glass of lemonade. What a good lunch!)
- Have students write their paragraphs in their notebooks.

Reaching All Students—Emergent Learners: Work with students in small groups to complete the activity.

- Have students work in pairs. Have them read their paragraphs to each other.

  Reaching All Students—Auditory Learners: Have several students read their paragraphs aloud for the rest of the class.

Grammar 2, page 127

Some and any

Preparation

- Write the following dialogue on the board as a way of presenting the grammar focus in context.

  Maria: We *don't* have *any* apples.
  Mother: You're right. Let's buy *some* apples. We need *some* lettuce, too.

- Read the dialogue aloud as students follow along. Then have the class read aloud with you.
- Call on two students to dramatize the dialogue for the rest of the class.

Presentation

- Have students look at the grammar chart.
- Call on an individual student to read aloud across both rows in the chart, using the word or words in each column.
- Have another student read aloud the Remember note at the bottom of the chart.

Practice

Exercise A

- Call on a volunteer to read the first item with the sample answers. Ask the student to explain why the answers are correct. (The first sentence is affirmative; therefore, you use *some*. The second sentence is negative; therefore, you use *any*.)
- Have students copy the sentences into their notebooks and fill in the blanks with *some* or *any*.

  Reaching All Students—Emergent Learners: First, have students do the exercise orally. Then have them copy the sentences into their notebooks. Last, have them complete the sentences. Provide help as needed.

- Review the answers with the class.

Exercise B

- Have students look at Maria's handwritten shopping list. Call on a student to read aloud the items on the list.
- Tell students that they will read questions about Maria's shopping list. They will need to write the answers to those questions.
- Call on a student to read the first question and the sample answer. Have the student explain why the answer is correct. (*Potatoes* is not on Maria's shopping list. The statement is negative; therefore, you use *any* in the answer.)
- Follow the same procedure for the second sample answer. (*Crackers* is on Maria's list. The statement is positive; therefore, you use *some* in the answer.)
- Have students number a sheet of paper in their notebooks from 1 to 5. Then have them write the answers to the questions.

  Reaching All Students—Emergent Learners: Have students work in pairs or small groups. Provide help as needed.

- Review the answers with the class.

Word Study, page 128

Long Vowel Sound: /ō/

Preparation

- Write the words *go*, *Joe*, *those*, *coat*, and *know* on the board.
- Call on volunteers to identify the names of the consonants and vowels in the words.

- Pronounce the words and have students repeat them after you.

Presentation

- Explain to students that they are going to study the five most common spellings for the long vowel sound /ō/: *o*, *oe*, *o_e*, *oa*, and *ow*.
- Begin by reviewing the spelling *o*.
- Point to the word *go* on the board. Say the word. Then call on a volunteer to say the first sound (/g/) and then the second sound (/ō/).
- Ask students, "How many sounds does the word have?" (Two.) "How many letters does the word have?" (Two.)
- Follow the same procedure for the words *Joe*, *those*, *coat*, and *know*.
- Have students look at the instruction box. Read the sentence aloud as students follow along.

Practice
Exercise A

Have students use the learning strategy *Sound Out*, as well as the pictures, to read the words with the long vowel sound /ō/.

> **Reaching All Students—Emergent Learners:** Complete this activity as a class. After students have an approximation of the pronunciation, say the words correctly to provide a model. Have students repeat after you.

Exercise B

- First, have students read the sentences aloud. Then have them copy the sentences into their notebooks. Last, have them circle the letters that stand for the long vowel sound /ō/.
- Review the answers as a class. Point out that items 1, 2, and 3 each have two words with the long vowel sound /ō/.

Optional Activity: Have students close their texts. Ask them to number a page in their notebooks from 1 to 8. Then ask them to listen carefully to the words you read and to write the words. Then dictate the following words:

1. window   5. cold
2. toe   6. hose
3. yellow   7. oak
4. toast   8. stove

- After the dictation, write the words on the board. Then have students check their words.

- Have students record the number of correct words in their notebooks; for example, *I wrote (7) out of 8 dictated words with the long vowel sound /ō/ correctly*. Write this example on the board as a model.

Exercise C

- Have students skim the dialogue on pages 124–125 in their texts, looking for words with the long vowel sound /ō/. Remind students to look for the spellings they learned: *o, oe, o_e, oa,* and *ow*. Then have them write the four words in their notebooks.

Answers

Answers will vary. Possible answers include:

Okay   don't
so   total
potatoes   Pablo
Oh   o'clock
almost   go

Optional Activity: On a sheet of paper in their notebooks, have students head columns with the spellings for the long vowel sound /ō/: *o, oe, o_e, oa,* and *ow.* Then have them write as many words as they can that have the long vowel sound /ō/. (Set a time limit of 5–10 minutes.) Encourage students to use a dictionary, the text, or their vocabulary lists for help.

Reaching All Students—Auditory Learners: Encourage students to say the words aloud as they write them.

Have students share their lists with the class.

Grammar 3, page 129

Conjunctions: *and, but,* and *so*

Preparation

- Write the following dialogue on the board as a way of presenting the grammar focus in context.

> **Mei:** We're thirsty, *so* we want to go to Ricky's.
> **Sophie:** I want a glass of milk, *and* Mei wants a glass of lemonade.
> **Mei:** We're going to have some cookies, too.
> **Carmen:** I want some lemonade, *but* I don't want any cookies.

- Read the dialogue aloud as students follow along. Then have the class read aloud with you.

- Call on three students to dramatize the dialogue for the rest of the class.

Presentation

- Have students look at the grammar chart. Call on individual students to read aloud across each of the three rows of the chart, using the words in the columns.

- Call on a student to read aloud the Remember note at the bottom of the chart. Write on the board:
  and = 2 similar ideas
  but = 2 different ideas
  so = one idea comes from another idea

- Tell students that they can test whether *so* is appropriate in a sentence by deleting the word *so* and using *Because* before the first clause. Write the example from the chart on the board as an example:
  Mei is hungry, so she's eating some cookies.
  Because Mei is hungry, she's eating some cookies.

Practice

Exercise A

- Call on a volunteer to read the first sentence with the sample answer. Have the student explain why the answer is correct. (The two ideas are similar. Therefore, you use *and* to connect them.)

- Have students copy the sentences into their notebooks. Then have them fill in the blanks with *and, but,* or *so.*

Reaching All Students—Emergent Learners: First, have students do the exercise orally. Then have them copy the sentences into their notebooks. Last, have them complete the sentences with *and, but,* or *so*. Provide help as needed.

- Review the answers with the class.

Answers
1. and   3. so   5. so
2. but   4. but

Exercise B

 Have students listen to the conversation, or read it aloud with an advanced student.

Reaching All Students—Kinesthetic Learners: Act out the conversation with an advanced student, or call on volunteers to act out the conversation.

Practice
Exercise C

- Tell students that for this exercise they will first practice the conversation in Exercise B. Then they will make their own conversations.

- Have students work in pairs. Have each pair first practice the conversation in Exercise B.

- Next, refer students to page 222 in the Vocabulary Handbook for the names of other food items and drinks they might include in their own conversations.

- Then, as a class, brainstorm the names of food items and drinks students might use in their own conversations. Write them on the board. Be sure to teach or elicit the word *vegetables* as a substitute for *fruit* in the conversation.

- Have two advanced students model their conversation.

- Have pairs practice their conversations.

  Reaching All Students—Kinesthetic Learners: Call on volunteer pairs to act out their conversations.

Reading, pages 130–131

Before You Read

Presentation

- Have students look at the Before You Read section. Read the text aloud as students follow along.

- Review that *Use Selective Attention* can help them find information they need. To use the strategy, they need to look for key ideas and words as they read.

Practice

Ask students to brainstorm a list of ideas or words that could answer the question. Write students' responses on the board. Read them aloud, and have students repeat them after you.

Read This!

At Ricky's

Preparation

Note: Students will encounter the following new words in the reading: *French fries, hamburger, salad, soda, water, customer, counter, everything, glass, line, moment, decide, order, share, think (thought), enough, cashier, hurry up, cup.*

Practice

- Have students listen to the story, or read it aloud to them. Provide help with content, vocabulary, etc. as needed. Remind students to use *Use Selective Attention* to answer the questions.

  Reaching All Students—Emergent Learners: Work with emergent learners in small groups while the other students work independently. Read aloud as students follow along in their texts. Monitor their comprehension by interrupting the reading with questions such as, "Who works at Ricky's?" (Paco works at Ricky's.) "Who didn't have enough money for fries?" (Mei didn't have enough money for fries.) "Who is behind Carmen?" (Other customers are behind Carmen.) "Why did Carmen only order a glass of water?" (She wasn't hungry.) "It's almost six o'clock. Where does everyone have to go?" (Everyone has to go to the fountain.)

- Encourage students to answer the questions using complete sentences.

After You Read

Self-Evaluation
Exercise A
- Read the directions aloud as students follow along in their texts.
- Write the Before You Read question on the board. ("Who works at Ricky's?") Read it aloud as students follow along.
- Call on a volunteer to tell if he or she used *Use Selective Attention* to find the answer to the question. Then ask the student to read the key idea from the story that helps to answer the question. ("Yes, I know," said Maria. "Paco works here.") Have the student write the answer on the board. *(Paco works at Ricky's.)*
- Have students copy the answer into their notebooks.

Exercise B
- Read the directions aloud as students follow along in their texts. Assign four advanced students the roles of Mei, Maria, Carmen, and Paco. Have them act out the first part of the story for the rest of the class. (Note: The first part begins on page 130 and ends with the next-to-last line on page 130.) Encourage students to use appropriate facial expressions and gestures as they act out the story.
- Have students form groups of five. Have each student in a group choose a role in the story: Mei, Maria, Carmen, Paco, or Carlos. Have students act out the story in their groups.
  > **Reaching All Students—Kinesthetic Learners:** Choose one or more groups to act out the dialogue in front of the class.

Exercise C
- Have students number a sheet of paper in their notebooks from 1 to 4.
- Read the first question aloud. Call on a volunteer to answer. Write the answer on the board.
  > **Reaching All Students—Auditory Learners:** Call on advanced students to read the remaining questions before students write their answers.

- Have students write their answers in their notebooks. Encourage students to answer the questions with complete sentences.
  > **Reaching All Students—Emergent Learners:** Have students work in pairs, or work with them in small groups, to complete the exercise.
- Call on students to give their answers and write them on the board.
- Have students count the number of correct answers and write that number in their notebooks.

> **Answers**
> 1. He's a cashier.
> 2. She ordered a hamburger, French fries, and a soda.
> 3. She didn't have enough money.
> 4. She wasn't hungry.

Expansion

Call on volunteers to tell how they have been applying the strategy *Use Selective Attention* in their other classes. Write their responses on the board. Review them with the rest of the class.

Writing, page 132

Before You Write

Preparation *(See Transparencies 17 and 46–47.)*

Explain to students that they are going to write a paragraph about a favorite food.

Practice
Exercise A
- Focus students' attention on the handwritten paragraph.
  > **Reaching All Students—Auditory Learners:** Call on an advanced student to read the paragraph aloud as the other students follow along in their texts.
- Ask students what kind of information is included in the sample paragraph. (Name of the favorite food, where the student eats it, when the student eats it, and how the food is cooked or eaten.) Write students' responses on the board. Read them aloud as students follow along.

Presentation

Exercise B

- Draw students' attention to the Before I Write checklist. Call on an advanced student to read aloud the points in the checklist.

- Refer students to page 222 in the Vocabulary Handbook for the names of different types of foods they could write about.

- Call on volunteers to name some of their favorite foods. Write these names on the board. As a class, brainstorm the names of other foods and related vocabulary they could include in their paragraphs. Write these names and words on the board.

- Have students look at the word map. As a class, work through another example of making a word map. Draw the word map on the board.

- Have students follow the Before I Write checklist and draw a word map in their notebooks.

    Reaching All Students—Emergent Learners: Work with students in small groups. Guide them in drawing a word map.

Write This!

Presentation

- Draw students' attention to the While I Write checklist. Call on volunteers to read aloud the points in the checklist.

- Explain and model on the board each of the writing points in this section while you write a paragraph about your favorite food. As you write, do a "think aloud" about how you are following the While I Write checklist.

Practice

- Have students write their paragraphs in their notebooks, using their word maps and the While I Write checklist for help.

- Circulate while students are writing and encourage them to ask you for help with new words.

After You Write

Exercise A

- Draw students' attention to the After I Write checklist. Call on students to read aloud the points in the checklist.

- Have students use the After I Write checklist to evaluate their writing. Have them circle and then correct any errors.

Exercise B

Have students read their paragraphs to a classmate. Encourage them to make suggestions for improvement.

Exercise C

Have students write a final copy of their paragraphs in their notebooks.

Expansion

Reaching All Students—Kinesthetic Learners: Have a few students read their paragraphs for the rest of the class.

Learning Log, page 133

See How to Use the Learning Log on page xiii.
(See Transparencies 20 and 72.)

Chapter 12
He's the cutest guy at school.

Objectives

Language:

- Listen to a dialogue for comprehension.
- Understand familiar vocabulary and grammar structures by listening to a dialogue.
- Develop new vocabulary and grammar structures by listening to a dialogue.
- Act out a dialogue.
- Use the comparative and superlative forms of adjectives.
- Make original conversations using new vocabulary and grammar structures.
- Evaluate one's own learning of new vocabulary, grammar, and oral language.

Literacy:

- Read a dialogue for comprehension.
- Understand familiar vocabulary and grammar structures by reading a dialogue.
- Develop new vocabulary and grammar structures by reading a dialogue.
- Complete sentences with the comparative and superlative forms of adjectives.
- Decode words with the long vowel sound /yoo/.
- Read a short story for comprehension.
- Understand familiar vocabulary and grammar structures by reading a short story.
- Develop new vocabulary and grammar structures by reading a short story.
- Plan, write, revise, edit, proofread, and make a final copy of lyrics for a song.
- Use the comparative and superlative forms of adjectives, rhyme, repetition, and feeling words when writing lyrics for a song.
- Evaluate one's own learning of reading skills, reading comprehension, and writing skills.

Learning Strategies:

- Use cooperation with a classmate to read a dialogue and study new vocabulary.
- Use cooperation with a classmate to practice conversations.

- Use the strategy *Sound Out* to decode words.
- Use the strategy *Use What You Know* to understand a short story.
- Use cooperation with a classmate to check a song one has written.
- Evaluate one's own learning of the strategies *Use What You Know* and *Sound Out*.
- Identify easy and difficult material in a chapter and the different ways to learn the difficult material.

Opening Dialogue, pages 134–135

Getting Ready

Preparation *(See Transparency 17.)*

- Have students look at the illustrations and identify words for the items in the illustrations. (Examples: music store, CDs, store window, jeans, T-shirts.) Write the names of the items on the board or a poster. Read the words, one at a time, and have students repeat each one after you.
- Ask students to make sentences about what they see and what the characters are doing. (Examples: Those are CDs. Liliana and Sophie are shopping.) Write students' responses on the board. If needed, model complete sentences. Read the sentences and have students repeat them after you.

   Reaching All Students—Emergent Learners: Point to each character, one at a time, and ask what the character is doing. Have students repeat. Call on students to respond. If needed, model the response. Have students repeat.

Listening and Reading

I Love R&B!

Presentation

Exercise A

- Read the directions and the prelistening question aloud as students follow along in their texts.
- 🎧 Have students listen to the dialogue, or read the dialogue aloud to them. Have

students look at the appropriate illustrations as they listen.

- Explain any vocabulary that students do not understand.
- Ask the prelistening question, "How much money does Sophie want to borrow?" Call on a volunteer to respond. (She wants to borrow three dollars.)

Exercise B

Have students read the dialogue. Provide help with content, vocabulary, etc. as needed.

Reaching All Students—Emergent Learners: Work with emergent learners in small groups while the other students work independently. Read aloud as students follow along in their texts. Monitor their comprehension by interrupting the reading with questions such as, "What kind of music do both Sophie and Liliana like?" (R&B.) "Who likes rock music?" (Paco does.) "Is Paco older than Sophie and Liliana?" (Yes, he is.) "What kind of guys does Sophie like?" (She likes guys her own age. *or* She likes younger guys.) "What does Sophie want to buy?" (She wants to buy a Beyoncé CD.) "Does she have enough money?" (No, she doesn't.) "Does Liliana really want to buy the rock CD?" (No, she doesn't.) "How much money does Liliana give Sophie?" (She gives her three dollars.)

 Pair and Group Work

Practice

Have students who can read on their own form pairs. Have one student in the pair take the role of Sophie; have the other student take the role of Liliana. Then have them read the dialogue aloud. Provide help as needed.

Reaching All Students—Emergent Learners: Work in small groups with students who cannot read on their own. Model each sentence and have individual students "echo" your reading. Make sure that students look at the sentences as you read them.

Reaching All Students—Kinesthetic Learners: Choose one or more pairs to act out the dialogue in front of the class.

Vocabulary

Practice

Exercise A

Have students read and say the words and expressions. Provide assistance with pronunciation as needed. Then have students copy the words and expressions into their notebooks.

Reaching All Students—Auditory Learners: Encourage students to say the words and expressions as they write them in their notebooks.

Exercise B (See Transparencies 85–87.)

- Have students turn to page 250 in their texts.
- Have students work through Steps 1–2 (recognizing letters and finding syllables) with the words in the box on page 135 if further practice is needed.
- Have students work in pairs on Step 3, identifying letters or letter combinations that follow patterns or make unexpected sounds. Encourage students to ask questions and to discover as much as they can on their own.

Exercise C

Have students find the words and expressions in the dialogue. Have them read the sentences aloud.

Optional Activity: Call on a volunteer to read the first sentence aloud. Then, to check the student's understanding of the word or expression, ask the student to substitute a synonym, or equivalent word or expression, for the vocabulary word in the sentence. Have the student say the sentence with the synonym aloud for the rest of the class. Continue the procedure for the other words and expressions.

Exercise D

- Pair students and have them decide which classmate will go first.
- Tell students that, without speaking, the first student will choose five words from the word box and draw pictures of the words. The second student will look at the pictures and guess the words. Then the students will reverse roles.

Reaching All Students—Emergent Learners: Have two advanced students model doing the exercise.

- Have students take turns drawing and guessing the words. Circulate to answer any questions about the words.
- Have students write five sentences in their notebooks, using each of these new words. Call on students to read their sentences to the class.

Grammar 1, page 136

Comparative Adjectives

Preparation

- Write the following dialogue on the board as a way of presenting the grammar focus in context.
  Carolina: How old are you, Paco?
      Paco: I'm nineteen.
  Carolina: You're *older than* Sophie.
- Read the dialogue aloud as students follow along. Then have the class read aloud with you.
- Call on two students to dramatize the dialogue for the rest of the class.

Presentation

- Have students look at the first grammar chart. Read the explanation and the examples aloud as students follow along.
- Call on a volunteer to describe two students in the class, using the expression *taller than*. Follow the same procedure for the expression *shorter than*.
- Have students look at the second grammar chart. Read the explanations and examples aloud as students follow along.
- Write the words *loud, large,* and *hungry* on the board. Call on volunteers to tell you how to form the comparative of each adjective. Write the adjectives and their comparative forms on the board.

Practice

Exercise A

- Call on a volunteer to read aloud the first adjective and sample answer. Have the student explain why the answer is correct. (You add -er to *long* to form the comparative.)
- Have students copy the six adjectives into their notebooks and write the comparative form for each.

Reaching All Students—Emergent Learners: Have students work in pairs. Provide help as needed.
- Review the answers with the class.

Answers	
1. longer	**4.** later
2. easier	**5.** earlier
3. harder	**6.** funnier

Exercise B

- Tell students that for this exercise they will complete sentences comparing Luis and Sam and then the cat and the dog.
- Call on a student to read aloud the first example with the sample answer and explain why it is correct. (You add -er to *young* to form the comparative.)
- Have students copy the six sentences into their notebooks and write the comparative form of each adjective in the blank.

  Reaching All Students—Emergent Learners: First, have students do the exercise orally. Then have them copy the sentences into their notebooks. Last, have them complete the sentences. Provide help as needed.
- Review the answers with the class.

Answers	
1. younger	**4.** smaller
2. older	**5.** larger
3. shorter	**6.** cuter

Grammar 2, page 137

Superlative Adjectives

Preparation

- Write the following dialogue on the board as a way of presenting the grammar focus in context.
      Bic: Hey, Carlos! I'm taller than you.
  Carlos: I see.
   Pablo: But I'm *the tallest!*
- Read the dialogue aloud as students follow along. Then have the class read aloud with you.
- Call on two students to dramatize the dialogue for the rest of the class.

Presentation

- Have students look at the first grammar chart. Read the explanation and the examples aloud as students follow along.
- Call on a volunteer to describe a student in the class, using the expression *the tallest.* Follow the same procedure for the expression *the shortest.*
- Have students look at the second grammar chart. Read the explanations and the examples aloud as students follow along.
- Write the words *great, cute,* and *silly* on the board. Call on volunteers to tell you how to form the superlative for each adjective. Write the adjectives and their superlative forms on the board.

Practice

Exercise A

- Call on a volunteer to read aloud the first adjective and sample answer. Have the student explain why the answer is correct. (You change the *y* to an *i* and add *-est* to form the superlative.)
- Have students copy the six adjectives into their notebooks and write the superlative form for each.

   Reaching All Students—Emergent Learners: Have students work in pairs. Provide help as needed.

- Review the answers with the class.

Answers	
1. easiest	4. oldest
2. hardest	5. largest
3. youngest	6. dirtiest

Exercise B

- Tell students that for this exercise they will complete sentences comparing Yolanda's, Trish's, and Betty's hair in the first set of pictures and then their hats in the second set of pictures. Tell students that they will need to choose the comparative form (*-er*) to compare two girls and the superlative form (*-est*) to compare all three girls.
- Call on a student to read aloud the first example with the sample answer and explain why it is correct. (You choose the superlative form (*-est*) because the sentence is comparing all three girls.)

- Have students copy the six sentences into their notebooks and write the correct form of each adjective in the blank.

   Reaching All Students—Emergent Learners: First, have students do the exercise orally. Then have them copy the sentences into their notebooks. Last, have them complete the sentences. Provide help as needed.

- Review the answers with the class.

Answers	
1. longest	4. funniest
2. shortest	5. prettier
3. longer	6. smaller

Expansion

- Prepare index cards, one for each student in the class. On each card, write one short adjective students have learned in class. (Examples: *small, large, tall, long, short, late, early, easy, hard, funny, silly, cute, old, new, young, dirty, hungry, pretty, busy, great, loud, dark, happy, angry, nice, lucky, smart.*)
- Hand out the cards to the students.
- Tell students that they will compete against each other in teams to make the comparative and superlative forms of adjectives. The first team that finishes making the comparative and superlative forms correctly is the winner.
- Divide the class into two teams. Have each team stand on one side of the room facing the board.
- Have the first student on each team come to the board and write his or her adjective and then the comparative and superlative forms of the adjective. Encourage the students to write their answers quickly. When each student has finished writing the three forms on the board correctly, have the student "tag" the next person in line. The tagged student then goes to the front and writes his or her adjective and its comparative and superlative forms on the board. The competition continues in this way.
- The first team to complete writing the adjectives and their comparative and superlative forms correctly is the winner.

Word Study, page 138

Long Vowel Sound: /yōō/

Preparation

- Write the words *use, unit,* and *few* on the board.
- Call on volunteers to identify the names of the consonants and vowels in the words.
- Pronounce the words and have students repeat them after you.

Presentation

- Explain to students that they are going to study the three most common spellings for the long vowel sound /yōō/: *u_e, u,* and *ew*.
- Begin by reviewing the spelling *u_e*.
- Point to the word *use* on the board. Say the word. Then call on a volunteer to say the first sound (/yōō/) and the second sound (/z/).
- Ask students, "How many sounds does the word have?" (Two.) "How many letters does the word have?" (Three.)
- To help students understand why the word has three letters but only two sounds, underline the vowel *e* in the word. Point out that the *e* does not represent a sound in the word *use*. Instead, it acts as a marker or signal that the vowel before it probably stands for a long vowel sound—in this case, the sound /yōō/. Write on the board *u_e*.
- Follow the same procedure for the words *unit* and *few*.
- Have students look at the instruction box. Read the sentence aloud as students follow along.

Practice

Exercise A

Have students use the learning strategy *Sound Out*, as well as the pictures, to read the words with long vowel sound /yōō/.

> **Reaching All Students—Emergent Learners:** Complete this activity as a class. After students have an approximation of the pronunciation, say the words correctly to provide a model.

Exercise B

- First, have students read the sentences aloud. Then have them copy the sentences into their notebooks. Last, have them circle the letters that stand for the long vowel sound /yōō/.
- Review the answers as a class.

Answers
1. I want a f(ew) slices of cheese.
2. Does Mei have a men(u)?
3. She is a very c(u)t(e) baby.
4. I like to listen to m(u)sic.
5. Put an ice c(u)b(e) in his soda.
6. That ship is h(u)g(e)!

Optional Activity: Have students close their texts. Ask them to number a page in their notebooks from 1 to 8. Then ask them to listen carefully to the words you read and to write the words. Then dictate the following words:

1. huge	4. music	7. uniform
2. few	5. cute	8. January
3. cube	6. menu	

- After the dictation, write the words on the board. Then have students check their words.
- Have students record the number of correct words in their notebooks; for example, *I wrote (7) out of 8 dictated words with the long vowel sound /yōō/ correctly.* Write this example on the board as a model.

Exercise C

- Have students look at Exercise A. Have them choose three words with the long vowel sound /yōō/. Have them write a sentence for each word in their notebooks.

> **Reaching All Students—Emergent Learners:** Review the meanings of the words in Exercise A. Call on a volunteer to model a sample sentence on the board.

- Have students share their sentences with the class.

Answers
Answers will vary.

Optional Activity: On a sheet of paper in their notebooks, have students head columns with the spellings for the long vowel sound /yōō/: *u_e, u,* and *ew*. Then have them write as many words as they can that have the long vowel sound /yōō/. (Set a time limit of 5–10 minutes.) Encourage students to use a dictionary, the text, or their vocabulary lists for help.

Reaching All Students—Auditory Learners: Encourage students to say the words aloud as they write them.

Have students share their lists with the class.

Grammar 3, page 139

Comparatives and Superlatives with *more* and *most*

Preparation

- Write the following dialogue on the board as a way of presenting the grammar focus in context.

  Sophie: Why does Paco think rock music is *more interesting* than R&B?

  Liliana: I don't know. I think R&B is the *most interesting* music of all!

- Read the dialogue aloud as students follow along. Then have the class read aloud with you.
- Call on two students to dramatize the dialogue for the rest of the class.

Presentation

- Have students look at the grammar chart.
- Call on volunteers to read the example sentences. Then call on another volunteer to read the Remember note.
- Point out that the first column of the chart shows the adjective, the second column shows the comparative form, and the third column shows the superlative form. Explain any new words in the chart.
- Have three students read aloud across each row in the chart. Have the first student read the adjective, the second student read the comparative form, and the third student read the superlative form.

Practice

Exercise A

- Have students look at the illustration. Then tell students that they will write *True* for each true statement about the illustration and *False* for each false statement about the illustration. They will also correct each false statement.

- Read the first item aloud, "Betty's hat is the most beautiful." Ask, "Is that statement true or false?" Call on a student to read the sample answer. (False. Trish's hat is the most beautiful.) Ask the student why the answer is correct. (In the illustration, Trish's hat is the most beautiful of the three hats.)

  Reaching All Students—Auditory Learners: Call on advanced students to read the remaining sentences before students complete the activity.

- Have students number a sheet of paper in their notebooks from 1 to 5. Then have them write the answers.
- Review the answers with the class.

Answers

1. False. Trish's hat is the most beautiful.
2. True
3. True
4. False. Betty's hat is more casual than Trish's hat.
5. False. Trish's hat is the most formal.

Exercise B

Have students listen to the conversation, or read it aloud with an advanced student as the other students follow along in their texts.

Reaching All Students—Kinesthetic Learners: Act out the dialogue with an advanced student, or call on volunteers to act out the dialogue.

Exercise C

- Tell students that for this exercise they will first practice the conversation in Exercise B. Then they will make their own conversations.
- Have students work in pairs. Have each pair first practice the conversation in Exercise B.
- Then, as a class, brainstorm other items students might use in their own conversations. (Examples: shirt, sweater, jeans, pants, jacket, dress, skirt, shoes, belt, cap.) Write the names of the items on the board.
- Have two advanced students model their conversation.
- Have pairs practice their conversations.

  Reaching All Students—Kinesthetic Learners: Call on volunteer pairs to act out their conversations.

Expansion

- Bring in a few teen fashion magazines.
- Have students work in groups of three to make a poster comparing three outfits. Have them cut the three outfits from the magazines and paste them onto the poster. Then have them write three sentences describing the outfits, using an adjective, its comparative form, and its superlative form from the grammar chart. (Example: This red dress is *expensive*. This green dress is *more expensive* than the red dress. This blue dress is the *most expensive* dress of all.)
- Have each group share its poster with the class, and have each student in a group read one of the sentences.

Reading, pages 140–141

Before You Read

Preparation *(See Transparency 20.)*

- Tell students that they will use the learning strategy *Use What You Know* to understand the story.
- Ask students what they remember about this strategy. Write their responses on the board. (When we read, we can use what we already know about people and places to help us understand the story better.)

Practice

- Have students look at the Before You Read section. Read the first item aloud and call on a volunteer to answer the question. (The story is about Pablo.)
- Read the second item aloud and have students work in pairs to discuss what they already know about Pablo.
- Call on volunteers to share their responses with the class. Write students' responses on the board. (Examples: Pablo plays the guitar. He also writes and sings his own songs.)
- Read the third item aloud as students follow along in their texts.

Read This!

Pablo's Surprise

Preparation

Note: Students will encounter the following new words in the reading: *audience, author, people,*

performer, singer, storyteller, darkness, fireflies, kitten, hand, poem, stage, blink, clap (clapped), yell (yelled), good job.

Practice

- 🎧 Have students listen to the story, or read it aloud to them. Provide help with content, vocabulary, etc. as needed.
- Encourage students to use the strategy *Use What You Know* to help them understand the story.

   Reaching All Students—Emergent Learners: Work with emergent learners in small groups while the other students work independently. Read aloud as students follow along in their texts. Monitor their comprehension by interrupting the reading with questions such as, "What did the friends see in front of the fountain?" (They saw a stage and a lot of people.) "Who was the first performer?" (Sally Miller was the first performer.) "How did Sally look?" (She looked nervous.) "What is Pablo's big secret?" (He's a performer. *or* He's a singer.) "What was the love song about?" (It was about a beautiful girl.) "Who is the author of the poem?" (Jorge Elías Luján is the author of the poem.) "Did people like Pablo's songs and poem?" (Yes, they did.) "What does Carmen want to do?" (She wants to get something to eat.) Encourage students to answer the questions using complete sentences.

After You Read

Self-Evaluation

Exercise A *(See Transparency 20.)*

Refer students to After You Read. Read the first two questions aloud and call on volunteers to answer. Read the third question aloud and have students write their responses in their notebooks. Then call on individual students to give their responses.

> **Answers**
> *Answers will vary. Possible answers:*
> Pablo is a performer. He can sing funny and love songs very well. He likes poems. Everyone liked his songs and poem. Pablo is a good performer.

Exercise B

- Have students number a sheet of paper in their notebooks from 1 to 5.
- Tell students that they will write *True* for true statements and *False* for false statements. They will also correct the false statements.
- Call on a student to read the first item aloud. Call on another student to tell whether the statement is true or false. (False.) Have the student correct the sentence. (Pablo's friends were a little late for the show.) Ask the student to explain where in the story this information is found. (First and third sentences: "The friends arrived at the fountain at ten minutes after six o'clock." 'We're a little late,' said Mei.")

   Reaching All Students—Auditory Learners: Call on advanced students to read the remaining statements aloud before students complete the activity.
- Have students write their answers in their notebooks.
- Call on students to write their corrected sentences on the board and read them aloud.
- Have students count the number of correct answers and write that number in their notebooks.

Answers
1. False. Pablo's friends were a little late for the show.
2. True
3. True
4. False. Pablo's friends thought Pablo's song was funnier than Sally Miller's story.
5. False. Sophie thought Pablo's second song was the prettiest.

Expansion

Ask students to explain how they have been applying the strategy *Use What You Know* in their other classes. Write their responses on the board.

Writing, page 142

Before You Write

Preparation *(See Transparencies 48–49.)*
Tell students that they are going to write a song.

Exercise A

- Focus students' attention on the handwritten song.

   Reaching All Students—Auditory Learners: Call on a student to read the song aloud as the other students follow along in their texts.
- Ask students to tell what kind of song it is. (A love song.) Write *rhyme* and *repetition* on the board. Tell them that songs often have words that rhyme, or sound similar, at the end of lines. Point out that *brightest* and *lightest* rhyme. Ask students to find the word that rhymes with *are. (Far.)* Tell students that poems also have *repetition,* or lines that are repeated several times. Ask them to find the line that is repeated. *(Wherever you are.)*

Presentation
Exercise B

- Draw students' attention to the Before I Write checklist. Call on students to read aloud the points in the checklist.
- Refer students to page 223 of the Vocabulary Handbook for adjectives they might use in their songs.
- As a class, brainstorm "feeling words" students could include in their own songs. Write students' responses on the board. (Examples: *excited, wonderful, sad, shy*.)
- Model following the steps in the Before I Write checklist. Write your notes on the board.
- Have students follow the Before I Write checklist and make notes in their notebooks.

   Reaching All Students—Emergent Learners: Work with students in small groups. Guide them in following the steps in the checklist.

Write This!

Presentation

- Draw students' attention to the While I Write checklist. Call on students to read aloud the points in the checklist.
- Model following the While I Write checklist. Refer to the notes you took in your earlier modeling. As you write, do a "think aloud" about how you are following the While I Write checklist.

Practice

- Have students write their songs in their notebooks, using their notes and the While I Write checklist for help.
- Circulate while students are writing and encourage them to ask you for help if needed.

After You Write

Exercise A

- Draw students' attention to the After I Write checklist. Call on students to read aloud the points in the checklist.
- Have students use the After I Write checklist to evaluate their writing. Have them circle and then correct any errors.

Exercise B

Have students read their songs to a classmate. Encourage them to make suggestions for improvement.

Exercise C

Have students write a final copy of the song in their notebooks.

Expansion

- Call on volunteers read their song lyrics for the rest of the class.
- Encourage musically inclined students to create tunes to go with their songs and to present them to the class at a later date when ready.

Learning Log, page 143

See How to Use the Learning Log on page xiii.
(See Transparencies 20 and 73.)

UNIT 5 FRIENDS & FAMILY

Unit Opener, pages 144–145

Preview

- Call on a student to read aloud the unit title, "Friends & Family." Tell students that this unit is about activities with friends and family.

- Have students look at the photos and identify the people, settings, actions, and objects. (Examples: Friends at a barbecue, a daughter and mother laughing together, a father and son talking together.) Provide help as needed. Write students' responses on the board. Read the responses aloud, and have the class repeat.

- Ask students what kinds of activities they enjoy doing with their friends and family. Provide help with vocabulary as needed. Write students' responses on the board. Read the responses aloud, and have the class repeat.

- Read the unit goals aloud as students follow along in their texts. Answer any questions they may have.

Chapter 13
He's going to fall!

Objectives

Language:
- Listen to a dialogue for comprehension.
- Understand familiar vocabulary and grammar structures by listening to a dialogue.
- Develop new vocabulary and grammar structures by listening to a dialogue.
- Act out a dialogue.
- Use *be going to* for the future in affirmative and negative statements, *yes/no* questions, and information questions.
- Give commands, using *please* to be polite.
- Make original conversations using new vocabulary and grammar structures.
- Evaluate one's own learning of new vocabulary, grammar, and oral language

Literacy:
- Read a dialogue for comprehension.
- Understand familiar vocabulary and grammar structures by reading a dialogue.
- Develop new vocabulary and grammar structures by reading a dialogue.
- Complete and write affirmative and negative statements, *yes/no* questions, and information questions using *be going to* for the future.
- Decode words with the vowel sound /$\overline{oo}$/.
- Write commands.
- Read a short story for comprehension.
- Understand familiar vocabulary and grammar structures by reading a short story.
- Develop new vocabulary and grammar structures by reading a short story.
- Plan, write, revise, edit, proofread, and make a final copy of a dialogue.
- Use *be going to* for the future and the conjunction *so* in writing a dialogue.
- Evaluate one's own learning of reading skills, reading comprehension, and writing skills.

Learning Strategies:
- Use cooperation with a classmate to read a dialogue and study new vocabulary.
- Use cooperation with a small group to act out a dialogue.
- Use cooperation with a classmate to practice conversations.
- Use the strategy *Sound Out* to decode words.
- Use the strategy *Make Inferences* to understand a short story.
- Use cooperation with a classmate to check a dialogue one has written.
- Evaluate one's own learning of the strategies *Sound Out* and *Make Inferences*.
- Identify easy and difficult material in a chapter and the different ways to learn the difficult material.

Opening Dialogue, pages 146–147

Getting Ready

Preparation (See Transparency 17.)

Have students look at the illustrations. Have them talk about the characters, situation, actions, and objects. Encourage students to use full sentences. (Examples: Carlos, Carmen, Liliana, Maria, and Bic are skating in the park. / Maria skates well.) Write students' responses on the board. Read the responses aloud, and have students repeat.

> **Reaching All Students—Emergent Learners:** Ask students questions about the illustrations. Call on students to respond. If needed, model the response. Have students repeat.

Listening and Reading

The Accident

Presentation

Exercise A
- Read the directions and the prelistening question aloud as students follow along in their texts.
- Have students listen to the dialogue, or read the dialogue aloud to them. Have students look at the appropriate illustrations as they listen.
- Explain any vocabulary that students do not understand.

- Ask the prelistening question, "Where are they skating?" Call on a volunteer to respond. (They're skating at Jackson Park.)

Exercise B

 Have students read the dialogue. Provide help with content, vocabulary, etc. as needed.

Reaching All Students—Emergent Learners: Work with emergent learners in small groups while the other students work independently. Read aloud as students follow along in their texts. Monitor their comprehension by interrupting the reading with such questions as, "What did Carmen say to Carlos?" (She said, "Be careful, Carlos! You're going to fall and break your leg!") "Who skates really well?" (Maria does.) "What kind of lessons does Liliana want?" (She wants skating lessons.) "What does Carlos want to do?" (He wants to race Bic.) "What happened to Carlos?" (He fell.) "What did Carlos hurt?" (He hurt his arm and leg.) "What number does Carmen call?" (She calls 911.) "What street is the park on?" (It's on State Street.) Have students repeat the questions, then the answers.

Pair and Group Work

Practice

Exercise A

Have students who can read on their own form pairs. Have one student in the pair take the roles of Carlos and Liliana; have the other student take the roles of Carmen and Bic. Then have them read the dialogue aloud. Provide help as needed.

Reaching All Students—Emergent Learners: Work in small groups with emergent readers. Model each sentence and have individual students "echo" your reading. Make sure that students look at the sentences as you read them.

Exercise B

Have students form groups of four. Group students heterogeneously so that each group is made up of weak readers, average readers, and strong readers. Have each student choose a role in the dialogue. Have students practice acting out the dialogue in their groups.

Reaching All Students—Kinesthetic Learners: Choose one group to act out the dialogue in front of the class.

Vocabulary

Presentation

Read the vocabulary words and expressions aloud and have students repeat them. Check students' understanding of the words and expressions.

Practice

Exercise A

Have students read and say the words and expressions. Provide assistance with pronunciation as needed. Then have students copy the words and expressions into their notebooks.

Reaching All Students—Auditory Learners: Encourage students to say the words and expressions as they write them in their notebooks.

Exercise B *(See Transparencies 85–87.)*

- Have students turn to page 250 in their texts.
- Have students work through Steps 1–2 (recognizing letters and finding syllables) with the words in the box on page 147 if further practice is needed.
- Have students work in pairs on Step 3, identifying letters or letter combinations that follow patterns or make unexpected sounds. Encourage students to ask questions and to discover as much as they can on their own.

Exercise C

Have students find the words and expressions in the dialogue. Have them read the sentences aloud.

Exercise D

- Pair students and have them decide which classmate will go first.
- Tell students that, without speaking, the first student will choose a word from the word box and draw a picture of it. The second student will look at the picture and guess the word. Then the students will reverse roles.

  Reaching All Students—Emergent Learners: Have two advanced students model doing the exercise first.

- Have students take turns drawing and guessing the words. Circulate to answer any questions about the words.
- Have several students draw their pictures on the board. Call on volunteers to guess the words illustrated.

Grammar 1, page 148

Future Tense with *be going to*: Statements

Preparation

- Write the following dialogue on the board as a way of presenting the grammar focus in context.

  Liliana: *Are* you *going to call* your parents?
  Carmen: Yes, *I am.*
  Carlos: Ouch!
  Liliana: Hang in there, Carlos. The ambulance *is going to be* here in a minute.

- Read the dialogue aloud as students follow along. Then have the class read aloud with you.
- Call on two students to dramatize the dialogue for the rest of the class.

Presentation

- Have students look at the grammar chart. Explain that the left part of the chart shows affirmative statements with the future tense with *be going to*. The right part shows negative statements.
- Call on an individual student to read aloud across each row of the affirmative statements in the left part of the chart. Then call on another student to read aloud the negative statements in the right part of the chart.

  Reaching All Students—Auditory/ Cooperative Learners: Have pairs of students take turns reading sentences from the chart. Have the first student read an affirmative sentence from the left part of the chart and the second student read the corresponding negative sentence from the right part of the chart. Have them continue until they have read all the sentences.

- Have students look at the contractions box. Point out that *isn't* is the contraction of *is not; aren't* is the contraction of *are*

not. Explain that *am not* does not have a contraction.

  Reaching All Students—Auditory/ Cooperative Learners: Have volunteers take turns reading sentences from the Negative Statements chart, substituting *isn't* for *is not* and *aren't* for *are not*.

Practice

- Read the first sentence with the sample answer aloud. Have students repeat. Have a volunteer explain why the answer is correct. (Add *be going to* for the future. The form of the verb *be (is)* matches the subject *(Carlos)*.)
- Have students copy the sentences into their notebooks and fill in the blanks with the correct form of *be going to* for the future.

  Reaching All Students—Auditory Learners: Call on advanced students to read the remaining sentences before students write their answers.

  Reaching All Students—Emergent Learners: First, have students do the exercise orally. Then have them copy the incomplete sentences into their notebooks. Last, have them complete the sentences. Provide help as needed.

- Review the answers with the class.

> **Answers**
> 1. is going to
> 2. is going to
> 3. are not going to / aren't going to
> 4. are going to
> 5. is not going to / isn't going to

Future Tense with *be going to*: Yes/No Questions

Presentation

- Have students look at the grammar chart. Explain that the left part of the chart shows how to make *yes/no* questions with *be going to* for the future (read the first row as an example). The middle part shows affirmative answers (read the first row as an example). The right part shows negative answers (read the first row as an example).

  Reaching All Students—Auditory/ Cooperative Learners: Have groups of three students take turns reading sentences from the chart. Have the first student read the question, the second student read the affirmative answer, and the third student read the negative answer. Have them continue until they have read all the questions and responses.

- Have students work in pairs or small groups to develop a rule that tells how to make *yes/no* questions with *be going to* for the future. Call on students to give their rules. Write the rule on the board. (Example: *Be* + subject + *going to* + verb. The verb *be* matches the subject. *Going to* doesn't change. The main verb is in the base form.)

Practice

- Have students number a sheet of paper in their notebooks from 1 to 5.
- Tell students that they will write a *yes/no* question with *be going to* for the future for each statement.
- Call on a student to read the first statement aloud. Call on another student to read the sample answer aloud. Have the student explain why the answer is correct. (The subject becomes *you*. *Are* matches the subject. *Are* comes before the subject to make the *yes/no* question.)
- Have students write the questions in their notebooks.

    > **Reaching All Students—Emergent Learners:** First, have students do the exercise orally. Then have them copy the sentences into their notebooks. Last, have them write the questions. Provide help as needed.

- Review the answers with the class. Have the class repeat each question after you. Help with pronunciation and intonation as needed.

Answers
1. Are you going to watch TV tonight?
2. Is the teacher going to be at school tomorrow?
3. Are you going to do homework after school?
4. Is your family going to go the movies this weekend?
5. Are you going to clean your room this weekend?

Expansion

- Tell students that they will take turns asking and answering the questions with a classmate. Tell them that they should give true short answers.

- Work with two students through a model of asking and answering the first two questions. (Examples: Are you going to watch TV tonight? Yes, I am. / Is the teacher going to be at school tomorrow? No, she's not.)
- Divide the class into pairs.
- Have pairs practice asking and answering the questions.
- Call on different volunteer pairs to ask and answer each of the questions for the rest of the class.

Grammar 2, page 149

Future Tense with *be going to*: Information Questions

Preparation

- Write the following dialogue on the board as a way of presenting the grammar focus in context.

    Maria: *What are* you *going to do* now?
    Sophie: I'm going to go home. I'm going to go shopping with my mom tonight.
    Maria: Oh, yeah? *Where are* you *going to go?*
    Sophie: We're going to go to the mall.

- Read the dialogue aloud as students follow along. Then have the class read aloud with you.
- Call on two students to dramatize the dialogue for the rest of the class.

Presentation

- Have students look at the grammar chart. Explain that this chart shows how to make information questions with *be going to* for the future. Remind students that information questions ask *who, what, when, where, why,* and *how*.
- Call on a pair of students to read aloud across each row in the chart. Have the first student read the question on the left and the second student read the answer on the right. Have them continue until they have read all the questions and answers.

Practice

Exercise A

- Tell students that for this exercise they will write four questions for a short dialogue. They will need to look at speaker A's cues and speaker B's responses before writing each question.

- Read speaker A's cue for item 1 aloud. Call on a volunteer to read speaker B's reply. Call on another volunteer to read the sample answer. Have the student explain why the answer is correct. (Add *be going to* for the future. The subject is *you*. *Are* matches the subject.)
- Have students write the dialogue questions in their notebooks.

    Reaching All Students—Emergent Learners: Work with students in small groups to complete the activity.

- Review the answers with the class.

    Reaching All Students—Advanced Learners: Call on pairs of students to act out the dialogue for the rest of the class.

Answers
1. What are you going to do this weekend?
2. When are you going to go?
3. What are you going to see?
4. Where are you going to see it?

Exercise B

 Have students listen to the conversation or read it aloud with a classmate.

Reaching All Students—Kinesthetic Learners: Call on volunteers to act out the conversation for the rest of the class.

Practice
Exercise C

- Tell students that for this exercise they will first practice the conversation in Exercise B. Then they will make their own conversations.
- Have students work in pairs. Have each pair practice the conversation in Exercise B.
- Next, have students check page 222 of the Vocabulary Handbook for other activities they might include in their own conversations.
- Then, as a class, brainstorm other activities students could use in their own conversations. (Examples: go shopping, go out to eat, meet a friend, play baseball, watch TV, play a computer game, baby-sit.) Write the names of the activities on the board.
- Have two advanced students model their conversation for the class.
- Have pairs practice their conversations aloud.

    Reaching All Students—Kinesthetic Learners: Call on volunteer pairs to act out their conversations for the rest of the class.

Word Study, page 150

Other Vowel Sound: /o͞o/
Preparation

- Write the words, *school, rule, true,* and *new* on the board.
- Call on volunteers to identify the names of the consonants and vowels in the words.
- Pronounce the words and have students repeat them after you.

Presentation

- Explain to students that they are going to study four common spellings for the long vowel sound /o͞o/: *oo, u-e, ue,* and *ew*.
- Begin by reviewing the spelling *u-e*.
- Point to the word *rule* on the board. Say the word. Then call on a volunteer to say the first sound (/r/), the second sound (/o͞o/), and the third sound (/l/).
- Ask students, "How many sounds does the word have?" (Three.) "How many letters does the word have?" (Four.)
- To help students understand why the word has four letters but only three sounds, underline the vowels *u-e* in the word. Point out that the letters *u-e* stand for the vowel sound /o͞o/.
- Follow the same procedure for the words *school, true,* and *new*.
- Have students look at the instruction box. Read the sentence aloud as students follow along.

Practice
Exercise A

- Have students use the learning strategy *Sound Out,* as well as the pictures, to read the words with the vowel sound /o͞o/.

    Reaching All Students—Emergent Learners: Complete this activity as a class if students need help. After students have an approximation of the pronunciation, say the words correctly to provide a model.

Exercise B

- First, have students read the sentences aloud. Then have them copy the sentences into their notebooks. Last, have them circle the letters that represent the vowel sound /o͞o/.

- Review the answers as a class.

Answers
1. In J(u)n(e), Pablo is going to go fishing with his dad.
2. The birds fl(ew) over the house.
3. Does Anita have any gl(ue) I can borrow?
4. There is a lot of f(oo)d on the table.
5. Carolina has a new shamp(oo).
6. Carmen bought a bl(ue) shirt for Carlos.

Optional Activity: Have students close their texts. Ask them to number a page in their notebooks from 1 to 8. Then ask them to listen carefully to the words you read and to write the words. Then dictate the following words:

1. flew	5. drew
2. moon	6. blue
3. June	7. food
4. glue	8. shampoo

- After the dictation, write the words on the board. Then have students check their words.
- Have students record the number of correct words in their notebooks; for example, *I wrote (7) out of 8 dictated words with the vowel sound /$\overline{oo}$/ correctly.* Write this example on the board as a model.

Exercise C

- Have students look at Exercise A. Have them choose two words with the vowel sound /$\overline{oo}$/. Then have them write a sentence for each word in their notebooks.

   Reaching All Students—Emergent Learners: Review the meanings of the words in Exercise A. Call on a volunteer to write a sample sentence on the board. Then have students write the two sentences in their notebooks. Provide help as needed.

- Have students share their sentences with the class.

Answers
Answers will vary.

Expansion

- On a sheet of paper in their notebooks, have students write column headings with the spellings for the vowel sound /$\overline{oo}$/: *u-e, ue, ew,* and *oo.* Then have them write as many words as they can that have the vowel sound /$\overline{oo}$/ under each heading. (Set a time limit of 5–10 minutes.) Encourage students to use a dictionary, their texts, or their vocabulary lists for help.

   Reaching All Students—Auditory Learners: Encourage students to say the words aloud as they write them.

- Have students share their lists with the class.

Grammar 3, page 151

Commands

Preparation

- Write the following dialogue on the board as a way of presenting the grammar focus in context.

   Carmen: Can I sign your cast, Carlos?
   Carlos: Sure. But *don't hurt my arm.*
   Carmen: I won't. Now *please don't move.*
   Carlos: Okay. What are you writing?
   Carmen: I'm writing, *"Ask Maria for skating lessons!"*

- Read the dialogue aloud as students follow along. Then have the class read aloud with you.
- Call on two students to dramatize the dialogue for the rest of the class.

Presentation

- Have students look at the grammar chart.
- Explain to students that the chart shows how to form affirmative and negative commands. It also shows how to form commands using the word *Please.*
- Read aloud across the first row of affirmative commands without the word *Please* as students follow along in their texts. Then read aloud across the same row with the word *Please.* Call on a volunteer to explain the effect of using the word *Please* with the command. (It makes the command polite.)
- Follow the same procedure for the row of negative commands.
- Read aloud the Remember note at the bottom of the chart as students follow along.

Practice
Exercise A

- Have students number a sheet of paper in their notebooks from 1 to 8.

- Have students look at the commands in the box. Read the commands aloud, and have students repeat after you.
- Next, have students look at the illustrations. Tell them that they will choose the command in the box that matches the action in each illustration.
- Have students look at the illustration for item 1. Call on a volunteer to read aloud the sample answer. If needed, call on a volunteer to give the answer to item 2.
- Have students complete the exercise individually, in pairs, or in small groups.

   Reaching All Students—Emergent Learners: First, have students do the exercise orally. Then have them complete the exercise in their notebooks. Provide help as needed.
- Review the answers with the class.

Answers

1. Don't talk.	**5.** Look up.
2. Open your book.	**6.** Close your book.
3. Don't sit down.	**7.** Smile.
4. Stand up.	**8.** Raise your hand.

Exercise B

- Read the directions aloud as students follow along in their texts.
- Divide students into small groups. Have each group choose a leader. Have the leader keep his or her text open while the other students close their texts.
- Work with one group through a model game. Have the leader say a command from the box in the text with or without the word *Please*. The other students should follow the command only if the leader uses the word *Please* with the command. If the leader does not use the word *Please* with the command, the other students should not follow the command.
- Have the leader of each group begin the game, using the eight commands in the box in the text.
- If a student makes a mistake, he or she is out of the game.
- The last student left is the winner. He or she then becomes the new leader of the group.

Expansion

   Optional Activity: Have students break into small groups. Have each group choose a

leader. Tell the groups that they will now play a game called "Do the opposite." Explain that the opposite of the command "Smile." is the command "Do not smile." The opposite of the command "Don't move." is the command "Move." Call on volunteers to say other opposite commands. (Examples: "Raise your hand." / "Don't raise your hand."; "Open your book." / "Close your book."; "Sit down." / "Don't sit down."; "Look up." / "Don't look up.")
- Have the leader in each group say a command from the box in the text. The other students should do the *opposite* of what the leader says. If the leader says, "Raise your hand.", the other students should keep their hands down. The leader should watch group members to make sure they all do the *opposite*. Anyone who does not do the opposite is out of the game. The last student left is the winner. He or she becomes the new leader of the group.
- Do a couple of examples as a class to make sure that students understand the game.

Reading, pages 152–153

Before You Read

Preparation

- Tell students that they will use the learning strategy *Make Inferences* to understand the story.
- Ask students what they remember about the strategy *Make Inferences*. Write their responses on the board. (Example: We can often guess what new words or ideas mean by looking at the other words or sentences around them.)
- Have students look at the Before You Read part in their texts. Call on volunteers to read the steps for the strategy.
- As a refresher, briefly model the strategy by reading aloud the first few sentences of the story. Do a "think aloud," following the strategy steps for the words *cloudy* and *blue*.

Read This!

The Visitors

Preparation

- Note: Students will encounter the following new words in the reading: *ankle, wrist, actor, visitor, cast, hospital, outside, pain, voice, leap, rest, shout, sleep, sprain, visit, yawn, awake, "blue," bored, cloudy, tired, weak, weakly, happen.*

- Call on a student to read aloud the title of the story.
- Have students look at the pictures and study them. Tell them that they can also use the pictures to help them guess, or make inferences about, new words.

Practice

Have students listen to the story, or read it aloud to them. Remind them to write new words in their notebooks and to use the strategy *Make Inferences* to guess the meaning of the words. Circulate to answer any questions.

Reaching All Students—Emergent Learners: Work with emergent learners in small groups while the other students work independently. Guide them in using the strategy *Make Inferences* for each of the new words.

After You Read

Self-Evaluation
Exercise A

- Refer students to After You Read.
- Read the question in item 1 aloud as students follow along.
- On the board, write the headings *New Words* and *Inferences*. Call on volunteers to say the new words they found in the story. Write the words under the heading *New Words*. Then ask volunteers to give the inferences they made for the meanings of the words. Write these under the heading *Inferences*. Be sure students point out the words or sentences in the story that led them to make the inferences.
- Have students write the new words and the inferences in their notebooks.
- Read the question in item 2 aloud as students follow along. Call on a volunteer to answer the question.

Answers
1. *Answers will vary.*
2. Liliana thinks that he is acting. At first, he said he hurt a lot. He also spoke weakly. When his friends said, "We'll come back later," he said he felt great and was not in pain.

Exercise B

- Have students number a sheet of paper in their notebooks from 1 to 5.
- Read item 1 aloud as students follow along. Call on a student to give the answer. (He broke his wrist and sprained his ankle.) Ask the student to find the supportive statements in the story. (Carlos . . . says, "I broke my wrist and sprained my ankle.")

    Reaching All Students—Auditory Learners: Call on a student to read the remaining questions aloud as the other students follow along in their texts.

- Have students write their answers in their notebooks.
- Call on students to give their answers and write them on the board. Be sure they also give the supporting statements from the story.
- Have students count the number of correct answers and write that number in their notebooks.

Answers
1. He broke his wrist and sprained his ankle.
2. He watched TV, rested, and slept.
3. No, he didn't. He watched TV all day.
4. Yes, he was.
5. Liliana and Maria made him cookies. Samir and Bic bought him a new CD. Pablo brought his guitar to play a new song he wrote.

Expansion

- Have students create a timeline for what happened to Carlos.
- Write the names of these days down a column on the board: *Sunday, Monday, Tuesday.* Have students write the names of the days down a column in their notebooks.
- Have students complete their timeline individually, in pairs, or in small groups.
- Review the answers with the class.

Answers
Sunday: Carlos watched TV all day.
Monday: Carlos watched TV, rested, and slept.
Tuesday: Carlos was bored and "blue," but then his friends came to visit him.

Writing, page 154

Before You Write

Preparation (See Transparencies 24 and 50-51.)
Explain to students that they are going to write a telephone dialogue.

Exercise A

- Focus students' attention on the handwritten dialogue.

    Reaching All Students—Auditory Learners: Call on two students to read the dialogue aloud as the other students follow along in their texts.

- Ask students to tell what kind of information the writer included in the sample dialogue. (A greeting, an invitation, questions and answers about the activity, good-byes.) Write students' responses on the board.

Presentation

Exercise B

- Draw students' attention to the Before I Write checklist. Call on students to read aloud the points in the checklist.
- Refer students to page 222 of the Vocabulary Handbook for activities they could include in their dialogue.
- As a class, brainstorm with students other vocabulary they could include in their dialogues. Write students' responses on the board.
- Model following the steps in the Before I Write checklist to plan your own sample dialogue.
- Have students follow the Before I Write checklist and make notes in their notebooks.

    Reaching All Students—Emergent Learners: Work with students in small groups. Guide them in following the steps in the checklist.

Write This!

Presentation

- Draw students' attention to the While I Write checklist. Call on students to read aloud the points in the checklist.
- Model following the While I Write checklist. Refer to the notes you took in your earlier modeling. As you write, do a "think aloud"

about how you are following the While I Write checklist.

Practice

- Have students write their dialogues in their notebooks, using their notes and the While I Write checklist for help.
- Circulate while students are writing and encourage them to ask you for help with new words.

After You Write

Presentation

Exercise A

- Draw students' attention to the After I Write checklist. Call on students to read aloud the points in the checklist.
- Model following the steps in the After I Write checklist, checking your own dialogue.
- Have students use the After I Write checklist to evaluate their writing. Have them circle and then correct any errors.

Exercise B

Have students read their dialogues with a classmate. Encourage them to make suggestions for improvement.

Exercise C

Have students write a final copy of the dialogue in their notebooks.

Expansion

Have students work in pairs to practice the dialogues they wrote.

Reaching All Students—Kinesthetic Learners: Have a few pairs of students act out their dialogues for the rest of the class.

Learning Log, page 155

See How to Use the Learning Log on page xiii.
(See Transparencies 20 and 74.)

Chapter 14
Hey! The lights went out!

Objectives

Language:

- Listen to a dialogue for comprehension.
- Understand familiar vocabulary and grammar structures by listening to a dialogue.
- Develop new vocabulary and grammar structures by listening to a dialogue.
- Act out a dialogue.
- Use the past continuous tense in affirmative and negative statements, *yes/no* questions, and information questions.
- Use possessive pronouns and questions with *Whose*.
- Make original conversations using new vocabulary and grammar structures.
- Evaluate one's own learning of new vocabulary, grammar, and oral language.

Literacy:

- Read a dialogue for comprehension.
- Understand familiar vocabulary and grammar structures by reading a dialogue.
- Develop new vocabulary and grammar structures by reading a dialogue.
- Write sentences using new vocabulary.
- Complete and write affirmative and negative statements, *yes/no* questions, and information questions using the past continuous.
- Decode words with the vowel sound /o͞o/.
- Write and complete statements and questions using possessive pronouns.
- Read a short story for comprehension.
- Understand familiar vocabulary and grammar structures by reading a short story.
- Develop new vocabulary and grammar structures by reading a short story.
- Plan, write, revise, edit, proofread, and make a final copy of a narrative paragraph.
- Use the past continuous and simple past to write a narrative paragraph about a personal event.
- Use question marks for direct speech in a narrative paragraph.

- Evaluate one's own learning of reading skills, reading comprehension, and writing skills.

Learning Strategies:

- Use cooperation with a classmate to read a dialogue and study new vocabulary.
- Use cooperation with a small group to act out a dialogue.
- Use cooperation with a classmate to practice conversations.
- Use the strategy *Sound Out* to decode words.
- Use the strategy *Use Selective Attention* to understand a short story.
- Use cooperation with a classmate to check a paragraph one has written.
- Evaluate one's own learning of the strategies *Sound Out* and *Use Selective Attention.*
- Identify easy and difficult material in a chapter and the different ways to learn the difficult material.

Opening Dialogue, pages 156–157

Getting Ready

Preparation *(See Transparency 17.)*

- Have students look at the illustrations and identify the characters. Then ask them to name the items in the illustrations. Write the names and the words on the board or a poster. Say the names and words, and have students repeat.

- Ask students to make sentences about what they see and what the people are doing. Write students' responses on the board. If needed, model complete sentences. Read the sentences, and have students repeat them after you.

    Reaching All Students—Emergent Learners: Point to the first illustration and ask, "Where are they?" Have students repeat. Call on students to respond. If needed, model the response. (They're in science class.) Have students repeat. Then ask students to make other sentences about what they see and what the people are doing.

Listening and Reading

The Storm

Presentation

Exercise A

- Read the directions and the prelistening question aloud as students follow along in their texts.
- Have students listen to the dialogue, or read the dialogue aloud to them. Have students look at the appropriate illustrations as they listen.
- Explain any vocabulary words that students do not understand.
- Ask the prelistening question, "Why is the principal closing the school for the rest of the day?" Call on a volunteer to respond. (The school's electricity is off.)

Exercise B

Have students read the dialogue. Provide help with content, vocabulary, etc. as needed.

Reaching All Students—Emergent Learners: Work with emergent learners in small groups while the other students work independently. Read aloud as students follow along in their texts. Monitor their comprehension by interrupting the reading with such questions as, "What is Mrs. Kim's science lesson on?" (It's on weather.) "What happened to the lights?" (They went out.) "What is Carlos not sure he can find?" (He's not sure he can find his seat.) "Why is the electricity off?" (A tree fell on a power line.) "What's going to be at the school soon?" (The buses are going to be at the school soon.) "What was Pablo doing when the lights went out?" (He was watching a video in history class.) "What was Carmen doing?" (She was listening to Mrs. Kim.) "Who needs an umbrella?" (Carmen does.) Have students repeat the questions, then the answers.

Pair and Group Work

Practice

Exercise A

Have students who can read on their own form pairs. Have students take turns reading each of the lines in the dialogue aloud. Provide help as needed.

Reaching All Students—Emergent Learners: Work in small groups with emergent readers. Model each sentence and have individual students "echo" your reading. Make sure that students look at the sentences as you read them.

Exercise B

Have students form groups of six. Group students heterogeneously so that each group is made up of weak readers, average readers, and strong readers. Have each student choose a role in the dialogue. Have students practice acting out the dialogue in their groups.

Reaching All Students—Kinesthetic Learners: Choose one or more groups to act out the dialogue in front of the class.

Vocabulary

Presentation

- Read the vocabulary words and expressions aloud and have students repeat them.
- Check students' understanding of the words and expressions.

Practice

Exercise A

Have students read and say the words and expressions. Provide assistance with pronunciation as needed. Then have students copy the words and expressions into their notebooks.

Reaching All Students—Auditory Learners: Encourage students to say the words and expressions as they write them in their notebooks.

Exercise B (See Transparencies 85–87.)

- Have students turn to page 250 in their texts.
- Have students work through Steps 1–2 (recognizing letters and finding syllables) with the words in the box on page 157 if further practice is needed.
- Have students work in pairs on Step 3, identifying letters or letter combinations that follow patterns or make unexpected sounds. Encourage students to ask questions and to discover as much as they can on their own.

Exercise C

Have students find the words and expressions in the dialogue. Have them read the sentences aloud.

Exercise D

- Ask students to choose five words from the word box. In their notebooks, have them write five sentences using these new words. Have students underline the new vocabulary word in each sentence.
- Call on students to read their sentences aloud.

Answers
Answers will vary.

Expansion

- Pair students and have the first student choose a word from the word box to illustrate.
- Tell students that, without speaking, the first student will draw a picture of his or her word. The second student will look at the picture and guess the word.
- Have students take turns drawing and guessing the words. Circulate to answer any questions about the words.
- Have several students draw their pictures on the board. Call on volunteers to guess the words illustrated.

Grammar 1, page 158

Past Continuous Tense: Statements

Preparation

- Write the following dialogue on the board as a way of presenting the grammar focus in context.

  Pablo: Where were you? The bus almost left without you.
  Sophie: I *was looking* for my umbrella.
  Pablo: Did you find it?
  Sophie: No. It was so dark, I got lost. I *was walking* up and down the halls.
  Pablo: Poor Sophie.

- Read the dialogue aloud as students follow along. Then have the class read aloud with you.
- Call on two students to dramatize the dialogue for the rest of the class.

Presentation

- Have students look at the grammar chart. Explain that the left part of the chart shows affirmative statements with the past continuous. The right part shows negative statements.
- Call on an individual student to read aloud across each row of the affirmative statements in the left part of the chart. Then call on another student to read aloud the negative statements in the right part.

  Reaching All Students—Auditory/Cooperative Learners: Have pairs of students take turns reading sentences from the chart. Have the first student read an affirmative sentence from the left part of the chart and the second student read a negative sentence from the right part of the chart. Continue for the remaining sentences.

- Call on volunteers and have each choose a sentence to read aloud from the chart.
- Read aloud the Remember note at the bottom of the chart as students follow along.
- Refer students to the contractions box. Read the contractions aloud and have students repeat.
- Write a sentence in the present continuous tense on the board. (I am studying English now.) Call on a volunteer to tell you how to change it into the past continuous to talk about yesterday morning. (I was studying English yesterday morning.) Then call on another volunteer to tell you how to change it into a negative statement. (I was not studying English yesterday morning.)

Practice

- Have students number a sheet of paper in their notebooks from 1 to 5.
- Tell students that they will need to use the cues to write true affirmative or negative past continuous statements.
- Read the cue for item 1 aloud. Call on a student to read the sample answer aloud. Ask students to raise their hand if they were not playing soccer on Saturday morning. Tell them that they will write a negative answer. Ask students to raise their hand if they were playing soccer on Saturday morning. Tell them that they will write an affirmative statement. Call on a volunteer to give the affirmative statement. (I was playing soccer on Saturday morning.) Write the statement on the board.
- Have a student read the remaining cues aloud. Make sure students understand them. Remind students to use contractions in their statements.

- Have students write their statements.

    Reaching All Students—Emergent Learners: First, have students do the exercise orally. Then have them write the sentences in their notebooks. Provide help as needed.

- Call on individual students to share their answers with the class.

Answers

1. I (was/wasn't) playing soccer Saturday morning.
2. It (was/wasn't) raining Sunday afternoon.
3. The teacher (was/wasn't) sleeping yesterday in class.
4. I (was/wasn't) watching TV Friday evening.
5. My parents (were/weren't) reading the newspaper last night.

Past Continuous Tense: Yes/No Questions

Presentation

- Have students look at the grammar chart. Explain that the left part of the chart shows *yes/no* questions in the past continuous (read the first row as an example). The middle part shows affirmative answers (read the first row as an example). The right part shows negative answers (read the first row as an example).

    Reaching All Students—Auditory/ Cooperative Learners: Have three students take turns reading sentences from the chart. Have the first student read the question, the second student read the affirmative answer, and the third student read the negative answer.

- Have students work in pairs or small groups to develop a rule that tells how to make *yes/no* questions in the past continuous. Call on students to give their rules. Write the rule on the board. (Example: *Was/were* + subject + verb (+ *ing*). *Was/Were* matches the subject. The main verb uses the *-ing* form.)

Practice

- Have students number a sheet of paper in their notebooks from 1 to 5.
- Tell students that they will write five *yes/no* questions in the past continuous for the answers they wrote in the previous exercise.
- Call on a student to read the example question aloud. Have the student explain why

the answer is correct. (The subject becomes *you*. *Were* matches the subject. *Were* comes before the subject to make a question.)

- Have students change the statements into questions and write them in their notebooks.
- Review the answers with the class.

Answers

1. Were you playing soccer Saturday morning?
2. Was it raining Sunday afternoon?
3. Was the teacher sleeping yesterday in class?
4. Were you watching TV Friday evening?
5. Were your parents reading the newspaper last night?

Expansion

- Tell students that they will take turns asking and answering the questions with a classmate. Tell them that they should give true short answers.
- Work with two students through a model of asking and answering the first two questions.
- Divide the class into pairs. Tell students the first classmate will ask the five questions, and the second student will answer. Then they will change roles.
- Have pairs practice asking and answering the questions.
- Call on different volunteer pairs to ask and answer each of the questions for the rest of the class.

Grammar 2, page 159

Past Continuous Tense: Information Questions

Preparation

- Write the following dialogue on the board as a way of presenting the grammar focus in context.

    Sophie: Paco just came to my house five minutes ago. He *was looking* for Carmen. I was so embarrassed!

    Mei: Why? *What were* you *doing?*

    Sophie: I *was dancing.*

    Mei: So?

    Sophie: I'm not a very good dancer!

- Read the dialogue aloud as students follow along. Then have the class read aloud with you.

- Call on two students to dramatize the dialogue for the rest of the class.

Presentation

- Have students look at the grammar chart. Tell them that this chart shows how to make information questions in the past continuous tense. If needed, remind them that information questions ask *who, what, when, where, why,* and *how.* Explain any new words.
- Call on pairs of students to read aloud across the rows in the chart. Have one student read the question on the left part and the other read the answer on the right part.

Practice

Exercise A

- Have students look at the illustration. Ask questions to elicit the situation in the picture, such as: "What happened?" (The lights went out.) "When did they go out?" (They went out last night.) "What were the boy and his sister doing when the lights went out?" (They were playing a game.) "What was the father doing?" (He was reading a book and eating an apple.) "What was the mother doing? (She was writing a letter and drinking a cup of coffee.)
- Have students number a sheet of paper in their notebooks from 1 to 5.
- Tell students that they will write questions about what David was doing when the lights went out.
- Call on a volunteer to read aloud the statement and question word for the first item. Call on a second volunteer to read aloud the sample answer and explain why it is correct. (*What + was +* subject + *doing? Was* matches the subject, David. *Doing* asks about the activity and replaces *playing a game.*)
- Have students write the questions in their notebooks.

> **Reaching All Students—Emergent Learners:** Work with students in small groups to complete the activity.

- Review the answers with the class.

Answers
Answers may vary. Possible answers:
1. What was David doing?
2. When was he playing it?
3. Where was he playing it?
4. Who was he playing with?
5. What else was he doing?

Exercise B

- Tell students that they will ask and answer questions about what David's mother and father were doing when the lights went out.
- Write the question words *What, When, Where, Who,* and *What else* on the board.
- Work with two students through a model of asking and answering two questions about David's mother. Encourage the students to refer to the grammar chart if needed.
- Divide the class into pairs. Tell students that the first classmate will ask four questions about David's mother, and the second student will answer them. Then they will change roles to ask and answer questions about David's father.
- Have pairs practice asking and answering the questions.

> **Reaching All Students—Emergent Learners:** First, have students tell you what David's mother and father were doing when the lights went out. Write the verb phrases on the board. Then have them work in pairs to ask and answer the questions. Provide help as needed.

- Call on different volunteer pairs to ask and answer four questions about David's mother and then four questions about David's father for the rest of the class.

Answers
Answers will vary. Possible answers:
What was David's mother doing? She was writing a letter.
When was she writing it? She was writing it last night.
Where was she writing it? She was writing it in the living room.
What else was she doing? She was drinking a cup of coffee.
What was David's father doing? He was reading a book.
When was he reading it? He was reading it last night.
Where was he reading it? He was reading it in the living room.
What else was he doing? He was eating an apple.

Word Study, page 160

Other Vowel Sound: /o͞o/

Preparation

- Write the word *look* on the board.
- Call on a volunteer to identify the names of the consonants and vowels in the word.
- Pronounce the word and have students repeat it after you.

Presentation

- Underline the vowels *oo* in *look* on the board and ask students to pronounce the sound. Ask them if they hear the /o͞o/ sound.
- Point to the word *look* on the board. Say the word. Then call on a volunteer to identify the first sound (/l/), the second sound (/o͞o/), and the third sound (/k/).
- Explain that the vowels *oo* together stand for one vowel sound, /o͞o/.

Practice

Exercise A

Have students use the learning strategy *Sound Out*, as well as the pictures, to read the words with the vowel sound /o͞o/.

> **Reaching All Students—Emergent Learners:** Complete this activity as a class if students need help. After students have an approximation of the pronunciation, say the words correctly to provide a model.

Exercise B

- First, have students read the sentences aloud. Then have them copy the sentences into their notebooks. Last, have them circle the letters that represent the vowel sound /o͞o/.
- Review the answers as a class.

> **Answers**
> 1. Did Carlos hurt his f(oo)t?
> 2. Carolina and Carmen were baking c(oo)kies yesterday.
> 3. Is this Liliana's noteb(oo)k?
> 4. There are two fish on Pablo's h(oo)k.
> 5. What are they going to c(oo)k for dinner?
> 6. Pedro is saying g(oo)d-bye to Samir.

Optional Activity: Ask students to number a page in their notebooks from 1 to 6. Then ask them to listen carefully to the words you read and to write the words next to the correct numbers. Then dictate the following words:

1. cook		4. cookie	
2. notebook		5. good-bye	
3. hook		6. foot	

- After the dictation, write the answers on the board. Then have students check their answers.
- Have students record the number of correct answers in their notebooks; for example, *I wrote (5) out of 6 dictated words with vowel sound /o͞o/ correctly.* Write this example on the board as a model.

Exercise C

- Have students look at Exercise A. Have them choose two words with the vowel sound /o͞o/. Then have them write a sentence for each word in their notebooks.

> **Reaching All Students—Emergent Learners:** Review the meanings of the words in Exercise A. Call on a volunteer to write a sample sentence on the board. Then have students write the two sentences in their notebooks. Provide help as needed.

- Have students share their sentences with the class.

> **Answers**
> *Answers will vary.*

Expansion

- In their notebooks, have students head a column with this spelling for the vowel sound /o͞o/: *oo.* Then have them write as many words as they can under the heading. (Set a time limit of 5–10 minutes.) Encourage students to use a dictionary, their texts, or their vocabulary lists for help.

> **Reaching All Students—Auditory Learners:** Encourage students to say the words aloud as they write them.

- Have students share their lists with the class.

Grammar 3, page 161

Possessive Pronouns

Preparation

- Write the following dialogue on the board as a way of presenting the grammar focus in context.

  Carmen: There's a dollar bill on the table. *Whose* is this?

  Carlos: It's *mine.*

  Carmen: I don't think so. I think it's mom's.

  Carlos: No, it's not *hers.* It's *mine.*

  Paco: What are you two talking about? That's my money.

  Carmen: Ha! I knew it wasn't *yours,* Carlos.

- Read the dialogue aloud as students follow along. Then have the class read aloud with you.
- Call on two students to dramatize the dialogue for the rest of the class.

Presentation

- Have students look at the grammar chart.

  Reaching All Students—Auditory/Cooperative Learners: Have pairs of students take turns reading aloud sentences from the chart. Have the first student read a sentence with a possessive adjective from the left part of the chart and the second student read the corresponding sentence with a possessive pronoun from the right part of the chart. Continue for the remaining sentences.

- Point out several different objects in the room (a female student's pen, a male student's desk, your book, the class board). Say sentences about the objects using a possessive adjective. (Example: It's Maria's pen.) Call on volunteers to rephrase the sentences, using a possessive pronoun. (It's hers.)

Practice

- Have students number a sheet of paper in their notebooks from 1 to 5.
- Tell students that they will change the phrases with possessive adjectives in parentheses into possessive pronouns to complete the sentences.
- Call on a volunteer to read aloud the first sentence with the sample answer.
- Have students write the five sentences with possessive pronouns in their notebooks.

Reaching All Students—Emergent Learners: Have students work in pairs or small groups. Provide help as needed.

- Review the answers with the class.

> **Answers**
> 1. Those umbrellas are theirs.
> 2. This money is hers.
> 3. That house is ours.
> 4. This calculator is mine.
> 5. These pens are yours.

Questions with *whose*

Presentation

- Have students look at the grammar chart in their texts. Explain that questions with *Whose* ask who owns an item.
- Read aloud the questions and answers and have students repeat.
- Have students work in pairs or small groups to develop a rule that tells how to make *Whose* questions with demonstrative pronouns (*this, that, these, those*). Call on students to give their rules. Write the rule on the board. (Example: *Whose* + subject + verb *(be)* + demonstrative pronoun. The verb *be* and the demonstrative pronoun match the subject.)

Practice
Exercise A

- Have students number a sheet of paper in their notebooks from 1 to 5.
- Tell students that they will change the five statements from the previous exercise into *Whose* questions and that they will write short answers using possessive pronouns.
- Call on a student to read the previous statement aloud. Call on another student to read the example answer aloud. Have the student explain why the example is correct. (Make a question with *Whose* + subject (*umbrellas*) + verb *(be)* + demonstrative pronoun (*those*). *Are* and *those* match the subject. For the short answer, *they* and *are (they're)* match the subject. *Theirs* is the possessive pronoun for *their umbrellas.*)
- Have students change the statements into questions and write them in their notebooks. Have them also write the short answers. Tell students to use contractions in their short answers.

Reaching All Students—Emergent Learners: First, have students do the exercise orally. Then have them write the questions and short answers in their notebooks. Provide help as needed.

- Review the answers with the class. Have the class repeat each question and answer after you. Help with pronunciation and intonation as needed.

Answers

1. Whose umbrellas are those? They're theirs.
2. Whose money is this? It's hers.
3. Whose house is that? It's ours.
4. Whose calculator is this? It's mine.
5. Whose pens are these? They're yours.

Exercise B

Have students listen to the conversation, or read it aloud with an advanced student as the other students follow along in their texts.

Reaching All Students—Kinesthetic Learners: Act out the dialogue with an advanced student, or call on volunteers to act out the dialogue.

Exercise C

- Tell students that for this exercise they will first practice the conversation in Exercise B. Then they will make their own conversations.
- Have students work in groups of three. Have each group first practice the conversation in Exercise B.
- Then, as a class, brainstorm other items students might use in their own conversations.
- Have advanced students model their conversation.
- Have groups practice their conversations.
  Reaching All Students—Kinesthetic Learners: Call on volunteer groups to act out their conversations.

Expansion

Optional Activity: Tell the class that they will now play a game called "Whose is this?"

- Call on three students to come to the front of the room, each one with two personal objects. Have them put their objects on a table or desk. Then add two objects that belong to you. Have the students stand in a semi-circle around you, facing the class. Tell students that you're going to be the leader. Explain that you'll go around the circle, asking about the items. If a student can't answer in four seconds or makes a mistake, that student is out of the game. Pick up one or two of the objects and turn to the first student in the circle and ask, "Whose is this?" or "Whose are these?" Have the class repeat. Hand the object or objects to that student and have the student answer ("It's <u>hers</u>." or "They're <u>hers</u>."), prompting if needed. Have the class repeat. Direct the student to hand the object or objects to the owner. Continue going around the circle, asking questions, until all objects have been handed back to their owner. Model choosing the fastest student to be the next leader.

- Have students stand in groups of five or six. Have them choose a leader. Then have them play the game.
  Reaching All Students—Emergent Learners: Work with emergent learners in a group. Provide help as needed.

Reading, pages 162–163

Before You Read

Preparation

- Tell students that they will use the learning strategy *Use Selective Attention* to understand the story.
- Have students look at the Before You Read section in their texts. Read the text aloud as students follow along.

Practice

Ask students to brainstorm a list of ideas or words that could answer the question, "What did Carlos and Carmen's mother not want them to do?" Write students' responses on the board. Read them aloud, and have students repeat them after you.

Read This!

Mother's Plan

Preparation

Note: Students will encounter the following new words in the reading: *thunderstorm, end, broken, dangerous, perfect, rain, sunny, completely, instead, plan (n.), stop.*

Practice

🎧 Have students listen to the story, or read it aloud to them. Provide help with content, vocabulary, etc. as needed. Remind students to *Use Selective Attention* to answer the question, "What did Carlos and Carmen's mother not want them to do?"

Reaching All Students—Emergent Learners: Work with emergent learners in small groups while the other students work independently. Read aloud as students follow along in their texts. Monitor their comprehension by interrupting the reading with such questions as, "Did Carmen and Carlos think it was a perfect day to do homework?" (No, they didn't.) "When is it dangerous to watch TV or talk on the phone?" (It's dangerous during a thunderstorm.) "What does Carlos want to do instead of cleaning his room?" (He wants to do his homework.) "What did Carmen have to do?" (She had to clean Carlos's room.) "What did Carmen do after dinner?" (She talked on the phone with Liliana.) "What did Carlos do on Saturday?" (He went to the park with his friends.) Encourage students to answer the questions using complete sentences.

After You Read

Self-Evaluation
Exercise A

- Read the directions aloud as students follow along in their texts.
- Write the Before You Read question on the board ("What did Carlos and Carmen's mother not want them to do?") Read it aloud as students follow along.
- Call on a volunteer to tell if he or she used *Use Selective Attention* to find the answer to the question. Then ask the student to read the key idea from the story that helps to answer the question. ("Their mother did not think this was a good idea. She said, 'Turn off the TV.'") Have the student write the answer on the board. (Their mother did not think it was a good idea. She told them to turn off the TV.)
- Have students discuss their answers with a classmate.

Exercise B

- Have students number a sheet of paper in their notebooks from 1 to 5.
- Read the directions aloud as students follow along in their texts.
- Ask students whether the first sentence is true or false. (True.) Ask students to identify the statement in the story that supports their responses. (But she really did not want them to watch so much TV.)

Reaching All Students—Auditory Learners: Call on a volunteer to read the remaining sentences aloud before students complete the activity.

- Have students complete the exercise.
- Review the answers with the class. Be sure students give supportive statements from the text for their answers.
- Have students count the number of correct answers and write that number in their notebooks.

Answers
1. True.
2. False. Carmen and Carlos wanted to watch TV.
3. True.
4. False. After dinner, Carmen talked on the phone with Liliana.
5. False. On Saturday, Carmen did her homework.

Expansion

Point out that good readers use several strategies at one time to understand what they are reading. List the strategies students have learned on the board—*Make Predictions, Use Selective Attention, Use What You Know, Make Inferences,* and *Sound Out.* As you read the name of each strategy, ask students to raise their hand if they used the strategy while they read the story. Encourage students to use the strategies when reading in all of their classes.

Writing, page 164

Before You Write

Preparation *(See Transparencies 24 and 52–53.)*
Explain to students that they are going to write a paragraph about something that happened to them.

Exercise A

- Focus students' attention on the handwritten paragraph.

  Reaching All Students—Auditory Learners: Call on a student to read the paragraph aloud as the other students follow along in their texts.

- Ask students to tell what kind of information is in the paragraph. (A description of an accident, when it happened, where it happened, how it happened, what happened after the accident.) Write students' responses on the board.

Presentation

Exercise B

- Draw students' attention to the Before I Write checklist. Call on students to read aloud the points in the checklist.

- As a class, brainstorm with students other possible events they could write about. (Examples: an accident they had or saw; an achievement, such as playing in a sporting event or performing in a musical or theatrical event; an embarrassing moment; an exciting event they attended, such as a concert or famous play.) For each category, have students brainstorm words that could tell when, where, and how it happened. Write students' responses on the board.

- Model following the steps in the Before I Write checklist to plan your own paragraph.

- Have students follow the Before I Write checklist and make notes in their notebooks.

  Reaching All Students—Emergent Learners: Work with students in small groups. Guide them in following the steps in the checklist.

Write This!

Presentation

- Draw students' attention to the While I Write checklist. Call on students to read aloud the points in the checklist.

- Model following the While I Write checklist. Refer to the notes you took in the earlier modeling. As you write, do a "think aloud" about how you are following the While I Write checklist.

Practice

- Have students write their paragraphs in their notebooks, using their notes and the While I Write checklist for help.

- Circulate while students are writing and encourage them to ask you for help if needed.

After You Write

Presentation

Exercise A

- Draw students' attention to the After I Write checklist. Call on students to read aloud the points in the checklist.

- Model following the steps in the After I Write checklist, checking your own paragraph.

- Have students use the After I Write checklist to evaluate their writing. Have them circle and then correct any errors.

Exercise B

Have students read their paragraphs to a classmate. Encourage them to make suggestions for improvement.

Exercise C

Have students write a final copy of their paragraphs in their notebooks.

Expansion

- Have students illustrate their paragraphs and post them on a bulletin board.

- Set aside a time for students to read the other paragraphs on the bulletin board.

Learning Log, page 165

See How to Use the Learning Log on page xiii.
(See Transparencies 20 and 75.)

Chapter 15
We'll have a study group.

Objectives

Language:

- Listen to a dialogue for comprehension.
- Understand familiar vocabulary and grammar structures by listening to a dialogue.
- Develop new vocabulary and grammar structures by listening to a dialogue.
- Act out a dialogue.
- Use *will* in affirmative and negative statements about the future, *yes/no* questions, and information questions.
- Use *may* and *might* to talk about the possible future.
- Make original conversations using new vocabulary and grammar structures.
- Evaluate one's own learning of new vocabulary, grammar, and oral language.

Literacy:

- Read a dialogue for comprehension.
- Understand familiar vocabulary and grammar structures by reading a dialogue.
- Develop new vocabulary and grammar structures by reading a dialogue
- Complete and write *yes/no* questions, information questions, and affirmative and negative statements about the future using *will*.
- Decode words with the vowel sound /ô/.
- Complete and write sentences using *may* or *might* to talk about the possible future.
- Read a short story for comprehension.
- Understand familiar vocabulary and grammar structures by reading a short story.
- Develop new vocabulary and grammar structures by reading a short story.
- Plan, write, revise, edit, proofread, and make a final copy of paragraphs listing steps for reaching a goal.
- Create a step-by-step list, and use *will* to talk about the future in writing about reaching a goal.
- Evaluate one's own learning of reading skills, reading comprehension, and writing skills.

Learning Strategies:

- Use cooperation with a classmate to read a dialogue and study new vocabulary.
- Use cooperation with a small group to act out a dialogue.
- Use cooperation with a classmate to practice conversations.
- Use the strategy *Sound Out* to decode words.
- Use the strategy *Personalize* to understand a short story.
- Use cooperation with a classmate to check a dialogue one has written.
- Evaluate one's own learning of the strategies *Sound Out* and *Personalize*.
- Identify easy and difficult material in a chapter and the different ways to learn the difficult material.

Opening Dialogue, pages 166–167

Getting Ready

Preparation *(See Transparency 17.)*

- Have students look at the illustrations and identify the characters. Then ask them to name the items in the illustrations. Write the names and the words on the board or a poster. Say the names and words, and have students repeat.

- Ask students to make sentences about what they see and what the people are doing. Write students' responses on the board. If needed, model complete sentences. Read the sentences, and have students repeat them after you.

  Reaching All Students—Emergent Learners: Point to the first illustration and ask, "What are they doing?" Have students repeat. Call on students to respond. If needed, model the response. (They're having Mr. Gomez's class.) Have students repeat. Then ask students to make other sentences about what they see and what the people are doing.

Listening and Reading
Help for Maria
Presentation
Exercise A

- Read the directions and the prelistening question aloud as students follow along in their texts.

- Have students listen to the dialogue, or read the dialogue aloud to them. Have students look at the appropriate illustrations as they listen.

- Ask the prelistening question, "What can the students do to get ready for the exam?" Call on a volunteer to respond. (They can have a study group. They can study the vocabulary words and review the stories in their book.)

Exercise B

Have students read the dialogue. Provide help with content, vocabulary, etc. as needed.

> **Reaching All Students—Emergent Learners:** Work with emergent learners in small groups while the other students work independently. Read aloud as students follow along in their texts. Monitor their comprehension by interrupting the reading with such questions as, "What might Mr. Gomez give the students?" (He might give them extra homework.) "What does the class need to talk about?" (They need to talk about their final exam in reading.) "Who is worried about the exam?" (Maria is.) "Who will help Maria?" (Samir, Bic, and Carmen will.) "What will they do at the meeting?" (They will make plans for the study group.) "Who does Mei want to ask to come?" (She wants to ask her grandmother.) Have students repeat the questions, then the answers.

Pair and Group Work
Practice
Exercise A

Have students who can read on their own form pairs. Have students take turns reading each of the lines in the dialogue aloud. Provide help as needed.

> **Reaching All Students—Emergent Learners:** Work in small groups with emergent readers. Model each sentence and have individual students "echo" your

reading. Make sure that students look at the sentences as you read them.

Exercise B

Have students form groups of seven. Group students heterogeneously so that each group is made up of weak readers, average readers, and strong readers. Have each student choose a role in the dialogue. Have students practice acting out the dialogue in their groups.

> **Reaching All Students—Kinesthetic Learners:** Choose one or more groups to act out the dialogue in front of the class.

Vocabulary
Presentation

- Read the vocabulary words and expressions aloud and have students repeat them.
- Check students' understanding of the words and expressions.

Practice
Exercise A

Have students read and say the words and expressions. Provide assistance with pronunciation as needed. Then have students copy the words and expressions into their notebooks.

> **Reaching All Students—Auditory Learners:** Encourage students to say the words and expressions as they write them in their notebooks.

Exercise B (See Transparencies 85–87.)

- Have students turn to page 250 in their texts.
- Have students work through Steps 1–2 (recognizing letters and finding syllables) with the words in the box on page 167 if further practice is needed.
- Have students work in pairs on Step 3, identifying letters or letter combinations that follow patterns or make unexpected sounds. Encourage students to ask questions and to discover as much as they can on their own.

Exercise C

Have students find the words and expressions in the dialogue. Have them read the sentences aloud.

Exercise D

- Have students choose five words or expressions from the Vocabulary box. Have them write five questions to ask a classmate in their notebooks, using these new words. Have students underline the new vocabulary word in each sentence.

> **Reaching All Students—Emergent Learners:** As a class, brainstorm questions students could ask using the new vocabulary.

- Call on a pair of students to model asking and answering their questions. One student will ask a question and the other will answer it; then they'll change roles.
- Have students work in pairs to take turns asking and answering their questions.
- Call on pairs to share their questions and answers with the class.

Answers
Answers will vary.

Expansion

- Have students choose one of their questions to memorize.
- Have students put away their notebooks, stand, and ask their question to as many classmates as possible.

Grammar 1, page 168

Future Tense with *will*: Statements

Preparation

- Write the following dialogue on the board as a way of presenting the grammar focus in context.
  Mr. Gomez: Liliana wasn't in class today. She doesn't know about the meeting.
  Will someone *call* her tonight?
  Maria: Yes, I *will*.
  Mr. Gomez: Good. Please don't forget to call her.
  Maria: I *won't forget*. I promise.
- Read the dialogue aloud as students follow along. Then have the class read aloud with you.
- Call on two students to dramatize the dialogue for the rest of the class.

Presentation

- Have students look at the grammar chart. Explain that the left part of the chart shows affirmative statements with the future tense using *will*. The right part shows negative statements.
- Call on an individual student to read aloud across each row of the affirmative statements in the left part of the chart. Then, call on another student to read aloud the negative statements in the right part of the chart.

  > **Reaching All Students—Auditory/ Cooperative Learners:** Have pairs of students take turns reading sentences from the chart. Have the first student read an affirmative sentence from the left part of the chart and the second student read a negative sentence from the right part of the chart. Continue for the remaining sentences.

- Read aloud the Remember note at the bottom of the chart.
- Write a present tense sentence with a regular verb on the board. (I review.) Call on a volunteer to tell you how to change it into the future tense using *will*. (I will review.) Follow the same procedure for a negative statement. (I watch TV. / I won't watch TV.)
- Direct students' attention to the contractions box. Tell students that these are contractions for *will*. Point out that for affirmative statements, you just add *'ll* to the subject. Point out that the negative contraction *won't* is the same for every subject. Read the contractions aloud and have students repeat.
- Call on volunteers to read a sentence from the chart, substituting a contraction.

Practice

- Read the first sentence aloud. Have students repeat. Have a student read the sample answer aloud. Ask why the answer is correct. (When you're hungry, you want to eat, so it's an affirmative statement. You use *I'll*.)
- Have students copy the sentences into their notebooks and fill in the blanks, using contractions.

  > **Reaching All Students—Emergent Learners:** First, have students do the exercise orally. Then have them copy the incomplete sentences into their notebooks. Last, have them complete the sentences with the correct affirmative or negative *will* statements.

Provide help as needed, guiding them use the chart to find the answers.

- Review the answers with the class.

Answers
1. I'll
2. I won't
3. I'll
4. I won't
5. I'll

Future Tense with *will*: Yes/No Questions

Presentation

- Have students look at the grammar chart. Explain that the left part of the chart shows *yes/no* questions with *will* for the future (read the first row as an example). The middle part shows affirmative answers (read the first row as an example). The right part shows negative answers (read the first row as an example).

    Reaching All Students—Auditory/ Cooperative Learners: Have three students take turns reading sentences from the chart. Have the first student read the question, the second student read the affirmative answer, and the third student read the negative answer.

- Have students work in pairs or small groups to develop a rule that tells how to make *yes/no* questions with *will* for the future. Call on students to give their rules. Write the rule on the board. (Example: *Will* + subject + verb. *Will* is the same for all subjects. The main verb is in the plain form.)

Practice

- Have students number a sheet of paper in their notebooks from 1 to 5.
- Tell students they will change five statements into *yes/no* questions with *will* for the future.
- Call on a student to read the first statement aloud. Call on another student to read the sample answer aloud. Have the student explain why the answer is correct. (The subject becomes *you*. *Will* comes before the subject to make a question.)
- Have students change the statements to questions and write them in their notebooks.

    Reaching All Students—Emergent Learners: First, have students do the

exercise orally. Then have them copy the sentences into their notebooks. Last, have them write the questions. Provide help as needed.

- Review the answers with the class. Have the class repeat each question after you. Help with pronunciation and intonation as needed.

Answers
1. Will you study harder?
2. Will you keep your room cleaner?
3. Will you go to bed earlier?
4. Will you speak English a lot?
5. Will you do your homework every afternoon?

Grammar 2, page 169

Future Tense with *will*: Information Questions

Preparation

- Write the following dialogue on the board as a way of presenting the grammar focus in context.

    Maria: I'll bring some snacks to the study group.
    Liliana: Great! *What kind of* snacks *will* you *bring?*
    Maria: I'll bring some potato chips.
    Liliana: Sounds good!

- Read the dialogue aloud as students follow along. Then have the class read aloud with you.
- Call on two students to dramatize the dialogue for the rest of the class.

Presentation

- Have students look at the grammar chart. Tell them that this chart shows how to make information questions with *will*. If needed, remind them that information questions ask *who, what, when, where, why,* and *how*.
- Call on a pair of students to read aloud across each row in the chart. Have one student read the question on the left side and the other read the answer on the right side.

Practice

Exercise A

- Tell students that in this exercise, they'll match the questions on the left to the answers on the right. Tell them that they'll write the letter of the correct answer in their notebooks.

> **Reaching All Students—Auditory Learners:** Call on a student to read aloud all of the questions in the left-hand column as students follow along in their texts. Have another student read aloud all of the responses in the right-hand column.

- Read the question for item 1 aloud. Call on a volunteer to read aloud the correct letter and response. Have the student say why the answer is correct. (The response in *c* answers the *What* question. The pronoun for *Sophie* is *she,* and *c* has the pronoun *she.*)
- Have students number a sheet of paper in their notebooks from 1 to 5 and write the letters of the correct answers.
- Review the answers with the class.

```
Answers
1. c      4. a
2. e      5. d
3. b
```

Exercise B

 Have students listen to the conversation or read it aloud with a classmate.

> **Reaching All Students—Kinesthetic Learners:** Call on volunteers to act out the conversation for the rest of the class.

Exercise C

- Tell students that for this exercise they will first practice the conversation in Exercise B. Then they will make their own conversations.
- Divide the class into pairs. Have each pair practice the conversation in Exercise B.
- Have students check page 226 of the Vocabulary Handbook for other ideas for foods they might include in their own conversations.
- Then, as a class, brainstorm other foods students could use in their own conversations. (Examples: enchiladas, tortilla chips, vanilla ice cream, cookies, chili, sandwiches, iced tea.) Write them on the board.
- Work with two advanced students through a model conversation.
- Have students practice the conversation, using their own information.

> **Reaching All Students—Kinesthetic Learners:** Call on volunteer pairs to act out the conversation, using their own phrases, for the rest of the class.

Expansion

<u>Optional Activity:</u> Have students form small groups and select a group leader. Have students role play saying what snacks and drinks they'll bring to a study group. Have the group leader make notes of what each member will bring. Have one group model part of this activity for the class if needed. When groups have finished planning, call on group leaders to read their list to the class. Have the class vote on which study group is going to have the best snacks and drinks.

Word Study, page 170

Other Vowel Sound: /ô/

Preparation

- Write the words *auditorium* and *saw* on the board.
- Call on volunteers to identify the names of the consonants and vowels in the words.
- Pronounce the words and have students repeat them after you.

Presentation

- Underline the vowel *a* in *saw* on the board and ask students to pronounce the sound. Ask them if they hear the /ô/ sound. Repeat for the vowel sound in *auditorium.*
- Refer students to the instruction box in their texts. Tell them that they will look at two ways to form the vowel sound /ô/. Read the instruction box aloud and have the class repeat the example words.
- Point to the word *saw* on the board. Call on a volunteer to identify the first sound (/s/) and the second sound (/ô/).
- Ask students, "How many sounds does the word have?" (Two.) "How many letters does the word have?" (Three.) Tell them the letters *aw* together stand for one vowel sound, /ô/.
- Repeat the *Sound Out* strategy with the word *auditorium.*

Practice

Exercise A

Have students use the learning strategy *Sound Out*, as well as the illustrations, to read the words with the vowel sound /ô/.

Reaching All Students—Emergent Learners: Complete this activity as a class if students need help. After students have an approximation of the pronunciation, say the words correctly to provide a model.

Exercise B

- First, have students read the sentences aloud. Then have them copy the sentences into their notebooks. Last, have them circle the letters that represent the vowel sound /ô/.
- Review the answers as a class.

> **Answers**
> 1. What did she dr(aw) today?
> 2. The (au)dience really liked the show.
> 3. I need a str(aw) for my soda, please.
> 4. What are you going to do in (Au)gust?
> 5. She y(aw)ned at the end of the movie.
> 6. Our cat hurt its p(aw).

<u>Optional Activity:</u> Have students close their texts. Ask them to number a page in their notebooks from 1 to 8. Then ask them to listen carefully to the words you read and to write the words. Then dictate the following words:

1. draw	5. yawn
2. paw	6. autumn
3. author	7. straw
4. August	8. audience

- After the dictation, write the words on the board. Then have students check their words.
- Have students record the number of correct words in their notebooks; for example, *I wrote (7) out of 8 dictated words with the vowel sound /ô/correctly*. Write this example on the board as a model.

Exercise C

- Have students look at Exercise A. Have them choose two words with the vowel sound /ô/. Then have them write a sentence for each word in their notebooks. Have them underline the letters that represent the vowel sound /ô/.

  Reaching All Students—Emergent Learners: Review the meanings of the words in Exercise A. Call on a volunteer to write a sample sentence on the board. Then have students write the two sentences in their notebooks. Provide help as needed.

- Have students share their sentences with the class.

> **Answers**
> *Answers will vary.*

Expansion

- In their notebooks, have students head two columns with these spellings for the vowel sound /ô/: *au, aw*. Then have them write as many words as they can under the correct headings. (Set a time limit of 5–10 minutes.) Encourage students to use a dictionary, their texts, or their vocabulary lists for help.

  Reaching All Students—Auditory Learners: Encourage students to say the words aloud as they write them.

- Have students share their lists with the class.

Grammar 3, page 171

Statements with *may* and *might*

Preparation

- Write the following dialogue on the board as a way of presenting the grammar focus in context.

  Maria: What are you going to do this weekend?

  Liliana: I'm not sure. I *may* go to the movies with Sophie.

  Maria: Oh yeah?

  Liliana: Yeah. We *might* see the new Antonio Banderas movie.

- Read the dialogue aloud as students follow along. Then have the class read aloud with you.
- Call on two students to dramatize the dialogue for the rest of the class.

Presentation

- Have students look at the grammar chart.
- Explain that the left part of the chart shows affirmative statements with *may* or *might* and the right part shows negative statements.

- Call on a pair of students to read aloud across each row in the chart. Have one student read the affirmative statement on the left and the other read the negative statement on the right.
- Read aloud the Remember note at the bottom of the chart.
- Have students work in pairs or small groups to develop a rule that tells how to make statements with *may* and *might*. Call on students to give their rules. Write the rule on the board. (Example: Subject + *may/might* + verb. *May/might* doesn't change. The main verb is in the base form.)

Practice

Exercise A

- Read the directions aloud as students follow along in their texts. Ask students if they should use *going to, may,* or *might* for Pablo's statements. (*May* or *might*.) Ask the same question about Bic. (*Be going to.*) Point out that students will complete either affirmative or negative sentences.
- Call on two students to read the first two sentences in the dialogue aloud. Ask why the answer is correct. (It is an affirmative sentence. Pablo has possible plans, so he uses *may* or *might*.) Point out that either *may* or *might* is correct. Remind students to use *be going to, may,* and *might* at least once each.
- Have students copy the dialogue into their notebooks and fill in the blanks.

    Reaching All Students—Emergent Learners: First, have students do the exercise orally. Then have them copy the dialogue into their notebooks and complete it. Provide help as needed.

- Review the answers with the class.

Answers
1. might (or may)
2. might (or may)
3. might not (or may not)
4. may (or might)
5. am going to

Expansion

- Read the dialogue aloud and have students repeat.
- Have students practice the dialogue in pairs.

Exercise B

- Read the directions for Exercise B aloud as students follow along in their texts. Tell students that they will write true sentences about their weekend plans.
- Refer students to page 222 of the Vocabulary Handbook for other activities.

    Reaching All Students—Emergent Learners: As a class, brainstorm vocabulary for other activities they could write about. Write them on the board. Say the items as sentences with *going to, may,* or *might,* and have students repeat.

- Have students write six sentences in their notebooks about their weekend plans. Remind them to use *be going to, may,* and *might* at least once each.
- When students have finished writing, have them form pairs. Have students take turns telling their plans to a classmate.
- Call on volunteers to tell the class about their weekend plans.

Expansion

- Give students a moment to study and memorize their plans.
- On the board, write *What are you going to do this weekend?* Also write several phrases for showing interest such as *Oh really? Yeah? Sounds fun. That's great.*
- Tell students they will now close their notebooks and practice a conversation about their weekend plans.
- Call on a volunteer to model a conversation with you for the class. Ask the question on the board. As the student tells about his or her plans, respond with the phrases for showing interest written on the board. When the student has finished, have the student ask what you are going to do this weekend. Encourage the student to respond using the phrases for showing interest on the board.
- Have students stand and talk to as many classmates as possible about their weekend plans.
- Call on a volunteer pair to perform their conversation for the class.

Reading, pages 172–173

Before You Read

Presentation *(See Transparency 16.)*

- Have students look at the Learning Strategy box *Personalize*. Call on a student to read the Learning Strategy box aloud.

- Ask students to tell you some of their favorite movies. Ask if they thought about what the character in the movie was thinking and feeling. Ask if this made the movie more fun to watch. Ask students to tell you some of their favorite books or stories. Ask if they thought about what the characters were thinking and feeling.

- Point out that thinking about what a character is feeling, thinking, and doing is to *Personalize*. Tell them that they can use this as a strategy to understand what they read. It makes reading more interesting and will help them remember information in the story.

- Have students look at the Before You Read section. Call on a volunteer to read aloud the questions as students follow along in their texts.

Read This!

Grandmother Chu

Preparation

Note: Students will encounter the following new words in the reading: *chin, ear, eye, life, translator, Vietnamese, go ahead, hold, light (lit) up, nod, translate, whisper, lovely, proud, softly, quietly.*

Practice

Have students listen to the story, or read it aloud to them. Provide help with content, vocabulary, etc. as needed. Ask students individually if they are using the strategy *Personalize* to understand the story.

Reaching All Students—Emergent Learners: Work with emergent learners in small groups while the other students work independently. Read aloud as students follow along in their texts. Monitor their comprehension by interrupting the reading with such questions as, "What does Mei's grandmother tell stories about?" (She tells stories about her life in China.) "Can Mei's grandmother speak English well?" (No, she can't.) "Why didn't she go to school?" (She had to work.) "How did she learn to read Chinese?" (Mei's mother taught her.) "Who did Mei want to make proud?" (She wanted to make her grandmother proud.) "Who will have a study group for Mei and her friends?" (Mei's grandmother will.) Encourage students to answer the questions using complete sentences.

After You Read

Self-Evaluation

Exercise A

- Read the questions aloud. Have students discuss their answers with a classmate.

- When students have finished writing, call on volunteers to share their responses.

> **Answers**
> *Answers will vary.*

Exercise B

- Call on a student to read the first question aloud. Call on another student to give the answer. Have the student identify the statement in the story that support his or her response. (At night, she tells me stories about her life in China.)

    Reaching All Students—Auditory Learners: Call on a student to read the remaining questions aloud as the other students follow along in their texts.

- Have students number a page in their notebooks from 1 to 4 and write answers to the questions.

    Reaching All Students—Emergent Learners: Have students work in pairs or in small groups. Provide help as needed.

- Review the answers with the class. Be sure students give supportive statements from the text for their answers.

- Have students count the number of correct answers and write that number in their notebooks.

Expansion

Ask students how the strategy *Personalize* helped them understand the story.

Writing, page 174

Before You Write

Preparation *(See Transparencies 21 and 54–55.)*

Explain to students that they are going to write a few paragraphs about a goal. Give several examples of goals. (Examples: doing well in school, getting a job, playing a sport well, speaking English well.)

Exercise A

- Focus students' attention on the handwritten paragraphs.

   Reaching All Students—Auditory Learners: Call on a student to read the paragraphs aloud as the other students follow along in their texts.

- Ask students to tell what kind of information is included in the paragraphs. (A goal, a list of ways to reach the goal, the easiest and hardest steps.) Write students' responses on the board.

Presentation

Exercise B

- Draw students' attention to the Before I Write checklist. Call on students to read aloud the points in the checklist.
- As a class, brainstorm with students other goals they could write about. Write students' responses on the board.
- Brainstorm a structure students could use for their writing (a paragraph introducing the goal; a numbered list of steps needed to reach the goal; a paragraph about which steps are the easiest and hardest and how they feel reaching the goal).
- Have students follow the Before I Write checklist and make notes in their notebooks.

Reaching All Students—Emergent Learners: Work with students in small groups. Guide them in following the steps in the checklist.

Write This!

Presentation

- Draw students' attention to the While I Write checklist. Call on students to read aloud the points in the checklist.
- Explain and model on the board each of the writing points in this section while you write a few lines about reaching a goal. As you write, do a "think aloud" about how you are following the While I Write checklist.

Practice

- Have students write their goals and steps in their notebooks, using their notes and the While I Write checklist for help.
- Circulate while students are writing and encourage them to ask you for help if needed.

After You Write

Presentation

Exercise A

- Draw students' attention to the After I Write checklist. Call on students to read aloud the points in the checklist.
- Model following the steps in the After I Write checklist, checking your own paragraphs.
- Have students use the After I Write checklist to evaluate their writing. Have them circle and then correct any errors.

Exercise B

Have students read their paragraphs to a classmate. Encourage them to make suggestions for improvement.

Exercise C

Have students write a final copy of their paragraphs in their notebooks.

Expansion

Call on volunteers to come to the front of the class and read their paragraphs aloud.

Learning Log, page 175

See How to Use the Learning Log on page xiii. *(See Transparencies 20 and 76.)*

FEELINGS & HOBBIES

Unit Opener, pages 176–177

Preview

- Call on a student to read aloud the unit title, "Feelings & Hobbies." Tell students that in this unit they'll practice talking about hobbies and feelings.

- Have students look at the photos and identify the people, objects, activities, and settings. (Examples: There's a boy in a school band. He's playing a piccolo. He's wearing a band uniform. A boy is smiling happily. A girl is in class at school. She's thinking about something. She might be thinking about a test, a boyfriend, etc. She might feel sad.) Provide help as needed. Write students' responses on the board. Read the responses aloud and have the class repeat.

- Write the word *feelings* on the board. Give a few examples of feeling words (*happy, sad, miserable*). Then have students call out as many different feeling words as they can. Write students' responses on the board. Write the word *hobbies* on the board. Explain that hobbies are fun activities you do in your free time and give some examples (playing in a band, skateboarding, taking skating lessons). Then call on students to tell you some of their hobbies. List these on the board. Provide help with vocabulary as needed.

- Read the unit goals aloud as students follow along in their texts. Answer any questions they may have.

Chapter 16
I sometimes study with my friends.

Objectives

Language:

- Listen to a dialogue for comprehension.
- Understand familiar vocabulary and grammar structures by listening to a dialogue.
- Develop new vocabulary and grammar structures by listening to a dialogue.
- Act out a dialogue.
- Use adverbs of frequency before regular verbs and after *be*.
- Ask *How often* questions and use expressions of frequency.
- Use gerunds as objects of verbs.
- Make original conversations using new vocabulary and grammar structures.
- Ask for and give information.
- Evaluate one's own learning of new vocabulary, grammar, and oral language.

Literacy:

- Read a dialogue for comprehension.
- Understand familiar vocabulary and grammar structures by reading a dialogue.
- Develop new vocabulary and grammar structures by reading a dialogue.
- Write a dialogue using new vocabulary.
- Complete and write sentences using adverbs of frequency before regular verbs and after *be*.
- Complete and write statements with expressions of frequency.
- Decode words with the vowel sound /oi/.
- Write sentences using gerunds as objects of verbs.
- Read a short story for comprehension.
- Understand familiar vocabulary and grammar structures by reading a short story.
- Develop new vocabulary and grammar structures by reading a short story.
- Write interview questions about a classmate's hobby.
- Plan, write, revise, edit, proofread, and make a final copy of a descriptive paragraph about a classmate's hobby.
- Use gerunds, adverbs of frequency, and expressions of frequency in writing a paragraph about a classmate's hobby.
- Evaluate one's own learning of reading skills, reading comprehension, and writing skills.

Learning Strategies:

- Use cooperation with a classmate to read a dialogue and study new vocabulary.
- Use cooperation with a small group to act out a dialogue.
- Use cooperation with a classmate to practice conversations.
- Use the strategy *Sound Out* to decode words.
- Use the strategy *Use What You Know* to understand a short story.
- Use cooperation with a classmate to check a paragraph one has written.
- Evaluate one's own learning of the strategies *Sound Out* and *Use What You Know*.
- Identify easy and difficult material in a chapter and the different ways to learn the difficult material.

Opening Dialogue, pages 178–179

Getting Ready

Preparation *(See Transparency 17.)*

- Have students look at the illustrations and identify the characters. Then ask them to name the items in the illustrations. Write the names and the words on the board or a poster. Say the names and the words, and have students repeat.
- Ask students to make sentences about what they see and what the people are doing. Write students' responses on the board. If needed, model complete sentences. Read the sentences, and have students repeat them after you.

  Reaching All Students—Emergent Learners: Point to the first illustration and ask "Where are they?" Have students repeat. Call on students to respond. If needed, model the response. (They're in a living room.) Have students repeat. Then ask students to make other sentences about what they see and what the people are doing.

Listening and Reading

The Study Group

Presentation

Exercise A

- Read the directions and the prelistening question aloud as students follow along in their texts.
- Have students listen to the dialogue, or read the dialogue aloud to them. Have students look at the appropriate illustrations as they listen.
- Ask the prelistening question, "When does Sophie have dance class?" Call on a volunteer to respond. (She has dance class every afternoon.)

Exercise B

Have students read the dialogue. Provide help with content, vocabulary, etc. as needed.

Reaching All Students—Emergent Learners: Work with emergent learners in small groups while the other students work independently. Read aloud as students follow along in their texts. Monitor their comprehension by interrupting the reading with such questions as, "Why was Carlos late?" (Soccer practice went a little longer than usual.) "What does Carlos do at soccer practice?" (He sometimes helps the coach.) "What is Carlos always thinking about?" (He's always thinking about food.) "Why is Maria worried?" (She has such a hard time with English.) "How often does Carmen study?" (She studies about three times a week.) "Who isn't at the study group yet?" (Sophie isn't.) Have students repeat the questions, then the answers.

Pair and Group Work

Practice

Exercise A

Have students who can read on their own form pairs. Have one student in the pair take the roles of Carlos, Pablo, and Mei; have the other student take the roles of Carmen and Maria.

Then have them read the dialogue aloud. Provide help as needed.

Reaching All Students—Emergent Learners: Work in small groups with emergent readers. Model each sentence and have individual students "echo" your reading. Make sure that students look at the sentences as you read them.

Exercise B

Have students form groups of five. Group students heterogeneously so that each group is made up of weak readers, average readers, and strong readers. Have each student choose a role in the dialogue. Have students practice acting out the dialogue in their groups.

Reaching All Students—Kinesthetic Learners: Choose one or more groups to act out the dialogue in front of the class.

Vocabulary

Presentation

- Read the vocabulary words and expressions aloud and have students repeat them.
- Check students' understanding of the words and expressions.

Practice

Exercise A

Have students read and say the words and expressions. Provide assistance with pronunciation as needed. Then have students copy the words and expressions into their notebooks.

Reaching All Students—Auditory Learners: Encourage students to say the words and expressions as they write them in their notebooks.

Exercise B *(See Transparencies 85–87.)*

- Have students turn to page 250 in their texts.
- Have students work through Step 1–2 (recognizing letters and finding syllables) with the words in the box on page 179, if further practice is needed.
- Have students work in pairs on Step 3, identifying letters or letter combinations that follow patterns or make unexpected sounds. Encourage students to ask questions and to discover as much as they can on their own.

Exercise C

Have students find the words and expressions in the dialogue. Have them read the sentences aloud.

Exercise D

- Tell students that they will write five sentences using five words from the word box in their notebooks.

    Reaching All Students—Emergent Learners: Work with students in small groups.

    Reaching All Students—Advanced Learners: Challenge advanced students to use as many words from the list as they can.

- Have students work in pairs to read their sentences.

> **Answers**
> *Answers will vary.*

Grammar 1, page 180

Adverbs of Frequency

Preparation

- Write the following dialogue on the board as a way of presenting the grammar focus in context.

    Carmen: Are you going to study English this afternoon?

    Samir: No, I *always* go to basketball practice in the afternoon.

    Carmen: When do you *usually* do homework?

    Samir: I *usually* do homework after dinner. But I *sometimes* get up early and do it in the morning.

    Carmen: In the morning? That's strange. I *never* do that!

- Read the dialogue aloud as students follow along. Then have the class read aloud with you.

- Call on two students to dramatize the dialogue for the rest of the class.

Presentation

- Have students look at the grammar chart. Explain that the bars illustrate the adverbs of frequency.

- Call on an individual student to read aloud the adverbs of frequency on the left part of the chart.

- Ask the class questions using frequency adverbs to make sure they understand them. (Examples: "Who always gets up at six? Raise your hand." / "Who often gets up at six? Raise your hand.")

- Read aloud the Remember note at the bottom of the chart.

Practice

- Read the first sentence and adverb aloud. Have a student read the sample answer aloud. Ask why the answer is correct. (Adverbs of frequency usually go before regular verbs.)

- Have students number a page in their notebooks from 1 to 5 and write sentences using the frequency adverbs in parentheses.

    Reaching All Students—Auditory Learners: Call on advanced students to read each of the remaining sentences before students write their answers.

- Review the answers with the class.

> **Answers**
> 1. Sophie usually eats dinner at six.
> 2. Carlos and Carmen sometimes study together.
> 3. Maria always worries about tests.
> 4. Mei and Sophie often think about Paco.
> 5. Pablo never goes to bed early.

Adverbs of Frequency with *be*

Presentation

- Refer students to the grammar chart in their texts.

- Read aloud the Remember note at the bottom of the grammar chart.

- Call on students to read aloud the sentences from the chart.

Practice

- Read the directions aloud as students follow along in their texts.

- Read the first sentence aloud. Call on a student to read the sample answer. Ask if the student is always, usually, often, sometimes, or never hungry after school. Ask the same question to several different students to generate different responses.

- Have students write true sentences in their notebooks using the frequency adverbs.

    Reaching All Students—Auditory Learners: Call on advanced students to read each of the remaining sentences before students write their answers.

    Reaching All Students—Emergent Learners: First, have students do the exercise orally. Then have them write the sentences in their notebooks.

- Have students form pairs when they have finished writing. Have students take turns reading each of their sentences.
- Call on volunteers to share their answers with the class.

Answers
Answers will vary.
1. I'm (always/usually/often/sometimes/never) hungry after school.
2. I'm (always/usually/often/sometimes/never) tired in the morning.
3. I'm (always/usually/often/sometimes/never) late.
4. I'm (always/usually/often/sometimes/never) a good student.
5. I'm (always/usually/often/sometimes/never) silly.

Grammar 2, page 181

How often and Expressions of Frequency

Preparation

- Write the following dialogue on the board as a way of presenting the grammar focus in context.
  Pablo: I'm going to go fishing this afternoon.
    Bic: Oh really? *How often do* you *go fishing*?
  Pablo: I go fishing *once or twice a week*.
- Read the dialogue aloud as students follow along. Then have the class read aloud with you.
- Call on two students to dramatize the dialogue for the rest of the class.

Presentation

- Have students look at the grammar chart. Point out that the first part of the chart shows a *How often* question. Read the question aloud and have students repeat. Tell

them that the second part of the chart shows ways to tell how often something happens. Explain that both *one time* and *once* are correct, as are *two times* and *twice*.
- Call on a student to read aloud across each row in the second part of the chart.
- Call on another student to make new sentences combining the words in the middle section of the first part of the chart (*once time/once, twice*, etc.) with different words in the right section of the second part of the chart (*a day, a month*, etc.).
- Point out that, unlike adverbs of frequency, expressions of frequency go after regular verbs.

Practice
Exercise A

- Read the first sentence aloud. Call on a student to read aloud the sample answer. Ask the student, "How often do you *really* clean your room?" Ask the same question to several different students to generate different responses.
- Have students write true sentences in their notebooks using the expressions of frequency.

    Reaching All Students—Auditory Learners: Call on students to read aloud each of the remaining sentences before students write their answers.

    Reaching All Students—Emergent Learners: First, have students do the exercise orally. Then have them write the sentences in their notebooks.

- Review the answers with the class.

Answers
Answers will vary.

Exercise B

- Tell students that they will ask and answer *How often* questions for each of the items in Exercise A.
- Call on two students to model asking and answering *How often* questions.
- Have students work in pairs to ask and answer *How often* questions.

    Reaching All Students—Emergent Learners: Have students form the questions orally before working in pairs.

- Call on a few pairs to share their questions and answers with the class.

Exercise C

- Read the instructions aloud. Then read the cues in the box aloud and have students repeat.

  Reaching All Students—Emergent Learners: Call on two students to model asking and answering *How often* questions with a couple of the items in the box before the class works in pairs.

- Have students work in pairs. Have them ask and answer *How often* questions based on the items in the box.

- Call on pairs to share their questions and answers with the class.

Expansion

Optional Activity: Have students close their books and stand. Tell them that they will form pairs with as many different classmates as possible. Each student will ask and answer a *How often* question, then form a pair with a different classmate to ask and answer a *How often* question. Give students a minimum number of classmates to pair with (for example, at least five different classmates) if needed.

Word Study, page 182

Other Vowel Sound: /oi/

Preparation

- Write the words *voice* and *enjoy* on the board.
- Call on volunteers to identify the names of the consonants and vowels in the words.
- Pronounce the words and have students repeat them after you.

Presentation

- Underline the vowels *oi* in *voice* on the board and ask students to pronounce the sound. Ask them if they hear the /oi/ sound. Repeat for the vowel sound in *enjoy*.
- Refer students to the instruction box in their texts. Tell them that they will look at the most common ways to form the vowel sound /oi/. Read the instruction box aloud as students follow along.
- Point to the word *voice* on the board. Call on a volunteer to identify the first sound (/v/), the second sound (/oi/), and the third sound (/s/).

- Ask students, "How many sounds does the word have?" (Three.) "How many letters does the word have?" (Five.)
- Explain that the vowels *oi* together stand for one vowel sound, /oi/. This sound is called a diphthong. A diphthong is a sound in which the mouth moves from one position to another while the sound is being made. Exaggerate and extend the /oi/ sound to show students how the mouth position changes. Have students repeat and touch their mouths to feel the shift.
- Repeat the *Sound Out* strategy with the word *enjoy*.

Practice
Exercise A

Have students use the learning strategy *Sound Out*, as well as the pictures, to read the words with the vowel sound /oi/.

  Reaching All Students—Emergent Learners: Complete this activity as a class if students need help. After students have an approximation of the pronunciation, say the words correctly to provide a model.

Exercise B

- First, have students read the sentences aloud. Then have them copy the sentences into their notebooks. Last, have them circle the letters that represent the vowel sound /oi/.
- Review the answers as a class.

Answers
1. Is R(oy) a new student in your class?
2. I like finding old c(oi)ns.
3. The water in the pot is b(oi)ling.
4. The b(oy)s are playing in the gym.
5. Did Sophie buy a t(oy) for the new baby?
6. You need to put more (oi)l in the pan.

Optional Activity: Have students close their texts. Ask them to number a page in their notebooks from 1 to 8. Then ask them to listen carefully to the words you read and to write the words. Then dictate the following words:

1. boy	5. toy
2. soil	6. Roy
3. boil	7. oil
4. coin	8. point

- After the dictation, write the words on the board. Then have students check their words.
- Have students record the number of correct words in their notebooks; for example, *I wrote (7) out of 8 dictated words with the vowel sound /oi/ correctly.* Write this example on the board as a model.

Exercise C

- Have students look at Exercise A. Have them choose two words with the vowel sound /oi/. Then have them write a sentence for each word in their notebooks.

    Reaching All Students—Emergent Learners: Review the meanings of the words in Exercise A. Call on a volunteer to write a sample sentence on the board. Then have students write the two sentences in their notebooks. Provide help as needed.

- Have students share their sentences with the class.

> **Answers**
> *Answers will vary.*

Expansion

- In their notebooks, have students head two columns with these spellings for the vowel sound /oi/: *oi, oy*. Then have them write as many words as they can under the correct headings. (Set a time limit of 5–10 minutes.) Encourage students to use a dictionary, their texts, or their vocabulary lists for help.

    Reaching All Students—Auditory Learners: Encourage students to say the words aloud as they write them.

- Have students share their lists with the class.

Grammar 3, page 183

Gerunds as Objects of Verbs

Preparation

- Write the following dialogue on the board as a way of presenting the grammar focus in context.
    Liliana: Do you like *cooking*?
    Mei: Yeah, I love *cooking*, especially Chinese food.

Liliana: Really? I hate *cooking*. I always burn everything!

- Read the dialogue aloud as students follow along. Then have the class read aloud with you.
- Call on two students to dramatize the dialogue for the rest of the class.

Presentation

- Have students look at the grammar chart. Call on a volunteer to read aloud the sentences in the chart. Point out the gerund in each sentence.
- Read aloud the information at the top of the chart.

Practice
Exercise A

- Read the directions aloud as students follow along in their texts. Write the words *love, enjoy, like, don't like,* and *hate* on one side of the board. On the other side of the board, write these symbols: + +, +, −, − −. Call on volunteers to rate each of the words with the symbols (love + +, enjoy +, like +, don't like −, hate − −).
- Read the first item aloud. Have a student read the sample answer aloud. Ask the student, "Do you *really* enjoy studying math?" Have the student choose the most appropriate verb from the board and say a true sentence. Ask several individual students to say a true sentence with "study math" to generate different responses.
- Have students write true sentences in their notebooks, using gerunds for the words shown.
- Call on volunteers to share their answers with the class.

> **Answers**
> *Answers will vary.*

Exercise B

- Read the directions aloud as students follow along in their texts.
- As a class, brainstorm other topics students could talk about. (Possible categories: hobbies and free time activities, activities at school, chores.) Write them on the board.

    Reaching All Students—Emergent Learners: Have several students form sentences orally using words on the

board before students write their
sentences.

- Have students write five sentences in their notebooks about things they like and don't like doing. Remind them to use the words *love, like, enjoy, don't like,* and *hate* at least once each.
- Have students form pairs and take turns reading their sentences to a classmate.
- Call on pairs to share their sentences with the class.

Exercise C

 Have students listen to the conversation, or read it aloud with a classmate.

Reaching All Students—Kinesthetic Learners: Call on volunteers to act out the conversation for the rest of the class.

Exercise D

- Tell students that for this exercise they will first practice the conversation in Exercise C. Then they will make their own conversations.
- Divide the class into pairs. Have each pair practice the conversation in Exercise C.
- Have students check page 226 of the Vocabulary Handbook for other ideas for foods they might include in their own conversations.
- Then, as a class, brainstorm other things students like or don't like doing that they could use in their own conversations. (Examples: playing tennis, washing the dog, shopping for clothes, cooking, singing.) Write them on the board.
- Work with two advanced students through a model conversation.
- Have students practice the conversation, using their own information.

    Reaching All Students—Kinesthetic Learners: Call on volunteer pairs to act out the conversation, using their own phrases for the rest of the class.

Expansion

Optional Activity: Write the following conversation on the board:
A: Do you enjoy *going to the movies?*
B: *Yes,* I *love going to the movies.*
Tell students that they will use the sentences they wrote in Exercise B to ask about their classmates' likes and dislikes. Call on two students to model taking turns changing one of their statements into a question, then answering. Then tell students to stand and form pairs

with as many different classmates as possible. Each student will ask and answer a *Do you enjoy* question from one of their sentences, then form a pair with a different classmate to ask and answer. Give students a minimum number of classmates to pair with (for example, at least five different classmates) if needed.

Reading, pages 184–185

Before You Read

Preparation (See Transparency 20.)

- Tell students that they will be using the learning strategy *Use What You Know* to understand the story.
- Ask students what they remember about this strategy. Write their responses on the board. (When we read, we can use what we already know about people and places to help us understand the story better.)

Practice

- Have students look at the Before You Read section. Read the first question aloud and call on a volunteer to answer. (The story is about Sophie.)
- Read the second question aloud and have students work in pairs to discuss what they know about Sophie.
- Call on volunteers to share their responses with the class. Write students' responses on the board.

Read This!

The Dancer

Preparation

Note: Students will encounter the following new words in the reading: *dancer, activity, balance, exercise, myself, balance (v.), enjoy, include, join, plan (v.), tell, friendly, intelligent, celebration, chore, club, festival, get together, memory, recreation center, relatives, town, practice (v.).*

Practice

 Have students listen to the story, or read it aloud to them. Provide help with content, vocabulary, etc. as needed. Ask students individually if they are using the strategy *Use What You Know* to understand the story.

Reaching All Students—Emergent Learners: Work with emergent learners in small groups while the other students work independently. Read aloud as students follow along in their texts. Monitor their comprehension by interrupting the reading with such questions as, "What did Sophie practice when she was a child?" (She practiced dances for the festivals.) "Why does Sophie think her friends should try taking dance lessons?" (Because it's fun, and it's great exercise.). "Why is it difficult for Sophie to join the study group?" (Because she needs time to do her house chores and homework.) "What is Sophie's mom probably right about?" (She says students have to balance school and fun.) "Does Sophie like being with other people when she studies?" (Yes, she does.) Encourage students to answer the questions using complete sentences.

After You Read

Self-Evaluation

Exercise A *(See Transparency 20.)*

- Read the first two questions aloud and call on volunteers to answer.
- Read the third question aloud and have students discuss their answers with a classmate. Then call on individual students to give their responses.

> **Answers**
> *Answers will vary. Possible answers include:* Sophie loves dancing. Dance is her favorite free-time activity. She is a very good dancer. She usually goes to dance club three times a week. She likes being with other people when she studies.

Exercise B

- Read the directions aloud as students follow along in their texts. Point out that this *true/false* activity includes the answer *I don't know* for statements that don't have clear answers in the story. Say, "For example, if the statement was, 'Sophie likes to go to the movies,' the answer is *I don't know* because the story doesn't say anything about movies."
- Call on a volunteer to read aloud the first sentence. Ask students whether the answer is *True, False,* or *I don't know.* (True.) Ask stu-

dents to identify the statement in the story that supports their response. (It was so much fun. Sophie says, "Dancing in the festivals is one of my favorite memories of my life in Haiti.")

> **Reaching All Students—Auditory Learners:** Call on a student to read the remaining sentences aloud as the other students follow along in their texts.

- Have students number a page in their notebooks from 1 to 5 and complete the exercise.
- Review the answers with the class. Be sure students give supportive statements from the text for their answers.

> **Answers**
> 1. True.   4. True.
> 2. True.   5. False.
> 3. I don't know.

Expansion

List all the strategies on the board—*Use What You Know, Make Predictions, Use Selective Attention, Make Inferences, Personalize,* and *Sound Out.* Ask students if they used any other strategies while they read this story. Have students raise their hands if they used the strategy. Remind students that good readers use more than one strategy to understand what they are reading.

Writing, page 186

Before You Write

Preparation *(See Transparencies 24 and 56–57.)*

Explain to students that they are going to write questions to ask a classmate about a hobby or interest. Then they are going to interview, or ask questions to, the classmate. Finally, they will write a paragraph about that classmate's hobby.

Exercise A

- Focus students' attention on the handwritten paragraph.

> **Reaching All Students—Auditory Learners:** Call on a student to read the paragraph aloud as the other students follow along in their texts.

- Ask students to tell what kind of information is in the paragraph. (Information about a classmate's hobby, how well she plays, how often she practices, how often she plays in tournaments, how often she wins, who she likes to pay with and why.) Write students' responses on the board.

Presentation

Exercise B

- Draw students' attention to the Before I Write checklist. Call on students to read aloud the points in the checklist.
- Have students look at the writing model and think what questions the writer could have asked to get that information. As a class, brainstorm 5 to 10 interview questions students could use to ask classmates about their hobbies. (Examples: What is your favorite hobby? How well do you do it? How often do you do it? When do you usually do it? Who do you do it with? What do you like about it? How did you learn your hobby?) Write the interview questions on the board.
- Have students write the interview questions in their notebooks.

Practice

Exercise C

- Call on two volunteers to model asking and answering a few of the interview questions. Have the interviewer take notes on the board.
- Have students work in pairs. Have them ask each other the interview questions, taking notes in their notebooks. Circulate to answer questions about spelling and vocabulary.

    Reaching All Students—Emergent Learners: Work with emergent learners in small groups. Guide them in conducting the interview and taking notes.

Write This!

Presentation

- Draw students' attention to the While I Write checklist. Call on students to read aloud the points in the checklist.

- Call on the interviewer who took notes on the board earlier. Tell the student to use the notes on the board to write the first two or three sentences of a model paragraph. Have the student write the sentences on the board.

Practice

- Have students write their paragraphs in their notebooks, using their notes and the While I Write checklist for help.
- Circulate while students are writing and encourage them to ask you for help if needed.

After You Write

Presentation

Exercise A

- Draw students' attention to the After I Write checklist. Call on students to read aloud the points in the checklist.
- Have students use the After I Write checklist to evaluate their writing. Have them circle and then correct any errors.

Exercise B

Have students read their paragraphs to a classmate. Encourage them to make suggestions for improvement.

Exercise C

Have students write a final copy of their paragraphs in their notebooks.

Expansion

- Have students illustrate their paragraphs and post them on a bulletin board.
- Set aside a time for students to read the other paragraphs on the bulletin board.

Learning Log, page 187

See How to Use the Learning Log on page xiii.
(See Transparencies 20 and 77.)

Chapter 17
You should get some rest.

Objectives

Language:
- Listen to a dialogue for comprehension.
- Understand familiar vocabulary and grammar structures by listening to a dialogue.
- Develop new vocabulary and grammar structures by listening to a dialogue.
- Act out a dialogue.
- Use the modals *should* and *shouldn't* in affirmative and negative statements and *yes/no* questions.
- Use the modal *could* to make suggestions.
- Use compound sentences with *because* clauses.
- Make original conversations using new vocabulary and grammar structures.
- Evaluate one's own learning of new vocabulary, grammar, and oral language.

Literacy:
- Read a dialogue for comprehension.
- Understand familiar vocabulary and grammar structures by reading a dialogue.
- Develop new vocabulary and grammar structures by reading a dialogue.
- Write a dialogue using new vocabulary.
- Write *yes/no* questions and affirmative and negative statements using *should* and *shouldn't*.
- Write sentences using *could* to make suggestions.
- Decode words with the vowel sound /ou/.
- Write compound sentences with *because* clauses.
- Read a short story for comprehension.
- Understand familiar vocabulary and grammar structures by reading a short story.
- Develop new vocabulary and grammar structures by reading a short story.
- Act out a short story.
- Plan, write, revise, edit, proofread, and make a final copy of letters to and from an advice columnist.

- Use letter format, *should*, and *because* to write letters to and from an advice columnist.
- Evaluate one's own learning of reading skills, reading comprehension, and writing skills.

Learning Strategies:
- Use cooperation with a classmate to read a dialogue and study new vocabulary.
- Use cooperation with a small group to act out a dialogue and a short story.
- Use cooperation with a classmate to practice conversations.
- Use the strategy *Grouping* to learn new vocabulary.
- Use the strategy *Sound Out* to decode words.
- Use the strategy *Use Selective Attention* to understand a short story.
- Use cooperation with a classmate to check letters one has written.
- Evaluate one's own learning of the strategies *Sound Out* and *Use Selective Attention*.
- Identify easy and difficult material in a chapter and the different ways to learn the difficult material.

Opening Dialogue, pages 188–189

Getting Ready

Preparation (See Transparency 17.)

- Have students look at the illustrations and identify the characters. Then ask them to name the items in the illustrations. Write the names and the words on the board or a poster. Say the names and words, and have students repeat.
- Ask students to make sentences about what they see and what the people are doing. Write students' responses on the board. If needed, model complete sentences. Read the sentences, and have students repeat them after you.

  Reaching All Students—Emergent Learners: Point to the first illustration and ask, "Where are they?" Have students repeat. Call on students to respond. If needed, model the response. (They're in Mr. Gomez's classroom.) Have students repeat. Then ask students to make other sentences about what they see and what the people are doing.

Listening and Reading

At the Nurse's Office

Presentation
Exercise A

- Read the directions and the prelistening question aloud as students follow along in their texts.
- Have students listen to the dialogue, or read the dialogue aloud to them. Have students look at the appropriate illustrations as they listen.
- Ask the prelistening question, "Will Maria go home today?" Call on a volunteer to respond. (Yes, she will.)

Exercise B

Have students read the dialogue. Provide help with content, vocabulary, etc. as needed.

Reaching All Students—Emergent Learners: Work with emergent learners in small groups while the other students work independently. Read aloud as students follow along in their texts. Monitor their comprehension by interrupting the reading with such questions as, "How does Maria feel?" (Terrible.) "Who is Ms. Cho?" (She's the school nurse.) "What's wrong with Maria?" (She has a sore throat, a stomachache, and a bad headache.) "How is English class going for Maria?" (It's very hard.) "What should Maria do?" (She should get a lot of rest. And she should drink plenty of water.) "Should she take medicine or call a doctor right now?" (No, she shouldn't.) "What could Maria do if she feels better tomorrow?" (She could come to school.) "What does Maria have tomorrow in Mr. Gomez's class?" (She has a test.) Have students repeat the questions, then the answers.

 Pair and Group Work

Practice
Exercise A

Have students who can read on their own form pairs. Have one student in the pair take the role of Maria; have the other student take all other roles (Mr. Gomez, Ms. Cho, Carmen, and Sophie). Then have them read the dialogue aloud. Provide help as needed.

Reaching All Students—Emergent Learners: Work in small groups with emergent readers. Model each sentence and have individual students "echo" your reading. Make sure that students look at the sentences as you read them.

Exercise B

Have students form groups of five. Group students heterogeneously so that each group is made up of weak readers, average readers, and strong readers. Have each student choose a role in the dialogue. Have students practice acting out the dialogue in their groups.

Reaching All Students—Kinesthetic Learners: Choose one or more groups to act out the dialogue in front of the class.

Vocabulary

Presentation

- Read the vocabulary words and expressions aloud and have students repeat them.
- Check students' understanding of the words and expressions.

Practice
Exercise A

Have students read and say the words and expressions. Provide assistance with pronunciation as needed. Then have students copy the words and expressions into their notebooks.

Reaching All Students—Auditory Learners: Encourage students to say the words and expressions as they write them in their notebooks.

Exercise B (See Transparencies 85–87.)

- Have students turn to page 250 in their texts.
- Have students work through Steps 1–2 (recognizing letters and finding syllables) with the words in the box on page 189 if further practice is needed.

- Have students work in pairs on Step 3, identifying letters or letter combinations that follow patterns or make unexpected sounds. Encourage students to ask questions and to discover as much as they can on their own.

Exercise C

Have students find the words and expressions in the dialogue. Have them read the sentences aloud.

Exercise D

- Tell students that they will be using the learning strategy *Grouping* to study new words in the dialogue. Tell students that *Grouping* is putting words that are similar together in the same group. This can help them learn new words.
- Write these headings on the board: *Feelings, Illnesses, Occupations, Verbs, Other Words.* Have students copy these headings into their notebooks.
- Have students look at the dialogue and find one new word for the Feelings category. Call on a volunteer to read the word he or she found. Have students write that word under the Feelings category in their notebooks.

Practice

- Have students work in pairs to complete each category in their notebooks.
- Call on five volunteers and assign a category to each one. Have the students write the words for their category on the board.
- As you check each category on the board, have students write any words they missed in their notebooks.
- For each category, ask students if they found other words not written on the board. Write correct responses on the board.

Answers
Possible answers include:

Feelings	Illnesses	
terrible	sore throat	
feel better	stomachache	
	headache	
Occupations	Verbs	Other Words
(school) nurse	stay	medicine
doctor		curious
		plenty
		a couple of
		by the way

Grammar 1, page 190

Statements with *should*

Preparation

- Write the following dialogue on the board as a way of presenting the grammar focus in context.

> **Carlos:** *Shouldn't* I see Ms. Cho, too? I feel terrible.
>
> **Mr. Gomez:** You look fine, Carlos. What's the matter?
>
> **Carlos:** I have a headache from all this studying.
>
> **Mr. Gomez:** Carlos, I think you *should* sit down.

- Read the dialogue aloud as students follow along. Then have the class read aloud with you.
- Call on two students to dramatize the dialogue for the rest of the class.

Presentation

- Have students look at the grammar chart. Explain that the left part of the chart shows affirmative statements with *should*. The right part shows negative statements.
- Call on an individual student to read aloud across each row of the affirmative statements in the left part of the chart. Then, call on another student to read aloud the negative statements in the right part.

> **Reaching All Students—Auditory/ Cooperative Learners:** Have pairs of students take turns reading sentences from the chart. Have the first student read an affirmative sentence from the left part of the chart and the second student read a negative sentence from the right part of the chart. Continue for the remaining sentences.

- Read aloud the Remember note at the bottom of the chart.

Practice

- Have students number a sheet of paper in their notebooks from 1 to 5.
- Tell students that in this exercise they will give advice about what Maria *should* or *shouldn't* do while she's sick.
- Read the first item aloud. Call on a student to read the sample answer aloud. Have the student explain why the answer is correct.

(When you're sick, you should get a lot of rest. You write an affirmative sentence.)

- Have students write the sentences in their notebooks, using *should* or *shouldn't*.

  Reaching All Students—Auditory Learners: Call on an advanced student to read each of the remaining items before students write their sentences.

  Reaching All Students—Emergent Learners: First, have students do the exercise orally. Then have them write the sentences in their notebooks. Provide help as needed.

- Review the answers with the class.

Answers
1. Maria should get a lot of rest.
2. Maria shouldn't walk home.
3. Maria should stay in bed.
4. Maria shouldn't go swimming.
5. Maria should drink plenty of water.

Yes/No Questions with *should*

Presentation

Have students look at the grammar chart. Explain that the left part of the chart shows how to make *yes/no* questions using *should* or *shouldn't*. The right part shows affirmative or negative answers. Read aloud the Remember note at the bottom of the chart.

> **Reaching All Students—Auditory/ Cooperative Learners:** Have three students take turns reading sentences from the chart. Have the first student read a question with *should* or *shouldn't*, the second student read the affirmative answer, and the third student read the negative answer.

Practice
Exercise A

- Have students number a sheet of paper in their notebooks from 1 to 5.
- Call on a student to read the directions aloud.
- Read the first item aloud. Have a student read the sample answer aloud. Tell students they could use either *should* or *shouldn't* in the question. If they really want to take medicine and want the nurse to say *yes*, they

could use *shouldn't*. If they just want general advice, they should use *should*.

> **Reaching All Students—Emergent Learners:** First, have students do the exercise orally. Then have them write the questions in their notebooks.

- Call on volunteers to share their answers with the class.

Answers
Answers will vary. Possible answers include:
1. Should I take medicine?
2. Shouldn't I go home?
3. Should I call a doctor?
4. Should I go to school tomorrow?
5. Shouldn't I drink plenty of soda?

Exercise B

- Call on a student to read the directions aloud.

  Reaching All Students—Emergent Learners: As a class, brainstorm the beginning of the role-play conversation. Write this example on the board:
  Nurse: Can you tell me how you feel?
  Student: I feel terrible. I have a headache, a stomachache, and a sore throat.
  Nurse: I'm sorry. You should rest here on the bed.
  Student: Shouldn't I go home?

- Work with two students through a model of the role play. Encourage the student playing the nurse to give answers that a nurse would give a sick person.
- Have students work in pairs to do the role play.

  Reaching All Students—Kinesthetic Learners: Call on pairs to act out their role plays for the class.

Grammar 2, page 191

Statements with *could*

Preparation

- Write the following dialogue on the board as a way of presenting the grammar focus in context.
  Carlos: Maria's not feeling well. I want to bring her a present. But what should I bring her?

Paco: Let's see . . . you *could* bring her some flowers.

Carlos: Flowers?

Paco: Yeah, you *could* bring her some roses.

- Read the dialogue aloud as students follow along. Then have the class read aloud with you.
- Call on two students to dramatize the dialogue for the rest of the class.

Presentation

- Have students look at the grammar chart. Tell them that this chart shows how to make suggestions with *could*. Point out that the verb *could* stays the same for each subject.
- Have two students take turns reading aloud sentences from the chart.

Practice

Exercise A

- Read the directions aloud as students follow along in their texts.
- Read the first sentence aloud. Then read the suggestions in the box and have students repeat. Have a student read the sample answer aloud. Ask why the answer is correct. (If you're worried about a test, you *could* study more so you feel more confident.)
- Have students number a page in their notebooks from 1 to 5 and write sentences with *could* and the suggestions listed in the box.

  Reaching All Students—Emergent Learners: First, have students do the exercise orally. Then have them write the sentences in their notebooks.

- Review the answers with the class.

Answers
1. You could study more.
2. You could drink some soda.
3. You could rest a while.
4. You could go to the movies.
5. You could make a sandwich.

Exercise B

 Have students listen to the conversation or read it aloud with a classmate.

Reaching All Students—Kinesthetic Learners: Call on volunteers to act out the conversation for the rest of the class.

Exercise C

- Divide the class into pairs. Have each pair practice the conversation in Exercise B.
- Tell students they will make conversations with *I'm bored, I'm hungry,* and *I'm thirsty,* and their own information. Write these three beginning statements on the board.
- As a class, brainstorm suggestions students could use in their conversations (free-time activities, snacks, and drinks). Write them on the board.
- Work with two advanced students through a model conversation.
- Have pairs practice the conversation, using their own information.

  Reaching All Students—Kinesthetic Learners: Call on volunteer pairs to act out the conversation, using their own phrases for the rest of the class.

Word Study, page 192

Other Vowel Sound: /ou/

Preparation

- Write the words *out* and *now* on the board.
- Call on volunteers to identify the names of the consonants and vowels in the words.
- Pronounce the words and have students repeat them after you.

Presentation

- Underline the vowels *ou* in *out* on the board and ask students to pronounce the sound. Ask them if they hear the /ou/ sound. Repeat for the vowel sound in *now*.
- Refer students to the instruction box in their texts. Tell them that they will look at the most common ways to form the vowel sound /ou/. Read the instruction box aloud as students follow along.
- Point to the word *out* on the board. Call on a volunteer to identify the first sound (/ou/) and the last sound (/t/).
- Ask students, "How many sounds does the word have?" (Two.) "How many letters does the word have?" (Three.) Explain that the vowels *ou* together stand for one vowel sound, /ou/.
- Ask students if they know what kind of sound this is. (It's a diphthong. The mouth moves

from one position to another while the sound is being made.) Exaggerate and extend the /ou/ sound to show students how the mouth position changes. Have students repeat and touch their mouths to feel the shift.

- Repeat the *Sound Out* strategy with the word *now*.

Practice
Exercise A

Have students work in pairs and use the learning strategy *Sound Out*, as well as the pictures, to read the words with the vowel sound /ou/.

Reaching All Students—Emergent Learners: Complete this activity as a class if students need help. After students have an approximation of the pronunciation, say the words correctly to provide a model.

Exercise B

- First, have students work in pairs to read the sentences aloud. Then have them copy the sentences into their notebooks. Last, have them circle the letters that represent the vowel sound /ou/.

- Review the answers as a class. Point out that *ab<u>out</u>* in item 4 also has the vowel sound /ou/.

Answers
1. We saw a huge gray cl(ou)d in the sky.
2. She has a br(ow)n cat.
3. There was a big cr(ow)d at the game.
4. She read her grandson a story ab(ou)t a m(ou)se.
5. We're going to go shopping in your t(ow)n tomorrow.
6. You can study at my h(ou)se after school today.

Optional Activity: Have students close their texts. Ask them to number a page in their notebooks from 1 to 8. Then ask them to listen carefully to the words you read and to write the words. Then dictate the following words:

1. cloud	5. round
2. eyebrow	6. brown
3. house	7. town
4. crowd	8. mouse

- After the dictation, write the words on the board. Then have students check their words.

- Have students record the number of correct words in their notebooks; for example, *I wrote (7) out of 8 dictated words with the vowel sound /ou/ correctly.* Write this example on the board as a model.

Exercise C

- Have students look at Exercise A. Have them choose two words with the vowel sound /ou/. Then have them write a sentence for each word in their notebooks. Have them underline the letters that represent the vowel sound /ou/.

Reaching All Students—Emergent Learners: Review the meanings of the words in Exercise A. Call on a volunteer to write a sample sentence on the board. Then have students write the two sentences in their notebooks. Provide help as needed.

- Have students share their sentences with the class.

Answers
Answers will vary.

Expansion

- In their notebooks, have students head two columns with these spellings for the vowel sound /ou/: *ou, ow*. Then have them write as many words as they can under the correct headings. (Set a time limit of 5–10 minutes.) Encourage students to use a dictionary, their texts, or their vocabulary lists for help.

Reaching All Students—Auditory Learners: Encourage students to say the words aloud as they write them.

- Have students share their lists with the class.

Grammar 3, page 193

Because Clauses
Preparation

- Write the following dialogue on the board as a way of presenting the grammar focus in context.

  Carlos: Let's go ride the new roller coaster at Seven Flags on Saturday.
  Samir: I'd like to go, but I have to go to my aunt's. Why don't you go with Carmen?

Carlos: Carmen won't ride roller coasters *because* she thinks they're scary.

- Read the dialogue aloud as students follow along. Then have the class read aloud with you.
- Call on two students to dramatize the dialogue for the rest of the class.

Presentation

- Have students look at the grammar chart.
- Call on a volunteer to read aloud the first two sentences in the grammar chart. Point out that the second sentence gives a *reason*; it tells why Maria should go home. Call on a volunteer to read the sentence with the *because* clause aloud.
- Read aloud the Remember note at the bottom of the chart.

Practice

Exercise A

- Tell students that in this exercise they will change two sentences into one sentence with a *because* clause.
- Call on a student to read the two sentences in item 1 aloud. Have another student read the sample answer and say why it is correct. (You add *because* after *games*. The second sentence uses the pronoun *they* for *games*.) Point out the contraction *they're* in the sample answer; tell students to use contractions in their sentences.
- Have students number a page in their notebooks from 1 to 4 and write sentences with *because* clauses.
- Review the answers with the class.

> **Answers**
> 1. Bic likes video games because he thinks they're exciting.
> 2. Sophie hates soccer because she thinks it's boring.
> 3. Liliana likes love stories because she thinks they're interesting.
> 4. Carlos doesn't like math because he thinks it's hard.

Exercise B

- Tell students that they'll write about their own feelings using *because* clauses. Call on a student to read the directions aloud as other students follow along in their texts.

- Write *love, like, enjoy, don't like,* and *hate* on the board.
- Read the first item aloud. Have a student read the example answer. Ask students who *love, like,* or *enjoy* roller coasters to raise their hands. Call on one or two individual students to say why they do, using a sentence with a *because* clause. Ask students who *don't like* or *hate* roller coasters to raise their hands. Ask one or two individual students to tell why they don't.
- Have students number a page in their notebooks from 1 to 6 and write their sentences.

  Reaching All Students—Emergent Learners: Work with a small group of emergent learners, or have students work in pairs.
- Call on students to share their answers with the class.

> **Answers**
> *Answers will vary.*

Exercise C

- Call on a student to read the directions aloud. As the student is reading, write the topics from Exercise B on the board (roller coasters, dancing, love stories, video games, math, watching TV).
- Call on four students to come to the front of the classroom to demonstrate the game. Have the first student make a statement with a *because* clause using one of the topics on the board. Have the second student report the first student's statement, then add another about a different topic. Have the third and fourth student do likewise. When a student makes a mistake, tell that student that he or she is out of the game. Have students continue until only one student is left. Tell the class that the group would then start the game again.
- Have students form groups of three to five students, standing or sitting in a circle. Have the groups play the game several times.
- Circulate to offer assistance with the game rules as needed.

Reading, pages 194—195

Before You Read

Presentation

- Tell students that they will be using the learning strategy *Use Selective Attention* to understand the story. Remind students that *Use Selective Attention* involves focusing on key words and ideas. You can use it to look for specific information in the story.
- Have students look at the Before You Read section in their texts. Call on a volunteer to read aloud the questions. Explain the word *discover* (understand something new).

Read This!

The Artist

Preparation

Note: Students will encounter the following new words in the reading: *artist, knock (n.), surprised, the day after tomorrow, have no idea, flower, smart, interrupt.*

Practice

Have students listen to the story, or read it aloud to them. Provide help with content, vocabulary, etc. as needed.

Reaching All Students—Emergent Learners: Work with emergent learners in small groups while the other students work independently. Read aloud as students follow along in their texts. Monitor their comprehension by interrupting the reading with such questions as, "Who went to see Maria?" (Carmen, Samir, and Sophie went to see Maria.) "When does Maria say she should be better?" (She says she should be better the day after tomorrow.) "Why does Samir think Maria will do well on the test?" (Because she works hard and she is smart.) "Did Maria's friends know she was an artist?" (No, they didn't.) "What did Carlos bring Maria?" (He brought her flowers.) "Is Maria going to take the test?" (Yes, she is.) Encourage students to answer the questions using complete sentences.

After You Read

Self-Evaluation
Exercise A

- Refer students to After You Read. Ask if students used the strategy *Use Selective Attention* to find the answers to the questions in the Before You Read section.

  Reaching All Students—Emergent Learners: Have students do the activity in pairs. Circulate to coach students and answer questions.

> **Answers**
> They think she's sick because she's worried about the test.
> They discover she is an artist.

- Call on individual students to read aloud the sentences in the story that give the answer to each question. Then ask students to discuss their answers with a classmate.

> **Answers**
> 1. "I'm worried about Maria," Samir said. "I think she's sick because she's worried about the test."
> 2. Everyone was surprised. They had no idea that Maria was an artist.

Exercise B

- Call on a student to read aloud the first step of the directions.
- Tell students that they are going to write their own *true/false* statements. Write the first one together as a class. First, locate information in the story and then ask volunteers for a true statement and a false statement about that information. (Example: "I'm worried about Maria," Samir said. = Samir is worried about Maria. / Samir is not worried about Maria.) Write the statements on the board and write *True* and *False* next to each.
  Samir is worried about Maria.   *True   False*
  Samir is not worried about Maria.   *True   False*
- Have students work in pairs to write five more *true/false* statements. Of the five statements, three should be true and two should be false. Write this on the board.

- Ask each pair of students to exchange their papers with a nearby pair of students. Tell pairs to circle *true* or *false* for each sentence. Demonstrate this on the board with the example sentences.
- Have pairs exchange and check each other's papers. Have students write a check mark next to correct answers and an X mark next to incorrect answers. Then have pairs return the checked questions.
- Have the pairs share several true/false statements with the rest of the class.
- Have students count the number of correct answers and write that number in their notebooks.

> **Answers**
> *Answers will vary.*

Expansion

Ask students if they used any other strategies while they read this story. List all the strategies on the board—*Use What You Know, Make Predictions, Use Selective Attention, Make Inferences, Personalize,* and *Sound Out.* Have students raise their hands if they used the strategy. Remind students that good readers use more than one strategy to understand what they are reading.

Writing, page 196

Before You Write

Preparation *(See Transparencies 23 and 58–59.)*

- Show a real newspaper advice column to the class. Explain that an advice column contains questions from readers about problems they have. The advice columnist gives advice about the problems. Ask if students ever read advice columns.
- Explain to students that they are going to write two short letters. The first letter will state a problem and ask for advice. The second letter will respond with advice and suggestions about what to do.

Exercise A

- Focus students' attention on the handwritten letters.

Reaching All Students—Auditory Learners: Call on two students to read the two letters aloud as the other students follow along in their texts.

- Ask students to tell what kind of information is included in each letter. (A letter asking for advice, explaining the problem and situation; a letter giving advice and suggestions about the problem.) Write students' responses on the board.

Presentation
Exercise B

- Draw students' attention to the Before I Write checklist. Call on students to read aloud the points in the checklist.
- As a class, brainstorm with students other problems they could write about. (Examples: worrying about grades or a test, being nervous about speaking English, missing one's home country, a disagreement with a friend or parent, a boyfriend/girlfriend problem.) Write students' responses on the board.
- Have students follow the Before I Write checklist and make notes in their notebooks.

  Reaching All Students—Emergent Learners: Work with emergent learners in small groups. Guide them in following the steps in the checklist. Have each student choose a problem to write about, then brainstorm possible causes and solutions for the problem.

Write This!

Presentation

- Draw students' attention to the While I Write checklist. Call on students to read aloud the points in the checklist.
- Explain and model on the board each of the writing points in this section while you write a few lines of a request for advice. As you write, do a "think aloud" about how you are following the While I Write checklist.

Practice

- Have students write their letters in their notebooks, using their notes and the While I Write checklist for help.
- Circulate while students are writing and encourage them to ask you for help if needed.

After You Write

Presentation

Exercise A

- Draw students' attention to the After I Write checklist. Call on students to read aloud the points in the checklist.
- Have students use the After I Write checklist to evaluate their writing. Have them circle and then correct any errors.

Exercise B

Have students read their letters to a classmate. Encourage them to make suggestions for improvement.

Exercise C

Have students write a final copy of their letters in their notebooks.

Expansion

Have students cut or tear out the letter asking for advice from their notebooks. Collect these and redistribute them. Have students write a response to the letter they receive. When students have finished writing, have them return the letter and their response to the writer.

Learning Log, page 197

See How to Use the Learning Log on page xiii. *(See Transparencies 20 and 78.)*

Chapter 18
It was too easy.

Objectives

Language:

- Listen to a dialogue for comprehension.
- Understand familiar vocabulary and grammar structures by listening to a dialogue.
- Develop new vocabulary and grammar structures by listening to a dialogue.
- Act out a dialogue.
- Use comparatives and superlatives for the irregular adjectives *good* and *bad*.
- Use *too* and *not enough* to state opinions.
- Use *used to* in affirmative and negative statements and yes/*no* questions.
- Make original conversations using new vocabulary and grammar structures.
- Evaluate one's own learning of new vocabulary, grammar, and oral language.

Literacy:

- Read a dialogue for comprehension.
- Understand familiar vocabulary and grammar structures by reading a dialogue.
- Develop new vocabulary and grammar structures by reading a dialogue.
- Write a dialogue using new vocabulary.
- Complete statements with comparatives and superlatives for the irregular adjectives *good* and *bad*.
- Complete statements using *too* and *not enough.*
- Decode words with the vowel sound /ûr/.
- Complete affirmative and negative statements using *used to.*
- Read a short story for comprehension.
- Understand familiar vocabulary and grammar structures by reading a short story.
- Develop new vocabulary and grammar structures by reading a short story.
- Plan, write, revise, edit, proofread, and make a final copy of a fictional story.
- Write an interesting fictional story with a title, a clear beginning and end, and correct punctuation.
- Evaluate one's own learning of reading skills, reading comprehension, and writing skills.

Learning Strategies:

- Use cooperation with a classmate to read a dialogue and study new vocabulary.
- Use cooperation with a small group to act out a dialogue.
- Use cooperation with a classmate to practice conversations.
- Use the strategy *Sound Out* to decode words.
- Use the strategy *Make Predictions* to understand a short story.
- Use cooperation with a classmate to check a fictional story one has written.
- Evaluate one's own learning of the strategies *Sound Out* and *Make Predictions.*
- Identify easy and difficult material in a chapter and the different ways to learn the difficult material.

Opening Dialogue, pages 198–199

Getting Ready

Preparation (See Transparency 17.)

- Have students look at the illustrations and identify the characters. Then ask them to name the items in the illustrations. Write the names and the words on the board or a poster. Say the names and words, and have students repeat.

- Ask students to make sentences about what they see and what the people are doing. Write students' responses on the board. If needed, model complete sentences. Read the sentences, and have students repeat them after you.

    Reaching All Students—Emergent Learners: Point to the first illustration and ask "What are they doing?" Have students repeat. Call on students to respond. If needed, model the response. (They're taking a test.) Have students repeat. Then ask students to make other sentences about what they see and what the people are doing.

Listening and Reading

The Test

Presentation

Exercise A

- Read the directions and the prelistening questions aloud as students follow along in their texts.
- Have students listen to the dialogue, or read the dialogue aloud to them. Have students look at the appropriate illustrations as they listen.
- Ask the prelistening question, "Did everyone *really* think the test was easy?" Call on a volunteer to respond. (No, they didn't.) Ask the follow-up question, "How do you know?" Call on a volunteer to answer. (Carlos says, "We're just teasing you. Of course the test was hard.")

Exercise B

Have students read the dialogue. Provide help with content, vocabulary, etc. as needed.

> **Reaching All Students—Emergent Learners:** Work with emergent learners in small groups while the other students work independently. Read aloud as students follow along in their texts. Monitor their comprehension by interrupting the reading with such questions as, "Why did the students have gloomy faces?" (They don't like tests.) "How does Maria think she did on the test?" (She thinks she missed a lot of questions.) "How does Carmen think she did on the test?" (She thinks maybe she did okay.) "Did Mei say the test was too hard?" (No, she said it was too easy.) "What should Maria do?" (She should just relax and wait to see her grade.) "What does Maria wonder?" (She wonders how she did on the comprehension questions.) Have students repeat the questions, then the answers.

Pair and Group Work

Practice

Exercise A

Have students who can read on their own form pairs. Have students take turns reading each of the lines in the dialogue aloud. Provide help as needed.

> **Reaching All Students—Emergent Learners:** Work in small groups with emergent readers. Model each sentence and have individual students "echo" your reading. Make sure that students look at the sentences as you read them.

Exercise B

Have students form groups of eight. Group students heterogeneously so that each group is made up of weak readers, average readers, and strong readers. Have each student choose a role in the dialogue. Have students practice acting out the dialogue in their groups.

> **Reaching All Students—Kinesthetic Learners:** Choose one or more groups to act out the dialogue in front of the class.

Vocabulary

Presentation

- Read the vocabulary words and expressions aloud and have students repeat them.
- Check students' understanding of the words and expressions.

Practice

Exercise A

Have students read and say the words and expressions. Provide assistance with pronunciation as needed. Then have students copy the words and expressions into their notebooks.

> **Reaching All Students—Auditory Learners:** Encourage students to say the words and expressions as they write them in their notebooks.

Exercise B (See Transparencies 85–87.)

- Have students turn to page 250 in their texts.
- Have students work through Steps 1–2 (recognizing letters and finding syllables) with the words in the box on page 199 if further practice is needed.
- Have students work in pairs on Step 3, identifying letters or letter combinations that follow patterns or make unexpected sounds. Encourage students to ask questions and to discover as much as they can on their own.

Exercise C

Have students find the words and expressions in the dialogue. Have them read the sentences aloud.

Exercise D

- Tell students that they will write a mini-dialogue with five words from the word box in their notebooks.
- Have students choose the names of two characters for their dialogues. Have students write the dialogues in their notebooks using five words or expressions from the word box. Have them underline the new vocabulary words in their dialogues.

    Reaching All Students—Emergent Learners: Work with students in small groups.

    Reaching All students—Advanced Learners: Challenge advanced students to use as many words from the list as they can.

- Have students work in pairs to read their dialogues.

    Reaching All Students—Kinesthetic Learners: Call on pairs to act out one or both of their dialogues in front of the class.

Answers
Answers will vary.

Grammar 1, page 200

Comparatives and Superlatives: Irregular Adjectives

Preparation

- Write the following dialogue on the board as a way of presenting the grammar focus in context.

    Carlos: Let's go to Pedro's and get a burrito.

    Carmen: Pedro's burritos are *the worst* in town.

    Carlos: How about Chico's? Their burritos are *better than* Pedro's.

    Carmen: Chico's burritos are okay. But Serrano has *the best burritos* in town!

- Read the dialogue aloud as students follow along. Then have the class read aloud with you.
- Call on two students to dramatize the dialogue for the rest of the class.

Presentation

- Have students look at the grammar chart. Read aloud the information at the top of the chart. Then read aloud across the three rows and have students repeat.
- Draw one, two, and three stars on the board, and draw one, two, and three Xs. Point to the star(s) and X(s) and call on individual students to say which word from the grammar chart goes next to each. Write students' responses on the board.

★ good	X bad
★★ better than	XX worse than
★★★ the best	XXX the worst

- Ask students which words are used to compare two things (better than, worse than) and which are used to compare three or more things (the best, the worst).

Practice

Exercise A

- Call on a student to read the instructions aloud.
- Have students look at the illustration "Carmen's Hamburger Guide." Tell students they'll use the guide to fill in the blanks in sentences 1–5.
- Call on a student to read the sample answer aloud. Have the student explain why the answer is correct. (Big Burger has three stars on Carmen's guide. They're the best hamburgers.)
- Have students number a sheet of paper in their notebooks from 1 to 5. Have them copy the sentences into their notebooks and fill in the blanks.

    Reaching All Students—Emergent Learners: First, have students do the exercise orally. Then have them copy the incomplete sentences into their notebooks. Last, have them complete the sentences. Provide help as needed.

- Review the answers with the class.

Answers
1. the best
2. better than
3. better than
4. worse than
5. the worst

Exercise B

 Have students listen to the conversation or read it aloud with a classmate.

Reaching All Students—Kinesthetic Learners: Call on volunteers to act out the conversation in front of the class.

Practice
Exercise C

- Divide the class into pairs. Have each pair practice the conversation in Exercise B.
- Tell students they will now make conversations with their own information.
- As a class, brainstorm suggestions students could use in the conversation (fast-food restaurants; Mexican, Salvadorian, Chinese, or Vietnamese restaurants; ice-cream parlors; coffee shops). For each, elicit at least two to three specific names of establishments (for example, McDonald's, Burger King, Wendy's) and some foods students could compare (hamburgers, French fries, fried chicken). Write them on the board.
- Work with two advanced students through a model conversation.
- Have pairs practice the conversation, using their own information.

   Reaching All Students—Kinesthetic Learners: Call on volunteer pairs to act out the conversation in front of the class, using their own phrases.

Grammar 2, page 201

Too and *not enough*

Preparation

- Write the following dialogue on the board as a way of presenting the grammar focus in context.

   Carlos: Carmen, Serrano's burritos are *too expensive.*
   Carmen: They cost a little more because they're so big. The burritos at Pedro's and Chico's are *too small*!
   Carlos: Okay, okay. Let's go to Serrano.

- Read the dialogue aloud as students follow along. Then have the class read aloud with you.
- Call on two students to dramatize the dialogue for the rest of the class.

Presentation

Have students look at the grammar chart. Read the information and sentences aloud as students follow along.

Practice

- Call on a student to read the directions aloud.
- Have students look at the picture for the first item. Ask students how the manager looks. (She looks angry.) Ask students why the manager is angry. (The table is not clean.)
- Call on a student to read the sample answers aloud. Ask why each answer is correct. (The table is dirty; *too* means more than necessary or desired, so the table is too dirty. The table is not clean, so the table is not clean enough.)
- Have students number a page in their notebooks from 1 to 4 and complete the exercise.

   Reaching All Students—Emergent Learners: First, have students do the exercise orally. Then have them write the incomplete sentences into their notebooks. Last, have them complete the sentences.

- Review the answers with the class.

Answers
1. The table is too dirty.
   The table isn't clean enough.
2. The plate is too small.
   The plate isn't big enough.
3. The coffee is too hot.
   The coffee isn't cool enough.
4. The children are not tall enough.
   The children are too short.

Expansion

Optional Activity: Tell students that they will write five true sentences using *too, not enough,* or *enough.* As a class, brainstorm some topics students could write about and some adjectives they could use. (Examples: the last English class—easy/hard; the weather—hot/warm/cool/cold; the school—big/small; the student—tall/short; the student's room—dirty/clean; school lunches—small/big.) Write these on the board. Call on a student to make three sentences for one of the topics using *too, not enough,* and *enough* as a model. Have students number a page in their notebooks from 1 to 5 and write their true sentences.

   Reaching All Students—Emergent Learners: Work with emergent learners in small groups while the other students work independently. When students have finished writing, have students work in pairs to take turns reading their sentences to each other. Then call on individual students to share one or two of their sentences with the class.

Answers
Answers will vary.

Word Study, page 202

Other Vowel Sound: /ûr/

Preparation

- Write the words *hurt*, *first*, and *her* on the board.
- Call on volunteers to identify the names of the consonants and vowels in the words.
- Pronounce the words and have students repeat them after you.

Presentation

- Underline the *ur* in *hurt* on the board and ask students to pronounce the sound. Ask them if they hear the /ûr/ sound. Repeat for the vowel sound in *first* and *her*.
- Ask students, "What is the short vowel sound for the letter *u*?" (/u/ as in *hut*.) "What is the long vowel sound for the letter *u*?" (/yoo/ as in *cute*). "Does *hurt* have the short or long /u/ sound?" (Neither.) Explain that when the consonant *r* follows a vowel, it often changes the vowel sound to what is called an *r*-controlled vowel sound. Explain that the *r* controls the sound of the vowel.
- Explain to students that they are going to study the three most common spellings for the *r*-controlled vowel sound /ûr/: *ur*, *ir*, and *er*.
- Point to the word *hurt* on the board. Call on a volunteer to identify the first sound (/h/), the second sound (/ûr/), and the third sound (/t/).
- Follow the same procedure for the words *first* and *her*.

Practice
Exercise A

Have students use the learning strategy *Sound Out*, as well as the pictures, to read the words with the vowel sound /ûr/.

Reaching All Students—Emergent Learners: Complete this activity as a class. After students have an approximation of the pronunciation, say the words correctly to provide a model.

Exercise B

- First, have students read the sentences aloud. Then have them copy the sentences into their notebooks. Last, have them circle the letters that represent the vowel sound /ûr/.
- Review the answers as a class. Point out that items 1 and 3 have two words each with the vowel sound /ûr/.

Answers
1. I got a lett(er) from my best friend yest(er)day.
2. Are they going to go to the library on Th(ur)sday?
3. My moth(er) is cooking dinn(er) right now.
4. Bic wants to buy a blue sh(ir)t at the mall.
5. Does she want to see the school n(ur)se?
6. How much is that p(ur)ple hat?

Optional Activity: Have students close their texts. Ask them to number a page in their notebooks from 1 to 8. Then ask them to listen carefully to the words you read and to write the words. Then dictate the following words:

1. bird   5. mother
2. letter   6. shirt
3. Thursday   7. winter
4. purple   8. nurse

- After the dictation, write the words on the board. Then have students check their words.
- Have students record the number of correct words in their notebooks; for example, *I wrote (7) out of 8 dictated words with the vowel sound /ûr/ correctly*. Write this example on the board as a model.

Self-Evaluation

- Have students work in pairs to reread the words in Exercise A. Then ask them to count the number of words they read correctly. Have them write their scores in their notebooks; for example, *I read (6) out of 8 words with the vowel sound /ûr/ correctly*.
- Have students work in pairs. Have them dictate the eight words from the lesson to each other, one student dictating the eight words at a time. Next, have students exchange pa-

pers and then correct each other's paper. After students receive their paper back, have them write their scores in their notebooks; for example, *I wrote (6) out of 8 dictated words with the vowel sound /ûr/ correctly.*

Exercise C

- Have students look at Exercise A. Have them choose two words with the vowel sound /ûr/. Then have them write a sentence for each word in their notebooks.

    Reaching All Students—Emergent Learners: Review the meanings of the words in Exercise A. Call on a volunteer to write a sample sentence on the board. Then have students write the two sentences in their notebooks. Provide help as needed.

- Have students share their sentences with the class.

Answers
Answers will vary.

Expansion

- In their notebooks, have students head two columns with these spellings for the *r*-controlled vowel sound /ûr/: *ur, ir, er*. Then have them write as many words as they can under the correct headings. (Set a time limit of 5–10 minutes.) Encourage students to use a dictionary, their texts, or their vocabulary lists for help.

    Reaching All Students—Auditory Learners: Encourage students to say the words aloud as they write them.

- Have students share their lists with the class.

Grammar 3, page 203

Statements with *used to*

Preparation

- Write the following dialogue on the board as a way of presenting the grammar focus in context.

    Mei: Do you miss El Salvador, Maria?
    Maria: Sometimes. I *used to* go to parties all the time there.
    Mei: Really? I *didn't use to* go to many parties in China. I go to a lot more here.

- Read the dialogue aloud as students follow along. Then have the class read aloud with you.
- Call on two students to dramatize the dialogue for the rest of the class.

Presentation

- Have students look at the grammar chart.
- Read aloud the Remember note at the bottom of the chart. Point out that the left part of the chart shows how to make affirmative sentences with *used to*. The right part shows how to make negative sentences.
- Have two students take turns reading aloud sentences from the chart. Have the first student read affirmative statements with *used to* and the second student read negative statements with *didn't use to*.
- Write *used to* and *didn't use to* on the board. Point out that *used to* is in past tense, so there is an *-ed* on the end. Point out that for *didn't use to*, *didn't* shows the past tense, so *use to* is in the base form.

Practice

- Tell students that in this exercise they will fill in the blanks to make an affirmative sentence with *used to* or a negative sentence with *didn't use to*.
- Call on a student to read the sample answer aloud. Ask why the answer is correct. (You should make an affirmative sentence, so you write *used to* in the blank.)
- Have students number a page in their notebooks from 1 to 5 and complete the exercise.

    Reaching All Students—Emergent Learners: First, have students do the exercise orally. Then have them fill in the blanks in their notebooks.

- Review the answers with the class.

Answers
1. Carlos used to live in a smaller city.
2. Samir didn't use to walk to school, but now he does.
3. Sophie used to dance in festivals when she was younger.
4. Mei used to eat more Chinese food when she lived in China.
5. Liliana didn't use to like hamburgers, but now she does.

Yes/No Questions with *used to*

Presentation

- Have students look at the grammar chart. Point out that the first part of the chart shows how to make *yes/no* questions with *used to*. The second and third parts show how to make short affirmative and negative answers. Point out that in *yes/no* questions, *Did* shows the past tense, so *use to* is in the base form.
- Have three students take turns reading aloud sentences from the chart. Have the first student read *yes/no* questions with *used to*, the second student read short affirmative answers, and the third student read short negative answers.

Exercise A

 Have students listen to the conversation or read it aloud with a classmate.

Practice
Exercise B

- Divide the class into pairs. Have each pair practice the conversation in Exercise A.
- Tell students that they will make conversations with their own information. As a class, brainstorm suggestions students could use in the conversation. Brainstorm things they used to do but don't do now (play with toys, watch cartoons, eat more Mexican food, study Spanish, live in a bigger/smaller city, go to a lot of parties, like children's music, have long hair). Brainstorm things they didn't used to do but they do now (speak English, like boys/girls, like reggae, have friends from different countries, have short hair). Write them on the board.
- Tell students that when they both used to do the same thing, they can say, "So did I" or "I did, too." When they both didn't use to do the same thing, they can say, "I didn't either." Write these phrases on the board.
- Work with two advanced students through a model conversation.
- Have pairs practice the conversation, using their own information.

  Reaching All Students—Kinesthetic Learners: Call on volunteer pairs to act out the dialogue, using their own phrases.

Reading, pages 204–205

Before You Read

Preparation *(See Transparency 22.)*

- Tell students they will be using the learning strategy *Make Predictions* to understand the story.
- Have students look at the Before You Read section in their texts. Call on a student to read each of the strategy steps in the text.

Practice

- Have students work independently to follow the first four steps of the strategy *Make Predictions*. Have them make notes about their predictions in their notebooks.

  Reaching All Students—Emergent Learners: Have students do the activity in pairs.

- Call on individual students to share their predictions with the class. Write students' predictions on the board.

Read This!

The Last Day

Preparation

Note: Students will encounter the following new words in the reading: *elbow, shoulder, push, world, find out, pass back, promote, reply, shake (shook), brave, pale, stunned, whole, before, Congratulations.*

Practice

- Have students listen to the story, or read it aloud to them. Provide help with content, vocabulary, etc. as needed.
- Ask students individually how they are using strategies to understand the story.

  Reaching All Students—Emergent Learners: Work with emergent learners in small groups while the other students work independently. Read aloud as students follow along in their texts. Monitor their comprehension by interrupting the reading with such questions as, "What do the students find out today?" (They find out what their test grades were.) "Does Maria want to go into the classroom?" (No, she doesn't.) "What was the surprise?" (There was a party in Mr. Gomez's classroom.) "What can't Maria believe?" (She can't believe she passed.) "What does Maria think about her grade?" (She's really happy.) "Where are Maria's best friends?" (They're right there at Washington School.) Encourage students to answer the questions using complete sentences.

After You Read

Self-Evaluation

Exercise A *(See Transparency 22.)*

- Refer students to the After You Read section. Call on a student to read the questions aloud.
- Have students work in pairs to take turns asking and answering each question.
- Call on individual students to share their responses with the class.

Answers
Answers will vary.

Exercise B

- Call on a student to read the first question aloud. Call on another student to answer. Have the student identify the statements in the story that support his or her response. ("Today we find out what our test grades are," Bic told his friends. / "I'm not going in there . . . .," she [Maria] said. "I'm not brave enough.")
  Reaching All Students—Auditory Learners: Call on a student to read the remaining questions aloud.
- Have students number a page in their notebooks from 1 to 4 and write answers to the questions.
  Reaching All Students—Emergent Learners: Have students work in pairs or in small groups. Provide help as needed.
- Review the answers with the class. Be sure students give supportive statements from the text for their answers.
- Have students count the number of correct answers and write that number in their notebooks.

Answers
Answers will vary. Possible answers include:
1. She was worried she failed the test.
2. They found a party.
3. Everyone passed the final test.
4. She is more relaxed. She is less homesick. She feels at home with her new school and friends.

Writing, page 206

Before You Write

Preparation *(See Transparencies 23 and 60–61.)*
Explain to students that they are going to write a story about one of the main characters in the text. Call on volunteers to say the names of the characters (Carlos, Carmen, Maria, Bic, Pablo, Sophie, Samir, Liliana, Mei). Write students' responses on the board.

Exercise A

- Focus students' attention on the handwritten story.
  Reaching All Students—Auditory Learners: Call on a student to read the story aloud as the other students follow along in their texts.
- Ask students to tell what the story is about and what kind of information is included in the story. (It's about Samir; he is worried about what he will study in college and what he will do in his life; he is baby-sitting his brother, and his brother says, "You're a good teacher." Samir decides he will become a teacher.) Write students' responses on the board.

Presentation
Exercise B

- Draw students' attention to the Before I Write checklist. Call on students to read aloud the points in the checklist.
- Ask students to think a moment and decide which character they will write about. Have them write the character's name in their notebooks. Call on several volunteers to tell you which character they will write about. Ask them what they know about the character.
- As a class, brainstorm with students story lines they could write about by calling on

volunteers to say what they will write about. Write students' responses on the board.

- Have students follow the Before I Write checklist and make notes in their notebooks.

   Reaching All Students—Emergent Learners: Work with students in small groups. Guide them in following the steps in the checklist.

Write This!

Presentation

- Draw students' attention to the While I Write checklist. Call on students to read aloud the points in the checklist.
- Explain and model on the board each of the writing points in this section while you write a few lines of a story. As you write, do a "think aloud" about how you are following the While I Write checklist.

Practice

- Have students write their stories in their notebooks, using their notes and the While I Write checklist for help.
- Circulate while students are writing and encourage them to ask you for help if needed.

After You Write

Presentation

Exercise A

- Draw students' attention to the After I Write checklist. Call on a student to read aloud each point in the checklist.
- Have students use the After I Write checklist to evaluate their writing. Have them circle and then correct any errors.

Exercise B

Have students read their stories to a classmate. Encourage them to make suggestions for improvement.

Exercise C

Have students write a final copy of their stories in their notebooks.

Learning Log, Page 207

See How to Use the Learning Log on page xiii. *(See Transparencies 20 and 79.)*

FOCUS ON CONTENT

Life Science, pages 210–211

Note: This reading should be presented after students have completed Unit 1.

Before You Read

Preparation *(See Transparency 17.)*

- Write the following exercise goals on the board and read them aloud:

Goals
—*Read a life science textbook selection*
—*Learn about ecosystems and food chains*
—*Learn science vocabulary as you read*
—*Get as much meaning as you can from the reading*

- Tell students that this reading selection is similar to one they might find in a life science textbook. Point out that because textbooks are teaching new topics, they include a lot of vocabulary that is new, even to a native speaker. Let students know that the text itself will provide definitions for much of the science vocabulary. Tell them that they will go back and study the vocabulary in more detail after the reading. Finally, explain to students that their goal is to try and get as much meaning from the text as possible, rather than to try and understand every word.

- Write *Sound Out* on the board and remind students that this strategy can help them read new words. Call on a student to model how to use *Sound Out* for the title of the life science reading. (See How to Teach the Focus on Content Lessons on page xiv for additional strategy suggestions.)

- Refer students to the prereading instructions. Read the steps aloud as students follow along in their texts.

- Have students look at the pictures and identify any words they know for the objects in the pictures. Write the words on the board or a poster. Read the words, one at a time, and have students repeat each one after you.

- Point to objects in the pictures that students didn't mention and ask, "What's this?" Write the responses on the board or a poster. Read the responses and have students repeat them.

While You Read

How Nature Works: Ecosystems and Food Chains

Practice

🎧 **Reaching All Students— Emergent Learners:** Have students listen to the first half of the passage (page 210), or read it aloud to them. Have students follow along in their texts.

- Have students read the first half of the passage aloud, either chorally as a class, in small groups, or softly to themselves. Remind students that as they read, they can *Sound Out* unfamiliar words.

- Have students silently read the first half of the passage. Tell them to try to understand as much as they can.

  Reaching All Students—Emergent Learners: Work with emergent readers in small groups while the other students work independently. If students need moderate support, have them read with a partner or small group. Pair proficient readers with students who are less proficient.

- Have students answer the Before You Go On question. Encourage students to go back and reread if needed. (Plants and animals are living things. Sunlight, air, rocks, and soil are non-living things.)

  🎧 **Reaching All Students— Emergent Learners:** Have students listen to the second half of the passage (page 211), or read it aloud.

- Have students read the second half of the passage aloud. When they have finished, tell them to read the passage silently to themselves.

After You Read

Self-Evaluation

Vocabulary

- Refer students to the instructions in their texts. Read the instructions aloud as students follow along in their texts.

- Have students look through the reading again. Tell them to write the words they don't understand in their notebooks.

- Have students try to guess the meaning of the unknown words, using context clues from the words around them and information from the photos.

- After students have worked on their own, have students work in pairs or small groups to discuss and decipher the words they couldn't figure out.

- Finally, have students use their dictionaries to find the definitions of any words they couldn't decipher. (Refer to the How to Use a Dictionary section on page 256 of the Student Book.)

- Call on volunteers to share the meanings for some of the most important new vocabulary in the passage.

Comprehension

- Have students take out their notebooks and number a sheet of paper from 1 to 5.

- Call on a student to read the first item aloud. Then call on a volunteer to answer the question. Ask the student to find the supportive statement in the passage.

  Reaching All Students—Emergent/ Auditory Learners: Call on advanced students to read the questions aloud.

- Have students write the answers in their notebooks.

  Reaching All Students—Emergent Learners: Have students work in pairs, or work with them in small groups.

- After students complete the exercise, have them check their work by scanning the reading to find the answers and then correct any mistakes.

- Call on students to give their answers and write them on the board. Be sure they also give statements to support their answers from the passage.

- Have students count the number of correct answers and write that number in their notebooks.

Answers
1. Ecosystems are all around us.
2. Ecosystems have both living and non-living things.
3. Animals need air, water, and food.
4. Each living thing is linked to the other living things in the food chain.
5. Yes, I am.

Expansion

- If available, use the Internet as a class to conduct research and view pictures of different ecosystems and food chains.
- As a class, brainstorm some examples of ecosystems (forests, deserts, oceans, lakes, etc.). Write these on the board. Then elicit the names of several organisms in each ecosystem. Allow students to use their dictionaries if needed. Finally, brainstorm an example of a food chain in one of these ecosystems. Write this on the board, using arrows to show that one organism is food for the next. Then have students work in small groups to create a chart showing another food chain in one of the ecosystems, using their dictionaries if needed. Call on groups to share their charts with the class.

Physical Science, pages 212–213

Note: This reading should be presented after students have completed Unit 2.

Before You Read

Preparation *(See Transparency 22.)*

- Write the following exercise goals on the board and read them aloud:

Goals

—*Read a physical science textbook selection*
—*Learn about the universe*
—*Learn science vocabulary as you read*
—*Get as much meaning as you can from the reading*

- Tell students that this reading selection is similar to one they might find in a physical science textbook. Point out that, because textbooks are teaching new topics, they often include a lot of vocabulary that is unfamiliar, even to a native speaker. Let students know that the text itself will provide definitions for much of the science vocabulary. Tell them that they will go back and study the vocabulary in more detail after the reading. Their goal is to try to get as much meaning from the text as possible, rather than try to understand every word.
- Remind students that using learning strategies can help them understand what they read. Ask students what strategies they have studied so far. *(Make Predictions, Use Selective Attention, Sound Out.)* Write the strategy names on the board. Call on students to give brief definitions or examples of how to use each strategy. If they need reminders, refer them to page 56 in the Student Book for *Make Predictions,* and page 66 for *Use Selective Attention.* (See How to Teach the Focus on Content Lessons on page xiv for additional strategy suggestions.)
- Refer students to the prereading instructions. Read the steps aloud as students follow along in their texts.
- Have students look at the title, the headings, and the pictures. Have them describe what they see. Ask them to consider what the reading is about.
- Have students *Use Selective Attention* to scan the text for words they already know in the reading.
- Have students form pairs and tell each other their predictions.

While You Read

The Universe:
Earth and the Milky Way

Practice

- **Reaching All Students— Emergent Learners:** Have students listen to the first half of the passage (page 212), or read it aloud to them. Have students follow along in their texts.
- Have students read the first half of the passage aloud, either chorally as a class, in small groups, or softly to themselves. Remind students that as they read, they can *Sound Out* unfamiliar words.
- Have students silently read the first half of the passage carefully. Tell them to try to understand as much as they can. Encourage students to use their prediction strategy to help them make guesses about the text and to see if they need to change their predictions as they read.

  Reaching All Students—Emergent Learners: Work with emergent readers in small groups while the other students work independently. If students need moderate support, have them read with a partner or small group to figure out the meaning of the passage.

Pair proficient readers with readers who are less proficient.

- Have students answer the Before You Go On question. Encourage them to go back and reread if needed. (The sun is a medium-size star.)
- Have students make predictions about what kind of information they will find in the next section.

  🎧 **Reaching All Students—Emergent Learners:** Have students listen to the second half of the passage (page 213), or read it aloud.

- Have students read the second half of the passage aloud. When they have finished, tell them to read the passage silently to themselves.

After You Read

Self-Evaluation
Vocabulary

- Refer students to the instructions in their texts. Read the instructions aloud as students follow along in their texts.
- Have them look through the reading again. Tell them to write the words they don't understand in their notebooks.
- Have students try to guess the meaning of the unknown words, using context clues from the words around them and information from the pictures.
- After students have worked on their own, have students work in pairs or small groups to discuss and decipher the words they couldn't figure out.
- Finally, have students use their dictionaries to find the definitions of any words they couldn't decipher. (Refer to the How to Use a Dictionary section on page 256 of the Student Book.)
- Call on volunteers to share the meanings for some of the most important new vocabulary in the passage.

Comprehension

- Have students take out their notebooks and number a sheet of paper from 1 to 5.
- Call on a student to read the first item aloud. Then ask a volunteer to answer the question. Ask the student to find information in the passage that supports the answer.

Reaching All Students—Emergent/ Auditory Learners: Call on advanced students to read the questions aloud.

- Have students write the answers in their notebooks.

  Reaching All Students—Emergent Learners: Have students work in pairs, or work with them in small groups.

- After students complete the exercise, have them check their work by scanning the reading to find the answers. Have them correct any mistakes.
- Call on students to give their answers and write them on the board. Be sure they also give statements from the passage to support their answers.
- Have students count the number of correct answers and write that number in their notebooks.

Answers
1. A star is a giant ball of hot gas.
2. The sun's core reaches up to 15 million degrees centigrade (27 million degrees Fahrenheit).
3. A galaxy is a very large group of stars.
4. About 200 billion stars are in our Milky Way.
5. Our galaxy is bigger than our solar system.

Expansion

- To help students get a sense of large numbers, such as the distance of the sun from Earth (150,000,000 kilometers), make comparative calculations like how far it is from your city to a distant location like Tokyo or Sydney. Find out how long an airline flight takes to reach that city from your nearest airport. Then look at how many times farther away the sun is from Earth.
- Check with local science teachers for "star charts" that can be projected in the room. If feasible, schedule a visit to a planetarium.
- If available, use the Internet as a class to conduct research and view pictures of the Milky Way and the planets.
- Have students work in cooperative learning groups to study one of the planets and present a report to the class. Encourage the use of visuals in class reports.

Math, pages 214–215

Note: This reading should be presented after students have completed Unit 3.

Before You Read

Preparation *(See Transparency 20.)*

- Share the objectives of the lesson with students. Write the following exercise goals on the board and read them aloud:

    Goals
    —Read a math textbook selection
    —Learn about math word problems
    —Learn math vocabulary as you read
    —Get as much meaning as you can from the reading

- Tell students that this reading selection is similar to one they might find in a math textbook. Point out that, as in a regular math book, some vocabulary may be unfamiliar. Tell students their goal is to try to get as much meaning as possible from the text.

- Ask students what strategies they have studied so far. *(Make Predictions, Use Selective Attention, Grouping, Use What You Know, Make Inferences, Sound Out.)* Write the strategy names on the board. Call on students to give brief definitions or examples of how some or all of these strategies are used. Make sure students understand the strategy *Use What You Know;* if necessary, refer them to page 98 in the Student Book. (See How to Teach the Focus on Content Lessons on page xiv for additional strategy suggestions.)

- Refer students to the prereading instructions. Read the steps aloud as students follow along in their texts.

- Discuss with students what they already know about math word problems. Write their responses on the board.

While You Read

Solving Word Problems: Mathematics in Everyday Life

Practice

🎧 **Reaching All Students— Emergent Learners:** Have students listen to the first half of the passage (page 214), or read it aloud to them. Tell them to follow along in their texts.

- Have students read the first half of the passage aloud, either chorally as a class, in small groups, or softly to themselves. Remind students that as they read, they can *Sound Out* unfamiliar words.

- Have students silently read the first half of the passage carefully. Tell them to try to understand as much as they can. Tell them to apply the strategy *Use What You Know* to understand the information.

    Reaching All Students—Emergent Learners: Work with emergent readers in small groups while the other students work independently. If students need moderate support, have them read with a partner or small group to figure out the meaning of the passage. Pair proficient readers with students who are less proficient.

- Have students answer the Before You Go On question. Encourage them to go back and reread if needed. (She can buy four pencils. Ten cents is left.)

    🎧 **Reaching All Students— Emergent Learners:** Have students listen to the second half of the passage (page 215), or read it aloud.

- Have students read the second half of the passage aloud. When they have finished, tell them to read the passage silently to themselves.

After You Read

Self-Evaluation

Vocabulary

- Refer students to the instructions in their texts. Read the instructions aloud as students follow along in their texts.

- Have them look through the reading again. Tell them to write the words they don't understand in their notebooks.

- Have students try to guess the meaning of the unknown words, using context clues from the words around them and information from the photos.

- After students have worked on their own, have students work in pairs or small groups to discuss and decipher the words they couldn't figure out.

- Finally, have students use their dictionaries to find the definitions of any words they couldn't decipher. (Refer to the How to Use a Dictionary section on page 256 of the Student Book.)

- Call on volunteers to share the meanings for some of the most important new vocabulary in the passage.

Comprehension

- Have students take out their notebooks and number a sheet of paper from 1 to 5.
- Call on a student to read the first item aloud. Then ask a volunteer to answer the question. Ask the student to find the supportive statement in the passage.

  Reaching All Students—Emergent/ Auditory Learners: Call on advanced students to read the questions aloud.

- Have students write the answers in their notebooks.

  Reaching All Students—Emergent Learners: Have students work in pairs, or work with them in small groups.

- After students complete the exercise, have them check their work by scanning the reading to find the answers. Have them correct any mistakes.
- Call on students to give their answers and write them on the board. Be sure they also give the supporting statements from the passage.
- Have students count the number of correct answers and write that number in their notebooks.

Answers

1. The five steps for solving a word problem are: rewrite the question, find the numbers you need, choose the operation, find the answer, check your answer.
2. Four mathematical operations are: addition, subtraction, multiplication, and division.
3. You can check a division answer by multiplying and then adding the remainder.
4. One way to simplify is to cross out unnecessary information.
5. The phrase "times" expresses a multiplication operation.

Expansion

- As a class, develop and solve math word problems that apply to the class. For example: Given the number of students, how many eyes are in the class? How many fingers? If the local pizza place has an extra large pizza that serves 8, how many pizzas would the class need to order to serve every-

one 1 piece? two pieces? How many pieces would be left over?

- Have each student bring in a word problem from his or her math textbook. Call on students one at a time to write their word problem on the board. Then have the class apply the strategy steps to the word problem. Alternately, use the word problems students bring in to play a "Math Bowl" game in which teams compete to be the first to have the correct answer. Encourage students to use the math vocabulary they learned in the reading.

Literature, pages 216–217

Note: This reading should be presented after students have completed Unit 4.

Before You Read

Preparation (See Transparency 17.)

- Write the following exercise goals on the board and call on a volunteer to read them aloud.

Goals

—*Read a literature textbook selection*
—*Read and appreciate a poem*
—*Learn literature vocabulary as you read*
—*Get as much meaning as you can from the text*

- Tell students that this reading selection is similar to one they might find in a literature textbook. As in a regular literature textbook, some vocabulary may be unfamiliar to students. Tell students their goal is to try to get as much meaning as possible from the text.
- Ask students what strategies they have studied so far. (*Make Predictions, Use Selective Attention, Grouping, Use What You Know, Make Inferences, Sound Out.*) Write the strategy names on the board. Call on students to give brief definitions or examples of how some or all of these strategies are used.
- Ask students to choose another strategy or strategies they would like to use to help them understand and remember information in the text. Have students write the strategy they chose in their notebooks. Call on a few students to identify the strategy and explain why they chose it.

- Refer students to the prereading instructions. Call on a volunteer to read the steps aloud as students follow along in their texts.

While You Read

Poetry: Understanding Images

Practice

- 🎧 **Reaching All Students— Emergent Learners:** Tell students to listen to the first half of the passage (page 216), or read it aloud to them. Have students follow along in their texts.
- Have students read the first half of the passage aloud, either chorally as a class, in small groups, or softly to themselves.
- Have students silently read the first half of the passage carefully. Encourage students to use their strategies and try to understand as much of the text as they can.

    Reaching All Students—Emergent Learners: Work with emergent readers in small groups while the other students work independently. If students need moderate support, have them read with a partner or small group to figure out the meaning of the passage. Pair proficient readers with readers who are less proficient.

- Have students answer the Before You Go On question. Encourage them to go back and reread if needed. (Line 2 has a simile: *one rolled away like a setting sun.*)

    🎧 **Reaching All Students— Emergent Learners:** Have students listen to the second half of the passage (page 217), or read it aloud.

- Have students read the second half of the passage aloud. When they have finished, tell them to read the passage silently to themselves.

After You Read

Self-Evaluation

Vocabulary

- Refer students to the instructions in their texts. Read the instructions aloud as students follow along in their texts.
- Have them look through the reading again. Tell them to write the words they don't understand in their notebooks.

- Have students try to guess the meaning of the unknown words, using context clues from the words around them and the information from the pictures.
- After students have worked on their own, have students work in pairs or small groups to discuss and decipher the words they couldn't figure out.
- Finally, have students use their dictionaries to find the definitions of any words they couldn't decipher. (Refer to the How to Use a Dictionary section on page 256 of the Student Book.)
- Call on volunteers to share the meanings for some of the most important new vocabulary in the passage.

Comprehension

- Have students take out their notebooks and number a sheet of paper from 1 to 5.
- Call on a student to read the first item aloud. Call on a volunteer to answer the question. Ask the student to find the supportive statement in the passage.

    Reaching All Students—Emergent/ Auditory Learners: Call on advanced students to read the questions aloud.

- Have students write the answers in their notebooks.

    Reaching All Students—Emergent Learners: Have students work in pairs, or work with them in small groups.

- After students complete the exercise, have them check their work by scanning the reading to find the answers. Have them correct any mistakes.
- Call on students to give their answers and write them on the board. Be sure they also give statements to support their answers from the passage.
- Have students count the number of correct answers and write that number in their notebooks.

Answers
1. You see pictures in your mind.
2. Poems use figures of speech to create images, or pictures.
3. A simile uses *like* or *as* to compare two unlike things. A metaphor links two things without using *like* or *as*.
4. What images do the words create in my mind? How do the images make me feel?
5. Answers will vary.

Expansion

- Have students describe and compare the images the poem brought to their minds. If students need help getting started, ask questions such as, "When you read about the table, what did the table in your mind look like? Was it wood, glass, metal; big or small; round or square?"

- Have students share their favorite line, phrase, or image in the poem. Encourage them to express what kind of feelings the poem brought out for them.

- Have students bring in a favorite poem or lyrics to a favorite pop song to read for the class. As a class, examine the images, similes, and metaphors in the poems or lyrics.

- Have students write poems using similes and/or metaphors. Students can work independently, in pairs, or in small groups.

Social Studies, pages 218–219

Note: This reading should be presented after students have completed Unit 5.

Before You Read

Preparation

- Share the objectives of the lesson with students. Write the following exercise goals on the board and read them aloud, or call on a student to read them aloud:

Goals

—*Read a social studies textbook selection*
—*Learn about reading maps of the United States*
—*Learn social studies vocabulary as you read*
—*Get as much meaning as you can from the reading*

- Tell students that this reading selection is similar to one they might find in a social studies textbook. Point out that, as in a regular social studies textbook, some vocabulary will be unfamiliar. Tell students their goal is to try to get as much meaning as possible from the text.

- Ask students what strategies they have studied so far. (*Make Predictions, Use Selective Attention, Grouping, Use What You Know, Make Inferences, Identify with a Character,*

Sound Out.) Write the strategy names on the board. Call on students to give brief definitions or examples of how some or all of these strategies are used.

- Refer students to the prereading instructions. Call on a student to read the steps aloud as students follow along in their texts. Then tell students to look at the title, headings, and pictures.

- Have students scan the text, looking for answers to these questions: *What is the main topic? What two kinds of maps will you read about?* Then call on volunteers to share any information they found. (The main topic is reading maps of the United States. We'll read about political and physical maps.)

Optional Activity: Ask students to choose another strategy or strategies they would like to use to help them understand and remember information in the text. Have students write the strategy they chose in their notebooks. Call on a few students to identify the strategy and explain why they chose it.

While You Read

The United States: Reading Maps of Our Country

Practice

> **Reaching All Students— Emergent Learners:** Have students listen to the first half of the passage (page 218), or read it aloud to them. Then tell them to follow along in their texts.

- Have students read the first half of the passage aloud, either chorally as a class, in small groups, or softly to themselves.

- Have students silently read the first half of the passage carefully. Tell them to try to understand as much as they can. Remind students that using their strategies can help them.

> **Reaching All Students—Emergent Learners:** Work with emergent readers in small groups while the other students work independently. If students need moderate support, have them read with a partner or small group to figure out the meaning of the passage. Pair proficient readers with readers who are less proficient.

- Have students answer the Before You Go On question. Encourage them to go back and reread if needed. (Answers will vary: The capital of my state is ___.)
  - 🎧 **Reaching All Students— Emergent Learners:** Have students listen to the second half of the passage (page 219), or read it aloud.
- Have students read the second half of the passage aloud. When they have finished, tell them to read the passage silently to themselves.

After You Read

Self-Evaluation
Vocabulary

- Refer students to the instructions in their texts. Read the instructions aloud as students follow along in their texts.
- Have them look through the reading again. Tell them to write the words they don't understand in their notebooks.
- Have students try to guess the meaning of the unknown words, using context clues from the words around them and information from the pictures.
- After students have worked on their own, have students work in pairs or small groups to discuss and decipher the words they couldn't figure out.
- Finally, have students use their dictionaries to find the definitions of any words they couldn't decipher. (Refer to the How to Use a Dictionary section on page 256 of the Student Book.)
- Call on volunteers to share the meanings for some of the most important new vocabulary in the passage.

Comprehension

- Have students take out their notebooks and number a sheet of paper from 1 to 5.
- Call on a student to read the first item aloud. Then ask a volunteer to answer the question. Ask the student to find information in the passage that supports the answer.
  - **Reaching All Students—Emergent/ Auditory Learners:** Call on advanced students to read the questions aloud. Have students write the answers in their notebooks.
  - **Reaching All Students—Emergent Learners:** Have students work in pairs, or work with them in small groups.

- After students complete the exercise, have them check their work by scanning the reading to find the answers. Have them correct any mistakes.
- Call on students to give their answers and write them on the board. Be sure they also give the supporting statements from the passage.
- Have students count the number of correct answers and write that number in their notebooks.

Answers
1. Alaska and Hawaii are not in the continental United States.
2. The capital of the United States is Washington, D.C.
3. It is about four hundred kilometers (two hundred and forty miles) from Washington, D.C., to New York City.
4. Two mountain ranges in the United States are the Appalachian Mountains and the Rocky Mountains.
5. Answers will vary.

Expansion

- If not already listed, help students plot their city on the map. Have them make a list of approximate distances from their city to other cities on the map.
- Have students work in cooperative learning groups to prepare reports on their state and/or other states they find to be of interest. Suggest that students write about the state's location in the United States (north, south, east, west), neighboring states, the state capital and other major cities, distances between cities, and state landforms. Students can illustrate their reports with a state map showing physical and political features, as well as a compass and scale.

History, pages 220–221

Note: This reading should be presented after students have completed Unit 6.

Before You Read

Preparation (See Transparencies 18 and 25.)

- Write the following exercise goals on the board and call on a volunteer to read them aloud:

Goals

—Read a history textbook selection
—Learn about Martin Luther King Jr.
—Learn history vocabulary as you read
—Get as much meaning as you can from the reading

- Tell students that this reading selection is similar to one they might find in a history textbook. Point out that, as in a history textbook, some vocabulary may be unfamiliar. Tell students their goal is to try to get as much meaning as possible from the text.

- Ask students what strategies they have studied so far. *(Make Predictions, Use Selective Attention, Grouping, Use What You Know, Make Inferences, Identify with a Character, Sound Out.)* Write the strategy names on the board. Call on students to give brief definitions or examples of how some or all of these strategies are used.

- Refer students to the prereading instructions. Call on a volunteer to read the steps aloud as students follow along in their texts.

- Tell students to record dates with significant events that are mentioned in the text as they read. Remind them not to write down everything in their notebooks, but just the most crucial dates and events. Point out that this will help them remember important information and will give them a framework for understanding the reading.

    Optional Activity: Along with taking notes, ask students to choose another strategy or strategies they would like to use to help them understand and remember information in the text. Have students write the strategy they chose in their notebooks. Call on a few students to identify the strategy and explain why they chose it.

While You Read

Martin Luther King Jr.: An American Hero

Practice

🎧 **Reaching All Students—Emergent Learners:** Have students listen to the first half of the passage (page 220), or read it aloud to them. Tell them to follow along in their texts.

- Have students read the first half of the passage aloud, either chorally as a class, in small groups, or softly to themselves.

- Tell students to silently read the first half of the passage carefully. Point out that they should try to understand as much as they can. Remind students to make notes of the most important events and dates mentioned in the text.

    Reaching All Students—Emergent Learners: Work with emergent readers in small groups while the other students work independently. If students need moderate support, have them read with a partner or small group to figure out the meaning of the passage. Pair proficient readers with students who are less proficient.

- Have students answer the Before You Go On question. Encourage them to go back and reread, if needed. (African Americans had to go to separate schools and eat in separate restaurants. They also had to sit at the back of buses.)

- Call on volunteers to share the notes they made for this section of the text. Write them on the board.

    🎧 **Reaching All Students— Emergent Learners:** Have students listen to the second half of the passage (page 221), or read it aloud.

- Have students read the second half of the passage aloud. When they have finished, tell them to read the passage silently to themselves.

- Call on volunteers to share the notes they made for this section of the text. Write them on the board.

After You Read

Self-Evaluation

Vocabulary

- Refer students to the instructions in their texts. Read them aloud as students follow along in their texts.

- Have them look through the reading again. Tell them to write the words they don't understand in their notebooks.

- Have students try to guess the meaning of the unknown words, using context clues from the words around them and information from the photos.

- After students have worked on their own, have them work in pairs or small groups to discuss and decipher the words they couldn't figure out.

- Finally, have students use their dictionaries to find the definitions of any words they couldn't decipher. (Refer to the How to Use a Dictionary section on page 256 of the Student Book.)
- Call on volunteers to share the meanings for some of the most important new vocabulary in the passage.

Comprehension

- Have students take out their notebooks and number a sheet of paper from 1 to 5.
- Call on a student to read the first item aloud. Then ask a volunteer to answer the question. Ask the student to find information in the passage that supports the answer.

  Reaching All Students—Emergent/ Auditory Learners: Call on advanced students to read the questions aloud. Have students write the answers in their notebooks.

  Reaching All Students—Emergent Learners: Have students work in pairs, or work with them in a small group.

- After students complete the exercise, have them check their work by scanning the reading to find the answers and then correct any mistakes.
- Call on students to give their answers and write them on the board. Be sure they also give statements from the passage to support their answers.

- Have students count the number of correct answers and write that number in their notebooks.

Answers
1. He was born on January 15, 1929.
2. They were fighting for equal rights for all Americans.
3. In 1963, he gave his most famous speech, called *I Have a Dream*.
4. The Civil Rights Act made it illegal to discriminate against people because of their color, religion, or the country they came from.
5. Answers will vary.

Expansion

Have students work in small groups using the Internet or other resources to research an example of discrimination in American history. For example, they might research Rosa Parks and the bus boycott in Montgomery, Alabama, in 1954–1955 or find out more about the life of Martin Luther King Jr. Have groups write a one-page report (or less) based on their research, and have them present their reports to the class.

WORKBOOK ANSWER KEY

GETTING STARTED

Introductions (page 1)

A.

Students write their names.

B.

1. *Hello*
2. Hi
3. What's
4. name
5. meet
6. Nice

Classroom Objects (page 2)

A.

1. *a notebook*
2. a table
3. a chair
4. a pencil
5. an eraser
6. a desk
7. a pen
8. a book
9. a bookcase

B.

1. A: What's this?
   B: *It's a pencil.*
2. A: What's this?
   B: It's a notebook.
3. A: What's this?
   B: It's an eraser.

Classroom Commands

(page 3)

A.

1. *Get your pen.*
2. Open your notebook.
3. Write your name.
4. Stand up.
5. Raise your hand.
6. Close your book.

B.

Students follow the commands.

Days of the Week (page 4)

A.

1. *Monday*
2. Tuesday
3. Wednesday
4. Thursday
5. Friday
6. Saturday
7. Sunday

B.

1–2. Students fill in the day of the week for Today and Tomorrow.

C.

1–15. *Sunday,* Monday, Tuesday, Wednesday, Thursday, Friday, Saturday, Sunday, Monday, *Tuesday,* Wednesday, Thursday, Friday, *Saturday,* Sunday

The Alphabet (page 5)

A.

Students write capital and lowercase letters.

B.

a,b,c,*d*,e,f,g,h,i,j,*k*,l,m,n,o,p,q,*r*,s,t, u,v,w,*x*,y,z

C.

1. *Mei Song*
2–5. Students write the names of four friends.

Numbers 1–20 (page 6)

A.

Students write the number words from *one* through *ten*.

B.

11 *eleven*	16 sixteen
12 twelve	17 seventeen
13 thirteen	18 eighteen
14 fourteen	19 nineteen
15 fifteen	20 twenty

C.

1. 18 − 7 = <u>11</u>, *eighteen − seven = eleven*
2. 6 + 13 = <u>19</u>, six + thirteen = nineteen
3. 17 − 5 = <u>12</u>, seventeen − five = twelve

Numbers 20–100 (page 7)

A.

20 twenty	70 seventy
30 thirty	80 eighty
40 forty	90 ninety
50 fifty	100 one hundred
60 sixty	

B.

1. *sixty-nine dollars*
2. fifty-five dollars
3. forty-seven dollars
4. sixty-four dollars
5. ninety-six dollars
6. twenty-five dollars

C.

1. 22 + 62 = <u>84</u>, twenty-two + sixty-two = eighty-four
2. 94 − 41 = <u>53</u>, ninety-four − forty-one = fifty-three
3. 39 + 57 = <u>96</u>, thirty-nine + fifty-seven = ninety-six

4. 76 − 48 = <u>28</u>, seventy-six − forty-eight = twenty-eight
5. 26 + 74 = <u>100</u>, twenty-six + seventy-four = one hundred

Time (page 8)

A.

1. three *forty-five*
2. eight <u>thirty</u>
3. two <u>oh five</u>
4. nine <u>fifteen</u>
5. five <u>o'clock</u>

B.

1. B: *It's six forty-five.*
2. B: It's eight o'clock.
3. B: It's eight thirty.
4. B: It's ten oh five.

C.

1. *7:00*
2–4. Students write the time they do the activities in Exercise B.

Months of the Year (page 9)

A.

Students circle the months of the year.

B.

Students write months from Exercise A in the calendar.

Dates (Ordinal Numbers 1st–31st) (page 10)

A.

Across

3. *11th, eleventh*
4. 5th, fifth
7. 2nd, second
8. 6th, sixth
9. 10th, tenth
10. 12th, twelfth

Down

1. 4th, fourth
2. 3rd, third
3. 8th, eighth
4. 1st, first
5. 7th, seventh
6. 9th, ninth

B.

Students write the ordinal numbers 1st–31st.

CHAPTER 1

Listening and Reading

(page 11)

1. *b*   2. a   3. a   4. a

Vocabulary (page 11)

A.

1. *teacher*   3. brother
2. students   4. okay

B. Answers will vary.

Grammar 1

Pronouns (page 12)

A.

1. we   3. he   5. I
2. she   4. they   6. it

B.

1. *it*   3. she   5. we
2. he   4. they   6. you

C.

1. *He* is the English teacher.
2. *They* are students.
3. *We* are students.
4. *It* is new.
5. *You* are from Mexico.
6. *They* are brother and sister.

Grammar 2

Present Tense of be: Statements (page 13)

A.

1. *are*   5. are   9. is
2. am   6. are   10. are
3. is   7. is   11. am
4. is   8. is   12. are

B.

1. *They're*   4. I'm
2. He's   5. You're
3. It's

C.

1. *He's not nervous.*
2. I'm not twelve.
3. We're not from the United States.
4. She's not my teacher.
5. They're not brother and sister.
6. You're not my brother.

Word Study

The Alphabet (page 14)

Students write capital and lowercase letters.

Consonants and Vowels (page 14)

A.

b,c,d,f,g,h,j,k,l,m,n,p,q,r,s,t,v,w,x,y,z

B.

a,e,i,o,u

C.

1. sp__ea__k   4. o__ka__y
2. n__a__me   5. te__ache__r
3. s__iste__r   6. st__uden__ts

Alphabetical Order (page 14)

1. *brother*   6. okay
2. English   7. pretty
3. he   8. sister
4. name   9. students
5. nice   10. teacher

Grammar 3

Present tense of be: Yes/No Questions (page 15)

A.

1. *Are you a student?*
2. Are they pretty?
3. Is he nervous?
4. Is it a pencil?
5. Is she from El Salvador?

B.

1. A: *Are*   6. A: Is
   B: *we are*   B: he is
2. A: *Is*   7. A: Is
   B: *he's not*   B: it is
3. A: Are   8. A: Are
   B: they're not   B: we're not
4. A: Is   9. A: Is
   B: she is   B: he isn't
5. A: Are   10. A: Is
   B: they are   B: it isn't

C.

Answers will vary.

Reading (page 16)

A.

1. *b*   3. b   5. b
2. b   4. a   6. b

B.

1. *new*   3. pretty   5. Nice
2. very   4. speaks   6. school

CHAPTER 2

Listening and Reading

(page 19)

Carmen's Schedule:

1–2. lunch, P.E., math, science, music

Liliana's Schedule:

3–4. P.E., lunch, math, science, music

Maria's Schedule:

5. music, lunch, math, science, P.E.

Vocabulary (page 19)

1. same   4. after
2. different   5. schedules
3. together   6. almost

Grammar 1

Present Tense of have: Affirmative Statements (page 20)

A.

1. *has*   3. has   5. have
2. have   4. have   6. have

B.

1. *has, math*
2. has, P.E.
3. have, English
4. have, math, English
5. have, math, P.E.
6. have, math, music

C.

1–5. Sentences may vary.

Grammar 2

Present Tense of have: Negative Statements (page 21)

1. *don't have*
2. doesn't have
3. don't have
4. don't have
5. don't have

Present Tense of have: Yes/No Questions (page 21)

A.

1. *Do*   3. Does   5. Do
2. Does   4. Does

B. Questions and answers may vary.

Word Study (page 22)

Short Vowel Sounds: /a/, /i/, /o/

A.

1. m__a__p   4. h__a__t   7. s__i__x
2. h__o__t   5. h__i__t   8. c__a__t
3. p__i__g   6. c__a__p

B.

1. (It's), __not__, (his), [hat]
2. [have], (six), (big), [caps]
3. [cat], [has], [hat]
4. [map], (is), __not__, (big)

5. had, big, hit, with, his, bat
6. have, big, map

C.

1–3. Sentences may vary.

Grammar 3

Plural Nouns (page 23)

1. *names*	6. classes
2. boxes	7. students
3. lunches	8. schools
4. days	9. brushes
5. cats	10. schedules

Possessive Adjectives (page 23)

A.

1. *Your*	3. Our
2. Her	4. Their

B.

1. *My*	4. my	7. my
2. my	5. His	8. Their
3. Her	6. my	9. Our

Reading (page 24)

A.

1. b   2. b   3. b   4. b   5. a

B.

1. every	4. also
2. classes	5. favorite
3. languages	

CHAPTER 3

Listening and Reading

(page 27)

1. b   2. a   3. b   4. b   5. a

Vocabulary (page 27)

1. borrow	4. fun
2. wallet	5. calculator
3. things	

Grammar 1

Articles: *a* and *an* (page 28)

A.

a,e,i,o,u,*y*

B.

1. *a*	5. a	9. a
2. *an*	6. an	10. an
3. a	7. a	11. an
4. an	8. a	12. a

Demonstrative Pronouns: *this* and *that* (page 28)

1. *c*	3. a	5. d
2. e	4. b	6. f

Grammar 2

Demonstrative Pronouns: *these* and *those* (page 29)

A.

1. *These are*	4. These are
2. This is	5. Those are
3. That is	6. Those are

B.

1. *That is an apple.*
2. These are erasers.
3. Those are notebooks.
4. This is a backpack.
5. These are brushes.
6. Those are boxes.

Word Study (page 30)

Short Vowel Sounds: /e/ and /u/

A.

1. b<u>e</u>d	4. n<u>e</u>t	7. d<u>e</u>sk
2. b<u>u</u>s	5. s<u>u</u>n	8. c<u>u</u>p
3. p<u>e</u>n	6. t<u>e</u>n	

B.

1. *no*   2. yes   3. yes   4. no

C.

1–4. Sentences may vary.

Grammar 3

Possessive of Singular and Plural Nouns (page 31)

A.

1. *my mother's*	4. Mrs. Smith's
2. Anna's	5. Thomas's
3. my brother's	

B.

1. *The girls' umbrellas*
2. My brother's backpack
3. Mr. Gomez's students
4. The students' schedules
5. Carmen's pen

C.

1. *My friend's dog is black.*
2–3. Sentences may vary.

Reading (page 32)

A.

1. a   2. b   3. a   4. b   5. a

B.

1. again	4. asks
2. says	5. right
3. problem	

CHAPTER 4

Listening and Reading

(page 35)

1. *False*	4. False
2. True	5. False
3. True	6. True

Vocabulary (page 35)

1. downstairs	4. other
2. lost	5. next to
3. cafeteria	

Grammar 1

Prepositions of Location: *in, on, under, next to* (page 36)

A.

1. c   2. a   3. d   4. b

B.

Sentences may vary. Examples:
1. *The notebooks are next to the cup.*
2. The backpack is on the desk.
3. The pencils are in the cup.
4. The book is in the backpack.
5. The binder is under the backpack.

C.

1–3. Sentences may vary.

Grammar 2

Where Questions with *be* (page 37)

A.

1. A: *Where's*
   B: *She's*
2. A: Where are
   B: They're
3. A: Where's
   B: He's
4. A: Where am
   B: You're
5. A: Where are
   B: You're
6. A: Where are
   B: I'm

B.

1. A: *Where's Tom?*
   B: *He's in*
2. A: Where's the cafeteria?
   B: It's next to
3. A: Where are Sam and Chen?
   B: They're in
4. A: Where's Robert?
   B: He's in
5. A: Where's the library?
   B: It's across from
6. A: Where's the music room?
   B: It's next to

C.

1–5. Questions and answers may vary.

Word Study (page 38)

Consonant Sounds: /ch/ and /sh/

A.

1. fi*sh*
2. ben*ch*
3. *sh*ip
4. *ch*in
5. di*sh*
6. lun*ch*
7. in*ch*
8. *sh*op

B.

1. fi*sh*, *ch*ins
2. hairbru*sh*, ben*ch*
3. lun*ch*, *sh*ip

Grammar 3

There is and **There are** (page 39)

A.

1. *There is*
2. There are
3. There are
4. There is
5. There are

B.

1. *There are some books on the bed.*
2. There's a computer on the desk.
3. There are (some) pencils in the cup.
4. There's a desk next to the bed.
5. There's a toy ship next to the computer/on the desk.

C.

1–2. Sentences will vary.

Reading (page 40)

A.

1. a   2. a   3. b   4. a   5. a

B.

1. live
2. like
3. nice
4. a lot of
5. go

CHAPTER 5

Listening and Reading

(page 43)

1. b   2. a   3. b   4. b

Vocabulary (page 43)

A.

Name: Carmen, Carlos
Address: 316 Fifth Street
Phone: 555-2377

B.

1. come   2. directions   3. need

Grammar 1 (page 44)

What **Questions with** *be*

A.

1. *What's*
2. What are
3. What's
4. What are
5. What's

B.

1. A: *What's your favorite class?*
2. A: What's his phone number?
3. A: What's this?
4. A: What's her brother's name?
5. A: What's your address?

C.

1–2. Questions and answers may vary.

Grammar 2

Present Tense of Regular Verbs: Statements (page 45)

A.

1. *needs*
2. live
3. want
4. speak
5. likes
6. asks

B.

1. *Laura doesn't want a new backpack.*
2. Anna and Mary don't like tests.
3. I don't listen to music in school.
4. We don't need new notebooks.
5. Mrs. Perez doesn't speak Chinese.
6. Julio doesn't live in Peru.

Present Tense of Regular Verbs: Yes/No Questions (page 45)

1. A: Does
   B: *he does*
2. A: Do
   B: I don't
3. A: Do
   B: they do
4. A: Do
   B: I don't
5. A: Does
   B: she does
6. A: Do
   B: we don't

Word Study (page 46)

Consonant Blends

A.

1. *cl*ock
2. *dr*ess
3. *bl*ack
4. *sw*im
5. *dr*um
6. *st*op
7. *fl*ag
8. *st*airs

B.

1. swim, class
2. black, dress
3. station, store
4. flag, clock, classroom

C.

1–3. Sentences may vary.

Grammar 3

Statements with *can* (page 47)

1. *can*
2. can't
3. can
4. can
5. can't
6. can't

Yes/No **Questions with** *can* (page 47)

A.

1. *Can we come to your party?*
2. Can he swim?
3. Can they speak Spanish?
4. Can she play the drums?
5. Can I read Vietnamese?
6. Can you answer the question?

B.

1. A: *Can Miguel read Chinese?*
   B: *No, he can't*
2–6. Questions and answers may vary.

Reading (page 48)

A.

1. b   3. a   5. b
2. b   4. a

B.

1. job
2. sad
3. dance
4. baby-sit
5. children

CHAPTER 6

Listening and Reading

(page 51)

1. b   3. b   5. b
2. b   4. a

Vocabulary (page 51)

1. late
2. sick
3. take out
4. starts
5. today

Grammar 1

What **Questions with** *do* (page 52)

A.

1. *does*
2. do
3. does
4. do
5. do

B.

1. A: *What does he like?*
2. A: What do you have?
3. A: What does she want?
4. A: What do you play?
5. A: What do you need?

C.

1–2. Questions and answers may vary.

Grammar 2

What + Noun (page 53)

A.

1. *What class do you have next?*
2. What color do you like?
3. What classes does your friend have?
4. What books do you need for school?

B.

1. A: *What school do you go to?*
2. A: What classes do you have?
3. A: What time do your classes start?
4. A: What time do you go home?

C.

1–4. Answers will vary.

Word Study (page 54)

Consonant Blends

A.

1. pl<u>ant</u>   5. be<u>lt</u>
2. ma<u>sk</u>   6. la<u>mp</u>
3. <u>g</u>ift   7. <u>t</u>ent
4. ha<u>nd</u>   8. de<u>sk</u>

B.

1. *plant*   3. lamp
2. mask/desk   4. hand

C.

1–4. Sentences may vary.

Grammar 3

Past Tense of *be*: Statements (page 55)

A.

1. *You were late*
2. I was very silly
3. The class wasn't hard
4. Mrs. Moore was funny
5. Ted and Ann weren't in school
6. You weren't sick

B.

1. *wasn't*
2–6. Answers will vary.

Past Tense of *be*: Yes/No Questions (page 55)

1. A: *Was your English teacher angry yesterday?*
   B: *No, she wasn't.*
2. A: Were you late to school yesterday?
   B: Answers may vary.
3. A: Were your best friends in school yesterday?
   B: Answers may vary.
4. A: Was your English class hard yesterday?
   B: Answers may vary.
5. A: Were you in the library after school yesterday?
   B: Answers may vary.
6. A: Were your friends at lunch yesterday?
   B: Answers may vary.

Reading (page 56)

A.

1. b   3. b   5. c
2. c   4. b

B.

1. easy   4. early
2. bad   5. tomorrow
3. watch

CHAPTER 7

Listening and Reading

(page 59)

1. Yes, he does.
2. No, he can't.
3. Yes, she is.
4. No, she can't.
5. No, she isn't.
6. Yes, she can.

Vocabulary (page 59)

1. *Carlos's father is changing a lightbulb.*
2. Carmen is making the bed.
3. Carlos is cooking.
4. David is cleaning the windows.
5. Carolina is washing her hair.

Grammar 1

Present Continuous Tense: Statements (page 60)

A.

helping Mr. Green, changing a lightbulb, writing on the board, dancing, cleaning the floor, eating a snack, listening to music

B.

1. Renee *is helping Mr. Green.*
2. Mr. Green <u>is changing a lightbulb</u>.
3. Abdul <u>is writing on the board</u>.
4. Anna <u>is listening to music</u>.
5. Manuel and Lee <u>are eating a snack</u>.
6. Flavio <u>is cleaning the floor</u>.

C.

1. *She isn't cleaning the table.*
2. He isn't changing a lightbulb.
3. We aren't writing in our notebooks.
4. You aren't reading a book.
5. They aren't making enchiladas.

Grammar 2

Present Continuous Tense: *What* Questions (page 61)

A.

1. *What's*   4. What are
2. What are   5. What's
3. What's   6. What are

B.

1. *What are they eating?*
2. What is he writing?
3. What is she studying?
4. What are they making?

Present Continuous Tense: Yes/No Questions (page 61)

1. *No, he isn't. He's studying math.*
2. No, she isn't. She's cleaning the window.
3. No, they aren't. They're making cookies.

Word Study (page 62)

Long Vowel Sounds /ā/, /ī/, /ō/, /yōo/

A.

1. n<u>o</u>se   5. c<u>u</u>be
2. b<u>i</u>ke   6. n<u>a</u>me
3. c<u>u</u>te   7. ph<u>o</u>ne
4. c<u>a</u>ke   8. wr<u>i</u>te

B.

1. likes, ice, cubes
2. cute, nose
3. open, phone, page
4. cake, ice, cream

C.

1–3. Sentences may vary.

Grammar 3

Object Pronouns (page 63)

A.

1. *(Carlos and his grandmother) I'm helping them.*
2. (Carlos) She's helping him.
3. (the enchiladas) They're burning them.
4. (his mother) He's asking her.
5. (a cake) We're making it.
6. (Carlos and me) She's cooking with us.
7. (a cake) When is your mother baking it?
8. (your sister) Where are you going with her?
9. (you and your friend) What's he making for you?

B.

1. *Are you drying the dishes?*
   Yes, I'm drying them.
2. Is your mother reading this book?
   Yes, she's reading it.
3. Are your brother and sister eating the cookies?
   Yes, they're eating them.
4. Is your brother asking your father?
   Yes, he's asking him.
5. Are your sisters helping you and your brother?
   Yes, they're helping us.
6. Are you studying with Bob and Carlos?
   Yes, I'm studying with them.
7. Are you cleaning your room?
   Yes, I'm cleaning it.
8. Are you eating with your grandmother?
   Yes, I'm eating with her.

Reading (page 64)

A.

1. *b*   3. a   5. e
2. c   4. d

B.

1. helping   4. knocking
2. later   5. turning
3. get ready   6. cool

CHAPTER 8

Listening and Reading

(page 67)

1. *b*   3. c   5. a
2. b   4. a   6. b

Vocabulary (page 67)

1. *tonight*   4. too bad
2. go out   5. Would
3. work   6. another

Grammar 1

Simple Present Tense and Present Continuous Tense (page 68)

A.

1. *am talking*   6. is washing
2. makes   7. go out
3. am studying   8. call
4. watches   9. am doing
5. are burning

B.

1. *am making*   6. Do, make
2. Do, make   7. make
3. make   8. make
4. are, making   9. make
5. am making

Grammar 2

Sentences with *like, have,* and *want* + Infinitive (page 69)

A.

1. *likes*   3. wants   5. want
2. have   4. has   6. like

B.

1. *My brother doesn't have to work today.*
2. I don't like to write letters.
3. My father doesn't like to dance.
4. My sisters don't want to wash the dishes.
5. My friends don't have to study tonight.

C.

1–3. Sentences may vary.

D.

1–3. Sentences may vary.

Word Study (page 70)

Long vowel sound: /ā/

A.

1. r<u>ai</u>n   5. s<u>ay</u>
2. pl<u>ay</u>   6. tr<u>ai</u>n
3. m<u>ai</u>l   7. c<u>ake</u>
4. g<u>a</u>m<u>e</u>   8. p<u>age</u>

B.

lake, train, lake, makes, lake, play, games, train

Grammar 3

What Questions with *like, have,* and *want* + Infinitive (page 71)

1. A: *What does Marco like to do?*
   B: *He likes to ride his bike.*
2. A: *What do Marco and Ken want to do?*
   B: *They want to go to the movies.*
3. A: What does Marco have to do?
4. B: Kim wants to visit his grandmother.
5. B: Kim and Ken like to play soccer.
6. A: What does Kim have to do?

Yes/No Questions with *like, have,* and *want* + Infinitive (page 71)

1–6. Answers will vary.

Reading (page 72)

A.

1. Yes, she does.
2. She misses her friends, her big sister, and her school.
3. She draws and paints pictures.
4. No, she doesn't.
5. She works. She baby-sits.

B.

Name: *Maria Lopez*
Age: fifteen
Country: United States / El Salvador
School: *Washington School*
Likes to: draw and paint pictures

C.

1. feel   4. homesick
2. homework   5. sometimes
3. draw

CHAPTER 9

Listening and Reading

(page 75)

1. They are sixteen.
2. They are twins.
3. No, they don't.
4. He wants to dance with Carmen.
5. They want to dance with Maria.

Vocabulary (page 75)

1. Let's   4. introduce
2. both   5. twins
3. wrong

Grammar 1

Past Tense of Regular Verbs: Affirmative Statements (page 76)

A.

1. *laughed*
2. danced
3. wanted
4. asked
5. liked
6. arrived
7. talked
8. washed
9. studied
10. cooked
11. changed
12. played
13. helped
14. needed

B.

1. *We cleaned the house yesterday.*
2. We listened to music yesterday.
3. He watched TV yesterday.
4. They played soccer yesterday.
5. She studied history yesterday.

C.

1–3. Sentences will vary.

Grammar 2

Past Tense of Irregular Verbs: Affirmative Statements (page 77)

A.

1. came
2. ate
3. said
4. sang
5. taught
6. read
7. wrote
8. made
9. did
10. went
11. knew
12. had

B.

1. *We ate lunch at twelve o'clock yesterday.*
2. I went to the movies last Saturday.
3. I sang in the bathroom last night.
4. I had breakfast at seven o'clock yesterday.
5. My teacher said "Good Morning!" this morning.
6. Ms. Smith taught math yesterday.

C.

1–3. Sentences may vary.

Word Study (page 78)

Long Vowel Sound: /ē/

A.

1. m**ee**t
2. cit**y**
3. f**ie**ld
4. m**e**
5. bab**y**
6. cl**ea**n
7. r**ea**d
8. tr**ee**

B.

1. We, happy, see
2. trees, city

3. reading, feet
4. He, me, clean, field

C.

1–3. Sentences may vary.

Grammar 3

Past Tense: Negative Statements (page 79)

A.

1. _c_ *Maria didn't go to the movies on Saturday.*
2. _a_ Carmen didn't eat ice cream at the party.
3. _f_ Carlos and Samir didn't ask Carmen to dance.
4. _e_ Pablo didn't play the drums.
5. _b_ The party wasn't at Maria's house.
6. _d_ Liliana didn't talk to Paco.

B.

1–5. Sentences will vary.

Past Tense: *Yes/No* Questions (page 79)

A.

1. *Did you eat ice cream yesterday?*
2. Did you do homework last night?
3. Did you go out with your friends on Saturday?
4. Did you clean your room this morning?
5. Did you watch TV Sunday morning?
6. Did you help your mother on Sunday?

Reading (page 80)

A.

1. Yes, they did.
2. He (Pablo) wrote the song.
3. They talked about Paco.
4. No, they didn't.
5. They had to go home at twelve o'clock.

B.

Across

5. *embarrassed*
6. cute

Down

1. Everybody
2. midnight
3. delicious
4. promised

CHAPTER 10

Listening and Reading (page 83)

1. Pablo needs a shirt and a pair of pants.
2. It's a secret.
3. No, he doesn't.
4. He wants a dark color.
5. He needs to try on the pants.

Vocabulary (page 83)

1. expensive
2. try on
3. girlfriend
4. clothes
5. secret

Grammar 1

Information Questions with *be*: Present Tense (page 84)

1. *What is*
2. Where is
3. When is
4. Who is
5. Why is
6. How is

Information Questions with *be*: Past Tense (page 84)

A.

1. A: *Where were*
2. A: Why were
3. A: When was
4. A: Who was
5. A: How was
6. A: What are

B.

1–5. Sentences may vary.

Grammar 2

Information Questions with *do*: Present Tense (page 85)

A.

1. d
2. f
3. b
4. c
5. e
6. a

B.

1. *What does your sister do on Saturday?*
2. Where does she go?
3. Why does she go there?
4. Who does she go with?
5. When do you go shopping?
6. What do you buy?

Information Questions with *do*: Past Tense (page 85)

1. *How did they look?*
2. How much did it cost?
3. When did the movie start?
4. What did you want to do?

5. Who did you play baseball with?
6. Where did your friend go shopping?

Word Study (page 86)

Long Vowel Sound: /ī/

A.

1. pie
2. nine
3. child
4. cry
5. light
6. dry
7. night
8. bike

B.

1. yes
2. yes
3. no
4. yes

C.

1–3. Sentences will vary.

Grammar 3

Questions with *how much* (page 87)

A.

1. *does*
2. do
3. are
4. does
5. is
6. do
7. is

B.

1. A: *How much do these shoes cost?*
   B: *They're $32.50.*
2. A: *How much is this shirt?*
   B: *It's $16.99.*
3. A: How much are these pants?
   B: They're $24.50.
4. A: How much does this jacket cost?
   B: It's $49.95.
5. A: How much is this belt?
   B: It's $12.99.
6. A: How much are these socks?
   B: They're $3.25.

Reading (page 88)

A.

1. Maria wanted a new dress.
2. Maria had forty dollars.
3. They had to be at the fountain at six because they had to meet Pablo.

B.

Across
2. color
4. found
5. price tag
7. suddenly

Down
1. shopping
3. supermarket
6. only

CHAPTER 11

Listening and Reading

(page 91)

1. Yes, she does.
2. She needs a dozen eggs.
3. She wants to eat some crackers because she's hungry.
4. They have to meet Pablo.
5. She isn't hungry anymore because she ate some crackers.

Vocabulary (page 91)

1. dozen
2. hungry
3. else
4. finished
5. total

Grammar 1

Count and Non-Count Nouns (page 92)

A.

Circled items: *potatoes,* carrots, cookies, apples, eggs, onions, bananas, enchiladas, crackers

Boxed items: *milk,* lemonade, bread, beef, cheese, coffee, rice, lettuce, broccoli

B.

1. *six carrots*
2. *two pounds of beef*
3. a gallon of milk
4. an onion
5. a pound of coffee
6. a dozen eggs
7. two slices/pieces of cheese
8. four glasses of lemonade
9. a cup of coffee
10. three cookies
11. four slices of bread
12. a piece of pie

Grammar 2

Some and any (page 93)

A.

Students will check: 1. *onions*
2. apples, 3. lettuce, 6. carrots, 8. milk, 9. lemonade, 11. eggs, 13. beef

B.

1. *Yes, she has some onions.*
2. *No, she doesn't have any cheese.*

3. No, she doesn't have any broccoli.
4. Yes, she has some milk.
5. Yes, she has some carrots.
6. Yes, she has some beef.

C.

1–4. Sentences will vary.

Word Study (page 94)

Long Vowel Sound: /ō/

A.

1. coat
2. window
3. toe
4. toast
5. hose
6. cold
7. rose
8. yo-yo

B.

1. those, yellow, roses
2. cold, toast, stove
3. cold, so, go, coat
4. Oh, those, notebook, so

C.

1–3. Sentences may vary.

Grammar 3

Conjunctions: *and, but,* and *so* (page 95)

A.

1. *b*
2. d
3. e
4. f
5. a
6. c

B.

1. *but*
2. so
3. but
4. and
5. and
6. so

C.

1. *We need some lettuce, but we don't need any carrots.*
2–6. Sentences may vary.

Reading (page 96)

A.

1. Mel, Maria, and Carmen went to Ricky's to get something to eat.
2. Paco was the cashier at Ricky's.
3. There were other customers behind Carmen.
4. Carmen ordered a cup of water.

B.

1. *salad*
2. enough
3. customers
4. cashier
5. ordered
6. receipt

C.

Carmen: I don't know, Paco. I can't decide.

CHAPTER 12

Listening and Reading

(page 99)

1. Sophie likes the CD store because it has the best R&B music section.
2. She likes R&B music.
3. He likes rock music.
4. She wanted to buy Beyoncé's CD.
5. Liliana gave Sophie three dollars.

Vocabulary (page 99)

1. kidding
2. age
3. have time
4. own
5. section

Grammar 1

Comparative Adjectives (page 100)

A.

1. *funnier*
2. taller
3. shorter
4. cuter
5. prettier
6. older
7. younger
8. nicer
9. sillier
10. larger
11. smaller
12. earlier
13. later
14. easier
15. harder

B.

1. *Ken is shorter than Yoko.*

2–4. Sentences may vary.

Examples:

2. Lenora is older than Yoko.
3. Ken is younger than Yoko.
4. Yoko is taller than Ken.

C.

1. *My sister is funnier than my brother.*

2–4. Sentences may vary.

Grammar 2

Superlative Adjectives (page 101)

A.

1. *latest*
2. earliest
3. smallest
4. largest
5. easiest
6. loudest
7. silliest
8. nicest
9. funniest
10. tallest
11. shortest
12. cutest
13. prettiest
14. hardest
15. happiest

B.

1. *funny*
2. harder
3. nicest
4. earlier
5. shortest
6. loud
7. taller

Word Study (page 102)

Long Vowel Sound /yōō/

A.

1. m<u>u</u>l<u>e</u>
2. c<u>u</u>b<u>e</u>
3. f<u>ew</u>
4. men<u>u</u>
5. h<u>u</u>g<u>e</u>
6. b<u>u</u>gle
7. m<u>u</u>seum
8. n<u>ew</u>

B.

1. cute, mule
2. new, uniform
3. Andrew, blew, bugle
4. few, menus

C.

1–5. Sentences may vary.

Grammar 3

Comparatives and Superlatives with *more* and *most* (page 103)

A.

1. *more interesting, most interesting*
2. *harder, hardest*
3. more difficult, most difficult
4. more formal, most formal
5. bigger, biggest
6. more casual, most casual
7. more expensive, most expensive
8. older, oldest

B.

1. *more expensive*
2. oldest
3. more casual
4. more formal
5. most expensive

Reading (page 104)

A.

1. b
2. a
3. b
4. a
5. b

B.

1. *storyteller*
2. audience
3. section
4. stage
5. performer
6. author

Pablo was the best <u>singer</u> in the show!

CHAPTER 13

Listening and Reading

(page 107)

1. True
2. True
3. False
4. False
5. False

Vocabulary (page 107)

1. emergency
2. fast
3. fell
4. broke
5. hurts

Grammar 1

Future Tense with *be going to*: Statements (page 108)

A.

1. *I'm not going to stay home on Saturday.*
2. My sister is going to baby-sit tomorrow.
3. My family isn't going to go out for dinner tonight.
4. We are going to eat Chinese food on Sunday.

B.

1. *My sister is going to go to her dance lesson.*

2–4. Sentences will vary.

Future Tense with *be going to*: *Yes/No* Questions (page 108)

1. *Are, going to; I'm not.*
2. Is, going to; he isn't.
3. Are, going to; we're not.
4. Are, going to; they are.
5. Is, going to; he isn't/she isn't.

Grammar 2

Future Tense with *be going to go*: Information Questions (page 109)

A.

1. *I'm going to get up at seven.*

2–5. Answers will vary.

B.

1. *b*
2. c
3. d
4. e
5. a

C.

1–2 Answers will vary.

Word Study (page 110)

Other Vowel Sound: /ōō/

A.

1. gl<u>ue</u>
2. fl<u>ew</u>
3. m<u>oo</u>n
4. J<u>u</u>n<u>e</u>

Copyright © 2005 by Pearson Education, Inc.

5. dr<u>ew</u>   7. fl<u>ute</u>
6. sch<u>oo</u>l   8. sp<u>oo</u>n

B.

June, tune, flute, blue, moon

C.

1–2. Sentences may vary.

Grammar 3

Commands (page 111)

A.

1. c	4. g	7. d
2. f	5. b	
3. a	6. e	

B.

1. *Please sit down.*
2. Please be quiet.
3. Close your book.
4. Close the window!
5. Don't look up!

Reading (page 112)

A.

1. *sprained his ankle*
2. watched TV
3. brought him his homework
4. came to visit him
5. brought some cookies
6. gave him a CD
7. brought his guitar
8. hurt a lot

B.

Across

3. pain
6. shout
7. awake

Down

1. leap
2. visit
4. bored
5. weak

CHAPTER 14

Listening and Reading

(page 115)

A.

1. He saw a big storm.
2. A tree fell on the power line.
3. He was watching a video in history class.

B.

2, <u>5</u> 1, <u>3</u>, <u>4</u>

Vocabulary (page 115)

1. continue
2. soon
3. storm

Grammar 1

Past Continuous Tense: Statements (page 116)

A.

1. *They were talking. They weren't eating lunch.*
2. They were playing a game. They weren't studying.
3. She was listening to music. She wasn't reading.

B.

1–4. Sentences may vary.

Past Continuous: *Yes/No* Questions (page 116)

1. *Were; No, I wasn't.*
2–5. Answers will vary.

Grammar 2

Past Continuous Tense: Information Questions (page 117)

A.

1. b	3. d	5. c
2. e	4. a	

B.

1. Q: *What was David doing at ten?*
2. Q: Where was David playing basketball?
3. Q: When was David eating lunch?
4. Q: Who was David meeting at the library?
5. Q: Who else was David meeting at the library?
6. Q: When was David eating dinner?

Word Study (page 118)

Other Vowel Sound: /o͝o/

A.

1. c<u>oo</u>kie	5. c<u>oo</u>k
2. g<u>oo</u>d-bye	6. h<u>oo</u>k
3. f<u>oo</u>t	7. b<u>oo</u>k
4. noteb<u>oo</u>k	8. h<u>oo</u>d

B.

1. no	3. no
2. no	4. yes

C.

1–3. Sentences may vary.

Grammar 3

Possessive Pronouns (page 119)

1. *mine*	4. hers
2. yours	5. theirs
3. his	6. ours

Questions with *whose* (page 119)

1. *It's his.*
2. *They're theirs.*
3. They're theirs.
4. Whose notebook is that?
5. Whose videos are those?
6. It's his.

Reading (page 120)

A.

1. True	5. True
2. False	6. False
3. False	7. True
4. False	8. False

B.

1. *ending*	5. raining
2. completely	6. closed
3. perfect	7. instead
4. weather	8. sunny
	electricity

CHAPTER 15

Listening and Reading

(page 123)

1. *study group*	4. stories
2. meeting	5. read
3. vocabulary	

Vocabulary (page 123)

1. extra	4. final
2. exam	5. group
3. review	6. meeting

Grammar 1

Future Tense with *will*: Statements (page 124)

A.

1. *he'll study a lot*
2. we'll buy some soda
3. I'll clean my room
4. she'll go to bed early
5. they'll finish their homework

B.

1. *I won't*	3. I won't
2. it won't	4. they won't

Future Tense with *will*: Yes/No Questions (page 124)

1. A: *Will you go to bed early tonight?*
   B: *No, I won't.*
2. A: Will it rain tomorrow?
   B: Answers will vary.
3. A: Will you call a friend tonight?
   B: Answers will vary.
4. A: Will they start a study group?
   B: Answers will vary.

Grammar 2

Future Tense with *will*: Information Questions (page 125)

A.

1. *Who will make plans for the study group?*
2. Where will they meet?
3. What will they study?
4. When will they meet?
5. What will they bring?
6. What else will they bring?

B.

1. A: *When will you visit Guatemala again?*
2. A: Who will go with you?
3. A: Where will you stay?
4. A: Who will you visit?
5. A: What will you see?
6. A: What else will you see?

Word Study (page 126)

Other Vowel Sound: /ô/ (page 126)

A.

1. author   5. straw
2. paw   6. yawn
3. draw   7. laundry
4. August   8. strawberry

B.

1. audience, yawning
2. author, laundry
3. saw, Paul, autumn
4. August, strawberry, straw

C.

1–3. Sentences may vary.

Grammar 3

Statements with *may* and *might* (page 127)

A.

Definite plans
going to
not going to
will
won't

Possible plans
may
may not
might
might not

B.

1. *We may not go shopping.*
2. I may go out with my friends.
3. He might be late.
4. They might not have a party.
5. She may not buy a dress.
6. They might have a study group on Thursday.

C.

1. *I might wear a blue sweater and jeans.*
2–4. Sentences will vary.

Reading (page 128)

1. Mei lives with her father, two sisters, three brothers, and her grandmother.
2. Mei's grandmother speaks Chinese.
3. She didn't want to go because her English is so bad.
4. She always wanted to go to school.
5. Mei's mother taught her grandmother to read Chinese.

B.

1. nodded   4. translator
2. lit up   5. whispered
3. softly

CHAPTER 16

Listening and Reading

(page 131)

1. He likes eating the snacks.
2. She wants to start studying.
3. He studies about three times a week.
4. She has to study every day.
5. She has dance class every afternoon.

Vocabulary (page 131)

1. mind   4. chance
2. practice   5. typical
3. especially

Grammar 1

Adverbs of Frequency (page 132)

A.

always, usually, often, sometimes, never

B.

1. *usually*   4. often
2. always   5. never
3. sometimes

C.

1. Sentences will vary.

Adverbs of Frequency with *be* (page 132)

1. *She's always on time for school.*
2. They're never late for the movies.
3. He's often bored on weekends.
4. I'm sometimes nervous before a test.
5. She's usually shy at parties.
6. We're always happy to baby-sit.

Grammar 2

How often and Expressions of Frequency (page 133)

A.

1. *I go to the movies twice a month.*
2–5. Answers will vary.

B. and C.

1–3. Questions and answers will vary.

Word Study (page 134)

Other Vowel sound: /oi/

A.

1. soil   5. toy
2. coin   6. boil
3. boy   7. Roy
4. point   8. foil

B.

1. *coin, soil*
2. oil, soil
3. oil, foil
4. Roy, enjoys, coins
5. boy, pointing, toy
6. oil, boil

C.

1–2. Sentences may vary.

Grammar 3

Gerunds as Objects of Verbs (page 135)

A.

1–5. Sentences will vary.

B.

1–5. Questions and answers will vary.

Reading (page 136)

A.

1. a   3. b   5. a
2. b   4. b

B.

Across

4. snack
6. exercise
8. dancer
10. dancing

Down

1. intelligent
2. myself
3. friendly
5. celebration
7. including
9. join

CHAPTER 17

Listening and Reading

(page 139)

1. *Maria tells Mr. Gomez she feels terrible.*
2. Mr. Gomez tells Maria to go see the school nurse/Ms. Cho.
3. Mr. Gomez tells Carmen to walk with Maria to the nurse's office.
4. Maria has a sore throat, a stomachache, and a bad headache.
5. Ms. Cho says English is a hard class.
6. Ms. Cho tells Maria she should get a lot of rest and drink plenty of water.
7. Ms. Cho tells Maria to call a doctor tomorrow if she doesn't feel better.
8. Ms. Cho tells Maria she should go home.

Vocabulary (page 139)

1. c   2. b   3. a

Grammar 1

Statements with *should* (page 140)

1. *You should drink a lot of water and juice.*
2. You should see a doctor.
3. You shouldn't go to school.
4. You should get plenty of rest.
5. You shouldn't play soccer.

Yes/No Questions with *should* (page 140)

A. and B.

Questions and answers will vary.

Grammar 2

Statements with *could* (page 141)

A.

1. B: *You could go to the cafeteria.*
2. B: You could baby-sit.
3. B: You could get a book at the library.
4. B: You could ride your bike to school.
5. B: You could start a study group.
6. B: You could get some rest.

B.

1. a   2. d   3. b   4. c   5. e

Word Study (page 142)

Other Vowel Sound: /ou/

A.

1. m**ou**se   5. t**ow**n
2. cr**ow**d   6. eyebr**ow**
3. h**ou**se   7. **ow**l
4. cl**ou**d   8 m**ou**th

B.

1. f**ou**nd, m**ou**se, c**ou**ch.
2. cr**ow**d, h**ou**se
3. **ow**l

C.

1–4. Sentences may vary.

Grammar 3

Because Clauses (page 143)

A.

1. f   3. b   5. d
2. a   4. e   6. c

B.

1. Pablo likes having a study group because it's boring studying alone.
2. Carlos was late for the study group because he was at soccer practice.
3. Maria should go to the school nurse because she feels terrible.
4. Maria is worried because she has a test tomorrow.
5. Sophie was late because she had a dance lesson.
6. Carlos likes snacks because he's always hungry.

Reading (page 144)

A.

1. They were worried because she's sick.
2. They think she'll do well because she studied for the test, she worked hard, and she's smart.
3. They learned she's an artist.
4. She feels a lot better.

B.

1. surprised   4. knock
2. flowers   5. smart
3. idea   6. stay

There was plenty of food at the surprise party.

CHAPTER 18

Listening and Reading

(page 147)

1. a   3. a   5. b
2. b   4. b

Vocabulary (page 147)

1. e   3. d   5. a
2. c   4. b

Grammar 1

Comparatives and Superlatives: Irregular Adjectives (page 148)

A.

1. *better than*
2. the best
3. worse than
4. the worst
5. the best
6. better than

B.

1–5. Sentences will vary.

Grammar 2

Too and *not enough* (page 149)

A.

1. *are too long, aren't short enough*
2. is too dirty, isn't clean enough
3. too short, not tall enough
4. are too small, aren't big enough

B.

1–2. Sentences will vary.
   Example: Last July I thought the weather was too hot / wasn't cool enough.
   Example: The questions on the test were too difficult / weren't easy enough.

Word Study (page 150)

Other Vowel Sound: /ûr/

A.

1. winter
2. shirt
3. mother
4. letter
5. bird
6. Thursday
7. girl
8. turtle

B.

mother, nurse, skirt, purse, hurt

C.

Sentences may vary.

Grammar 3

Statements with *used to* (page 151)

1. *didn't use to*
2. *used to*
3. *didn't use to*
4. *used to*
5. *used to*
6. *didn't use to*

Yes/No Questions with *used to* (page 151)

1. A: *Did you use to watch cartoons a lot?*
   B: *Yes, I did. I used to watch Scooby Doo.*
2–6. Questions and answers will vary.

Reading (page 152)

A.

1. There was a party.
2. All the students passed the test.
3. She couldn't believe she passed.
4. She used to be nervous about everything.
5. She's more relaxed now.

B.

1. world
2. stunned
3. tease
4. Congratulations
5. grade wondering

READER'S COMPANION: Life Science

Use What You Know (page 157)

Possible answers: food, water, warmth, light, vitamins, and minerals.

Language Link (page 157)

Students should circle *non-living*. not living; not alive

Learning Strategy: Compare (page 157)

Students should underline *soil, water, and sunlight* and *air, water, and food*. They should circle and write *water*.

Check Your Understanding (page 158)

Students should underline *plant* or *leaves* and number it 1. They should underline *rabbit* and number it 2. They should underline *fox* and number it 3. A food chain is a chain or group of living things in which each thing serves as food for the next—the first thing in the chain is food for the second thing in the chain, the second thing is food for the third thing, and so on.

Language Link and Learning Strategy: Compare (page 158)

Students should circle *smaller*. It compares the size of foxes with the size of other animals.

READER'S COMPANION: Physical Science

Use What You Know (page 160)

Possibilities include the sun, the moon, the planets, and the stars.

Learning Strategy: Picture (page 160)

Students should underline *small lights* and *a giant ball of hot gas*. They should use these details to try to picture stars in their minds.

Learning Strategy: Picture (page 160)

It is a group of stars shaped like a large spoon with a curved handle.

Language Link (page 161)

Students should circle *solar*. The solar system is the sun and the planets that go around it.

Check Your Understanding (page 161)

Students should underline *a very large group of stars*. Earth is part of the Milky Way galaxy.

READER'S COMPANION: Math

Use What You Know (page 163)

Among the situations that students may name are shopping, banking, paying fares or admission fees, measuring things, and paying bills.

Check Your Understanding (page 163)

Students should circle *Movie tickets cost $6 each. Mark has $40. How many tickets can Mark buy?* A word problem is a math problem that is expressed in words.

Learning Strategy: Selective Attention (page 163)

Students should underline *$6* and *$40*.

Check Your Understanding (page 164)

Students should circle the four boxed operations, division

Language Link (page 164)

Students should circle the equals sign in the equation. An equation is a mathematical statement that shows what something equals.

Check Your Understanding (page 164)

The *r* stands for the "remainder," the amount left when a number cannot be divided evenly.

Learning Strategy: Selective Attention (page 165)

Key words are *long* and *wide*. The key numbers are *36* and *28.5*.

Language Link (page 165)

Students should circle *unnecessary*. It means "not necessary" or "not needed."

Check Your Understanding (page 165)

multiplication

READER'S COMPANION: Literature

Use What You Know (page 167)

Students' responses will vary. Some may focus on content; others on style elements such as imagery, diction, or rhyme.

Language Link (page 167)

Students should circle *unlike*. not alike; not similar

Learning Strategy: Images, Similes, and Metaphors (page 167)

Students should circle *stars* and *bright diamonds*. They glow, glitter, sparkle, and twinkle with light.

Learning Strategy: Images, Similes, and Metaphors (page 168)

Students should underline *one rolled away like a setting sun*.

Students should circle *one* and *setting sun*. Both are round and seem to roll slowly away.

Check Your Understanding (page 168)

Students should put a number 1 near *one* in line 2, a number 2 near *another* in line 3, the numbers 3–5 (or 3, 4, 5) near *three* in line 4, and 6–12 (or 6, 7, 8, 9, 10, 11, 12) near *seven* in line 5.

Learning Strategy: Images, Similes, and Metaphors (page 168)

Students might put boxes around *twelve oranges, the table, one rolled away, setting sun, another came to rest, a chair, two or three remain there in the middle* [of the table], *still speeding,* and *open pathways*. Responses to the other question will vary. In response to the second question, some students may find the images fresh and bright; some may say the images make them hungry.

Language Link (page 169)

Students should circle *simile* and put a line over the e. They should also say it out loud, pronouncing the final long e sound.

Students should circle *read, reread, see, meaning, we,* and *create* and put lines over the *ea, e* and *ea, ee, ea, e,* and *e,* respectively. They should also say the six words out loud.

Check Your Understanding (page 169)

Students should underline *explains*. If you don't fully understand it, you should just try to enjoy the images it creates.

READER'S COMPANION: Social Studies

Use What You Know (page 171)

Students may write the names of any American cities and may or may not include the states.

Learning Strategy: Preview (page 171)

Students should circle "Reading Maps of Our Country" and "How to Read a Map." The headings show that there will be information on how to read a map.

Check Your Understanding (page 171)

Students should mark off the scale on the edge of their papers and then use the papers to calculate the distance between Chicago and Santa Fe. It is about 1,000 miles.

Language Link (page 172)

Students should circle *political* and *continental*.

political: related to politics

continental: of a continent; related to a continent

Check Your Understanding (page 172)

Miami

Learning Strategy: Preview (page 173)

Students should circle "Physical Map." The page is about physical features on maps.

Check Your Understanding (page 173)

Atlantic Ocean and Pacific Ocean

Language Link (page 173)

It means "a flat place."

READER'S COMPANION: History

Use What You Know (page 175)

Among the many rights students may list are the right to vote; the right of free speech; the right to practice a religion; the right to do things like buy a house or go to a restaurant without regard to race, religion, or ethnic background; and the right to equal protection under the law.

Language Link (page 175)

Students should underline *separate*. They should circle *They had to go to separate schools, had to eat at separate restaurants,* and *had to sit at the back of buses,* and number the circled examples 1, 2, and 3, respectively.

Learning Strategy: Relate (page 175)

Most students are likely to express resentment or anger at the unfair treatment. Many are likely to express a strong desire to fight the system or correct the situation.

Check Your Understanding (page 176)

Students should underline *equal rights for all Americans.*

The Civil Rights movement was the struggle for equal rights for all Americans.

Learning Strategy: Relate (page 176)

Students may express feelings of excitement or awe at being part of the large crowd, joy in the comradeship of fighting for a cause, resentment at the injustices exposed, and inspiration on hearing King's powerful words.

Language Link (page 176)

Students should circle *illegal*.

illegal: not legal; against the law

Check Your Understanding (page 177)

Students should underline *courage* and *leadership*. Students may say that King was a famous man leading an important movement, that his courage and leadership were deeply admired all over the world, and/or that many people who had been denied their rights relied on him to change the situation.

Learning Strategy: Relate (page 177)

Possible responses include working to make peace in the world, fighting to end terrorism, working for a cleaner environment, feeding the hungry, and getting better medical care for people who need it.

Grammar Reference and Practice

Present Tense of *be* (page 179)

A.

1. *We're*
2. She's
3. It's
4. You're
5. He's
6. They're
7. I'm

B.

1. *She's not a student in our school.*
2. They're not sisters.
3. He's not our math teacher.
4. We're not from the United States.
5. It's not on the desk.

Present Tense of *have* (page 180)

A.

1. *have*
2. has
3. have
4. have
5. have
6. has
7. have

Copyright © 2005 by Pearson Education, Inc.

B.

1. *They don't have math class after lunch.*
2. *Mr. Gomez doesn't have four new students.*
3. Maria doesn't have a new P.E. teacher.
4. The girls don't have the same schedule.
5. We don't have science together.
6. I don't have a sister.

Present Tense of Regular Verbs (page 181)

A.

1. *eat*
2. need
3. live
4. listens
5. likes
6. borrows

B.

1. *My friends and I don't eat lunch in the cafeteria at the same time.*
2. The boys don't need directions to the party.
3. I don't live next to the school.
4. My father doesn't listen to music every night after dinner.
5. Carmen doesn't like the same things her brother likes.
6. My sister doesn't borrow my new backpack every Sunday.

Present Continuous Tense (page 182)

1. *What's Luz eating?*
2. What are they writing?
3. What's she hitting?
4. What's she making?

B.

1. speaking
2. using
3. pointing
4. eating
5. sitting
6. listening
7. sweeping
8. writing

Simple Present Tense and Present Continuous Tense (page 183)

A.

1. *Simple Present*
2. Simple Present
3. Simple Present
4. Present Continuous
5. Present Continuous
6. Simple Present
7. Simple Present
8. Present Continuous

B.

1. walks
2. is playing
3. call
4. is eating

---

5. is playing
6. studies
7. are raising
8. are cleaning

Past Tense of *be* (page 184)

1. were
2. wasn't
3. were
4. wasn't
5. were
6. weren't
7. was
8. were
9. weren't
10. was
11. wasn't

Past Tense of Regular Verbs (page 185)

A.

1. asked
2. liked
3. changed
4. watched
5. lived
6. copied
7. helped
8. changed

B.

1. *wanted*
2. danced
3. studied
4. needed
5. played
6. introduced
7. cleaned
8. borrowed

Past Tense of Irregular Verbs (page 186)

A.

1. A: *went*
   B: was
   A: were
2. A: knows
   A: taught
3. A: made
   B: ate

B.

1. On Wednesday, *he went to his brother's soccer game.*
2. On Thursday, he wrote his science report.
3. On Friday, he ate at Gino's with his friends.
4. On Saturday, he went to the movies with Becky.
5. On Sunday, he read his history book all day.

Past Tense: Negative Statements (page 187)

A.

1. *Cara's brother didn't go to the movies with her yesterday.*
2. Min didn't have a good time at the party.
3. Hannah's friends didn't eat lunch with her in the school cafeteria.

---

4. You didn't go out to dinner last night.
5. Marco didn't study at the library after school.

B.

1. *He didn't go to his brother's soccer game on Wednesday.*
2. He didn't write his science report on Thursday.
3. He didn't eat at Gino's with his friends on Friday.
4. He didn't go to the movies with Becky on Saturday.
5. He didn't read his history book all day on Sunday.

C.

1–2. Sentences may vary.

Statements with *used to* (page 188)

A–B.

Phrases and sentences may vary. Check to see that students use *used to* and *didn't use to* properly.

Past Continuous Tense (page 189)

A.

Sentences may vary.
Sample sentences:

1. *Jon was riding his bike last Saturday. He wasn't playing soccer.*
2. Kim was cleaning the house last Sunday. She wasn't making cookies.
3. Jen was painting last Saturday. She wasn't playing soccer.
4. Tania was playing video games last Saturday. She wasn't shopping.

B.

Answers will vary.

Future Tense with *be going to* and *will* (page 190)

Sentences may vary.
Sample sentences:

1. *Miranda and Arturo are going to have a birthday.*
2. Arturo won't baby-sit.
3. Miranda will visit a friend.
4. Miranda isn't going to go to the library.
5. Delia is going to buy clothes.
6. Miranda and Delia will baby-sit.

Introduction to the Tests

The assessment materials for *Keys to Learning: Skills and Strategies for Newcomers* include a Diagnostic Test, eighteen Chapter Tests, and six Unit Tests.

Description of the Tests

Diagnostic Test

The Diagnostic Test will help you determine your students' level of competence. It is based on readiness for the language skills taught in Units 1–3 (Chapters 1–9) of the Student Book. It includes a listening passage with comprehension questions, a grammar section, a word study section, a reading passage with comprehension questions, and a writing assignment. For the listening comprehension, grammar, and word study sections, the test format is multiple-choice, fill-in-the blank, or short answer; for the reading section it is true-false.

Chapter Tests

The Chapter Tests measure students' proficiency with the listening vocabulary, grammar, word study skills, and reading vocabulary presented in each chapter. Each Chapter Test begins and ends with a vocabulary section. One section includes words and expressions selected from the opening dialogue in the Student Book. The other includes words and expressions selected from the reading passage in the Student Book. All of these words and expressions can be found in the Learning Log at the end of the Student Book chapter. In both vocabulary sections, the words and expressions are tested in context—usually in sentences, short dialogues, or passages similar to those presented in the Student Book. The grammar section of each Chapter Test covers grammar points introduced in the Student Book. Students are asked to complete sentences by writing target forms correctly. The Word Study sections of most of the Chapter Tests have picture prompts and ask students to write or mark the letters that represent the target sounds.

Unit Tests

Each Unit Test covers grammar, reading, and writing skills presented in three consecutive Student Book chapters. The first section of each test measures students' proficiency with the grammar topics. The format is similar to that of the grammar sections of the Chapter Tests. The second section of each Unit Test includes a reading passage that is similar to the reading passages in the Student Book. Comprehension is tested in a variety of formats, including multiple-choice, sentence completion, and true-false. The third section of each Unit Test is a writing assignment similar to those writing assignments in the Student Book. A model is presented. Then students are asked to follow the same kind of process they used to complete the writing assignments in the Student Book.

Administering the Tests

The following are general guidelines. They can be modified, depending on your preferences and your students' experiences and needs.

Before You Administer a Test

Review the test to familiarize yourself with its contents. Make copies of the test for students and yourself. The Diagnostic Test has a listening passage (see below) that is included on the *Keys to Learning* audio program. To use it, have the CD and CD-player or audiocassette and tape-player available. Alternatively, you may read the dialogue aloud—with a colleague as the second speaker, if possible.

Diagnostic Test Listening Script

Antonio: Hello.

Vicky: Hi. I'm Vicky. What's your name?

Antonio: My name's Antonio. Nice to meet you, Vicky.

Vicky: Nice to meet you, too. Are you a new student?

Antonio: Yes, I am.

Vicky: Where are you from?

Antonio: I'm from Mexico. What about you?

Vicky: I'm from Colombia. Maybe we have some classes together. Do you have your schedule?

Antonio: No, I don't have it yet. It's in the school office, but I'm lost. I can't find the office.

(continued)

Vicky:	The office? I can help you. We're on the second floor now. The office is downstairs, on the first floor. It's next to the auditorium and across from the library.
Antonio:	Oh, okay. I was on the first floor, and I saw the library. Do you know what time it is now?
Vicky:	Yes. It's seven forty-five.
Antonio:	And when does the first class start?
Vicky:	It starts at eight o'clock.
Antonio:	Oh, no! I have to go to the office now. And then I have to find my first class.
Vicky:	Okay, Antonio. See you later.

When You Are Ready to Administer a Test

Make sure that students' desks are clear and that they have pens or pencils for completing their tests. The Unit Tests have writing sections that instruct students to make notes and then write paragraphs on separate pieces of paper. You will need to make sure that lined paper is available for these writing assignments. Distribute copies of the test to students and have them write their name and the date on each page of the test. Describe the contents of the test or the section of the test that you are administering. Point out the directions and example answers and make sure that students understand how to complete each section. Answer any questions that students may have and then start the test.

If you set a time limit for the test, tell students how much time they have for the test session and write the ending time on the board. Give students a five-minute warning before the test session ends.

After the Test

Score the test. The Answer Key and Tested-Skills Chart for the Diagnostic Test begins on page 285. The Answer Key for the Chapter Tests begins on page 287, and the Answer Key for the Unit Tests begins on page 293. The total possible number of points on each test varies. (Include example items in adding up the number of items in a test.) To score the writing sections of the Diagnostic and Unit Tests, see the section "Scoring the Writing Sections" below. To calculate students' other scores, follow this procedure:

1. Add up the total number of items answered correctly (for example, 41).
2. Divide by the total number of items in the test you are scoring (for example, 45).
3. Multiply by 100 to get the student's percent score (for example, $41 \div 45 \times 100 = 91\%$).

You may want to modify the scoring procedure by assigning more points to items or test sections that you consider to be more challenging or important for your students.

Scoring the Writing Sections

5 points:	The composition follows the model and/or expands on it appropriately. It is well organized, fluent, and complete. It demonstrates consistent control of word choice, sentence structure, spelling, capitalization, and punctuation.
4 points:	The composition follows the model and/or expands on it appropriately. It is complete and demonstrates a good, but not excellent, command of organization, word choice, sentence structure, spelling, capitalization, and punctuation.
3 points:	The composition shows some sense of organization and completeness. It shows an inconsistent command of word choice, sentence structure, spelling, capitalization, and punctuation.
2 points:	The composition lacks organization or completeness. It demonstrates considerable confusion about word choice, sentence structure, and so on.
1 point:	The student has attempted to write something but is unable to organize or complete the composition. There are numerous errors in word choice, sentence structure, and so on.
0 points:	The student has not attempted to write.

Copyright © 2005 by Pearson Education, Inc.

Name _____ Date _____

Diagnostic Test

 A. Vicky and Antonio are talking on the first day of school. Listen to the dialogue.

B. Complete the sentences about the dialogue. Circle the letter next to the correct word or words.

1. Antonio _____ a new student.

    (a.) is   b. is not

2. Vicky is from _____ .

    a. Mexico   b. Colombia

3. Antonio's schedule _____ in the school office.

    a. is   b. is not

4. Antonio and Vicky are on the _____ floor now.

    a. first   b. second

5. The office is _____ the library.

    a. across from   b. next to

6. It's _____ now.

    a. 7:45   b. 8:00

7. The first class starts at _____ .

    a. 7:45   b. 8:00

Name _____ Date _____

Complete each sentence. Circle the letter next to the correct word or words.

1. _____ am a student.

   (a.) I   b. You   c. We

2. _____ are a student.

   a. She   b. You   c. It

3. _____ is a student.

   a. She   b. He   c. It

4. _____ is a chair.

   a. She   b. He   c. It

5. He _____ from Mexico.

   a. be   b. is   c. are

6. Carlos and Carmen _____ from Mexico.

   a. be   b. is   c. are

7. We _____ from Peru.

   a. isn't   b. aren't   c. not

8. _____ he from Peru?

   a. Are   b. Does   c. Is

9. A: Are they from Colombia?

   B: No, they _____ .

   a. are   b. aren't   c. don't

10. The students _____ English class now.

    a. has   b. had   c. have

11. Maria _____ have a book.

    a. doesn't   b. isn't   c. not

12. _____ you have English class now?

    a. Are   b. Do   c. Does

13. I have two brothers. _____ names are Luis and Franco.

    a. Their   b. His   c. Theirs

14. My _____ name is Carmen.

    a. sister's   b. sister   c. sisters

15. Franco isn't here. Where _____ ?

    a. is   b. he is   c. is he

16. She _____ ten dollars.

    a. need   b. needs   c. needing

17. Franco _____ want a new watch.

    a. don't   b. isn't   c. doesn't

18. _____ speak Spanish?

    a. Is he   b. Does he   c. He

19. A: Does Luis live in Mexico?

B: No, he _____ .

a. don't   b. isn't   c. doesn't

20. Luis can _____ English.

a. speaks   b. speak   c. speaking

21. Can you _____ Spanish?

a. to speak   b. speak   c. speaking

22. What _____ want?

a. they   b. are they   c. do they

23. You _____ yesterday.

a. was late   b. were late   c. late

24. They _____ at school yesterday.

a. weren't   b. not   c. wasn't

25. Franco _____ his mother now.

a. helping   b. help   c. is helping

26. They _____ lunch now.

a. are not eating
b. not eating
c. not eat

27. What _____ doing?

a. do you   b. are you   c. you are

28. Is _____ English now?

a. studying   b. he study   c. he studying

29. A: What are you doing now?

B: I _____ TV.

a. am watching
b. watch
c. watching

30. I _____ home from school every afternoon.

a. am walking
b. walk
c. walking

31. Maria wants _____ to the party.

a. to go
b. go
c. that she goes

32. Does _____ study?

a. he like   b. he likes to   c. he like to

33. Maria _____ to Carmen yesterday.

a. talked   b. talk   c. talking

34. Franco _____ to school yesterday.

a. going   b. goes   c. went

35. We _____ play baseball yesterday.

a. didn't   b. weren't   c. don't

36. _____ he study yesterday?

a. Did   b. Does   c. Is

Word Study

A. Complete the alphabet. Fill in the blanks with the missing small letters.

a b _c_ ___ e f g ___ i j k ___ m n ___ p q r
    1. **2.**   **3.**   **4.**   **5.**

___ t ___ v w x ___ z
6. **7.**   **8.**

B. Complete the alphabet. Fill in the blanks with the missing capital letters.

_A_ B C D ___ ___ G H ___ J K L ___ N O
1.   **2.** **3.**   **4.**   **5.**

___ Q R S ___ U ___ W X Y Z
6.   **7.** **8.**

Name _____ Date _____

C. Write the names in the box in alphabetical order.

Chen	Elena	Tyler	Jennifer
Carlos	Paco	Lee	~~Anita~~

1. _____*Anita*_____

2. _____

3. _____

4. _____

5. _____

6. _____

7. _____

8. _____

D. Look at the pictures. Then complete each word. Write the missing letter.

1. _*h*_ at

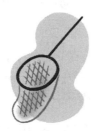

2. ___ et

3. ___ ap

4. ___ us

5. ___ ig

6. ___ un

E. Read the word in the box. Then choose the word with the same sound as the <u>underlined</u> letter or letters in the boxed word. Circle the letter next to the correct answer.

1. | c<u>a</u>t |
   a. came
   (b.) map
   c. may

2. | s<u>i</u>t |
   a. dime
   b. big
   c. pie

3. | h<u>o</u>t |
   a. cold
   b. nose
   c. stop

4. | b<u>e</u>d |
   a. net
   b. new
   c. key

5. | c<u>u</u>p |
   a. you
   b. cube
   c. sun

6. | m<u>a</u>th |
   a. cake
   b. chair
   c. class

7. | lun<u>ch</u> |
   a. chin
   b. school
   c. fish

8. | <u>sh</u>op |
   a. watch
   b. wash
   c. check

9. | m<u>a</u>ke |
   a. play
   b. mask
   c. small

10. | f<u>ee</u>t |
   a. fit
   b. eat
   c. net

Reading

A. Look at the picture. Then read the story.

A New Student

Today is Antonio's first day at Madison School. It's lunchtime, and he and Vicky are in the school cafeteria. Vicky says, "Hi, Antonio. It's nice to see you. How are you?"

Antonio answers, "Fine, thanks. I have my class schedule now."

Vicky says, "Oh, that's good. What class do you have after lunch?"

Antonio looks at his schedule. He answers, "I have math class."

Vicky says, "Great! I have math then, too. I have seven classes. I don't like all of them, but I like English and I love math. It's my favorite class. Do you like math?"

Antonio answers, "Well, I'm not sure. I'm not very good at it, so I am worried. Is the class difficult?"

"No, it isn't," says Vicky. "Our math teacher is Ms. King. She's really nice. She helps everyone."

"And you can help me too, right?" asks Antonio.

Vicky answers, "Right. Don't worry, Antonio. Math class is a lot of fun."

B. Read the statements about the story. Then circle *True* or *False*.

1. Antonio doesn't have his schedule yet.   True / (False)

2. Vicky has lunch after math class.   True / False

3. Math is Vicky's favorite class.   True / False

4. Antonio thinks that he is good at math.   True / False

5. Vicky thinks that math class isn't difficult.   True / False

6. Vicky can't help Antonio with math.   True / False

Name _____ Date _____

Writing

A. You are going to write a paragraph about yourself. First, read the paragraph below.

> My name is Ramon Ortiz. I am a student at North Valley School. I am from El Salvador. I speak English and Spanish. On weekends, I like to play soccer and baseball with my friends.

B. Before you write your paragraph, write answers to these questions about yourself.

1. What is your name? _____

2. What is the name of your school? _____

3. What country are you from? _____

4. What languages do you speak? _____

5. What do you like to do on weekends? _____

_____

C. Now write your paragraph on the lines below. In your paragraph, use the information you wrote in Exercise B. Use the paragraph in **Exercise A** as a model.

_____

_____

_____

_____

_____

_____

_____

_____

_____

_____

_____

_____

Copyright © 2005 by Pearson Education, Inc.

Chapter 1 Test

Dialogue Vocabulary

A. Complete the dialogue. Write the words and expressions from the box.

brother	sister
~~Hi~~	Spanish
Mexico	Thank you
Nice to meet you, too	very

Carlos: (1) _____*Hi*_____ ! My name is Carlos Alvarez. What's your name?

Pablo: My name is Pablo Cortez. Nice to meet you, Carlos.

Carlos: (2) _____ .

Pablo: Are you from (3) _____ ?

Carlos: Yes, I am. I speak English and

(4) _____ .

★ ★ ★ ★ ★

Carlos: Is Anna Cortez your

(5) _____ ?

Pablo: Yes, she is. We're (6)

_____ and sister.

Carlos: Anna is (7) _____ pretty.

Pablo: (8) _____ , Carlos.

Grammar

B. Read the words. Write the correct pronouns.

he	they	we
~~she~~	it	you

1. Maria _____*she*_____

2. Pablo and I _____

3. Carlos and you _____

4. Pablo _____

5. Carlos and Maria _____

6. the book _____

C. Complete the sentences. Write the pronoun and the correct form of *be*. Use contractions.

1. _____*We're*_____ from Peru. (We)

2. _____ from Colombia. (He)

3. _____ teachers. (They)

4. _____ students. (You)

5. _____ from Mexico. (It)

D. Change each sentence from the affirmative to the negative or from the negative to the affirmative. Write the new sentences on the lines.

1. We're from Mexico.

   We're not from Mexico.

2. He's not my brother.

   He's my brother.

3. She's not a teacher.

   _____

4. I'm nervous.

   _____

5. It's from the United States.

   _____

6. They're not students.

   _____

E. Change the sentences to questions. Write the questions on the lines.

1. Pablo is from Mexico.

   Is Pablo from Mexico?

2. You are a new student.

   _____

3. Anna and Pablo are from Peru.

   _____

4. She is nervous.

_____

5. You and Carmen are students.

_____

F. Read the questions. Then complete the short answers.

1. Is Maria from El Salvador?

Yes, *she is* _____ .

2. Is Mr. Gomez from Mexico?

No, _____ .

3. Are Pablo and Anna from Colombia?

Yes, _____ .

4. Are Carlos and Carmen from Peru?

No, _____ .

5. Is the book from the United States?

Yes, _____ .

Word Study

G. Fill in the blanks with the missing letters of the alphabet.

a (1) _b_ c d (2) ___ f g (3) ___ i
j k (4) ___ m n (5)___ (6) ___ q r
s (7) ___ u (8)___ w x (9)___ z

H. Write the names in alphabetical order.

1. Carlos	**1.** _Anna_
2. Samir	**2.** _____
3. Mei	**3.** _____
4. Edgar	**4.** _____
5. ~~Anna~~	**5.** _____
6. Maria	**6.** _____
7. Isabel	**7.** _____

Reading Vocabulary

I. Read the sentences below. Then match the sentences to the pictures. Write the correct letters.

a

b

c

1. ___ This is a new student. Her name is Isabel.

2. ___ This is El Salvador. Isabel is from El Salvador.

3. ___ This is Madison School.

Chapter 2 Test

Dialogue Vocabulary

A. Complete the dialogue. Write the words and expressions from the box.

Fine, thanks	almost	schedule
~~How are you~~	lunch	together
That's great		

Bic: Hi, Anna.

(1) _How are you_ ?

Anna: I'm fine. And you?

Bic: (2) _____ .
What's your schedule?

Anna: Well, I have (3) _____ now.

Bic: I have lunch now, too. We have
lunch (4) _____ .

Anna: (5) _____ !

Bic: What's your (6) _____ after
lunch?

Anna: I have art, P.E., and math.

Bic: I have art, science, and math. Our
classes are (7) _____ the
same!

Grammar

B. Complete the sentences. Write the correct form of *have*.

1. I _____have_____ science with Mrs. Kim.

2. He _____ an art class.

3. We _____ an English class together.

4. They _____ P.E. every day.

5. You _____ lunch now.

6. She _____ a music class.

C. Change each sentence from the affirmative to the negative. Write the new sentences on the lines. Use contractions.

1. We have the same classes.
   We don't have the same classes.

2. You have math with me.
   _____

3. She has science with Mrs. Kim.
   _____

4. I have music now.
   _____

5. He has P.E. with you.
   _____

D. Complete the questions with *have*. Then complete the short answers.

1. **A:** _____Does_____ he
   _____have_____ history now?
   B: No, _he doesn't_ .

2. **A:** _____ we
   _____ math together?
   B: Yes, _____ .

3. **A:** _____ they
   _____ P.E. after art?
   B: No, _____ .

4. **A:** _____ he
   _____ a music class?
   B: Yes, _____ .

5. **A:** _____ she
   _____ P.E. with you?
   B: No, _____ .

E. Write the plural form of each noun.

1. pencil _____pencils_____

2. student _____

3. box _____

4. brush _____

Name _____ Date _____

5. book _____

6. lunch _____

F. Complete the chart. Write the possessive adjectives.

Subject Pronoun	Possessive Adjective	
1. I	_my_	brother
2. you	_____	pencil
3. she	_____	schedule
4. he	_____	cap
5. it	_____	name
6. we	_____	teacher
7. they	_____	desks

Word Study

G. Complete the words. Write *a*, *i*, or *o*.

1. m _a_ p   **2.** c ___ p

3. h ___ t   **4.** h ___ t

5. h ___ t   **6.** p ___ g

Reading Vocabulary

H. Complete each sentence with the correct word. Write the word on the line.

1. Tito and Lin have art class every
_____ _day_ _____ .
(day / boys)

2. Tito and Lin love art class. They are
very _____ at
art. (day / good)

3. Tito speaks two _____ .
He speaks Spanish and English.
(languages / Puerto Rico)

4. Tito is from _____ .
(Spanish / Puerto Rico)

5. Lin speaks two languages, too. She
speaks _____
and English. (China / Chinese)

6. Lin is from _____ .
(China / Chinese)

Name _____   Date _____

Chapter 3 Test

Dialogue Vocabulary

A. Complete the sentences and dialogues.
Write the words or expressions from the
box.

dollars	know
I borrow your pen	Wait
wallet	~~this in English~~

1. How do you say _this in English_ ?

2. Excuse me, Luis. Is it okay if
_____ ?

3. I have a wallet with seven
_____ in it.

4. Oh, no! My _____ isn't
here.

5. **Anna:** This is my notebook.

   Bo: _____ ! That's my
   notebook. Your notebook is in
   your backpack.

6. **Bic:** Some of these words are hard.

   Mei: I _____ . They're hard
   for me, too.

Grammar

B. Complete the dialogue. Write *a* or *an*.

Mrs. Kim: Excuse me, Anna. Is this your
backpack?

Anna: Yes, it is.

Mrs. Kim: What's in it?

Anna: I have (1) _an_ orange, (2) ____
protractor, (3) ____ eraser, and
(4) ____ calculator. . . . Wait. . . . I
have more things in it. I have
(5) ____ hairbrush, (6) ____ folder,
and (7) ____ umbrella.

Mrs. Kim: Look in your backpack, Anna. Do
you have more things in it?

Anna: Oh, no! I have (8) ____ ice-cream
bar in here. Look! This isn't good.
I have (9) ____ problem.

C. Complete the sentences. Write *This, That,
These,* or *Those.*

1. _____ is   2. _____ is
a comb.   a pencil.

3. _____   4. _____
are erasers.   are pencils.

D. Complete the sentences. Write the
correct pronoun.

1. _____ _This_ _____ is my backpack.
(This/These)

2. _____ are their pens.
(That/Those)

3. _____ is his computer.
(That/Those)

4. _____ is her hairbrush.
(This/These)

5. _____ are our books.
(This/These)

E. Complete the sentences. Write the
correct possessive form of the noun.

1. My _____ _sister's_ _____ name is Anna.
(sister)

2. My _____ names are Franco and Edgar. (brothers)

3. The _____ pens are in his backpack. (boy)

4. The _____ wallets are in their backpacks. (girls)

5. This is _____ notebook. (Maria)

6. This is _____ schedule. (Luis)

Word Study

F. Look at the pictures. Then read the sentences. Write the letter of the picture that matches the sentence. Then circle the letter that stands for the short vowel sound /e/ or /u/.

a

b

c

d

e

f

1. _d_ This is my p(e)t.

2. ___ This is the sun.

3. ___ This is a net.

4. ___ This is a bus.

5. ___ This is a pup.

6. ___ This is a pen.

Reading Vocabulary

G. Complete the sentences about the pictures. Use the words from the box.

~~asks~~	comb	pens	worried
books	problem	answers	pencils

She (1) ___asks___ the teacher. The teacher (2) _____ .

She has two (3) _____ , three

(4) _____ , four

(5) _____ , and a

(6) _____ .

He has a (7) _____ . He's

(8) _____ .

Chapter 4 Test

Dialogue Vocabulary

A. Complete the dialogues. Use the words and expressions from the box.

~~best~~	downstairs
stairs	other building
lost	What about you
See you	

1. **Luis:** Is Elena your _____*best*_____ friend?

    Anna: Yes, she is. I really like her.

2. **Maria:** I have lunch now. Where's the cafeteria?

    Carmen: It isn't in this building. It's in the _____ .

3. **Lin:** Bic, you look worried. Do you have a problem?

    Bic: Yes, I do. I'm _____ . Where's the library?

    Lin: It's _____

    next to the auditorium. The

    _____ are

    next to room 201.

    Bic: Thank you, Lin. I'm not worried now.

4. **Carlos:** I have science now, then music.

    _____ ?

    Samir: I have math now. After math, I have music, too.

    Carlos: Great! _____ in music class.

Grammar

B. Look at the picture. Then, complete the sentences. Write *in, on, under,* or *next to*.

The box is (1) _____*on*_____ the

desk. The pencils are (2) _____

the box. The apple is (3) _____

the desk, too. The apple is

(4) _____ the box. The backpack

is (5) _____ the desk. The

notebooks are (6) _____ the

backpack. The chair is (7) _____

the desk. The calculator is

(8) _____ the chair. The

erasers are (9) _____

the chair.

C. Complete the questions. Write *where* and the correct form of the verb *be*.

1. _____*Where is*_____ the library?

2. _____ the computers?

3. _____ Liliana?

4. _____ Luis and Edgar?

5. _____ your book?

6. I'm lost. _____ I?

D. Complete the sentences. Write *there is* or *there are*.

1. ___*There are*___ two pens on the desk.

2. _____ one folder next to the pens.

3. _____ some chairs in the library.

4. _____ many new students at my school.

5. _____ a music room downstairs.

6. _____ four pencils and two books in my backpack.

7. _____ a pretty girl in Carlos's class.

Word Study

E. Complete the words. Write *ch* or *sh*.

1. ___s___ ___h___ ut

2. ___ ___ in

3. ___ ___ ip

4. in ___ ___

5. lun ___ ___

6. di ___ ___

7. ben ___ ___

8. fi ___ ___

Reading Vocabulary

F. Complete the paragraphs. Write the words from the boxes.

go	like	~~live~~	nice

Isabel and I are from El Salvador. We (1) ___*live*___ in the United States. We're students. We (2) _____ to Madison School. We (3) _____ our school. It's (4) _____ .

a lot of	use	small	library

Isabel and I have English and math together. Our English class is (5) _____ . It has seven students. There are twenty-seven students in math. It's a big class.

There are (6) _____ computers in the (7) _____. Isabel and I (8) _____ the computers after school every day. They're fun!

Name _____ Date _____

Chapter 5 Test

Dialogue Vocabulary

A. Match the questions and the answers. Write the correct letters.

1. Can my little brother come to the party, too? _d_

2. What's your address? ___

3. What's your phone number? ___

4. Can you find our house? ___

5. Can your sister come to the party? ___

a. No, I'm sorry. She can't come.

b. It's 555-0107.

c. Don't worry. I have a map and directions.

d. Sure. Your brother can come.

e. It's 469 First Street.

Grammar

B. Complete the questions. Write *what* and the correct form of *be*.

1. _____ *What is* _____ the teacher's name?

2. _____ these?

3. _____ that?

4. _____ your favorite class?

5. _____ her brothers' names?

C. Complete the sentences. Write the correct form of the verb.

1. Liliana ____ *lives* ____ in the United States. (live/lives)

2. They _____ their teacher. (like/likes)

3. Luis _____ a map. (don't want/doesn't want)

4. I _____ a new backpack. (don't need/doesn't need)

5. Our teacher _____ English and Chinese. (speak/speaks)

D. Change the sentences to questions. Write the questions on the lines. Then complete the short answers.

1. Pablo needs a map.

A: _Does Pablo need a map?_

B: Yes, _he does_ .

2. Elena likes P.E. class.

A: _____

B: No, _____ .

3. They speak English.

A: _____

B: Yes, _____ .

4. Anna lives next to the fire station.

A: _____

B: Yes, _____ .

5. Carlos and Carmen live in that building.

A: _____

B: No, _____ .

E. Change each sentence from the affirmative to the negative or from the negative to the affirmative. Write the new sentences on the lines.

1. Mei can play the drums.

Mei can't play the drums.

2. You can't come to the party.

You can come to the party.

3. Bic can't swim after school.

_____

4. Her brothers can speak Chinese.

_____

5. We can dance in the library.

_____

6. I can't speak two languages.

_____

F. Change the sentences to questions.
Write the questions on the lines. Then
complete the short answers.

1. Mei can swim.

A: _Can Mei swim?_____

B: Yes, _she can_____ .

2. You can play the drums.

A: _____

B: No, I _____ .

3. We can dance at the party.

A: _____

B: Yes, we _____ .

4. The teachers can speak Spanish.

A: _____

B: Yes, _____ .

5. Pablo can answer the question.

A: _____

B: No, _____ .

Word Study

G. Write the correct word for each picture.
Use the words from the box.

black	class	~~dress~~
clock	flag	glass

1. _dress_____   **2.** _____

3. _____

4. _____

5. _____

6. _____

Reading Vocabulary

H. Complete the sentences. Use the words
from the box.

eat and dance	practice	happy	sad
~~baby-sits~~	money	job	

1. Elena has a job. She

_____baby-sits_____ two
little children.

2. Paco has a _____ ,
too. He's a chef.

3. Lin needs a job. She needs

_____ for
CDs.

4. A party is fun. You can

_____ at a
party.

5. "A party? Great! I can come. I'm

_____ ."

6. "I'm sorry. I can't come to the

party. I'm _____ ."

7. These enchiladas aren't very good.
The chef still needs a lot of

_____ .

Chapter 6 Test

Dialogue Vocabulary

A. Complete the dialogue. Use the words from the box.

hall	sick	~~start~~	piece
late	sit	take out	today

Mrs. Kim: What time does class

(1) _____start_____ , Pablo?

Pablo: At one o'clock.

Mrs. Kim: And what time is it now?

Pablo: It's five minutes after one. I'm five

minutes (2) _____ to

class.

Mrs. Kim: Where were you?

Pablo: I was in the (3) _____ .

I'm sorry, Mrs. Kim. I have a

problem.

Mrs. Kim: Really? Are you

(4) _____ ?

Pablo: No, I'm not, but I'm very nervous.

Mrs. Kim: Don't worry, Pablo. Please

(5) _____ in your chair

now. And all of you

(6) _____ a

(7) _____ of paper.

Pablo: Oh, no! There *is* a test

(8) _____ . Now I'm

very, very nervous.

Grammar

B. First, read the answer. Then complete the question.

1. A: _____*What do*_____ you

_____*want*_____ ?

B: I want a new computer.

2. A: _____

Anna and Edgar _____ ?

B: They need a map.

3. A: _____

Elena _____ ?

B: She likes music.

4. A: _____

Mr. Gomez _____ ?

B: He has a student's backpack.

5. A: _____ you

_____ ?

B: We need a piece of paper.

C. Complete the questions. Use *do* or *does* and the cues.

1. What time _____*does class*_____

start? (class)

2. What time _____

eat lunch? (they)

3. What color _____

like? (you)

4. What class _____

like? (Maria)

5. What languages _____

speak? (the teacher)

6. What books _____

need for school today? (I)

D. Complete the sentences. Write the correct form of the verb.

1. I _____*wasn't*_____ late to class. (wasn't/weren't)

2. Carmen _____ in school yesterday. (was/were)

3. We _____ in the gym. (wasn't/weren't)

4. Pablo _____ sick yesterday. (wasn't/weren't)

5. You _____ with a new student. (was/were)

Copyright © 2005 by Pearson Education, Inc.

Chapter 6 Test   235

6. Samir and Bic _____ in the cafeteria. (was/were)

E. Complete each question. Write *was* or *were*. Then complete the short answer.

    1. A: _____*Were*_____ you and Sophie in the gym?

    B: No, *we weren't* _____ .

    2. A: _____ Pablo sick yesterday?

    B: Yes, _____ .

    3. A: _____ Elena with a new student?

    B: No, _____ .

    4. A: _____ the teachers at lunch with you?

    B: No, _____ .

    5. A: _____ you in English class yesterday?

    B: Yes, I _____ .

Word Study

F. Complete the words. Write *lt, mp, nd,* or *nt.*

1. te _*n*_ _*t*_

2. be ___ ___

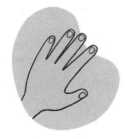

3. pla ___ ___

4. ha ___ ___

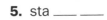

5. sta ___ ___

6. la ___ ___

Reading Vocabulary

G. Complete the sentences from a student's journal. Write the correct words.

    1. Today is Wednesday. _____*Tomorrow*_____ is Thursday. (Yesterday/Tomorrow)

    2. My P.E. class starts at 9:00 A.M. I was in the gym at 8:50 A.M. I was

    _____ for P.E. class. (early/late)

    3. My English class starts at 10:00 A.M. I wasn't early for English. I was in the classroom at 10:00 A.M. I was

    _____ . (on time/late)

    4. There were five problems on the math test today. The test was

    _____ . After the test, I was happy. (easy/hard)

    5. There were twenty-five questions on the science test today. The test was

    _____ . After that test, I wasn't happy. (easy/hard)

    6. My little brother is late to school almost every day. He doesn't have

    a _____ . He needs one. Then he can get to school on time. (watch/early)

Chapter 7 Test

Dialogue Vocabulary

A. Look at the pictures. Then complete the sentences. Use the words from the boxes.

changing
cleaning
making
~~washing~~

bed
~~hair~~
lightbulb
windows

1. She's ___washing___   **2.** He's _____

her ___hair___ .   a _____ .

3. He's _____   **4.** She's _____

his _____ .   the _____ .

Grammar

B. Complete the sentences. Write the present-continuous form of the verb.

1. She ___is cleaning___ the kitchen. (clean)

2. We _____ lunch. (eat)

3. I _____ cookies. (make)

4. Mei and Bic _____ ready for the party. (get)

C. Rewrite the sentences in **Exercise B** in the negative. Use *am not, isn't,* or *aren't.*

1. ___She isn't cleaning the kitchen.___

2. _____

3. _____

4. _____
_____

D. Complete the questions. Use the cues and the present-continuous tense.

1. What ___is he eating___ ?
(he, eat)

2. What _____ ?
(you, read)

3. What _____ ?
(they, study)

4. What _____ ?
(I, do)

E. Change the sentences to questions. Write the questions on the lines. Then complete the short answers.

1. They are making their beds.

A: ___Are they making their beds?___

B: Yes, ___they are___ .

2. Anna is washing her hair.

A: _____

B: No, _____ .

3. You are cleaning the windows.

A: _____

B: Yes, I _____ .

4. Bic and Mei are cooking enchiladas.

A: _____
_____

B: No, _____ .

F. Complete the sentences. Write the correct object pronoun.

1. Grandma is helping

_____*him*_____ . (Carlos)

2. Dad is helping _____ .
(Mom)

3. David is cleaning _____ .
(the windows)

4. I need _____ .
(a notebook)

5. You are helping _____ . (I)

6. Carolina isn't helping

_____ . (we)

Word Study

G. Complete the words. Write *a_e*, *i_e*, *o_e*, or *u_e*.

1. c __ t __   **2.** n __ s __

3. p __ g __   **4.** f __ v __

Reading Vocabulary

H. Look at the pictures. Then complete the sentences in the story. Use the words from the box.

~~living room~~	knocking	floor
entranceway	sweeping	rug
vacuuming	door	

My family is having a party today. It's three o'clock now. We're getting ready. My mother is in the kitchen. She's making a cake. My brother is in his bedroom. He's making his bed.

My sister is in the (1) _*living room*_ .

She's (2) _____ the

(3) _____ .

My father is in the hallway. He's

(4) _____ the

(5) _____ .

* * * * *

Now it's six o'clock. Our friends are here.

They're in the (6) _____ .

They're (7) _____ on the

(8) _____ . It's time for the party to start!

Chapter 8 Test

Dialogue Vocabulary

A. Complete the sentences. Use the words and expression from the box.

~~loud~~	excited	miserable
work	another	would you like to

1. My sister is vacuuming, and my little brothers are knocking on my door. It's very _____*loud*_____ here.

2. "There's a class party tonight. Anna, _____ come with me?"

3. Liliana is a student in the class. Mei is _____ student in the class.

4. Elena has a job. She has to _____ every Saturday.

5. The class is having a party. Elena wants to go, but she can't. She's _____ .

6. Isabel can go to the class party. She loves to go to parties. She's _____ .

Grammar

B. Complete each sentence. Choose the correct form of the verb. Write it on the line.

1. Mei and Liliana _____*talk*_____ (talk / are talking) on the phone every night.

2. Mei _____ (talks / is talking) to Liliana right now.

3. I _____ (walk / am walking) to school every morning.

4. My little brother _____ (walks / is walking) to school every morning, too.

5. Elena _____ (washes / is washing) her hair now.

6. She _____ (gets ready / is getting ready) to go to a party.

7. Sophie and I _____ (study / are studying) in the library right now.

8. We _____ (study / are studying) together every day.

C. Complete the sentences. Write the correct simple-present form of the verb. Use contractions.

1. I _____*don't like*_____ to clean my room. (like, negative)

2. Anna _____*wants*_____ to watch TV. (want, affirmative)

3. We _____ to study. (have, negative)

4. Pablo and Sophie _____ to talk on the phone. (like, affirmative)

5. David _____ to work. (have, affirmative)

6. She _____ to play baseball. (want, negative)

D. Complete each question. Use the correct simple-present form of the verb and the cues.

1. What _____*does Anna like*_____ to eat? (Anna, like)

2. What _____ to eat? (he, want)

3. What _____ to study? (we, have)

4. What _____ to read? (Carmen and Carlos, like)

5. What _____ to do? (you, want)

E. Change the sentences to *yes/no* questions. Write the questions on the lines.

   1. Edgar likes to play baseball.

     Does Edgar like to play baseball?
     _____

   2. You want to go out tonight.

     _____

   3. Elena has to work.

     _____

   4. We have to clean our rooms.

     _____

   5. Mei and Bic like to eat enchiladas.

     _____

     _____

Word Study

F. Look at the pictures. Then read the sentences that follow. Write the letter of the picture that matches the sentence. Then circle the letters that stand for the long vowel sound /ā/.

a

b

c

d

e

f

1. _c_ This is a d(ay).

2. ___ This is a train.

3. ___ We like to play.

4. ___ Here is the mail.

5. ___ This is a lake.

6. ___ This is a game.

Reading Vocabulary

G. Complete the sentences in Alberto's paragraphs. Use the words from the box.

learn	feel	homesick
miss	~~Sometimes~~	homework

   My name is Alberto. I'm fifteen years old. I come from Mexico. I live in the United States. I like the United States and my friends here.

   Most of the time, I'm happy. (1) ___Sometimes___, I (2) _____ very sad. I want to see my friends in Mexico, but I can't. I (3) _____ those friends. I want to live in Mexico, but I can't. I feel (4) _____ .

   I don't have time to be sad today. I have to do my (5) _____ for English class. I need to (6) _____ many new words. The words aren't difficult. I can do it.

Name _____ Date _____

Chapter 9 Test

Dialogue Vocabulary

A. Complete the sentences and dialogues. Use the words from the box.

| ~~came~~ | let's | twins |
| introduce | say | wrong |

1. Edgar ___*came*___ to the party. We talked to him there.

2. Yesterday was his brothers' birthday. They're both fourteen.

   They're _____ .

3. **Mei:** Lin, _____ eat now. I'm hungry.

   Lin: Okay. I'm hungry, too.

4. **Carmen:** Alberto, I didn't

   _____ my brother. This is Carlos.

   Alberto: Nice to meet you, Carlos.

   Carlos: Nice to meet you, too.

5. **Edgar:** So, Carmen, is that girl your sister?

   Carmen: Ha, ha, ha!

   Edgar: Did I _____

   something _____ ?

   Carmen: *That girl* is my mother!

Grammar

B. Complete the sentences. Write the past-tense form of the verbs.

1. Edgar ___*asked*___ a question. (ask)

2. I _____ at the funny movie. (laugh)

3. Paco _____ at the party. (dance)

4. Sophie and Lin _____ early this morning. (arrive)

5. We _____ together last night. (study)

6. David _____ baseball in the park. (play)

C. Complete the sentences. Write the past-tense form of the verbs.

1. Elena ___*knew*___ the answer. (know)

2. Our teacher _____ us some new words. (teach)

3. We _____ the words in our notebooks. (write)

4. You _____ the story in class yesterday. (read)

5. My class _____ a party. (have)

6. Grandma _____ a cake for the party. (make)

D. Change each sentence from the affirmative to the negative. Write the new sentences on the lines. Use contractions.

1. Bic played baseball yesterday.
   Bic didn't play baseball yesterday.

2. I talked to Pablo last night.
   _____

3. Anna and Edgar sang at the party.
   _____

4. You looked happy.
   _____

5. We did our homework on Saturday.
   _____

6. My little sister went to the movies.
   _____

E. Change each sentence to a question. Write the question on the line. Then complete the short answer.

1. The boys talked to Paco last night.

   A: _Did the boys talk to Paco last night?_

   B: No, _they didn't_ .

2. Carlos and Carmen had fun at the party.

   A: _____

   _____

   B: Yes, _____ .

3. You ate a piece of cake.

   A: _____

   B: Yes, I _____ .

4. Maria introduced them.

   A: _____

   B: No, _____ .

5. I said something wrong.

   A: _____

   B: No, you _____ .

3. _____ 4. _____

5. _____ 6. _____

Word Study

F. Write the correct word for each picture. Use the words from the box. Then circle the letter or letters that stand for the long vowel sound /ē/.

| city | ~~feet~~ | field | me | meat | tree |

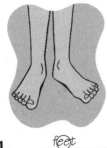

1. _feet_ 2. _____

Reading Vocabulary

G. Complete the sentences. Use the words from the box.

| agreed | delicious | ~~everybody~~ |
| boyfriend | embarrassed | grandson |

1. Tina asked, "Did ___everybody___ come to the party?" Luis answered, "Yes. There are fifteen students in our class, and fifteen students came."

2. Rosa is Luis's grandmother. Luis is Rosa's _____ .

3. Sara likes Luis. She goes to parties with him. Luis is Sara's

   _____ .

4. Lin said, "Edgar is so cute." Sophie _____ . "He is so cute," she said.

5. Lin said, "Edgar, you are so cute! Sophie and I both like you." Then Edgar looked _____ .

6. Edgar said, "Let's eat now. The food looks _____ ."

Chapter 10 Test

Dialogue Vocabulary

A. Complete the dialogues. Write the words and expressions from the box.

~~clothes~~	pair of	You're welcome
expensive	secret	May I help you
girlfriend		

Edgar: I need some cool new

(1) _____*clothes*_____ . I need

nice shirts and a

(2) _____ jeans, too.

Luis: Okay. Let's go shopping!

* * * * *

Salesclerk: (3) _____ ?

Edgar: Yes. How much is this shirt?

Salesclerk: It's not (4) _____ .
It's only $14.99.

Edgar: Great! Thank you.

Salesclerk: (5) _____ .

* * * * *

Sara: Why did Edgar want new
clothes?

Luis: I can't tell you. It's a

(6) _____ .

Sara: No, it isn't. He came to the party

with Isabel. He has a

(7) _____ !

Grammar

B. Read the answers. Then complete the questions. Write an information-question word (*who, what, when, where, why, or how*) and *is* or *are*.

1. A: _____*When is*_____ your
birthday?

B: It's July 17.

2. A: _____ your
gym shoes?

B: They're in my backpack.

3. A: _____ your
mother and father?

B: They're fine.

4. A: _____ that
guy?

B: He's Maria's brother.

5. A: _____ your
sister's name?

B: It's Anna.

6. A: _____ your
little brothers at home today?

B: They're home because they're sick.

C. Read the answers. Then complete the questions. Write an information-question word and *was* or *were*.

1. A: _____*Where were*_____
David and Sara last night?

B: They were at a party.

2. A: _____ the
math test?

B: It was yesterday.

3. A: _____ the
history test?

B: It was hard.

4. A: _____ you
at Grandma's house?

B: I was at Grandma's house because
she needed help.

D. Read the answers. Then complete the questions. Use the cues.

1. A: Where _____*does Luis work*_____ ?
(Luis)

B: He works at a computer store.

2. A: How _____ ?
(this dress)

B: It looks great.

Name _____ Date _____

3. A: When _____ ?
(you)

B: We study after school and on Saturday.

4. A: What _____ ?
(the girls)

B: They need new shoes.

5. A: Who _____ ?
(Isabel)

B: She likes Edgar.

E. Read the answers. Then complete the questions. Use the cues.

1. A: Where _did the girls go_ ?
(the girls)

B: They went to the gym.

2. A: When _____ ?
(Sophie)

B: She arrived at seven o'clock.

3. A: How _____ ?
(Anna and Lin)

B: They looked happy.

4. A: Who _____ ?
(you)

B: We asked the teacher.

5. A: Why _____ ?
(you)

B: I laughed because it was funny.

F. Complete the questions. Write *is, are, do,* or *does.*

1. How much _is_ that backpack?

2. How much _____ this book cost?

3. How much _____ those brown shoes?

4. How much _____ this sweater?

5. How much _____ those blue jeans cost?

G. Write the correct word for each picture. Use the words from the box. Then circle the letter or letters that stand for the long vowel sound /ī/.

child	dime	cry	pie

1. _____ **2.** _____

3. _____ **4.** _____

Reading Vocabulary

H. Look at the picture. Then write the correct words on the lines. Two words are not used.

skirt	pants	price tag
~~sweater~~	supermarket	window

1. _sweater_

2. _____

3. _____

4. _____

Copyright © 2005 by Pearson Education, Inc.

Chapter 11 Test

Dialogue Vocabulary

A. Complete the sentences in the dialogues. Write the correct words and expressions from the box.

anymore	total	~~hungry~~	Let's see
else	finished	Why don't you	

Anna: I didn't have lunch, so I'm

(1) _____*hungry*_____ .

Elena: I was hungry, but I ate some cookies.

I'm not hungry (2) _____ .

★ ★ ★ ★ ★

Anna: I can help you shop.

Elena: Great. (3) _____
get the broccoli and carrots?

Anna: Okay. What (4) _____
does your mom need?

Elena: Some milk. I can get it.

★ ★ ★ ★ ★

Anna: Do we have everything now?

Elena: Yes, we do. We're

(5) _____ .

★ ★ ★ ★ ★

Elena: How much did the vegetables cost?
Look at the receipt.

Anna: (6) _____ . . .

The broccoli was $2.30 and the

carrots were $1.90. The

(7) _____ was $4.20.

Grammar

B. Read the sentences. Underline the nouns. Then, for each noun, circle *count* or *non-count*.

1. I want an <u>apple</u>. (count)/ non-count)

2. She needs some rice.
(count / non-count)

3. Can I borrow your eraser?
(count / non-count)

4. Did you eat the cookies?
(count / non-count)

5. Do you like cheese?
(count / non-count)

6. We have one onion.
(count / non-count)

7. This coffee is good.
(count / non-count)

C. Look at the pictures. Then complete the sentences. Use the words from the box.

bread	coffee	milk
cheese	lemonade	rice

In the picture, there are three slices of

(1) _____ , one piece of

(2) _____ , two gallons

of (3) _____ , one glass

of (4) _____ , three cups of

(5) _____ , and one pound

of (6) _____ .

D. Complete the sentences. Write *some* or *any*.

1. I ate ____*some*____ cookies.

2. I didn't eat ____*any*____ bread.

3. She didn't want _____ lettuce.

4. She wanted _____ broccoli.

5. We need _____ beef.

6. We don't need _____ apples.

7. They don't have _____ bananas.

8. They have _____ crackers.

E. Complete the sentences. Write *and*, *but*, or *so*.

1. We need lots of things,

_____*so*_____ we're going to the store.

2. I need some eggs, _____ you need some potatoes.

3. Anna doesn't like broccoli,

_____ she likes carrots.

4. Elena likes broccoli, _____ Edgar likes broccoli, too.

5. Elena was very hungry, _____ she ate some cheese.

6. Edgar was very hungry, _____ Anna wasn't hungry.

Word Study

F. Look at the pictures. Then read the sentences that follow. Write the letter of the picture that matches the sentence. Then circle the letter or letters that stand for the long vowel sound /ō/.

a

b

c

d

1. ___ She's very cold.

2. ___ We have a new stove.

3. ___ This window is clean.

4. ___ The toast is ready.

Reading Vocabulary

G. Look at the pictures. Write the correct words on the lines. Use the words from the box.

French fries	counter	salad	~~cashier~~
hamburger	soda	customer	

1. _____*cashier*_____

2. _____

3. _____

4. _____

5. _____

6. _____

7. _____

Chapter 12 Test

Dialogue Vocabulary

A. Complete the dialogue. Write the correct expressions from the box.

~~section~~	I think so
I'm just kidding	have time
So do I	

Edgar: Do you have any CDs by Beyoncé?

Salesclerk: Yes. Her CDs are in the R&B music (1) _____*section*_____ .

Edgar: Hey, Luis. Look at this CD. I think it's the coolest.

Luis: (2) _____ . It's my favorite, too.

Edgar: I'm buying ten CDs.

Luis: Ten CDs! Really?

Edgar: No. (3) _____ . I don't have enough money.

Luis: Do we (4) _____ to stop for hamburgers on the way home?

Edgar: (5) _____ . We promised to be home by 6:00, but it's only 5:00 now.

Grammar

B. Complete the chart. Write the comparative and superlative form of the adjectives.

Adjective	Comparative	Superlative
1. tall	*taller*	*tallest*
2. hard	_____	_____
3. easy	_____	_____
4. cute	_____	_____
5. funny	_____	_____
6. new	_____	_____

C. Look at the information in the boxes. Then complete the sentences. Write the comparative form of the adjective.

line A _____
line B _____

1. Line A is ____*shorter*____ than line B. (short)

2. Line B is _____ than line A. (long)

Isabel is fifteen years old.
Anna is sixteen years old.

3. Anna is _____ than Isabel. (old)

4. Isabel is _____ than Anna. (young)

D. Look at the information in the boxes. Then complete the sentences. Write the correct form of the adjective.

line C _____
line D _____
line E _____

1. Line D is ____*shorter*____ than line C. (shorter/shortest)

2. Line E is the _____ line. (shorter/shortest)

3. Line C is the _____ line. (longer/longest)

Tommy is four years old.
Bobby is six years old.
Jerry is nine years old.

4. Jerry is the _____ boy. (older/oldest)

5. Jerry is _____ than Tommy. (older/oldest)

6. Bobby is _____ than Jerry.
(younger/youngest)

7. Tommy is the _____ boy.
(younger/youngest)

E. Complete the sentences. Write the correct form of the adjective.

Ted's shoes   **Jim's shoes**   **Pat's shoes**

1. Ted's shoes are _more casual_ than Jim's shoes.
(more casual / most casual)

2. Jim's shoes are _____ than Pat's shoes.
(more casual / most casual)

3. Ted has the _____ shoes. (more casual / most casual)

4. Pat's shoes are _____ than Jim's shoes.
(more formal / most formal)

5. Pat has the _____ shoes. (more formal / most formal)

Word Study

F. Write the correct word for each picture. Use the words from the box. Then circle the letter or letters that stand for the long vowel sound /yoo/.

~~cube~~	cute	few
huge	menu	music

1. _c(u)b(e)_   2. _____

3. _____   4. _____

5. _____   6. _____

Reading Vocabulary

G. Complete the sentences. Write the correct words from the box.

clapped	singer	storyteller
~~performers~~	stage	yelled
poem		

I went to a great show yesterday. All the
(1) _performers_ were wonderful. A man
on the (2) _____ introduced them.
First, a (3) _____ told funny
stories. Then a (4) _____ sang
beautiful songs. After he sang, he read a
(5) _____ . People in the
audience (6) _____ their hands
and (7) _____ , "Good job!"

Chapter 13 Test

Dialogue Vocabulary

A. Complete the dialogue. Write the correct words and expressions from the box.

fall	~~See you later~~	lessons
fast	That sounds like fun	

Maria: Bye, Alberto. (1) _See you later._

Alberto: Wait, Maria. Where are you going?

Maria: I'm going skating in the park. Would you like to come with me?

Alberto: (2) _____ , but I can't skate.

Maria: I can give you some skating

(3) _____ .

Alberto: I would like to learn how to skate, but I'm nervous.

Maria: Don't worry, Alberto. We aren't

going to skate

(4) _____ . You aren't

going to (5) _____ down

and break your arm or leg!

Grammar

B. Complete the sentences. For each verb, write the correct form of *be + going to* for the future.

1. Mei and Sophie _are going to study_ after school. (study)

2. I _____ a gift for her. (buy)

3. Bic _____ baseball. (play)

4. The test _____ hard. (be)

5. You _____ down. (fall)

C. Change the sentences in **Exercise B** to the negative form. Write the new sentences on the lines.

1. _Mei and Sophie are not going to study_ _after school._

2. _____

3. _____

4. _____

5. _____

D. Change the sentences below to questions. Write the questions on the lines. Then complete the short answers.

1. Bic and Luis are going to have a party.

A. _Are Bic and Luis going to have a party?_

B. No, _they aren't_ .

2. Mei is going to buy a gift.

A. _____

B. Yes, _____ .

3. Carolina is going to make her bed.

A. _____

B. No, _____ .

4. You are going to eat those cookies.

A. _____

B. No, I _____ .

5. They are going to play soccer.

A. _____

B. Yes, _____ .

E. Read the answers. Then complete the questions. Use the cues and *be + going to* for the future.

1. (Pablo / do / tonight?)

A. What _is Pablo going to do tonight?_

B. He's going to watch TV.

2. (you / help / your grandmother?)

A. When _____

B. I'm going to help her on Saturday.

3. (your brothers / play / baseball?)

    A. Where _____

    B. They're going to play at the park.

4. (Sophie / visit?)

    A. Who _____

    B. She's going to visit Carlos.

5. (we / get / at the store?)

    A. What _____

    B. We're going to get bread and milk.

F. Read the sentences. Then match the commands with the sentences.

1. Maria skates very well. _e_	**a.** Don't buy it.
2. Oh, no! I think you broke your leg. ___	**b.** Don't move.
3. It's time for class to begin. ___	**c.** Don't sit down.
4. The party is going to be fun. ___	**d.** Please come to it.
5. There's a cake on that chair. ___	**e.** ~~Look at her.~~
6. That CD is very expensive. ___	**f.** Please open your books.

Word Study

G. Write the correct word for each picture. Use the words from the box. Then circle the letter or letters that stand for the vowel sound /o͞o/.

drew	~~flew~~	glue
June	moon	shampoo

1. ___ _flew_ ___   **2.** _____

3. _____   **4.** _____

5. _____   **6.** _____

Reading Vocabulary

H. Match Carlos's sentences. Write the correct letters.

1. I had an accident and went to the hospital. _d_	**a.** I needed to rest.
2. I broke my wrist. ___	**b.** I wanted them to visit me.
3. I was very tired. ___	**c.** I wanted to do something.
4. I was bored. ___	**d.** ~~After that, I was feeling blue.~~
5. I missed my friends. ___	**e.** My friends think I'm an actor.
6. I'm not really in pain now, but I'm talking with a very weak voice. ___	**f.** There's a cast on it.

Chapter 14 Test

Dialogue Vocabulary

A. Complete the dialogue. Write the correct words and expressions from the box.

lights	soon	It sure is
power line	storm	~~Whoa~~

Luis: (1) _____Whoa_____ !

(2) _____ dark in here. I can't see a thing. What happened?

Tito: We had a big (3) _____ .

Something fell on the

(4) _____ and broke it.

The electricity went off, and the

(5) _____ went out.

Luis: Are they going to come back on

(6) _____ ?

Tito: I don't think so. I think it's going to be dark for a long time.

Grammar

B. Complete the sentences in the affirmative or negative. Write the correct past-continuous form of the verbs.

1. Mom __was cooking__ at six o'clock yesterday. (cook, affirmative)

2. She __was not watching__ TV. (watch, negative)

3. We _____ our homework. (do, affirmative)

4. I _____ math. (study, affirmative)

5. We _____ video games. (play, negative)

6. Dad _____ at six o'clock. (work, negative)

7. Dad and Luis _____ Grandma. (help, affirmative)

C. Write past-continuous *yes/no* questions. Then complete the short answers. Use the cues.

1. (you / watch / TV at six o'clock yesterday?)

   A: _Were you watching TV at six o'clock_
   yesterday?

   B: No, _I wasn't_ .

2. (David / play / video games?)

   A: _____

   B: Yes, _____ .

3. (your mom / help / your grandmother?)

   A: _____

   B: No, _____ .

4. (you and Luis / eat / at seven o'clock?)

   A: _____

   B: Yes, _____ .

5. (your parents / work / last Saturday?)

   A: _____

   B: No, _____ .

D. Complete the questions. Write the correct past-continuous form of the verb. Use the cues.

1. What _were you doing_ after school? (you, do)

2. Where _____ ? (the girls, study)

3. When _____ to Carlos? (Sophie, talk)

4. Who _____ a gift for? (David, buy)

5. What else _____ yesterday? (they, do)

E. Write the correct possessive pronouns.

1. This is *their* money. → It's __*theirs*__ .

2. This is *our* money. → It's _____ .

3. This is *your* money. → It's _____ .

4. This is *his* money. → It's _____ .

5. This is *her* money. → It's _____ .

F. Read the sentences. Then complete the questions and answers.

1. This is your pencil.

   A. Whose __*pencil is this*__ ?

   B. It's __*yours*__ .

2. That is their house.

   A. Whose _____ ?

   B. It's _____ .

3. These are my books.

   A. Whose _____ ?

   B. They're _____ .

4. Those are our CDs.

   A. Whose _____ ?

   B. They're _____ .

5. This is his room.

   A. Whose _____ ?

   B. It's _____ .

Word Study

G. Read the sentences. Circle the letters that stand for the vowel sound /o͝o/ as in *look*.

1. Carmen had a g**oo**d day today.

2. Is this yellow book yours, Paco?

3. Do you want cookies or toast?

4. Please try this brown shoe on your foot.

5. Your hook has a huge fish on it!

6. Mom's going to cook the food on our new stove.

Reading Vocabulary

H. Complete the sentences from the student's journal. Write the correct words from the box.

completely	Instead	~~thunderstorm~~
dangerous	perfect	

Yesterday, the weather was very bad. There was a big (1) __thunderstorm__ . It's (2) _____ to go outside during a thunderstorm, so I stayed in. The rain didn't stop (3) _____ until five o'clock!

Today, it was sunny and beautiful. It was a (4) _____ day to go to the park. I went to play soccer with my friends. Carlos came, but Carmen didn't come. (5) _____ , she stayed at home.

Name _____ Date _____

Chapter 15 Test

Dialogue Vocabulary

A. Complete the dialogue. Write the correct words and expressions from the box.

a few	~~extra~~	Of course
catch up	final	review

Luis: The math teacher gave us twenty

problems instead of ten, so we have

(1) _____*extra*_____ homework

tonight.

Anna: School was closed, and we missed a

lot of work. Now we have to

(2) _____ on it.

Luis: But we didn't miss many days. We only

missed (3) _____ days.

Anna: We need to get ready for our

(4) _____ exams.

Luis: I know. My English teacher told me to

(5) _____ the stories. That

means to read them again, right?

Anna: Right. Are you going to study the
vocabulary, too?

Luis: (6) _____ . They're very
important!

Grammar

B. Complete the sentences. Use *will* or
won't for the future with the verb in
parentheses.

1. It's cold, so I _*will wear*_
my coat. (wear)

2. I'm sick, so I _*won't go*_
to school today. (go)

3. He doesn't like parties, so he

_____ to our

party. (come)

4. She loves parties, so she

_____ to our

party. (come)

5. We want to help, so we

_____ the

dishes. (wash)

6. They're going to a movie, so they

_____ at

home tonight. (be)

C. Write *yes/no* questions with *will* for the
future. Use the cues. Then complete the
short answers.

1. (you / help / me?)

A: _Will you help me?_

B: Yes, _I will_ .

2. (Pablo / arrive / on time?)

A: _____

B: No, _____ .

3. (the students / read / more books?)

A: _____

B: Yes, _____ .

4. (we / have / a test next week?)

A: _____

B: Yes, you _____ .

5. (she / go / to bed early?)

A: _____

B: No, _____ .

D. Complete the questions. Use *will* for the
future and the cues.

1. Where _will we have_ _____
the study group? (we, have)

2. What time _____ ?
(it, start)

3. What kind of cake _____ ?
(Anna, make)

4. Who _____
the sandwiches? (make)

5. What _____ ?
(you, bring)

6. What else _____
for the study group? (we, need)

E. Read the sentences and the cues. Then complete the sentences. Write *may/might, may not/might not, is going to,* or *isn't going to.*

1. Edgar doesn't have a lot of money, so he __may not (or might not)__ buy anything. (possible plan)

2. Isabel has some money, so she _____ buy a CD. (possible plan)

3. Luis has a test tomorrow, so he _____ study tonight. (definite plan)

4. Pablo has a lot of homework, so he _____ watch TV tonight. (possible plan)

5. Anna isn't hungry, so she _____ eat lunch. (definite plan)

Word Study

F. Write the correct word for each picture. Use the words from the box. Then circle the letters that stand for the vowel sound /â/.

~~paw~~	August	author
straw	yawn	autumn

1. __p(aw)__   **2.** _____

3. _____   **4.** _____

5. _____   **6.** _____

Reading Vocabulary

G. Complete the sentences. Write the correct words from the box.

proud	~~translate~~	whispered
quietly	translator	

1. Lee's parents speak Vietnamese but not English. Lee speaks both languages. Lee can __translate__ from English to Vietnamese for his parents.

2. Kay likes her job. She translates from Chinese to English. She is a _____ .

3. Alberto _____ . That means that he spoke very softly.

4. Stop shouting. Please speak _____ .

5. I'll study a lot, and I'll do well on my exams. Then my parents will be _____ of me.

Chapter 16 Test

Dialogue Vocabulary

A. Complete the dialogue. Write the words and expressions from the box.

coach	especially	I hope so
practice	hard time	Do you mind if
~~typical~~		

Edgar: Tito was talking about soccer today.

Luis: That's (1) ____typical____ for Tito. He's always talking about soccer.

Edgar: I have a (2) _____ with soccer. I'm not good at it.

Luis: Tito's good at playing a lot of games. Bic is, too. Bic is (3) _____ good at playing baseball.

＊ ＊ ＊ ＊ ＊

Carolina: What do you do at baseball (4) _____ ?

Bic: We get ready for games. Mr. Diaz is our (5) _____ . He teaches us how to play the game.

＊ ＊ ＊ ＊ ＊

Carolina: (6) _____ I ask you a question?

Luis: What do you want to know?

Carolina: Is Bic going to play in the next game?

Luis: (7) _____ . I really want to watch him play.

Grammar

B. Read the sentences. Then rewrite them using the adverbs of frequency.

1. Anna goes to bed at nine o'clock. (sometimes)

Anna sometimes goes to bed at nine o'clock.

2. Our teacher is late to class. (never)

Our teacher is never late to class.

3. Carmen and Luis are hungry. (always)

_____

4. We study in the library. (usually)

_____

5. Maria has to work on Saturday. (often)

_____

6. Lin is bored in math class. (sometimes)

_____

C. Complete the questions. Then complete the answers. Use the cues.

1. (Anna / baby-sit?) (twice a month)

A: How often _does Anna baby-sit?_

B: She _baby-sits twice a month._

2. (you / eat rice?) (three times a day)

A: How often _____

B: I _____

3. (Tito / play soccer?) (two times a week)

A: How often _____

B: He _____

4. (the girls / go to the movies?) (once a week)

A: How often _____

B: They _____

5. (David / clean his room?) (once a year)

A: How often _____

B: He _____

D. Complete the sentences. Use the gerund form of the verb in parentheses.

1. Bic likes ____playing____ baseball. (play)

2. My father hates _____ to the movies. (go)

3. Luis and I enjoy _____ TV. (watch)

4. Mei finished _____ at ten o'clock. (study)

5. Please start _____ now. (write)

6. Lin loves _____ stories. (read)

Word Study

E. Look at the pictures. Then read the sentences. Write the letter of the picture that matches the sentence. Then circle the letters that stand for the vowel sound /oi/.

a

b

c

d

e

f

1. _d_ His first name is R(oy).

2. ____ Plants need good soil.

3. ____ Who wants to play with this toy?

4. ____ Is this coin a dime?

5. ____ You have to boil the water.

6. ____ This boy is ten years old.

Reading Vocabulary

F. Read the sentences and the cues. Then complete the sentences. Write the correct word or expression from the box.

friendly	free-time activity
by myself	join

1. Isabel is going to _____ us at the party. (She's going to come and be with us.)

2. I was _____ . (No one else was with me.)

3. Anna is _____ . (She's nice to people, and they like her.)

4. Reading is my favorite

_____ . (It's what I like to do when I'm not at school or working or studying.)

Chapter 17 Test

Dialogue Vocabulary

A. Complete the sentences. Write the correct words and expressions from the box.

couple of	~~headache~~	stomachache
feels better	sore	terrible
plenty of		

1. On Monday, Edgar's head hurt. He told the nurse, "I have a ___headache___ ."

2. His stomach hurt. He said, "I have a _____ , too."

3. His throat hurt, too. He said, "And I have a _____ throat."

4. He was very sick. He said, "I feel _____ ."

5. Edgar didn't go to school on Tuesday or Wednesday. He stayed home for a _____ days.

6. When he was at home, he stayed in bed, so he got _____ rest.

7. Edgar isn't sick now. He _____ .

Grammar

B. Read the students' problems. Then complete the sentences giving advice. Use *should* or *shouldn't* and the cues.

The students are worried about the test.

1. They ___shouldn't worry___ . (worry)

2. They _____ . (study / more)

I have a terrible stomachache.

3. You _____ . (take / this medicine)

4. You _____ . (eat / a lot of enchiladas)

Carlos fell down and hurt his arm and his leg. It's an emergency.

5. He _____ . (move)

6. His sister _____ . (call / 911)

C. Read the students' problems. Complete the *yes/no* questions. Use *should* or *shouldn't* and the cues. Then complete the short answers.

1. I have a sore throat and a headache. (I'm asking for advice.)

   A: ___Should I go___ swimming? (I / go)

   B: No, you _____ .

2. I have a sore throat and a headache. (I want you to say *yes*.)

   A: _____ in bed? (I / stay)

   B: Yes, you _____ .

3. Lin feels terrible. (I want you to say *yes*.)

   A: _____ the school nurse ? (she / see)

   B: Yes, she _____ .

4. Luis has a stomachache. (I'm asking for advice.)

   A: _____ to P.E. class today? (he / go)

   B: No, he _____ .

D. Complete the dialogues. Use *could* and the possibilities in the box.

get her some flowers	go out to eat
drink some lemonade	~~rest~~
watch TV	

1. **A:** I'm tired.

   B: You _could rest_ .

2. **A:** I'm bored.

   B: We _____ .

3. **A:** I'm thirsty.

   B: You _____ .

4. **A:** I don't want to cook tonight.

   B: We _____ .

5. **A:** I need a birthday gift for my mother.

   B: You _____ .

E. Read the pairs of sentences. Write each pair as one sentence with a *because* clause.

1. Anna is eating crackers. She's hungry.

   Anna is eating crackers because

   she's hungry.

2. We should study now. We have a test tomorrow.

   _____

   _____

3. I want to get a gift for my mother. Tomorrow's her birthday.

   _____

   _____

4. I don't want any soda. I'm not thirsty.

   _____

5. They need to rest now. They're tired.

   _____

F. Complete the words. Write *ou* or *ow*.

1. h __ __ se   **2.** cr __ __ d

3. cl __ __ d   **4.** t __ __ n

Reading Vocabulary

G. Complete the sentences from a student's vocabulary notebook. Write the correct word or expression from the box.

the day after tomorrow	~~smart~~
surprised	artists
flowers	

1. The word _____smart_____ can mean

   intelligent.

2. These are _____ .

3. Today is Tuesday. Thursday is

   _____ .

4. My friends planned this party for me, but they never told me about it. When it started, I was _____ .

5. People who write poems and stories are authors. People who draw and paint pictures are _____ .

Chapter 18 Test

Dialogue Vocabulary

A. Complete the dialogue. Write the correct words from the box.

~~expect~~	pass	comprehension
hope	tease	

Tito: Did you think the exam was hard?

Anna: Yes, I did. I didn't (1) ____*expect*____

it to be so hard. I (2) _____

that I didn't miss too many questions.

Tito: Why do our teachers give so many

(3) _____ questions on

tests?

Anna: They want to know how well we can understand the reading.

Pablo: If you miss too many questions

on the final exam, you won't

(4) _____ . You'll have to

take the exam again.

Tito: I know. My friend Patrick had to take the exam five times.

Anna: Oh, I don't believe you, Tito. That isn't

true. Don't (5) _____ us.

Grammar

B. Complete the sentences. Use the information in the chart. Write *better than, worse than, the best,* or *the worst.* (Four stars is the best.)

Pablo's CD Guide			
★★★★	★★★	★★	★
Luisa's CD	Betty's CD	Donna's CD	Trish's CD

1. Betty's CD is ____*better than*____ Donna's.

2. Luisa's CD is _____ .

3. Donna's CD is _____ Trish's.

4. Donna's CD is _____ Betty's.

5. Trish's CD is _____ .

C. Read the problems. Then complete the sentences. Use the cues and *too* or *not . . . enough.*

Everybody in the class got 100 percent on the test.

1. The test was ____*too easy*____ . (easy)

2. The test was _____ . (hard)

There is a lot of food on the plate. The food is falling onto the table.

3. The plate is _____ . (small)

4. The plate is _____ . (large)

The book has 350 pages. The students can't finish it in only two days!

5. The book is _____ . (short)

6. The book is _____ . (long)

D. Complete the sentences. Write *used to* or *didn't use to.*

1. I ____*didn't use to*____ like enchiladas, but now I do.

2. Liliana _____ live in Peru, but now she lives in the United States.

3. Alberto _____ play soccer, but now he plays soccer every day.

4. Anna _____ like Lin, but now they're best friends.

5. Edgar _____
want to be an artist, but now he wants
to be a teacher.

E. Write *yes/no* questions with *used to*. Use
the cues. Then complete the short
answers.

1. (you / read / comic books / ?)

A: *Did you use to read comic books?*

B: No, I _____ .

2. (your brothers / have / a lot of toys / ?)

A: _____

_____

B: Yes, they _____ .

3. (Maria / live / in Haiti / ?)

A: _____

_____

B: No, she _____ .

4. (you and Luis / study / together / ?)

A: _____

_____

B: Yes, we _____ .

5. lett ___ ___

6. n ___ ___ se

Reading Vocabulary

G. Complete the sentences. Write the
correct words from the box.

Congratulations	shook
~~found out~~	stunned
promoted	whole

1. Today we _*found out*_ our
grades. The teacher passed back our
exams, and our grades were on them.

2. I was in Mr. Gomez's class. I passed
the exam, and Mr. Gomez said,
"You're _____ ." That
means that next September I'll be in
Mrs. Ward's class.

3. At first, I was _____ . In
other words, I was very, very
surprised.

4. The _____ class came to
the party. In other words, all the
students were there.

5. Everybody was proud and happy. We
shouted, " _____ !" to our
friends.

6. Then we all _____ hands.

Word Study

F. Complete the words. Write *ur*, *ir*, or *er*.

1. Th _u_ _r_ sday

2. sh ___ ___ t

3. wint ___ ___

4. b ___ ___ d

Unit 1 Test

Grammar

A. Complete the sentences. Write the correct subject pronoun and *is* or *are*. Use the cues.

1. _____*She is*_____ very nervous. (Maria)

2. _____ a teacher. (Mr. Gomez)

3. _____ worried. (Lin and Mei)

4. _____ from Peru. (Liliana and I)

5. _____ in my backpack. (The pen)

6. _____ students. (Luis and you)

B. Write *yes/no* questions. Use the cues and the present tense of *be*. Then complete the short answers.

1. (you / from Mexico)

   A: __*Are you from Mexico?*__

   B: No, _____*I'm not*_____ .

2. (Maria / a new student)

   A: _____

   B: Yes, _____ .

3. (the books / in your backpack)

   A: _____

   B: Yes, _____ .

4. (Pablo / nervous)

   A: _____

   B: No, _____ .

C. Complete the sentences. Write the correct form of *have*.

1. I _____*have*_____ my schedule. (has/have)

2. You _____ lunch now. (doesn't have/don't have)

3. Carmen _____ science now. (has/have)

4. We _____ math together. (has/have)

5. He _____ his wallet. (doesn't have/don't have)

D. Change the sentences to questions. Write the questions on the lines. Then complete the short answers.

1. They have math together.

   A: __*Do they have math together?*__

   B: No, _____ .

2. You have your schedule.

   A: _____

   B: Yes, I _____ .

3. Anna has ten dollars.

   A: _____

   B: No, _____ .

4. We have the same math class.

   A: _____

   B: Yes, we _____ .

E. Write *a* or *an* before each noun.

1. _____*a*_____ page

2. _____ hat

3. _____ eraser

4. _____ story

5. _____ orange

6. _____ word

F. Write the plural form of each noun.

1. hat _____*hats*_____

2. school _____

3. problem _____

4. class _____

5. language _____

6. lunch _____

Name _____ Date _____

G. Complete the sentences. Write *This*, *That*, *These*, or *Those*.

1. ___*That*___ is your pencil.

2. _____ are my pencils.

3. _____ is my wallet.

4. _____ are his erasers.

5. _____ is her pen.

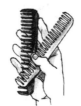

6. _____ are our combs.

H. Change each sentence to the plural. Write the new sentences on the lines.

1. This is a pen.
   These are pens.

2. That is a pencil.
   Those are pencils.

3. That is a wallet.

   _____

4. This is a comb.

   _____

5. This is a brush.

   _____

6. That is a calculator.

   _____

I. Read the first sentence in each pair of sentences. Then complete the second sentence. Write the correct possessive adjective. Use the <u>underlined</u> word or words as cues.

1. <u>Maria</u> has a backpack.
   That is ___*her*___ backpack.

2. <u>You</u> have a notebook.
   That is _____ notebook.

3. <u>We</u> have protractors.
   These are _____ protractors.

4. <u>Carlos</u> has a backpack.
   That is _____ backpack.

5. <u>Carmen and Bic</u> have folders.
   _____ folders are here.

6. <u>I</u> have a notebook and a backpack.
   _____ notebook is in _____ backpack.

J. Complete the sentences. Write the correct possessive form of the noun.

1. The ___*boy's*___ wallet is in his backpack. (boy)

2. The _____ schedules are the same. (girls)

3. The _____ names are Mei and Bic. (students)

4. Their _____ name is Mr. Gomez. (teacher)

5. This isn't _____ notebook. (Pablo)

6. That is _____ new cap. (Carlos)

Name _____ Date _____

Reading

A. Read the story about Tony and Anita. Then complete their class schedules below.

  Tony and Anita are students at Valley School. They are in their English classroom. Today is the first day of school. Anita says, "Good morning, Tony."

  Tony says, "Hey, Anita. You have English class with me!" Then he asks, "What classes do you have after English? Do you have your schedule?"

  Anita answers, "Yes, I do. It's in my backpack with my books. Wait, my schedule isn't in my backpack. It's in my folder. Here it is. After English, I have history and P.E. Then I have lunch. What's your schedule?"

  Tony says, "After English, I have science and math. Then I have lunch, too."

  Anita says, "That's great. After lunch, I have art, science, and math. What classes do you have after lunch?"

  Tony says, "I have music, history, and then P.E. I love P.E. It's my favorite class."

  Anita says, "I don't like P.E. I'm not good at it. My favorite class is art. It's fun."

Anita
1. English
2. history
3. P. E.
4.
5. art
6.
7. math

Tony
1.
2. science
3. math
4. lunch
5.
6.
7. P. E.

B. Complete the sentences about Tony and Anita and their schedules. Write the correct answers on the lines.

1. Tony and Anita are students at _____ Valley _____ School.

    Washington   Valley   English

2. Anita's schedule is in her _____ .

    folder   books   backpack

3. Anita and Tony have _____ together.

    English and lunch   art and math   English and science

4. After lunch, Tony and Anita have _____ classes.

    the same   almost the same   different

Name _____ Date _____

Writing

A. You are going to write two paragraphs, one about Sonia Karam and one about Andrew Tang. First, read the paragraph below.

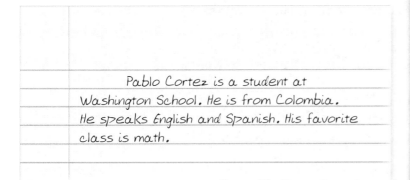

Pablo Cortez is a student at
Washington School. He is from Colombia.
He speaks English and Spanish. His favorite
class is math.

B. Read the *Before I Write* checklist.

Student: Sonia Karam
School: Valley School
Country: Lebanon
Languages: English and
            Arabic
Favorite class: science

Student: Andrew Tang
School: Madison School
Country: China
Languages: English and
            Chinese
Favorite class: music

C. Read the *While I Write* checklist. Then, on a separate piece of paper, write one paragraph about Sonia and one paragraph about Andrew. Use the model in **Exercise A** for help.

D. Read the *After I Write* checklist. Then check your work.

Tools for Writing

Before I Write

▶ Study the model.

▶ Look at the pictures of Sonia and Andrew.

▶ Read the information below the pictures.

While I Write

▶ Indent the first line of each paragraph.

    Pablo Cortez is a student at Washington School.

▶ Use a capital letter at the beginning of each sentence and at the beginning of the name of a person, place, country, or language.

    His favorite class is math.

    Pablo Cortez

    Washington School

    Colombia

    Spanish

▶ Use pronouns and possessive adjectives correctly.

    He is from Colombia.

    His favorite class is math.

After I Write

▶ Did I indent the first line of my paragraphs?

▶ Did I use capital letters correctly?

▶ Did I use pronouns and possessive adjectives correctly?

Unit 2 Test

Grammar

A. Look at the picture. Then complete the questions. Write *Where's* or *Where are*. Then complete the answers. Write *It's* or *They're* and the preposition *in, on, under*, or *next to*.

1. A: _____*Where's*_____ the cup?

 B: _____*It's on*_____ the table.

2. A: _____ the pens?

 B: _____ the cup.

3. A: _____ the folder?

 B: _____ the calculator.

4. A: _____ the books?

 B: _____ the cup.

5. A: _____ the wallet?

 B: _____ the books.

B. Read the answers. For each answer, write a question with *What's* or *What are*.

1. A: ___*What's his address?*___

 B: His address is 2403 Center Street.

2. A: _____

 B: Their names are Lin and Tito.

3. A: _____

 B: Her telephone number is 555-9415.

4. A: _____

 B: My favorite classes are science and music.

C. Complete the sentences in the affirmative or the negative. Write the correct simple present-tense form of the verb. Use contractions.

1. They ___*don't live*___ in Mexico. (live, negative)

2. We _____ directions. (need, negative)

3. You _____ in a nice house. (live, affirmative)

4. Pablo _____ Chinese. (speak, negative)

5. I _____ this lunch. (like, negative)

6. She _____ a new wallet. (want, affirmative)

7. They _____ French. (speak, affirmative)

D. Write *yes/no* questions in the simple present tense. Use the cues. Then complete the short answers.

1. (she / speak / Arabic)

 A: ___*Does she speak Arabic?*___

 B: No, _____ .

2. (they / need / directions)

 A: _____

 B: Yes, _____ .

3. (your brother / live / in Peru)

 A: _____

 B: Yes, _____ .

4. (you / want / a new watch)

 A: _____

 B: No, I _____ .

Name _____ Date _____

E. Complete the sentences. Use the cues and *can* or *can't.*

1. They _____ *can speak* _____ Arabic. (speak, affirmative)

2. He _____ the drums. (play, negative)

3. She _____ after school. (swim, affirmative)

4. I _____ my book. (find, negative)

5. You _____ in the cafeteria. (eat, affirmative)

6. We _____ that computer. (use, negative)

F. Write *yes/no* questions with *can*. Use the cues. Then complete the short answers.

1. (Carlos / swim)

A: _*Can Carlos swim?*_____

B: Yes, _____ .

2. (Mei / speak / French)

A: _____

B: No, _____ .

3. (they / come / to the party)

A: _____

B: No, _____ .

4. (you / play / the drums)

A: _____

B: Yes, I _____ .

G. Complete the questions. Write the correct words on the lines.

1. What _____ *do you* _____ need? (do you / does you)

2. What _____ want? (do Maria / does Maria)

3. What does _____ in his wallet? (he have / he has)

4. What language _____ speak? (do they / does they)

5. What books _____ need? (do he / does he)

6. What time does _____ ? (class start / class starts)

H. Complete the sentences in the affirmative or the negative. Write *was, wasn't, were,* or *weren't.*

1. Monday _____ *was* _____ a good day. (affirmative)

2. The test _____ hard. (negative)

3. I _____ happy. (affirmative)

4. Lin and Anna _____ sick yesterday. (affirmative)

5. They _____ in school. (negative)

6. We _____ worried. (affirmative)

I. Change the sentences to *yes/no* questions. Write the questions on the lines. Then complete the short answers.

1. They were late to class.

A: _*Were they late to class?*_____

B: No, _____ .

2. Pablo was at school on Monday.

A: _____

B: Yes, _____ .

3. You were sad yesterday.

A: _____

B: No, I _____ .

4. You and your brother were at the party.

A: _____

_____

B: Yes, _____ .

Name _____ Date _____

Reading

A. Read the dialogue.

Isabel: Hey, Edgar. There's a party at my house this Friday. Can you come?

Edgar: Yes, I can. What time does it start?

Isabel: At seven o'clock. Please don't be late.

Edgar: Don't worry. What's your address?

Isabel: It's 896 Grand Avenue.

Edgar: I'm sorry. I don't know where that is. I need directions to your house.

Isabel: Do you know where Cordell School is?

Edgar: Yes, I do.

Isabel: Well, there's a fire station across the street from it. I live next to the fire station.

Edgar: What color is your house?

Isabel: It's green. Do you have my phone number?

Edgar: No, I don't. I need that, too. What is it?

Isabel: It's 555-6514. See you at the party!

Edgar: Wait, Isabel. I have more questions. When is your birthday? Is it on Friday?

Isabel: Well . . . um, yes, it is.

Edgar: So the party is a birthday party! What do you want for your birthday?

Isabel: Oh, Edgar, don't be silly. I don't want a gift. I just want my friends to have fun at my party.

B. Complete the sentences below about the dialogue.

1. Isabel's party is on _____*Friday*_____ .

2. The party starts at _____ .

3. Isabel's address is _____ .

4. Isabel's house is next to _____ .

5. Isabel's phone number is _____ .

6. Isabel's birthday is on _____ .

Name _____ Date _____

Writing

A. You are going to write a paragraph about your day yesterday. First, read the student's journal below.

> Yesterday was a very good day. At ten o'clock, I was in the science classroom. There was a test. I was a little worried, but the test wasn't hard. At three o'clock, my friends and I were in the school gym. There was a ball game. It was fun, and I was happy. At seven o'clock, I was at home with my mother and my little brothers and sisters. Our dinner was very good. I was still happy.

B. Read the *Before I Write* checklist. Then write notes about yesterday below.

Kind of day: _____

Ten o'clock: _____

_____

_____

Three o'clock: _____

_____

_____

Seven o'clock: _____

_____

_____

How I felt: _____

_____

C. Read the *While I Write* checklist. Then, on a separate piece of paper, write a paragraph about yesterday. Use your notes and the paragraph in **Exercise A** for help.

D. Read the *After I Write* checklist. Then check your work.

Before I Write

▶ Study the model.

▶ Think about yesterday.

▶ Make notes about . . .
- the kind of day it was—good or bad.
- where I was at ten o'clock, three o'clock, and seven o'clock.
- how I felt.

While I Write

▶ Use *was* and *were* to write about the past.

  There **was** a test.

  My friends and I **were** in the school gym.

▶ Give details about time and place.

  At ten o'clock, I was **in the science classroom.**

▶ Use describing words to tell how you felt.

  I was still **happy**.

After I Write

▶ Did I use *was* and *were* to write about the past?

▶ Did I give details about time and place?

▶ Did I use describing words to tell how I felt?

Unit 3 Test

Grammar

A. Complete the sentences in the affirmative or the negative. Write the correct present continuous form of the verb.

1. Sophie ___is talking___ to Mei. (talk, affirmative)

2. Carolina ___is not helping___ me. (help, negative)

3. We _____ lunch now. (eat, affirmative)

4. My dad _____ a light bulb. (change, affirmative)

5. I _____ a story. (write, negative)

B. Read the answers. Then for each answer write a *What* question in the present continuous tense. Use *What's* or *What are* and the cues.

1. (Mr. Gomez)

   A: _What's Mr. Gomez cleaning?_

   B: He's cleaning the chalkboard.

2. (your sisters)

   A: _____

   B: They're making enchiladas.

3. (you)

   A: _____

   B: I'm reading a story.

C. Write *yes/no* questions in the present continuous tense. Use the cues. Then complete the short answers.

1. (you / make / cookies)

   A: _Are you making cookies?_

   B: No, ___I'm not___ .

2. (Paco / study / math)

   A: _____

   B: Yes, _____ .

3. (they / read / a story)

   A: _____

   B: No, _____ .

D. Rewrite the sentences. Use object pronouns for the underlined word or words.

1. David is cleaning the windows.

   David is cleaning them.

2. Dad is helping Carolina.

   _____

3. Pablo is reading the book.

   _____

4. Mr. Gomez is helping Maria and Sophie.

   _____

E. Complete the sentences. Write the simple present or present continuous form of the verb.

1. Mei ___is talking___ on the phone now. (talk)

2. She ___calls___ her friends every night. (call)

3. Maria _____ her homework every day. (do)

4. She _____ a picture right now. (draw)

F. Complete the sentences in the affirmative or the negative. Write the correct simple present form of the verb. Use contractions.

1. I ___don't have___ to work. (have, negative)

2. Sophie _____ to go out. (want, affirmative)

3. They _____ to cook. (like, negative)

4. I _____ to watch TV now. (want, affirmative)

5. Bic _____ to wash dishes. (like, negative)

G. Read the answers. Then complete the questions. Use the cues.

1. (you)

A: What _____ *do you like to eat* _____ ?

B: I like to eat cake and ice cream.

2. (we)

A: What _____ ?

B: We have to study math.

3. (your father)

A: What _____ ?

B: He likes to read history books.

4. (Carmen and Carlos)

A: What _____ ?

_____

B: They want to cook enchiladas.

H. Write *yes/no* questions in the simple present tense. Use the cues. Then complete the short answers.

1. (Sophie / want / to go out)

A: _____ *Does Sophie want to go out?* _____

B: Yes, _____ .

2. (they / have / to work tonight)

A: _____

B: No, _____ .

3. (you / like / to sing together)

A: _____

B: Yes, we _____ .

4. (Bic / want / to study now)

A: _____

B: No, _____ .

I. Complete the sentences. Write the simple past tense of the verbs.

1. Tito _____ *asked* _____ a question. (ask)

2. Anna _____ *knew* _____ the answer. (know)

3. We _____ to school early. (go)

4. They _____ at the party. (dance)

5. I _____ English and math. (study)

6. Pablo _____ his guitar. (play)

J. Change each sentence from the affirmative to the negative or from the negative to the affirmative. Write the new sentences on the lines. Use contractions.

1. Liliana called Mei last night.

_____ *Liliana didn't call Mei last night.* _____

2. I didn't ask the teacher.

_____

3. Sophie made the enchiladas.

_____

4. We didn't sing the song.

_____

K. Write *yes/no* questions in the simple past tense. Use the cues. Then complete the short answers.

1. (Maria / come / to the party)

A: _____ *Did Maria come to the party?* _____

B: Yes, _____ *she did* _____ .

2. (Paco / dance / with Carmen)

A: _____

B: No, _____ .

3. (you / eat / cake and ice cream)

A: _____

B: Yes, we _____ .

Reading

A. Read the letter.

December 15, 2004

Dear Tito,

     I went to our class party on Saturday night. The party was in the gym at school. All the students in the class came.
     At the party, I talked with my friends Diego and Andrew. Then Diego and Andrew danced with some of the girls. I wanted to ask Anna to dance with me. But I was very shy, so I didn't ask her.
     There was so much food at the party. Our mothers cooked it for us. They made enchiladas, chili, and cake. I liked the food, and I ate a lot.
     Our music teacher is Mr. Novato. He came to the party. He played his guitar, and we all sang. First, we sang songs in Spanish. I like those songs, but they made me feel a little sad and homesick for Mexico. Then he taught us some new songs in English. It was fun to learn those songs, and I started to feel happy again.
     I miss you and all of our friends in Mexico. Please write to me soon.

Your friend,
Alberto

B. Read the sentences below about the letter. Circle *True* or *False*. Then change the false sentences to make them true.

     Alberto
1. ~~Tito~~ wrote the letter.   True / (False)

2. Alberto's class party was on Saturday night.   True / False

3. Alberto asked Anna to dance with him.   True / False

4. The students' mothers made enchiladas, chili, and   True / False
cake for the party.

5. Singing songs in Spanish made Alberto feel happy.   True / False

6. Alberto misses Tito.   True / False

Writing

A. You are going to write a paragraph about yourself when you were five years old. First, read the paragraph below.

> When I was five years old, I liked to draw pictures. I liked to play in the park with my big brother and little sisters, too. We had a lot of fun together. I didn't like to go to bed early. I had to go to school every morning, but I didn't have to do homework. I had to help my mother sometimes, but I didn't have to cook. I wanted to be a singer.

Before I Write

▶ Study the model.
▶ Write answers to the questions.

While I Write

▶ Begin the first sentence with *When I was five years old, . . .*
▶ Use *liked, had,* and *wanted* + infinitive to write about the past.

  I **liked to play** in the park.

▶ Use correct affirmative and negative past-tense forms.

  I **had** to go to school every morning, but I **didn't have** to do homework.

B. Read the *Before I Write* checklist. Then write answers to these questions.

When you were five years old, . . .

what did you like to do? _____
_____
_____

what didn't you like to do? _____
_____
_____

what did you have to do? _____
_____
_____

what didn't you have to do? _____
_____
_____

what did you want to be? _____

After I Write

▶ Did I begin the first sentence with *When I was five years old, . . .*?
▶ Did I use *liked, had,* and *wanted* + infinitive to write about the past?
▶ Did I use correct affirmative and negative past-tense forms?

C. Read the *While I Write* checklist. Then, on a separate piece of paper, write your paragraph. Use your notes and the model in **Exercise A** for help.

D. Read the *After I Write* checklist. Then check your work.

Unit 4 Test

Grammar

A. Read the answers. Then complete the questions. Use *is* or *are*.

1. A: What _____*is your name*_____ ?

   B: My name is Elena.

2. A: When _____ ?

   B: The test is on Thursday.

3. A: How much _____ ?

   B: The shoes are $40.

4. A: Who _____ ?

   B: Paco is Maria's brother.

5. A: Why _____ ?

   B: I am angry because you are late.

B. Read the answers. Then write questions about the underlined words. Use *How, When, Where,* or *Why* and *was* or *were*.

1. A: _____*When was the party?*_____

   B: The party was <u>last Saturday</u>.

2. A: _____

   B: The boys were <u>at the park</u>.

3. A: _____

   B: The show was <u>wonderful</u>.

4. A: _____

   B: I was late <u>because I had to baby-sit</u>.

C. Read the answers. Then complete the questions using the simple present tense.

1. A: What _____*do they want*_____ ?

   B: They want hamburgers and sodas.

2. A: Where _____ ?

   B: Elena studies in her room.

3. A: When _____ ?

   B: We eat dinner at six o'clock.

4. A: How much _____ ?

   B: The book costs $10.

5. A: Why _____ ?

   B: Carmen likes Paco because he is cute.

D. Read the answers. Then write questions about the underlined words. Use *How, What, When,* or *Where* and the simple past tense.

1. A: _____*Where did Mei go?*_____

   B: Mei went <u>to the library</u>.

2. A: _____

   B: The boys went home <u>at ten o'clock</u>.

3. A: _____

   B: Carmen ate <u>crackers</u>.

4. A: _____

   B: Pablo looked <u>happy</u>.

E. Complete the lists. Write the words from the box in the correct columns.

~~bread~~	lettuce	pencil
~~carrot~~	milk	rice
cheese	onion	student
cookie		

Count Nouns	Non-Count Nouns
carrot	*bread*
_____	_____
_____	_____
_____	_____
_____	_____

F. Complete the sentences. Write *some* or *any*.

1. We need _____*some*_____ butter.

2. We don't need _____ bananas.

3. There are _____ cookies in the box.

Name _____ Date _____

4. I don't want _____ food.

5. I want _____ new clothes.

G. Complete the sentences. Write *and, but,* or *so.*

1. Mei is hungry, ____*and*____ Sophie is hungry, too.

2. Sophie wants some French fries, _____ she doesn't want a salad.

3. Mei wants a salad, _____ she wants some French fries, too.

4. Mei wants French fries, _____ she doesn't have enough money.

5. I don't want all of my French fries, _____ I can share them with Mei.

H. Write the missing forms.

Adjective	Comparative	Superlative
1. ___*tall*___	taller	___*tallest*___
2. cute	_____	_____
3. _____	older	_____
4. _____	_____	latest
5. early	_____	_____
6. _____	_____	dirtiest

I. Write the comparative or superlative forms of the adjectives.

1. (casual)

___*more casual*___ _____

2. (formal)

_____ _____

3. (beautiful)

_____ _____

J. Look at the boxes. Then use the cues to complete the sentences. Write the comparative or superlative form of the adjective.

Box A   Box B   Box C

1. Box A is ___*larger*___ than Box B. (large)

2. Box B is _____ than Box A. (small)

3. Box B is _____ than Box C. (large)

4. Box A is the _____ box. (large)

5. Box C is the _____ box. (small)

K. Read the information in the box. Then complete the sentences about the CDs. Write the comparative or superlative form of *expensive.*

CD 1 costs $7.
CD 2 costs $11.
CD 3 costs $18.

1. CD 2 is _____ than CD 1.

2. CD 3 is _____ than CD 2.

3. CD 3 is the _____ CD.

Copyright © 2005 by Pearson Education, Inc.

274 Unit 4 Test

Name _____ Date _____

Reading

A. Read the story.

There was a big show in the Madison School auditorium last Thursday evening. The first performer was Sara Ramos. She played the guitar and sang two love songs. Then Harry Chen came onto the stage. Harry is a storyteller. He told a funny story about getting lost at school. The students in the audience laughed. The next performer was Amelia Jackson. Amelia is the author of many poems, and she read two of them. The first poem was "The Promise," and the second one was "At Midnight." After Amelia finished, it was time for two brothers, Dave and Danny Salas, to sing. When they walked onto the stage, the audience was excited. Dave and Danny sang three R & B songs. After their songs, everyone clapped and yelled.

After the show, the students talked about it. Edgar said, "I liked Sara's songs because they were so pretty."

Isabel said, "I agree. Both her songs were pretty, but I think her second song was prettier than the first one."

Anna said, "I liked Harry's story because it was very funny. But Amelia was my favorite performer. I think her poems are wonderful."

Tito said, "Everyone in the show was good, but Dave and Danny were great!"

Alberto agreed, "Dave and Danny were great. They were my favorite performers because their songs were so cool. Their third song was the coolest song in the show."

B. Answer the questions below about the story. Write sentences.

1. Where was the show? *It was in the Madison School auditorium.* _____

2. When was the show? _____

_____

3. Who was the first performer? _____

_____

4. What was the title of Amelia's second poem? _____

_____

5. Why did Edgar like Sara's songs? _____

_____

6. Who were Alberto's favorite performers? _____

_____

7. Why were these performers Alberto's favorite performers? _____

_____

Name _____ Date _____

Writing

A. You are going to write a dialogue between a salesclerk and a customer. First, read the dialogue below.

Salesclerk:	May I help you?
Customer:	Yes. I'm looking for some casual clothes. Where are the jeans?
Salesclerk:	We have some jeans right over there. What color do you want?
Customer:	I like dark colors. Do you have any black or dark blue jeans?
Salesclerk:	We don't have any black jeans. Do you like these dark blue jeans?
Customer:	Those are cool. How much do they cost?
Salesclerk:	They cost ninety-five dollars. They're the most expensive jeans in the store.
Customer:	I like them, but I can't buy them. I only have fifty dollars. Do you have any other dark blue jeans?
Salesclerk:	What about these? They're only forty dollars.
Customer:	Those are nice, and they're darker than the other pair. I like them, too.
Salesclerk:	Do you want to try them on?
Customer:	Yes, I do. Thank you.

Tools for Writing

Before I Write

▶ Study the model.

▶ Think about shopping and the clothes you want to buy.

▶ Make notes about what you want to buy and the questions you and the salesclerk are going to ask.

While I Write

▶ Write questions correctly. Begin them with a capital letter. End them with a question mark.

What color do you want?

Do you like these dark blue jeans?

▶ Use *some* and *any* correctly.

*I'm looking for **some** casual clothes.*

*We don't have **any** black jeans.*

▶ Use comparative and superlative adjectives correctly.

*They're **darker** than the other pair.*

*They're the **most expensive** jeans in the store.*

After I Write

▶ Did I write questions correctly?

▶ Did I use *some* and *any* correctly?

▶ Did I use comparative and superlative adjectives correctly?

B. Read the *Before I Write* checklist. You are the customer in your dialogue. Then, on a separate piece of paper, make notes about what you want to buy and the questions you and the salesclerk are going to ask.

C. Read the *While I Write* checklist. Then, on a separate piece of paper, write a dialogue between you and a salesclerk. Use your notes and the dialogue in **Exercise A** for help.

D. Read the *After I Write* checklist. Then check your work.

Copyright © 2005 by Pearson Education, Inc.

Unit 5 Test

Grammar

A. Complete the sentences in the affirmative or the negative. Use the cues and the correct form of *be + going to* for the future.

1. We _____*are going to eat*_____ lunch soon. (eat, affirmative)

2. She _____ her homework tonight. (do, affirmative)

3. He _____ TV this evening. (watch, negative)

4. They _____ soccer after school. (play, negative)

5. I _____ to school early. (go, affirmative)

B. Complete the questions. Use the correct form of *be + going to* for the future. Then complete the short answers.

1. A: _*Is*_ Maria _____*going to*_____ work tonight?

B: No, _____*she isn't*_____ .

2. A: ___ you _____ wash the dishes?

B: Yes, I _____ .

3. A: ___ Pablo _____ sing?

B: Yes, _____ .

4. A: ___ your friends _____ go to the park?

B: No, _____ .

C. Complete the questions. Use the cues and the correct form of *be + going to* for the future.

1. (Pablo)

When _____*is Pablo going to*_____ sing?

2. (you)

Where _____ study tonight?

3. (Luis and Edgar)

What _____

_____ buy?

4. (Maria)

Who _____ visit?

D. Complete the sentences in the affirmative or the negative. Write the correct past continuous form of the verbs in parentheses. Use contractions.

1. It _____*wasn't raining*_____ at six o'clock. (rain, negative)

2. I _____ to school. (walk, affirmative)

3. We _____ on the phone. (talk, negative)

4. You _____ video games. (play, affirmative)

5. Maria _____ last Saturday night. (work, negative)

E. Change the sentences to *yes/no* questions. Write the questions on the lines. Then complete the short answers.

1. She was wearing a new dress.

A: _*Was she wearing a new dress?*_

B: Yes, _____ .

2. You were watching a video.

A: _____

B: No, we _____ .

3. It was raining at eight o'clock.

A: _____

B: No, _____ .

4. David and Carolina were helping you.

A: _____

_____

B: Yes, _____ .

F. Read the answers. Then complete the questions. Use the cues.

1. A: What ___*was Mei reading*___ ?
(Mei)

B: She was reading the newspaper.

2. A: When _____ ?
(Bic)

B: He was working yesterday morning.

3. A: Where _____ ?
(the children)

B: They were eating in the living room.

4. A: Who _____ ?
(you)

B: I was studying with Anita.

G. Complete the sentences in the affirmative or the negative. Use the cues and *will* for the future. Use contractions.

1. She ___*'ll share*___ her French fries. (share, affirmative)

2. He ___*won't skate*___ fast. (skate, negative)

3. We _____ you tomorrow. (visit, affirmative)

4. I _____ late. (sleep, negative)

5. You _____ fine tomorrow. (feel, affirmative)

H. Change the sentences to *yes/no* questions. Write the questions on the lines. Then complete the short answers.

1. I will come to the meeting.

A: ___*Will you come to the meeting?*___

B: Yes, I _____ .

2. Carlos will be late.

A: _____

B: No, _____ .

3. Maria's mother will make snacks.

A: _____
_____

B: Yes, _____ .

4. The students will leave early.

A: _____

B: No, _____ .

I. Read the answers. Then complete the questions. Use the cues.

1. (Maria's mother)

A: What ___*will Maria's mother make*___ ?

B: She'll make empanadas.

2. (Carlos)

A: Where _____
_____ ?

B: He'll get the potato chips from the market.

3. (you)

A: What kind of _____
_____ ?

B: I'll buy chocolate ice cream.

4. (the students)

A: What else _____ ?

B: They'll bring lemonade and soda.

J. Read the sentences. Circle the correct answer.

1. I (might / am going to) buy this CD. I'll decide later.

2. He definitely (may not / isn't going to) come to the party. He's going to work instead.

3. We (may / are going to) watch TV tonight. We don't have anything else to do.

4. They (might not / aren't going to) go out tonight. They don't have definite plans.

Name _____ Date _____

Reading

A. Read the story.

Elena's Plan

My name is Elena Sierra. I live with my father, mother, and three little brothers. We came to the United States from El Salvador. We speak Spanish at home, but I am learning English at school. Yesterday evening, there was a meeting for parents and teachers at my school. When I told my parents about the meeting, my father said, "I'm sorry, Elena. I want to go, but I can't. I have to work."

My mother was worried. She said, "I want to go, but I can't speak or understand English."

I was worried, too, but I wanted my mother to go to the meeting. I told her, "Don't worry. I can go with you."

My mother said, "Okay. You and I will go together."

When my mother and I arrived at the meeting, a teacher came over to us and asked, "Elena, does your mother speak English?"

I felt embarrassed. I said, "Maybe a little." Then I said, "Well, not really."

The teacher said, "That's not a problem. We have a translator for her. Her name is Ms. Bernal." My mother went to each of my classrooms and listened to all of my teachers. Ms. Bernal translated everything into Spanish for her. When my mother wanted to ask a question, she spoke in Spanish, and Ms. Bernal translated the question into English.

Ms. Bernal helped my mother learn more about my life at school in this country. When Ms. Bernal was translating for my mother, I was watching her and thinking about my future. Then I made a plan. When I finish school, I am going to be a translator. I will have to study hard and learn to speak English perfectly. It won't be easy, but I will do it because it will make me feel proud and happy to help people.

B. Read the sentences below about the story. Circle *True*, *False*, or *I don't know*. Change the false statements to make them true.

1. Elena came to the United States from El Salvador.   (True) / False / I don't know.

2. Elena's father didn't want to go to the meeting.   True / False / I don't know.

3. Elena's mother wanted to go to the meeting.   True / False / I don't know.

4. Elena thinks that she won't learn to speak English perfectly.   True / False / I don't know.

5. Ms. Bernal wants Elena to be a translator.   True / False / I don't know.

Writing

A. You are going to write a few short paragraphs about the job you want to have in the future and how you can reach your goal. First, read the paragraphs below.

> After I finish school, I want to be a music teacher. Here are some ways I can reach my goal:
>
> 1. I'll practice the guitar every day.
> 2. I'll ask my teachers for information about the job. I'll find out about the classes I'll need to take.
> 3. I'll study hard and do well on all my exams.
>
> The easiest step will be to practice every day. I love to sing and play the guitar. The hardest step will be to do well on all my exams. I do well on most of my exams, but some of them are very long and difficult to finish.
>
> It will be a lot of fun to teach music, so I'll keep on trying to reach my goal!

B. Read the *Before I Write* checklist. Then, on a separate piece of paper, make notes on some steps you can take to reach your goal.

C. Read the *While I Write* checklist. Then, on a separate sheet of paper, write a few paragraphs about the job you want to have in the future and how you plan to reach your goal. Use your notes and the model in **Exercise A** for help.

D. Read the *After I Write* checklist. Then check your work.

Tools for Writing

Before I Write

▶ Study the model.

▶ Think about the job I want to have in the future.

▶ Make notes on how I can reach my goal.

While I Write

▶ Make a step-by-step list for reaching my goal.

▶ Say which step will be the easiest and which will be the hardest.

▶ Use *will* or its contraction *'ll* with a verb to talk about the future.

  *I'll **practice** the guitar every day.*

After I Write

▶ Did I make a step-by-step list for reaching my goal?

▶ Did I say which step will be the easiest and which will be the hardest?

▶ Did I use *will* or its contraction *'ll* with a verb to talk about the future?

Unit 6 Test

Grammar

A. Read the sentences. Then rewrite them using the adverbs of frequency.

1. Isabel comes to class late. (never)

Isabel never comes to class late.

2. Isabel is late to class. (never)

_____

_____

3. Mei is early. (sometimes)

_____

4. Mei arrives at school early. (sometimes)

_____

_____

5. Carlos and Bic go to soccer practice after school. (usually)

_____

_____

6. Carlos and Bic are at soccer practice after school. (usually)

_____

_____

B. Complete the questions in the simple present tense. Then complete the answers. Use the cues.

1. (you / eat fish?) (once a week)

A: How often _____*do you eat fish*_____ ?

B: I _____*eat fish once a week*_____ .

2. (Lin / go shopping?) (two times a week)

A: How often _____ ?

B: She _____ .

3. (they / have meetings?) (twice a month)

A: How often _____ ?

B: They _____ .

4. (Edgar / buy flowers?) (once a year)

A: How often _____ ?

B: He _____ .

C. Complete the sentences. Use the gerund form of the verbs.

1. Maria loves _____*painting*_____ pictures. (paint)

2. They like _____ this game. (play)

3. It's going to start _____ . (rain)

4. I enjoyed _____ with you. (dance)

5. We'll finish _____ soon. (cook)

D. Complete the sentences. Use *should* or *shouldn't* and the cues.

1. You look tired. You
_____*should get*_____ some rest. (get)

2. You have a sore throat. You
_____ swimming. (go)

3. Maria is so nervous. She
_____ to relax. (try)

4. Luis has a stomachache. He
_____ today. (work)

5. Grandma needs help. We
_____ her. (help)

E. First, read the problems and the cues. Then complete the *yes/no* questions with *should* or *shouldn't*. Last, complete the short answers.

1. We're lost. (I'm asking for advice.)

A: _____*Should*_____ we ask someone for directions?

B: Yes, we _____ .

Name _____   Date _____

2. I feel terrible. (I want you to say *yes*.)

   A: _____ I
   stay home today?

   B: Yes, _____ .

3. Alberto is sick. (I'm asking for advice.)

   A: _____ he
   go to school today?

   B: No, _____ .

F. Complete the dialogues. Use *could* and the possibilities in the box.

join a study group   get a job
~~make a sandwich~~   go to a dance class

   1. A: Tito is hungry.

      B: He ___*could make a sandwich*___ .

   2. A: Anna wants to get some exercise.

      B: She _____

      _____ .

   3. A: Carmen needs money for CDs.

      B: She _____ .

   4. A: I don't like to study by myself.

      B: You _____

      _____ .

G. Complete the sentences. Use the information in the chart. Write *better than*, *worse than*, *the best*, or *the worst*. (Four stars is the best.)

Your Movie Guide			
★	★★	★★★	★★★★
Movie A	Movie B	Movie C	Movie D

   1. Movie C is ___*better than*___ Movie B.

   2. Movie D is _____ Movie C.

3. Movie B is _____ Movie C.

4. Movie A is _____ .

5. Movie D is _____ .

H. Complete the sentences. Use *used to* or *didn't use to*.

   1. I ___*used to*___ drink milk, but I don't drink it anymore.

   2. Tito _____ be homesick, but he isn't homesick anymore.

   3. Lin _____ like cheese, but she likes it now.

   4. We _____ stay up late, but now we often stay up until midnight.

   5. Alberto _____ play video games, but he doesn't play them anymore.

I. Complete the dialogues. Write *yes/no* questions with *used to*. Then complete the short answers.

   1. A: I know that Edgar doesn't play soccer now.

      ___*Did he use to play soccer?*___

      B: Yes, ___*he did*___ .

   2. A: I know that Anna doesn't like candy now. _____

      _____

      B: No, _____ .

   3. A: I know that you don't live in Peru now. _____

      _____

      B: Yes, we _____ .

   4. A: I know that you don't drink soda now. _____

      _____

      B: No, I _____ .

Reading

A. Read the story.

The Last Party?

Van Tran and his classmates were talking on the last day of school. Tom said, "We should have a party. We could all bring some food and drinks."

"That sounds like fun," Van said. "We could have it at my house. But you don't need to bring anything to eat."

Amy asked Van, "Shouldn't I bring some snacks?"

"No, Amy. It's nice of you to ask, but you shouldn't," replied Van.

When Van's classmates arrived at the party, they found a beautiful and delicious Vietnamese dinner waiting for them. Tom said, "Wow, Van! This food is wonderful. Who cooked it?"

Van said, "I did." Everyone was surprised because they didn't know that Van could cook.

"Who taught you how to cook?" Amy asked Van.

Van said, "I used to help my mother and grandmother in the kitchen. I learned how to cook from them. I love cooking. It's fun."

"You should become a chef," said Tom. "And you should have a cooking show on TV and teach everyone else how to cook."

Van laughed. "I used to want to be a chef. But my mother wanted me to be a doctor, so that's what I'm planning to do. I'm good at science, and I'll probably like being a doctor. But, to tell you the truth, sometimes I still want to be a chef."

Amy said, "You won't have to stop cooking when you're a doctor. Doctors have to balance work and fun, just like everyone else. You can cook in your free time."

"And will you come have dinner with me in your free time?" asked Van.

"Yes, I will," promised Amy.

B. Read the sentences about the story. Circle *True*, *False*, or *I don't know*. Change the false statements to make them true.

    didn't want
1. Van ~~wanted~~ his classmates to bring   True /(False)/ I don't know.
   food to the party.

2. Amy thought she should bring some   True / False / I don't know.
   snacks to the party.

3. Before the party, Tom knew that Van   True / False / I don't know.
   could cook.

4. Van's mother and grandmother taught   True / False / I don't know.
   him how to cook.

5. Van is planning to become a chef.   True / False / I don't know.

6. Amy wants to be a doctor.   True / False / I don't know.

Writing

A. You are going to write two paragraphs, one about the past and one about the present. First, read the paragraphs below.

When I was little, I used to draw cartoons a lot. I used to get ideas from TV shows. I sometimes drew cartoon animals, but I really liked drawing cartoon heroes like Spider-Man. I used to draw cartoons during class, and my teachers used to get upset.

I still like to draw cartoons, but I don't draw Spider-Man cartoons anymore. Now I draw cartoons from my own imagination. I often make up stories about a character named Fabula. I make comic books about Fabula for art class. Now I can draw every day in art class, and no one gets upset.

B. Read the *Before I Write* checklist. On a separate piece of paper, make notes about something you did in the past and about something you do now.

C. Read the *While I Write* checklist. Then, on a separate piece of paper, write two paragraphs, one about something you did in the past and one about something you do now. Use your notes and the model in **Exercise A** for help.

D. Read the *After I Write* checklist. Check your work.

Before I Write

▶ Study the model.
▶ Think about something I used to do.
▶ Think about something I do now.
▶ Make notes about what I used to do and what I do now.

While I Write

▶ Use *used to* with a verb to talk about the past.

   I **used to draw** cartoons a lot.

▶ Give specific examples.

   I really liked drawing cartoon heroes **like Spider-Man.**

▶ Compare the present with the past.

   I still like to draw cartoons, **but** I **don't** draw Spider-Man cartoons **anymore.**

After I Write

▶ Did I use *used to* with a verb to talk about the past?
▶ Did I give specific examples?
▶ Did I compare the present with the past?

Copyright © 2005 by Pearson Education, Inc.

DIAGNOSTIC TEST ANSWER KEY AND TESTED-SKILLS CHART

	ITEM	ANSWER	SCORE (Circle one.)		TESTED SKILL
Listening	1.	a.	0	1	Comprehension of a dialogue similar to the dialogues in the early chapters of the Student Book.
	2.	b.	0	1	
	3.	a.	0	1	
	4.	b.	0	1	
	5.	a.	0	1	
	6.	a.	0	1	
	7.	b.	0	1	
Grammar	1.	a.	0	1	Pronouns
	2.	b.	0	1	Pronouns
	3.	a.	0	1	Pronouns
	4.	c.	0	1	Pronouns
	5.	b.	0	1	Affirmative statements with simple present of *be*
	6.	c.	0	1	Affirmative statements with simple present of *be*
	7.	b.	0	1	Negative statements with simple present of *be*
	8.	c.	0	1	Yes/No questions with *be*
	9.	b.	0	1	Short answers with *be*
	10.	c.	0	1	Affirmative statements with *have*
	11.	a.	0	1	Negative statements with *have*
	12.	b.	0	1	Yes/No questions with *have*
	13.	a.	0	1	Possessive adjectives
	14.	a.	0	1	Possessive nouns
	15.	c.	0	1	Information questions with *be*
	16.	b.	0	1	Affirmative statements with lexical verbs
	17.	c.	0	1	Negative statements with lexical verbs
	18.	b.	0	1	Yes/No questions with lexical verbs
	19.	c.	0	1	Short answers with lexical verbs
	20.	b.	0	1	Statements with *can*
	21.	b.	0	1	Yes/No questions with *can*
	22.	c.	0	1	Information questions with *do*
	23.	b.	0	1	Affirmative statements with simple past of *be*
	24.	a.	0	1	Negative statements with simple past of *be*
	25.	c.	0	1	Affirmative statements with present continuous
	26.	a.	0	1	Negative statements with present continuous
	27.	b.	0	1	Information questions with present continuous
	28.	c.	0	1	Yes/No questions with present continuous
	29.	a.	0	1	Simple present vs. present continuous
	30.	b.	0	1	Simple present vs. present continuous
	31.	a.	0	1	Statements with verb + infinitive
	32.	c.	0	1	Yes/No questions with verb + infinitive
	33.	a.	0	1	Past tense of regular verbs, affirmative
	34.	c.	0	1	Past tense of irregular verbs, affirmative
	35.	a.	0	1	Past tense of regular verbs, negative
	36.	a.	0	1	Yes/No questions with past tense of regular verbs

(continued)

Word Study	A.					
		1.	c	0	1	Alphabet
		2.	d	0	1	Alphabet
		3.	h	0	1	Alphabet
		4.	l	0	1	Alphabet
		5.	o	0	1	Alphabet
		6.	s	0	1	Alphabet
		7.	u	0	1	Alphabet
		8.	y	0	1	Alphabet
	B.					
		1.	A	0	1	Alphabet
		2.	E	0	1	Alphabet
		3.	F	0	1	Alphabet
		4.	I	0	1	Alphabet
		5.	M	0	1	Alphabet
		6.	P	0	1	Alphabet
		7.	T	0	1	Alphabet
		8.	V	0	1	Alphabet
	C.					
		1.	Anita	0	1	Alphabetical order
		2.	Carlos	0	1	Alphabetical order
		3.	Chen	0	1	Alphabetical order
		4.	Elena	0	1	Alphabetical order
		5.	Jennifer	0	1	Alphabetical order
		6.	Lee	0	1	Alphabetical order
		7.	Paco	0	1	Alphabetical order
		8.	Tyler	0	1	Alphabetical order
	D.					
		1.	h	0	1	Initial *h*, /h/
		2.	n	0	1	Initial *n*, /n/
		3.	m	0	1	Initial *m*, /m/
		4.	b	0	1	Initial *b*, /b/
		5.	p	0	1	Initial *p*, /p/
		6.	s	0	1	Initial *s*, /s/
	E.					
		1.	b.	0	1	Short vowel sound /a/
		2.	b.	0	1	Short vowel sound /i/
		3.	c.	0	1	Short vowel sound /o/
		4.	a.	0	1	Short vowel sound /e/
		5.	c.	0	1	Short vowel sound /u/
		6.	c.	0	1	Short vowel sound /a/
		7.	a.	0	1	Consonant digraph /ch/
		8.	b.	0	1	Consonant digraph /sh/
		9.	a.	0	1	Long vowel sound /ā/
		10.	b.	0	1	Long vowel sound /ē/
Reading		1.	F	0	1	Comprehension of a story similar to the stories in the early chapters of the Student Book. Questions check understanding of affirmative and negative statements, a preposition of time, and pronoun references.
		2.	F	0	1	
		3.	T	0	1	
		4.	F	0	1	
		5.	T	0	1	
		6.	F	0	1	
Writing			See page 224.	0 1 2 3 4 5		Writing a simple paragraph similar to paragraphs assigned in the early chapters of the Student Book. Paragraph based on answers to personal-information questions.

CHAPTER TESTS ANSWER KEY

Chapter 1

Dialogue Vocabulary

A.
1. Hi
2. Nice to meet you, too
3. Mexico
4. Spanish
5. sister
6. brother
7. very
8. Thank you

Grammar

B.
1. she   3. you   5. they
2. we   4. he   6. it

C.
1. We're   4. You're
2. He's   5. It's
3. They're

D.
1. We're not from Mexico.
2. He's my brother.
3. She's a teacher.
4. I'm not nervous.
5. It's not from the United States.
6. They're students.

E.
1. Is Pablo from Mexico?
2. Are you a new student?
3. Are Anna and Pablo from Peru?
4. Is she nervous?
5. Are you and Carmen students?

F.
1. she is   4. they're not
2. he's not   5. it is
3. they are

Word Study

G.
1. b   4. l   7. t
2. e   5. o   8. v
3. h   6. p   9. y

H.
1. Anna   5. Maria
2. Carlos 6. Mei
3. Edgar   7. Samir
4. Isabel

Reading Vocabulary

I.
1. b   2. c   3. a

Chapter 2

Dialogue Vocabulary

A.
1. How are you   5. That's great
2. Fine, thanks   6. schedule
3. lunch   7. almost
4. together

Grammar

B.
1. have   3. have   5. have
2. has   4. have   6. has

C.
1. We don't have the same classes.
2. You don't have math with me.
3. She doesn't have science with Mrs. Kim.
4. I don't have music now.
5. He doesn't have P.E. with you.

D.
1. Does, have; he doesn't
2. Do, have; we do
3. Do, have; they don't
4. Does, have; he does
5. Does, have; she doesn't

E.
1. pencils   4. brushes
2. students   5. books
3. boxes   6. lunches

F.
1. my   5. its
2. your   6. our
3. her   7. their
4. his

Word Study

G.
1. map   3. hot   5. hat
2. cap   4. hit   6. pig

Reading Vocabulary

H.
1. day   4. Puerto Rico
2. good at   5. Chinese
3. languages   6. China

Chapter 3

Dialogue Vocabulary

A.
1. this in English
2. I borrow your pen
3. dollars
4. wallet
5. Wait
6. know

Grammar

B.
1. an   4. a   7. an
2. a   5. a   8. an
3. an   6. a   9. a

C.
1. This   3. Those
2. That   4. These

D.
1. This   4. This
2. Those   5. These
3. That

E.
1. sister's   4. girls'
2. brothers'   5. Maria's
3. boy's   6. Luis's

Word Study

F.
1. d; pet   4. b; bus
2. f; sun   5. a; pup
3. c; net   6. e; pen

Reading Vocabulary

G.
1. asks   5. pens
2. answers   6. comb
3. books   7. problem
4. pencils   8. worried

Chapter 4

Dialogue Vocabulary

A.
1. best
2. other building
3. lost, downstairs, stairs
4. What about you, See you

Grammar

B.

1. on	6. in
2. in	7. next to
3. on	8. on
4. next to	9. under
5. under	

C.

1. Where is	4. Where are
2. Where are	5. Where is
3. Where is	6. Where am

D.

1. There are	5. There is
2. There is	6. There are
3. There are	7. There is
4. There are	

Word Study

E.

1. shut	5. lunch
2. chin	6. dish
3. ship	7. bench
4. inch	8. fish

Reading Vocabulary

F.

1. live	5. small
2. go	6. a lot of
3. like	7. library
4. nice	8. use

Chapter 5

Dialogue Vocabulary

A.

1. d	3. b	5. a
2. e	4. c	

Grammar

B.

1. What is	4. What is
2. What are	5. What are
3. What is	

C.

1. lives	4. don't need
2. like	5. speaks
3. doesn't want	

D.

1. Does Pablo need a map?; he does
2. Does Elena like P.E. class?; she doesn't
3. Do they speak English?; they do

---

4. Does Anna live next to the fire station?; she does
5. Do Carlos and Carmen live in that building?; they don't

E.

1. Mei can't play the drums.
2. You can come to the party.
3. Bic can swim after school.
4. Her brothers can't speak Chinese.
5. We can't dance in the library.
6. I can speak two languages.

F.

1. Can Mei swim?; she can
2. Can you play the drums?; can't
3. Can we dance at the party?; can
4. Can the teachers speak Spanish?; they can
5. Can Pablo answer the question?; he can't

Word Study

G.

1. dress	4. black
2. flag	5. glass
3. clock	6. class

Reading Vocabulary

H.

1. baby-sits	5. happy
2. job	6. sad
3. money	7. practice
4. eat and dance	

Chapter 6

Dialogue Vocabulary

A.

1. start	5. sit
2. late	6. take out
3. hall	7. piece
4. sick	8. today

Grammar

B.

1. What do; want
2. What do; need
3. What does; like
4. What does; have
5. What do; need

C.

1. does class
2. do they
3. do you
4. does Maria
5. does the teacher
6. do I

D.

1. wasn't	4. wasn't
2. was	5. were
3. weren't	6. were

E.

1. Were; we weren't
2. Was; he was
3. Was; she wasn't
4. Were; they weren't
5. Were; I was

Word Study

F.

1. tent	4. hand
2. belt	5. stamp
3. plant	6. lamp

Reading Vocabulary

G.

1. Tomorrow	4. easy
2. early	5. hard
3. on time	6. watch

Chapter 7

Dialogue Vocabulary

A.

1. washing; hair
2. changing; light bulb
3. making; bed
4. cleaning; windows

Grammar

B.

1. is cleaning	3. am making
2. are eating	4. are getting

C.

1. She isn't cleaning the kitchen.
2. We aren't eating lunch.
3. I am not making cookies.
4. Mei and Bic aren't getting ready for the party.

D.

1. is he eating
2. are you reading
3. are they studying
4. am I doing

E.

1. Are they making their beds?; they are
2. Is Anna washing her hair?; she isn't
3. Are you cleaning the windows?; am

4. Are Bic and Mei cooking enchiladas?; they aren't

F.

1. him 3. them 5. me
2. her 4. it 6. us

Word Study

G.

1. cute 3. page
2. nose 4. five

Reading Vocabulary

H.

1. living room 5. floor
2. vacuuming 6. entranceway
3. rug 7. knocking
4. sweeping 8. door

Chapter 8

Dialogue Vocabulary

A.

1. loud
2. would you like to
3. another
4. work
5. miserable
6. excited

Grammar

B.

1. talk 5. is washing
2. is talking 6. is getting ready
3. walk 7. are studying
4. walks 8. study

C.

1. don't like 4. like
2. wants 5. has
3. don't have 6. doesn't want

D.

1. does Anna like
2. does he want
3. do we have
4. do Carmen and Carlos like
5. do you want

E.

1. Does Edgar like to play baseball?
2. Do you want to go out tonight?
3. Does Elena have to work?
4. Do we have to clean our rooms?
5. Do Mei and Bic like to eat enchiladas?

Word Study

F.

1. day; c 4. mail; f
2. train; e 5. lake; b
3. play; a 6. game; d

Reading Vocabulary

G.

1. Sometimes 4. homesick
2. feel 5. homework
3. miss 6. learn

Chapter 9

Dialogue Vocabulary

A.

1. came 4. introduce
2. twins 5. say; wrong
3. let's

Grammar

B.

1. asked 4. arrived
2. laughed 5. studied
3. danced 6. played

C.

1. knew 4. read
2. taught 5. had
3. wrote 6. made

D.

1. Bic didn't play baseball yesterday.
2. I didn't talk to Pablo last night.
3. Anna and Edgar didn't sing at the party.
4. You didn't look happy.
5. We didn't do our homework on Saturday.
6. My little sister didn't go to the movies.

E.

1. Did the boys talk to Paco last night?; they didn't
2. Did Carlos and Carmen have fun at the party?; they did
3. Did you eat a piece of cake?; did
4. Did Maria introduce them?; she didn't
5. Did I say something wrong?; didn't

Word Study

F.

1. feet 4. me
2. meat 5. tree
3. field 6. city

G.

1. everybody 4. agreed
2. grandson 5. embarrassed
3. boyfriend 6. delicious

Chapter 10

Dialogue Vocabulary

A.

1. clothes
2. pair of
3. May I help you
4. expensive
5. You're welcome
6. secret
7. girlfriend

Grammar

B.

1. When is 4. Who is
2. Where are 5. What is
3. How are 6. Why are

C.

1. Where were 3. How was
2. When was 4. Why were

D.

1. does Luis work
2. does this dress look
3. do you study
4. do the girls need
5. does Isabel like

E.

1. did the girls go
2. did Sophie arrive
3. did Anna and Lin look
4. did you ask
5. did you laugh

F.

1. is 4. is
2. does 5. do
3. are

Word Study

G.

1. pie 3. child
2. dime 4. cry

Reading Vocabulary

H.

1. sweater 3. price tag
2. window 4. skirt

Chapter 11

Dialogue Vocabulary

A.

1. hungry
2. anymore
3. Why don't you
4. else
5. finished
6. Let's see
7. total

Grammar

B.

1. apple; count
2. rice; non-count
3. eraser; count
4. cookies; count
5. cheese; non-count
6. onion; count
7. coffee; non-count

C.

1. bread
2. cheese
3. milk
4. lemonade
5. coffee
6. rice

D.

1. some
2. any
3. any
4. some
5. some
6. any
7. any
8. some

E.

1. so
2. and
3. but
4. and
5. so
6. but

Word Study

F.

1. c; c(o)ld
2. d; st(o)v(e)
3. a; wind(ow)
4. b; t(oa)st

Reading Vocabulary

G.

1. cashier
2. counter
3. customer
4. salad
5. hamburger
6. French fries
7. soda

Chapter 12

Dialogue Vocabulary

A.

1. section
2. So do I
3. I'm just kidding
4. have time
5. I think so

Grammar

B.

1. taller; tallest
2. harder; hardest
3. easier; easiest
4. cuter; cutest
5. funnier; funniest
6. newer; newest

C.

1. shorter
2. longer
3. older
4. younger

D.

1. shorter
2. shortest
3. longest
4. oldest
5. older
6. younger
7. youngest

E.

1. more casual
2. more casual
3. most casual
4. more formal
5. most formal

Word Study

F.

1. c(u)b(e)
2. men(u)
3. c(u)t(e)
4. f(ew)
5. h(u)g(e)
6. m(u)sic

Reading Vocabulary

G.

1. performers
2. stage
3. storyteller
4. singer
5. poem
6. clapped
7. yelled

Chapter 13

Dialogue Vocabulary

A.

1. See you later
2. That sounds like fun
3. lessons
4. fast
5. fall

Grammar

B.

1. are going to study
2. am going to buy
3. is going to play
4. is going to be
5. are going to fall

C.

1. Mei and Sophie are not going to study after school.
2. I am not going to buy a gift for her.
3. Bic is not going to play baseball.
4. The test is not going to be hard.
5. You are not going to fall down.

D.

1. Are Bic and Luis going to have a party?; they aren't
2. Is Mei going to buy a gift?; she is
3. Is Carolina going to make her bed?; she isn't
4. Are you going to eat those cookies?; 'm not
5. Are they going to play soccer?; they are

E.

1. is Pablo going to do tonight?
2. are you going to help your grandmother?
3. are your brothers going to play baseball?
4. is Sophie going to visit?
5. are we going to get at the store?

F.

1. e
2. b
3. f
4. d
5. c
6. a

Word Study

G.

1. fl(ew)
2. m(oo)n
3. gl(ue)
4. J(u)n(e)
5. shamp(oo)
6. dr(ew)

Reading Vocabulary

H.

1. d
2. f
3. a
4. c
5. b
6. e

Chapter 14

Dialogue Vocabulary

A.

1. Whoa
2. It sure is
3. storm
4. power line
5. lights
6. soon

Grammar

B.

1. was cooking
2. was not watching
3. were doing
4. was studying
5. were not playing

6. was not working
7. were helping

C.

1. Were you watching TV at six o'clock yesterday?; I wasn't
2. Was David playing video games?; he was
3. Was your mom helping your grandmother?; she wasn't
4. Were you and Luis eating at seven o'clock?; we were
5. Were your parents working last Saturday?; they weren't

D.

1. were you doing
2. were the girls studying
3. was Sophie talking
4. was David buying
5. were they doing

E.

1. theirs
2. ours
3. yours
4. his
5. hers

F.

1. pencil is this?; yours
2. house is that?; theirs
3. books are these?; mine
4. CDs are those?; ours
5. room is this?; his

Word Study

G.

1. g(oo)d
2. b(oo)k
3. c(oo)kies
4. f(oo)t
5. h(oo)k
6. c(oo)k

Reading Vocabulary

H.

1. thunderstorm
2. dangerous
3. completely
4. perfect
5. Instead

Chapter 15

Dialogue Vocabulary

A.

1. extra
2. catch up
3. a few
4. final
5. review
6. Of course

Grammar

B.

1. will wear
2. won't go
3. won't come
4. will come
5. will wash
6. won't be

C.

1. Will you help me?; I will
2. Will Pablo arrive on time?; he won't
3. Will the students read more books?; they will
4. Will we have a test next week?; will
5. Will she go to bed early?; she won't

D.

1. will we have
2. will it start
3. will Anna make
4. will make
5. will you bring
6. will we need

E.

1. may not/might not
2. may/might
3. is going to
4. may not/might not
5. isn't going to

Word Study

F.

1. p(aw)
2. (au)tumn
3. str(aw)
4. (Au)gust
5. (au)thor
6. y(aw)n

Reading Vocabulary

G.

1. translate
2. translator
3. whispered
4. quietly
5. proud

Chapter 16

Dialogue Vocabulary

A.

1. typical
2. hard time
3. especially
4. practice
5. coach
6. Do you mind if
7. I hope so

Grammar

B.

1. Anna sometimes goes to bed at nine o'clock.
2. Our teacher is never late to class.
3. Carmen and Luis are always hungry.
4. We usually study in the library.
5. Maria often has to work on Sunday.
6. Lin is sometimes bored in math class.

C.

1. does Anna baby-sit?; baby-sits twice a month
2. do you eat rice?; eat rice three times a day
3. does Tito play soccer?; plays soccer two times a week
4. do the girls go to the movies?; go to the movies once a week
5. does David clean his room?; cleans his room once a year

D.

1. playing
2. going
3. watching
4. studying
5. writing
6. reading

Word Study

E.

1. d; R(oy)
2. c; s(oi)l
3. f; t(oy)
4. e; c(oi)n
5. a; b(oi)l
6. b; b(oy)

Reading Vocabulary

F.

1. join
2. by myself
3. friendly
4. free-time activity

Chapter 17

Dialogue Vocabulary

A.

1. headache
2. stomachache
3. sore
4. terrible
5. couple of
6. plenty of
7. feels better

Grammar

B.

1. shouldn't worry
2. should study more
3. should take this medicine
4. shouldn't eat a lot of enchiladas
5. shouldn't move
6. should call 911

C.

1. Should I go; shouldn't
2. Shouldn't I stay; should
3. Shouldn't she see; should
4. Should he go; shouldn't

D.

1. could rest
2. could watch TV
3. could drink some lemonade
4. could go out to eat
5. could get her some flowers

E.

1. Anna is eating crackers because she's hungry.
2. We should study now because we have a test tomorrow.
3. I want to get a gift for my mother because tomorrow's her birthday.
4. I don't want any soda because I'm not thirsty.
5. They need to rest now because they're tired.

Word Study

F.

1. h<u>ou</u>se
2. cr<u>ow</u>d
3. cl<u>ou</u>d
4. t<u>ow</u>n

Reading Vocabulary

G.

1. smart
2. flowers
3. the day after tomorrow
4. surprised
5. artists

Chapter 18

Dialogue Vocabulary

A.

1. expect
2. hope
3. comprehension
4. pass
5. tease

Grammar

B.

1. better than
2. the best
3. better than
4. worse than
5. the worst

C.

1. too easy
2. not hard enough
3. too small
4. not large enough
5. not short enough
6. too long

D.

1. didn't use to
2. used to
3. didn't use to
4. didn't use to
5. used to

E.

1. Did you use to read comic books?; didn't
2. Did your brothers use to have a lot of toys?; did
3. Did Maria use to live in Haiti?; didn't
4. Did you and Luis use to study together?; did

Word Study

F.

1. Thu<u>r</u>sday
2. sh<u>ir</u>t
3. wint<u>er</u>
4. b<u>ir</u>d
5. lett<u>er</u>
6. n<u>ur</u>se

Reading Vocabulary

G.

1. found out
2. promoted
3. stunned
4. whole
5. Congratulations
6. shook

UNIT TESTS ANSWER KEY

Unit 1

Grammar

A.
1. She is
2. He is
3. They are
4. We are
5. It is
6. You are

B.
1. Are you from Mexico?; I'm not
2. Is Maria a new student?; she is
3. Are the books in your backpack?; they are
4. Is Pablo nervous?; he's not

C.
1. have
2. don't have
3. has
4. have
5. doesn't have

D.
1. Do they have math together?; they don't
2. Do you have your schedule?; do
3. Does Anna have ten dollars?; she doesn't
4. Do we have the same math class?; do

E.
1. a
2. a
3. an
4. a
5. an
6. a

F.
1. hats
2. schools
3. problems
4. classes
5. languages
6. lunches

G.
1. That
2. These
3. This
4. Those
5. That
6. These

H.
1. These are pens.
2. Those are pencils.
3. Those are wallets.
4. These are combs.
5. These are brushes.
6. Those are calculators.

I.
1. her
2. your
3. our
4. his
5. Their
6. My; my

J.
1. boy's
2. girls'
3. students'
4. teacher's
5. Pablo's
6. Carlos's

Reading

A.

	Anita		Tony
1.	English	1.	English
2.	history	2.	science
3.	P.E.	3.	math
4.	lunch	4.	lunch
5.	art	5.	music
6.	science	6.	history
7.	math	7.	P.E.

B.
1. Valley
2. folder
3. English and lunch
4. different

Writing

Answers will vary. Example:

Sonia Karam is a student at Valley School. She is from Lebanon. She speaks English and Arabic. Her favorite class is science.

Andrew Tang is a student at Madison School. He is from China. He speaks English and Chinese. His favorite class is music.

Unit 2

Grammar

A.
1. Where's; It's on
2. Where are; They're in
3. Where's; It's under
4. Where are; They're next to
5. Where's; It's on

B.
1. What's his address?
2. What are their names?
3. What's her telephone number?
4. What are your favorite classes?

C.
1. don't live
2. don't need
3. live
4. doesn't speak
5. don't like
6. wants
7. speak

D.
1. Does she speak Arabic?; she doesn't
2. Do they need directions?; they do
3. Does your brother live in Peru?; he does
4. Do you want a new watch?; don't

E.
1. can speak
2. can't play
3. can swim
4. can't find
5. can eat
6. can't use

F.
1. Can Carlos swim?; he can
2. Can Mei speak French?; she can't
3. Can they come to the party?; they can't
4. Can you play the drums?; can

G.
1. do you
2. does Maria
3. he have
4. do they
5. does he
6. class start

H.
1. was
2. wasn't
3. was
4. were
5. weren't
6. were

I.
1. Were they late to class?; they weren't
2. Was Pablo at school on Monday?; he was
3. Were you sad yesterday?; wasn't
4. Were you and your brother at the party?; we were

Reading

B.
1. Friday
2. seven o'clock
3. 896 Grand Avenue
4. the/a fire station
5. 555-6514
6. Friday

Writing

Answers will vary.

Unit 3

Grammar

A.
1. is talking
2. is not helping
3. are eating
4. is changing
5. am not writing

B.

1. What's Mr. Gomez cleaning?
2. What are your sisters making?
3. What are you reading?

C.

1. Are you making cookies?; I'm not
2. Is Paco studying math?; he is
3. Are they reading a story?; they aren't

D.

1. David is cleaning them.
2. Dad is helping her.
3. Pablo is reading it.
4. Mr. Gomez is helping them.

E.

1. is talking
2. calls
3. does
4. is drawing

F.

1. don't have
2. wants
3. don't like
4. want
5. doesn't like

G.

1. do you like to eat?
2. do we have to study?
3. does your father like to read?
4. do Carmen and Carlos want to cook?

H.

1. Does Sophie want to go out?; she does
2. Do they have to work tonight?; they don't
3. Do you like to sing together?; do
4. Does Bic want to study now?; he doesn't

I.

1. asked
2. knew
3. went
4. danced
5. studied
6. played

J.

1. Liliana didn't call Mei last night.
2. I asked the teacher.
3. Sophie didn't make the enchiladas.
4. We sang the song.

K.

1. Did Maria come to the party?; she did
2. Did Paco dance with Carmen?; he didn't
3. Did you eat cake and ice cream?; did

B.

1. False. *Alberto* wrote the letter.
2. True.
3. False. Alberto *didn't ask* Anna to dance with him.
4. True.
5. False. Singing songs in Spanish made Alberto feel *a little sad and homesick for Mexico.*
6. True.

Writing

Answers will vary.

Unit 4

Grammar

A.

1. is your name?
2. is the test?
3. are the shoes?
4. is Paco?
5. are you angry?

B.

1. When was the party?
2. Where were the boys?
3. How was the show?
4. Why were you late?

C.

1. do they want?
2. does Elena study?
3. do you eat dinner?
4. does the book cost?
5. does Carmen like Paco?

D.

1. Where did Mei go?
2. When did the boys go home?
3. What did Carmen eat?
4. How did Pablo look?

E.

Count Nouns: carrot; cookie; onion; pencil; student (Order may vary.)
Non-Count Nouns: bread; cheese; lettuce; milk; rice (Order may vary.)

F.

1. some
2. any
3. some
4. any
5. some

G.

1. and
2. but
3. and
4. but
5. so

H.

1. tall; tallest
2. cuter; cutest
3. old; oldest
4. late; later
5. earlier; earliest
6. dirty; dirtier

I.

1. more casual; most casual
2. more formal; most formal
3. more beautiful; most beautiful

J.

1. larger
2. smaller
3. larger
4. largest
5. smallest

K.

1. more expensive
2. more expensive
3. most expensive

Reading

B.

The wording of the answers may vary slightly.

1. It was in the Madison School auditorium.
2. It was last Thursday evening.
3. The first performer was Sara Ramos.
4. The title was "At Midnight."
5. He liked them because they were so pretty.
6. They were Dave and Danny.
7. They were his favorite because their songs were so cool.

Writing

Answers will vary.

Unit 5

Grammar

A.

1. are going to eat
2. is going to do
3. is not going to watch
4. are not going to play
5. am going to go

B.

1. Is . . . going to; she isn't
2. Are . . . going to; am
3. Is . . . going to; he is
4. Are . . . going to; they aren't

C.

1. is Pablo going to
2. are you going to
3. are Luis and Edgar going to
4. Maria going to

D.

1. wasn't raining
2. was walking
3. weren't talking
4. were playing
5. wasn't working

E.

1. Was she wearing a new dress?; she was
2. Were you watching a video?; weren't
3. Was it raining at eight o'clock?; it wasn't
4. Were David and Carolina helping you?; they were

F.

1. was Mei reading?
2. was Bic working?
3. were the children eating?
4. were you studying with?

G.

1. 'll share
2. won't skate
3. 'll visit
4. won't sleep
5. 'll feel

H.

1. Will you come to the meeting?; will
2. Will Carlos be late?; he won't
3. Will Maria's mother make snacks?; she will
4. Will the students leave early?; they won't

I.

1. will Maria's mother make?
2. will Carlos get the potato chips?
3. ice cream will you buy?
4. will the students bring?

J.

1. might
2. isn't going to
3. are going to
4. might not

Reading

B.

1. True
2. False. Elena's father *wanted* to go to the meeting.
3. True
4. False. Elena thinks that she *will* learn to speak English perfectly.
5. I don't know.

Writing

Answers will vary.

Unit 6

Grammar

A.

1. Isabel never comes to class late.
2. Isabel is never late to class.
3. Mei is sometimes early.
4. Mei sometimes arrives at school early.
5. Carlos and Bic usually go to soccer practice after school.
6. Carlos and Bic are usually at soccer practice after school.

B.

1. do you eat fish?; eat fish once a week
2. does Lin go shopping?; goes shopping two times a week
3. do they have meetings?; have meetings twice a month
4. does Edgar buy flowers?; buys flowers once a year

C.

1. painting
2. playing
3. raining
4. dancing
5. cooking

D.

1. should get
2. shouldn't go
3. should try
4. shouldn't work
5. should help

E.

1. Should; should
2. Shouldn't; you should
3. Should; he shouldn't

F.

1. could make a sandwich
2. could go to a dance class
3. could get a job
4. could join a study group

G.

1. better than
2. better than
3. worse than
4. the worst
5. the best

H.

1. used to
2. used to
3. didn't use to
4. didn't use to
5. used to

I.

1. Did he use to play soccer?; he did
2. Did she use to like candy?; she didn't
3. Did you use to live in Peru?; did
4. Did you use to drink soda?; didn't

Reading

B.

1. False. Van *didn't want* his classmates to bring food to the party.
2. True
3. False. Before the party, Tom *didn't know* that Van could cook.
4. True
5. False. Van is planning to become a *doctor*.
6. I don't know.

Writing

Answers will vary.

Graphic Organizers

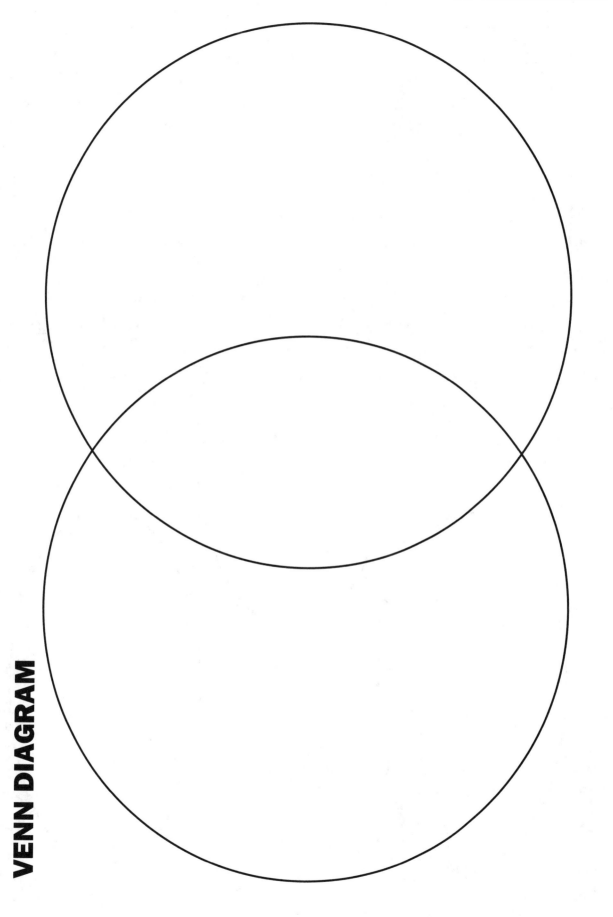

VENN DIAGRAM

WORD WEB

MAIN IDEA/SUPPORTING DETAILS WEB

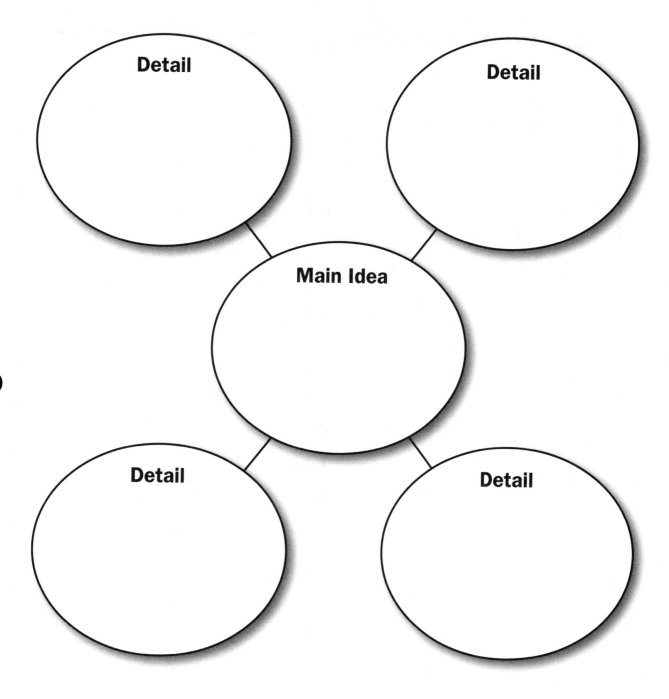

Name _____ Date _____

T-CHART

Name _____ Date _____

K-W-L-H CHART

K-What I Know	W-What I Want to Know	L-What I Learned	H-How I Learned

Name _____ Date _____

SEQUENCE-OF-EVENTS CHART

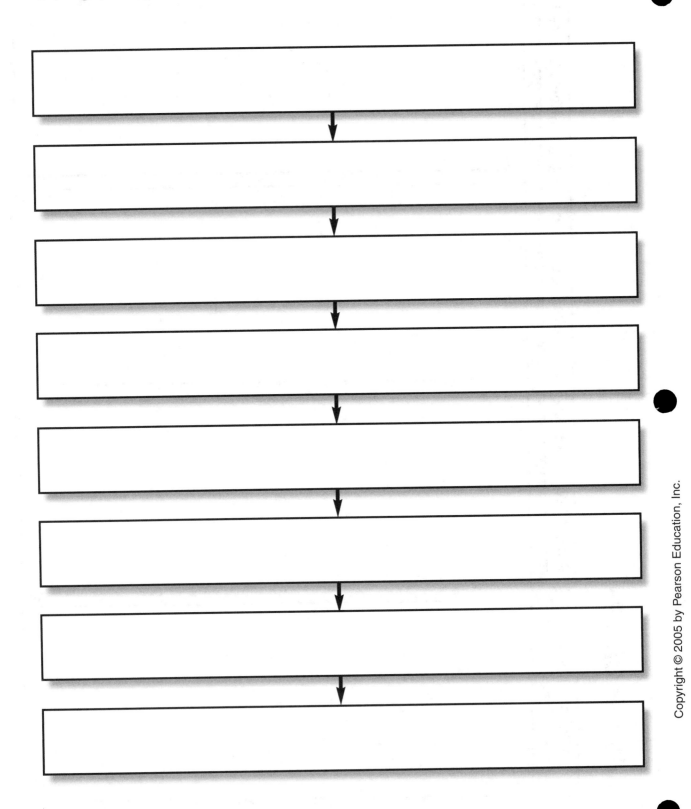

PREDICTION CHART

Pages	What I Predict	What Happens

CHARACTER/SETTING/PROBLEM/SOLUTION CHART

CHARACTER Who?	**SETTING** What time and place?
PROBLEM Conflict?	**SOLUTION** Resolution?

WH- QUESTION CHART

Who?	
What?	
Where?	
Why?	
When?	
How?	

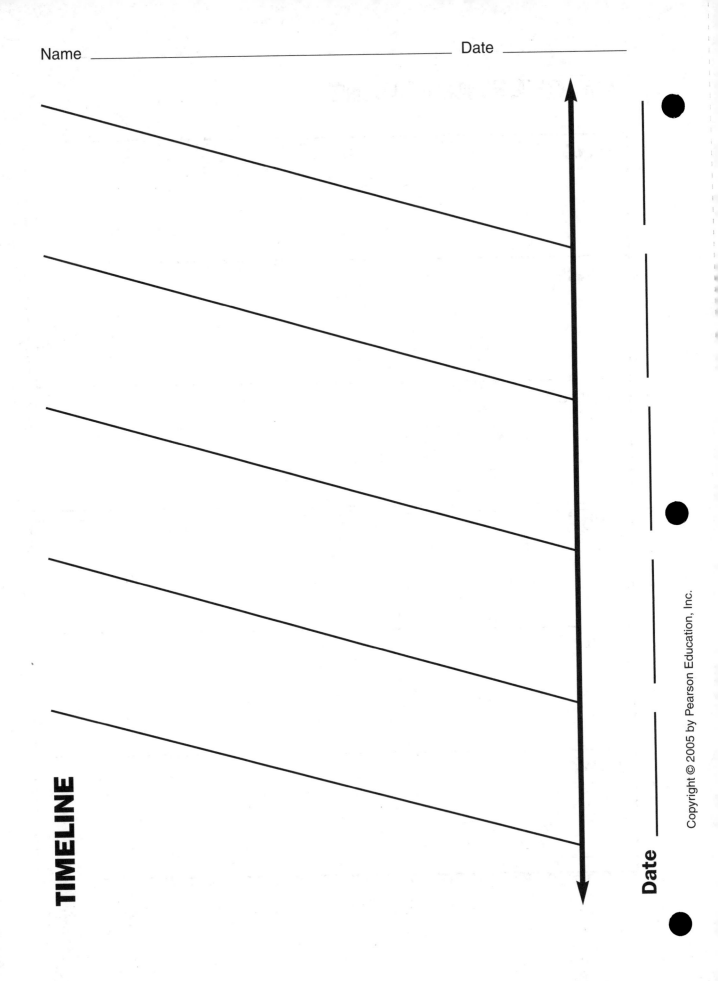

TIMELINE

Date _____